Asia Bible Commentary Series

JUDGES

GLOBAL LIBRARY

Asia Bible Commentary Series

JUDGES

Athena E. Gorospe
with
Charles Ringma

General Editor
Federico G. Villanueva

Old Testament Consulting Editors
Yohanna Katanacho, Tim Meadowcroft, Joseph Shao

New Testament Consulting Editors
Steve Chang, Andrew Spurgeon, Brian Wintle

© 2016 by Athena Evelyn Gorospe and Charles R. Ringma

Published 2016 by Langham Global Library
An imprint of Langham Publishing
www.langhampublishing.org

Langham Publishing and its imprints are a ministry of Langham Partnership

Langham Partnership
PO Box 296, Carlisle, Cumbria CA3 9WZ, UK
www.langham.org

Published in partnership with Asia Theological Association

ATA
QCC PO Box 1454 – 1154, Manila, Philippines
www.atasia.com

ISBNs:
978-1-78368-867-8 Print
978-1-78368-195-2 ePub
978-1-78368-197-6 PDF

Athena Evelyn Gorospe and Charles R. Ringma have asserted their right under the Copyright, Designs and Patents Act, 1988 to be identified as the Authors of this work.

All rights reserved. No part of this publication may be reproduced, stored in a retrieval system or transmitted, in any form or by any means, electronic, mechanical, photocopying, recording or otherwise, without the prior written permission of the publisher or the Copyright Licensing Agency.

Unless otherwise stated, Scripture quotations are from the New International Version, copyright © 2011. Used by permission. All rights reserved.

British Library Cataloguing in Publication Data
A catalogue record for this book is available from the British Library

ISBN: 978-1-78368-867-8

Cover & Book Design: projectluz.com

Langham Partnership actively supports theological dialogue and an author's right to publish but does not necessarily endorse the views and opinions set forth, and works referenced within this publication or guarantee its technical and grammatical correctness. Langham Partnership does not accept any responsibility or liability to persons or property as a consequence of the reading, use or interpretation of its published content.

CONTENTS

Series Preface ix

Authors' Preface xi

List of Abbreviations xiii

Introduction 1

Judges 1:1–3:6: Grappling with Failure 11
    Overview: Structure and Links 11
    1:1–36 Experiencing Failure 12
    2:1–5 Lack of Vigilance 22
    2:6–10 Acknowledging Yahweh 25
    2:11–21 Disobedience and Apostasy 28
    2:22–3:6 Failure and Testing 35
    Coping with Failure 39

Judges 3:7–31: The Role of Individual Deliverers 41
    3:7–11 Othniel the Ideal Deliverer 42
    3:12–30 Ehud the Unlikely Deliverer 49

Judges 4:1–5:31: Partnership and Solidarity in God's Work 57
    Story and the Poem 57
    4:1–24 Contours of an Upside-Down World:
        The Inversion of Roles 59
    5:1–31 Celebrating the Mighty Deeds of God in People's
        Participation 72
    The Singers and the Structure 73

Judges 6:1–8:29: The Use of Power: Empowerment, Abuse, and
    Violence 89
    Structure of the Gideon-Abimelech Cycle 90
    6:1–10 Disempowerment: The Economic Plunder of Israel 91

  6:11–7:25 The Growing of a Leader: Issues in Empowerment............94
  8:1–35 Difficulties and Resistances in the Transformation Process 111

Judges 8:30–9:57: The Pitfalls of Power...119
 8:30–35 Transitions: Honoring Leaders Rightly...............................120
 9:1–6 The Destructive Side of Family Ties.......................................122
 9:7–15 The Perils of Kingship...126
 9:16–20 Dealing with Integrity...132
 9:21–56 Retributive Justice...134

Judges 10:6–12:7: The Marginalization of Yahweh 139
 10:6–16 The Diminishment of Yahweh 140
 10:17–11:11 The Rise of a Self-Made Man......................................147
 11:12–28 Strong Leadership and Public Success 152
 11:29–40 Tragedy in the Midst of Victory 155
 12:1–7 Unresolved Issues..165

Judges 13:1–16:31: Reversal of Expectations 169
 Overall Narrative Structure...170
 The Samson Narrative as Dramatic Comedy:
  The Tragic Hero Who Overcomes 170
 13:1–25 Great Expectations and the Reversal of Roles....................172
 14:1–16:3 Comic Reversal in the Samson-Philistine Episodes..........187
 16:4–31 Comedy Turns to Tragedy and Then Comes Full Circle.....199
 13:1–16:31 Denouement: The Divine Trickster..............................206

Judges 17–18: The Domestication of God: Gods, Gold, and Goons........211
 Judges 17–21 Overview of Concluding Chapters 212
 Judges 17–18 Structure and Overview 217
 17:1–6 God's Domestication in Family Life....................................220
 17:7–13 God's Domestication in Religious Life..............................225
 18:1–31 God's Domestication in Economic-Political Life................230

Judges 19:1–20:7: When Home Becomes Unsafe 241
    19–21 Structure and Links in Judges 241
    19:1 Exposition: The Characters 244
    19:2a Inciting Moment: Leaving Home...245
    19:2b–21 Complications: Going Home..247
    19:22–26 Climax: Outcast and Disgrace Outside the Home 254
    19:27–29 Resolution: Going Home..259
    19:30–20:7 Epilogue: The Levite Tells the Story 262
Judges 20:1–21:25: A Society That Has Gone Awry 269
    20:1–17 A War between Brothers 270
    20:18–48 Parody of a Divine War..279
    21:1–23 Reparations for a Lost Tribe 290
    21:24–25 Epilogue: The Ironic and Incomplete Ending...................305
Bibliography...307

Topics

Vision and Reality: The Story in Asian Christian Realities 20
Likely and Unlikely Deliverers 55
Playing One's Part in Yahweh's Purposes 71
Cooperating in God's Work 87
God with Us – Key to Transformation 102
Empowering Asian Leaders 109
Taking the Spotlight Away from Yahweh 117
Nepotism in Asian Societies 123
The Ambiguity of Power 138
The False Gods of Asian Society 143
Harmful Effects of Ministering Out of Rejection 160
Using People and Using God 167
Children of Promise in Asian Culture 174
Spirituality of Presence 187
Humor in Filipino Culture and the Christian Life 196
God's Unexpected Ways 208
What is Offered to God Belongs to God 222
Patronage System in Asian Culture 229
The Domestication of Yahweh 239
Objectifying God and One Another 245
Justice: Restoring Agency and Empowering the Vulnerable 267
Just Reparations 297
Recovering Grace and Love in the Church 304

SERIES PREFACE

In recent years, we have witnessed one of the greatest shifts in the history of world Christianity. It used to be that the majority of Christians lived in the West. But now the face of world Christianity has changed beyond recognition. Christians are now evenly distributed around the globe. This has implications for the interpretation of the Bible. In our case, we are faced with the task of interpreting the Bible from within our respective contexts. This is in line with the growing realization that every theology is contextual. Our understanding of the Bible is influenced by our historical and social locations. Thus, even the questions that we bring into our reading of the Bible will be shaped by our present realities. There is a need therefore to interpret the Bible for our own contexts.

The Asia Bible Commentary Series addresses this need. In line with the mission of the Asia Theological Association Publications, we have gathered Asian evangelical Bible scholars in Asia to write commentaries on each book of the Bible. The mission is to "produce resources for pastors, Christian leaders, cross-cultural workers, and students in Asia that are biblical, pastoral, contextual, missional, and prophetic." Although the Bible can be studied for different reasons, we believe that it is given primarily for the edification of the Body of Christ (2 Tim 3:16–17). The ABCS is designed to help pastors in their sermon preparation, cell group leaders or lay leaders in their Bible study groups, Christian students in their study of the Bible, and Christians in general in their efforts to apply the Bible in their respective contexts.

Each commentary begins with an introduction that provides general information about the book's author and original context, summarizes the main message or theme of the book, and outlines its potential relevance to a particular Asian context. The introduction is followed by an exposition that combines exegesis and application. Here, we seek to speak to and empower Christians in Asia by using our own stories, parables, poems, and other cultural resources as we expound the Bible.

The Bible is actually Asian in that it comes from ancient West Asia and there are many similarities between the world of the Bible and traditional Asian cultures. But there are also many differences that we need to explore in some depth. That is why the commentaries also include articles or topics in which we bring specific issues in Asian church, social, and religious contexts into dialogue with relevant issues in the Bible. We do not seek to resolve every

Judges

tension but rather to allow the text to illumine the context and vice versa, acknowledging that in the end we do not have all the answers to every mystery.

May the Holy Spirit who inspired the writers of the Bible bring light to the hearts and minds of all who use these materials, to the glory of God and to the building up of the churches!

Federico G. Villanueva

General Editor

AUTHORS' PREFACE

The book of Judges will always be popular with Sunday School children because of its heroes, such as Gideon and Samson, and its dramatic stories. And feminist scholars have noted the book because it includes so many stories of women.

But to what extent will the faith community make use of this book in its teaching, preaching, and pastoral care? Is Judges simply too dark, too puzzling, and too difficult? We believe that this "troublesome book" mirrors back significant themes that have important messages for the contemporary faith community.

In co-authoring this book, we have tried to write it as a seamless whole, giving attention to the text and its setting, while also drawing implications for the church in Asia. We hope that the commentary will be read by scholars and theology students as well as pastors and laity.

Seamless writing poses a challenge, but also offers an enriching experience. We trust this will be evident as you engage this book. You may be interested to know that the writing of this commentary has taken place over a ten-year period and occurred in the face of serious illnesses for both of us, along with severe work challenges. We have worked on this book in the Philippines, Australia, the USA, and the UK.

We have many people and organizations to thank. First of all, we thank Asian Theological Seminary (ATS) for sabbaticals and the ATS community for their love and support. The SIL Guesthouse in Quezon City was a place of many collaborative writing sessions, and we thank the staff for their care.

In Australia, we are grateful to many friends for providing hospitality and accommodation – Rita Ringma, Irene Alexander, Chris and Marilyn Brown, and Sue Fairley from Grace College at the University of Queensland. Frequent use was also made of the library of Trinity College of the Uniting Church in Brisbane, and we especially thank the librarian, Alethea Hubley, who only understands the notion of going the second mile by going the third.

Other organizations with their support have played a key role in making this project possible. We thank Langham Partnership International, through Ian Shaw, for sponsoring the yearly International Research and Training Seminar, which enabled Athena to use the excellent research facilities of Wheaton College, Oxford University, Tyndale House in Cambridge, Trinity Theological College in Singapore, and Cambridge University.

Judges

Some of the last chapters were written at Fuller Theological Seminary in Pasadena, California through the Global Research Initiative of the Center for Missiological Research and at Ridley College in Cambridge. Special thanks to Bea and Peter Maglaya and Johnny Ching for opening their homes while Athena was in the US and to Scholar Leaders International, who provided additional support.

We acknowledge the roles played by Federico Villanueva and Bubbles Lactaoen, and we especially thank Karen Hollenbeck-Wuest for her comprehensive editorial work. For financial support of Karen's work, we thank Daniel Ong Kian Koc and his wife Bee Ching from Manila and Rosemary Toye and her husband Tim Klauke from Vancouver.

We feel honored to have been able to play our small part in the Asia Bible Commentary Series. We believe more than ever that in the fast-paced and pragmatic world of late modernity, we need to be attentive and reflective listeners of the biblical story. The future of our faith and that of the church lies first and foremost not in seeking to be relevant, but rather to be *different* as we are formed by the words of Scripture in the power of the Spirit. Only to this end can we be a transformational presence in the world.

Athena E. Gorospe and Charles Ringma

Manila, Philippines and Brisbane, Australia

LIST OF ABBREVIATIONS

BOOKS OF THE BIBLE

Old Testament
Gen, Exod, Lev, Num, Deut, Josh, Judg, Ruth, 1–2 Sam, 1–2 Kgs, 1–2 Chr, Ezra, Neh, Esth, Job, Ps/Pss, Prov, Eccl, Song, Isa, Jer, Lam, Ezek, Dan, Hos, Joel, Amos, Obad, Jonah, Mic, Nah, Hab, Zeph, Hag, Zech, Mal

New Testament
Matt, Mark, Luke, John, Acts, Rom, 1–2 Cor, Gal, Eph, Phil, Col, 1–2 Thess, 1–2 Tim, Titus, Phlm, Heb, Jas, 1–2 Pet, 1–2–3 John, Jude, Rev

BIBLE TEXTS AND VERSIONS

Divisions of the canon
NT	New Testament
OT	Old Testament

Ancient texts and versions
LXX	Septuagint
MT	Masoretic Text

Modern versions
ESV	English Standard Version
KJV	King James Version
NASB	New American Standard Bible
NIV	New International Version
NJB	New Jerusalem Bible
NJPS	Tanakh: The New JPS Translation
NKJV	New King James Version
NRSV	New Revised Standard Version

Journals, reference works, and series
AB	Anchor Bible
ABCS	Asia Bible Commentary Series
ABD	*Anchor Bible Dictionary*

AYBC	Anchor Yale Bible Commentary
Bib	*Biblica*
BDB	*The Brown-Driver-Briggs Hebrew and English Lexicon of the OT*
BerOl	Berit Olam
CBQ	*Catholic Biblical Quarterly*
DCH	*Dictionary of Classical Hebrew*
ExpTim	*Expository Times*
FOTL	Forms of the Old Testament Literature
GKC	*Gesenius Hebrew Grammar, A Grammar of Biblical Hebrew,* Joüon and Muraoka
HALOT	*Hebrew and Aramaic Lexicon of the Old Testament,* Koehler, Baumgartner and Stamm
HBT	*Horizons in Biblical Theology*
IBC	*Interpretation: A Bible Commentary for Teaching and Preaching*
ITC	International Theological Commentary
Int	*Interpretation*
JAAR	*Journal of the American Academy of Religion*
JANES	*Journal of the Ancient Near Eastern Society*
JBL	*Journal of Biblical Literature*
JPSTC	JPS Torah Commentary
JPT	*Journal of Pentecostal Theology*
JSOT	*Journal for the Study of the Old Testament*
JSOTSup	*Journal for the Study of Old Testament Supplement Series*
JTS	*Journal of Theological Studies*
NAC	New American Commentary
NCBC	New Century Bible Commentary
NIB	*The New Interpreter's Bible*
NIBC	New International Bible Commentary
NIDOTTE	New International Dictionary of Old Testament Theology and Exegesis
NIVAC	NIV Application Commentary
OTL	Old Testament Library
RevExp	*Review and Expositor*
SJOT	*Scandinavian Journal of the Old Testament*
TLOT	*Theological Lexicon of the Old Testament,* Jenni and Westermann

List of Abbreviations

TOTC	Tyndale Old Testament Commentaries
TynBul	*Tyndale Bulletin*
VE	*Vox Evangelica*
VT	*Vetus Testamentum*
WTJ	*Westminster Theological Journal*
WBC	Word Biblical Commentary
ZAW	*Zeitschrift für die alttestamentliche Wissenschaft*

INTRODUCTION

The book of Judges is a puzzle to many because of its strange stories. We wonder how God can use Samson (Judg 13–16) when he is such a moral failure – getting entangled repeatedly with women to the detriment of his calling. We are baffled when Jephthah makes a vow that leads to the sacrifice of his daughter, and then there is nothing in the story that explicitly states that this is wrong (Judg 11). Is the point of this story that we should be willing to sacrifice our loved ones in order to accomplish God's work? We are horrified when the Levite's concubine is raped and then her body is chopped into pieces (Judg 19), and so we are bewildered about how this story found its way into the "Holy Scriptures." Then we come to the bizarre story of virgins being kidnapped to provide wives for a decimated tribe (Judg 21). Because there is often no explicit evaluation of the characters' actions in the text, we are confounded about how to apply these bewildering narratives to our lives. So it is not surprising that many pastors do not preach from the book of Judges!

In this commentary we seek to help readers navigate the many puzzles of the book by providing an overall framework for reading Judges and by explaining a way of entering its stories so that that they can be appropriated in an Asian context.

A FRAMEWORK FOR READING JUDGES

A Cycle That Deteriorates

In reading the book of Judges, we are struck by the cyclical pattern that is repeated throughout the book and which frames the different stories. The pattern starts with *sin* ("the Israelites did evil in the eyes of the Lord"), which consequently brings *suffering* in the form of oppressive foreign nations that dominate Israel ("the Lord gave/sold them into the hands of [a foreign ruler or nation]"). This leads to *supplication* ("the Israelites cried out to the Lord"). In response, God brings *salvation* to Israel by sending a judge who delivers them from oppression. Then a period of peace follows ("the land had rest").[1] This pattern reveals both God's judgement for sin as well as God's mercy. As people cry out to God for help, God in compassion alleviates their distress through a deliverer. God's judgement ultimately seeks to restore Israel's relationship with Yahweh, which has been disrupted because of sin.

---

1. For an expanded explanation of this pattern, see pp. 42–48.

Israel, however, does not take advantage of the opportunity to have a new beginning. Despite God's repeated warnings and acts of compassionate deliverance, the Israelites and their leaders never learn. While continuing to pay lip service to Yahweh, they continually do evil by worshipping other gods and forgetting what Yahweh has done for them. Thus the cyclical pattern deteriorates as the book progresses.[2] In the earlier stories, the framework exhibits all the elements of this cyclical pattern, as seen in the Othniel (3:7–11), Ehud (3:12–30) and Deborah narratives (4:1–5:31). The cycle becomes less clear in the Gideon narrative (6:1–8:28), although the pattern is still complete. As the book moves towards the end, more elements of the cycle are missing, as can be seen in the Jephthah (10:6–12:7) and Samson narratives (13:1–16:31). In the last chapters (17:1–21:25), the pattern completely breaks down.

Along with the dissolution of this cyclical framework, there is deterioration in the socio-religious conditions of Israel, a decline in the quality of the judges, and an increasingly fragmented and divisive relationship among the Israelite tribes.[3] In addition, God is portrayed in a more ambivalent light,[4] becoming increasingly withdrawn and silent as the narrative progresses.[5] Thus "the pattern will not be simply cyclical: at every turn of the wheel Israel will become worse than they have ever been before."[6] Hence the movement becomes a downward spiral.[7]

The final chapters (17–21) trace stories of idolatry, rape, murder, and intertribal war, with everyone doing "as they saw fit" (17:6; 21:5). Here, God's judgement for sin is not direct and immediate, as it was with Israel's defeat and oppression by foreign nations. Rather, God's justice is slowly manifested as the people persistently refuse to obey God's commands, leading to foolish actions, internal strife, and institutional failure.

---

2. See J. P. U. Lilley, "A Literary Appreciation of the Book of Judges," *TynBul* 18 (1976): 101–102; Cheryl Exum, "The Centre Cannot Hold: Thematic and Textual Instabilities in Judges," *CBQ* 52 (1990): 412; D. W. Gooding, "The Composition of the Book of Judges," *Eretz Israel* 16 (1982): 70–79.
3. David Dorsey, "Judges," in *The Literary Structure of the Old Testament: A Commentary on Genesis to Malachi* (Grand Rapids, MI: Baker Academic, 1999), 107; Victor Matthews, *Judges & Ruth*, NCBC (Cambridge: Cambridge University Press, 2004), 8–10; Dennis T. Olson, "Judges," *NIB*, Vol. 2 (Nashville, TN: Abingdon, 1998), 725–726, 731–732; Daniel Block, *Judges, Ruth*, NAC (Nashville, TN: Broadman & Holman, 1999), 131–132.
4. Exum, "Thematic and Textual Instabilities," 411.
5. Ibid., 418, 422, 424, 426.
6. Gooding, "Composition," 72.
7. Dorsey, "Literary Structure," 120; Block, *Judges*, 145; Gregory Wong, *Compositional Strategy of the Book of Judges* (Leiden: Brill, 2006), 156–185.

Introduction

The stories increasingly express the sickness at the heart of Israel. Likewise, the characters from Gideon onwards show questionable qualities that are but manifestations of the dysfunction that has riddled the nation. Thus we should not regard the characters in the book as ethical ideals or examples to be followed. Rather, they raise possibilities about what can happen in the corporate body if the members continue to disobey and marginalize God.

The Use of Irony

Another important element in understanding Judges is to recognize the extensive use of irony.[8] In irony, one means the opposite of what is actually said.[9] Thus readers reject the surface meaning, even as they perceive a new meaning that "relies on and moves beyond that which has been stated."[10]

In the book of Judges, the narratives are told from a seemingly detached and neutral viewpoint, but the troubling and incongruous actions of the characters (especially in relation to God's covenantal stipulations) provide hints about evaluating their behavior. The characters' speeches may seem to give importance to the role of God, but their actions may actually contradict these claims. In these narratives, irony is used as a form of critique or protest, since it reveals the distance between what is and what ought to be.[11] Thus as we read the stories, we need to be mindful of this ironic tone and not take everything that is said or done by the characters – even in the name of God – as something that would meet with divine approval.

A NARRATIVE APPROACH

The approach in this commentary is to take seriously the narrative character of the book. Narrative has two major modes – the historical and the artistic literary work. The Judges narratives share characteristics of both these modes.

Historical References

The book refers to known peoples, places, and customs in ancient Israel and the ancient Near East. Places such as Jerusalem, Hebron, and Ashkelon

---

8. Lilian Klein, *The Triumph of Irony in the Book of Judges* (Sheffield: Almond Press, 1988), devotes extensive attention to this.
9. A good theoretical discussion of irony is found in Carolyn Sharp, *Irony and Meaning in the Hebrew Bible* (Bloomington, IN: Indiana University Press, 2009), although she does not deal with texts from the book of Judges. See also Klein's discussion of irony in *Triumph of Irony*, 195–199.
10. Sharp, *Irony and Meaning*, 24.
11. Edwin Good, *Irony in the Old Testament* (Philadelphia, PA: Westminster Press, 1965), 30.

are mentioned, which exist up to the present. Ancient peoples such as the Philistines, the Canaanites, the Moabites, and the Hittites are also cited. The book shows a polemic against Baal worship, which is known to have been pervasive in the Canaanite regions at this time, spreading to Egypt and the Mediterranean.[12] There is a broad chronological framework, although the events do not strictly follow each other in chronological order. There is also a desire to pay a debt to the past.[13] Biblical narratives, such as Judges, seek to address through historical memory "a people defined in terms of their past," and this "remembrance of the past devolves on the present and determines the future."[14]

Nevertheless, Judges is not like a modern historical book, which emphasizes the cause and effect of human events and excludes divine causation. Modern history includes a critical evaluation of sources, which is not found in biblical narratives.[15] What dominates the recounting of events is a theological purpose. The selection of events and how they are told involve interpretation and are creatively shaped with the use of imagination to achieve this theological purpose.

The book went through a long period of formation: from oral stories, to written sources of collected material, to the editing of the whole collection. Many scholars support the view that Judges is part of a corpus (Joshua-Kings) that received its final editing during the exile, although there are variations to this theory.[16] This corpus, known as the Deuteronomistic History, seeks to explain why Israel went into exile, despite God's promises to Abraham and David. It is called Deuteronomistic History because the interpretation of Israel's history is based on the covenant laws in Deuteronomy. Because the nation broke their covenant with Yahweh and failed to keep the deuteronomic laws, they experienced the curses accompanying the breaking of the

---

12. Karel van der Toorn, et al., *Dictionary of Deities and Demons in the Bible* (Leiden: Brill, 1995), 133, 137.
13. According to Paul Ricoeur, *Time and Narrative*, Vol. 3, trans. Kathleen Mclaughlin and David Pellauer (Chicago, IL: University of Chicago Press, 1988), 143, 152, 157.
14. Meir Sternberg, *The Poetics of Biblical Narrative* (Bloomington, IN: Indiana University Press, 1985), 31.
15. James Barr, *The Scope and Authority of the Bible* (London: SCM Press, 1980), 7–8. Barr points out that "history," as a classifying term, is not found in the Bible. History is a construct that developed from Greek historiography and one of its essential characteristics is the critical evaluation of sources (James Barr, *Old and New in Interpretation* [New York: Harper & Row, 1966], 71).
16. The idea of a deuteronomistic history was proposed by Martin Noth, *The Deuteronomistic History* (Sheffield: Almond Press, 1981).

Introduction

covenant (Deut 28). Thus God did not fail the nation, but rather the nation failed God.

Artistic Literary

Aside from a theological interpretation of the history of Israel, the book of Judges also displays features that show a literary concern. There is conscious artistry and symmetry in shaping the structure in order to communicate a certain message. Aside from the cyclical pattern discussed above, we see this in how the stories of the different judges are arranged geographically rather than chronologically, starting from the southern tribes, Judah (Othniel), then moving northward, and ending with Dan (Samson) in the far north. The northward movement is accompanied by deterioration in the quality of the judges.[17]

Literary techniques, such as suspense, humor, irony, flashback, and play of perspectives are utilized to reconstruct events. A verbatim dialogue is supplied even when no one could have known what was being said, except the characters themselves (e.g. Ehud and Eglon, the Moabite king; Samson and Delilah in the bedroom). The narrative also ascribes feeling, intentions, and motives to the characters. For example, Judges 3:1 explains the reason Israel is not able to drive out some of the inhabitants of the land: the Lord is testing them – pointing to divine causation rather than human factors in the unfolding of events.

Because Judges exhibits artistic literary features, we employ methods for reading poetic narratives, such as analysis of plot, characterization, point of view, time and place, dialogue, and style. We also look at the structure of the plot as a whole and discuss the parts in relation to the whole, although we acknowledge the presence of sources or oral traditions behind the narrative and attempt to hear the voices behind these sources and oral forms.

The Power of Stories

Stories capture our attention and speak to us more than propositional statements. They draw us because they move through time, just as our lives move through time. Moreover, we identify emotionally with the predicament that the characters face. We rejoice when they rejoice, and we grieve when they grieve. We are touched beyond the intellectual level as we ache, cry, and feel happiness or compassion for the characters.

---

17. Marc Zvi Brettler, *The Book of Judges* (London and New York: Routledge, 2002), 111–114. Brettler thinks this structure is intended to support the Davidic kingship.

Many parts of Asia are still predominantly oral. In these cultures, stories play a central role in social discourse. In order to be understood, stories need to be heard and read as a whole rather than being cut up into pieces. Asians belong to cultures that emphasize interconnectedness and holism, and so a reading of the text that cuts up the narrative into disjointed fragments and jumps from one place to another is very jarring to Asian sensibilities.[18]

In this commentary, we try to capture the power of the Judges story in its ancient context. Nevertheless, the primary purpose of the biblical text is not artistic or historiographical, but rather theological. Theology, however, is not just about "right thinking," but also about "right living." Thus we need to consider ethics.

Yet how can an ancient text show Christians in Asia how to live? In what way can the narratives of Judges speak to the issues of our times?

The Ancient and Asian Context

We do not read Scripture without bringing along our own presuppositions and preunderstandings. While our preunderstandings may provide lenses for understanding the biblical text, they can also act as blinders. The Bible has its own cultural and linguistic world, which is rooted in the cultural context and language of its time and it is distinct from our own cultural symbolic system. Without an understanding of the meaning of historical references, customs, symbols, and actions in the ancient setting, some parts of the narrative will not make sense to us, or we may impose our own cultural categories, which are alien to the world of the ancient text.

However, if the text is treated only as a historical document to be mined for information that can be used for historical reconstruction, then it is difficult to make the jump between the world of the text and our world. The historical gap is too big and the analogies do not work, since there are no exact parallels between the world of the ancient Israelites and our modern world. Even if we have understood the narrative in its original setting, our application will appear forced or strained.

On the other hand, those who regard the text as an artistic document see it as a closed linguistic system, without any relation to the outside world. What happens is a purely descriptive account of the artistic effects of the text

---

18. R. S. Sugirtharajah, *Asian Biblical Hermeneutics and Postcolonialism* (Maryknoll, NY: Orbis, 1998), 12, mentions how the Anglicist historical-critical approach replaced the Indian narrative approach, which views text as "authorless narrative wholes."

Introduction

without looking at how it affects the life of the reader. Moreover, Scripture is regarded as devoid of authority or theological relevance.[19]

In order for a narrative to speak to the Asian context, we need to pose real flesh-and-blood readers – us.[20] Athena is Filipino, while Charles is Australian; Athena lives in Manila, while Charles has lived in the Philippines and regularly teaches in Asia. Based on our social location and experience, we are filling in gaps in the narrative as we read, constructing coherence and meaning based on the formal structures and configurations of the narrative and its meaning within its own cultural world.[21] As we imaginatively engage the narrative, the process opens up thematic possibilities and connections that provide insight for those who live and work in Asia. These possibilities are not prescriptions, but rather thematic paradigms that can shape our personal and corporate experience.[22] "Thus, narratives do not tell us what to do, but point the way towards what is true of human experience, or what might be true of our own experience. Their function is not to inculcate in us a certain virtue, but to involve us in exploring possibilities that would help shape our identity."[23]

THEMES

The themes that orient our reading are those that resonate in the Asian setting. There are clues in the text that point these directions, although they may not be explicitly stated.

The book of Judges is concerned with how Yahweh has been replaced by other gods in the life of Israel. The ever-present element in the cyclical framework is, "they did evil in the eyes of the Lord" (2:11; 3:7, 12; 4:1; 6:1; 10:6; 13:1). Here, the evil that Israel does – which provokes Yahweh's anger – is abandoning Yahweh and following after other gods (see also Deut 4:25; 9:18;

---

19. See Brevard Childs, *Biblical Theology of the Old and New Testaments* (Minneapolis, MN: Fortress, 1992), 20.
20. Paul Ricoeur sees the importance of the real flesh-and-blood reader in the act of reading in *Time and Narrative*, Vol. 1, trans. Kathleen Mclaughlin and David Pellauer (Chicago, IL: University of Chicago Press, 1984), 171; *Time and Narrative*, Vol. 3, 164.
21. Athena Gorospe, "Old Testament Narratives in Context: Moses' Reverse Migration and the Hermeneutics of Possibility," in *The Gospel in Culture: Contextualization Issues through Asia Eyes*, ed. Melba Maggay (Mandaluyong City: OMF Lit, 2013), 189, 212.
22. Gorospe, "Old Testament Narratives," 215–217, based on Ricoeur's theory of narrative. See his article, "Imagination in Discourse and Action," in *From Text to Action: Essays in Hermeneutics, II*, trans. Kathleen Blamey (Evanston, IL: Northwestern University Press, 1991), 169–181.
23. Gorospe, "Old Testament Narratives," 216.

17:2). This does not mean that the Israelites no longer sacrifice to Yahweh. Rather, Israel looks to other gods (whether other deities, human beings, or themselves) as the source of their well being, security, deliverance, and hope. Hence Yahweh is marginalized from the center of life and relegated to the peripheries, while other allegiances and interests take over. Moreover, Israel projects onto Yahweh the way it regards its idols – as gods to be appeased and manipulated in order to bless one's plans and family. In this way, God is not only marginalized but also domesticated.

Another recurrent theme in Judges, which resonates in the Asian setting, is the use of power. The narrative shows how God rescues the powerless and the oppressed (despite their sins), uses those who are stereotyped as weak (Jael, Manoah), and empowers the insecure (Gideon).

While there is prophetic power in Deborah's words, and the spirit gives the judges the power to deliver, there is also misuse of power, including the power of one's position and accomplishments (Gideon), the power of words (Jephthah's vow), the power of kinship ties, religious establishment, and wealth (Abimelech), and the power of institutional mechanisms (the Israel tribes in chapters 20–21). These narratives provide a reflection on the temptations of power and how it can be put to good use as well as abused.

Lastly, Judges is distinctive because it includes a number of stories about women. Women are seen as initiators and leaders (e.g. Achsah, Deborah, Jael), but also victims of a culture that gives them no voice and power and treats them as objects (Jephthah's daughter, the Levite's concubine).[24]

Many of the stories in this book are dark, and some are quite depressing. They are not stories with Hollywood endings. The Bible tells it as it is – without varnish and without showing only the good side. We are often tempted to shut our ears, especially if a story we encounter is too terrible. We want to

---

24. For feminist perspectives on Judges, see the following: Mieke Bal, *Death and Dissymmetry: The Politics of Coherence in the Book of Judges* (Chicago, IL: University of Chicago Press, 1988) and *Murder and Difference: Gender, Genre, and Scholarship on Sisera's Death* (Bloomington, IN: Indiana University Press, 1988); Athalya Brenner, ed., *A Feminist Companion to Judges* (Sheffield: Sheffield Academic Press, 1993) and *Judges: A Feminist Companion to the Bible, Second Series* (Sheffield: Sheffield Academic Press, 1999); Phyllis Trible, *Texts of Terror: Literary Feminist Readings of Biblical Narratives* (Philadelphia, PA: Fortress, 1984). See also the following articles by Cheryl Exum: "Feminist Criticism: Whose Interests are Being Served?" in *Judges and Method: New Approaches in Biblical Studies*, 2d. ed., ed. Gale Yee, (Minneapolis, MN: Fortress, 2007), 65–89; "Samson's Women," in *Fragmented Women: Feminist (Sub)Versions of Biblical Narratives* (Valley Forge, PA: Trinity Press International, 1993), 61–93. The commentary of Tammi Schneider, *Judges*, BerOl (Collegeville, MN: Liturgical Press, 2000) gives detailed treatment of the women in Judges.

Introduction

turn off the TV, close the newspaper, and try to distract ourselves with other things when such disturbing narratives interrupt our carefully constructed and convenient world. Yet the Bible teaches us not run away from stories of pain and loss, but rather to develop the spiritual discipline of careful listening.

We hope that you will read this commentary with your Bible beside you. May the Word of God be like a sharp, two-edged sword that cuts through the diffidence, foolishness, and blindness of our hearts, while bringing healing and life.

JUDGES 1:1–3:6

Grappling with Failure

In the life of faith, we often experience both success and failure. But oftentimes, we only expect victory and success. This is especially true in relation to God's promises or God's work. We are oriented to the perspective that whenever we do God's work and claim the fulfillment of God's promises, we will automatically see the effects in term of a fruitful and victorious ministry, full of accomplishments and success stories.

When the Israelites enter the land, as recounted in the book of Joshua, they experience initial and spectacular success. Although there are some failures, overall they have the positive experience of seeing the fulfillment of God's promises. Hence, they expect that with much of the task of possessing the land behind them, they can now focus on putting structures in place that will enable them to live a fruitful life and flourish in the land

Nevertheless, the opening of the book of Judges shows that there is still land to be conquered and occupied. The task of occupying is not quite finished. Rather than a concerted overall Israelite effort, the task is delegated to the various tribes. However, contrary to the predominant success story in Joshua, the opening chapters of Judges trace a story of initial success, followed by a story of partial success/partial failure, ending with a story of complete failure. The introduction (Judg 1:1–3:6) tries to grapple with this failure by offering several explanations about why, despite God's promises and power, Israel fails to possess the land fully.

OVERVIEW: STRUCTURE AND LINKS

Judges 1:1–3:6 can be divided into five sections. The first section (1:1–33) reports about the failure to possess the land after some initial successes. The middle sections (2:1–5, 6–10, 11–21) grapple with and explain this failure from different angles. The tone is overtly theological and condemnatory.[1] Instead of mentioning specific people groups, there is a generalized reference to the inhabitants of the land and the nations around Israel.

---

1. Block, *Judges*, 76. However, Block groups 3:1–6 with 2:1–23.

In 2:1–5, the emissary of Yahweh accuses Israel of disobeying Yahweh by making a covenant with the Canaanites. This offense seems to be linked to Israel's failure to possess the land fully, although these two situations are not directly interconnected. Instead, the emissary says that the failure to dispossess is something that Israel has been forewarned about, implying that they should have been more vigilant about the challenges and dangers that faced them in entering the land.

The next two sections (2:6–10, 11–21) explicitly bring together Israel's offense and subsequent punishment. In 2:6–10, the narrator traces Israel's lack of success in fully occupying the land to the new generation's failure to acknowledge Yahweh and Yahweh's deeds, in contrast to the practice of their predecessors. In the next section (2:11–21), the narrator expounds upon the consequences of this failure to acknowledge Yahweh in a sermon that accuses Israel of doing evil by abandoning Yahweh and worshipping other gods. In this latter section, the failure to dispossess the Canaanites is identified clearly as Yahweh's punishment for Israel's disobedience and defection.

The last section (2:22–3:6) introduces a theological reason for Israel's failure to possess the land completely, explaining that by allowing the non-Israelite nations to remain, Yahweh is testing Israel and training his people in the context of war. The matter-of-fact tone of the first section (1:1–33) matches the reportorial quality of this final section (2:22–3:6). Both sections are also linked by references to specific people groups living in the land, with whom Israel is forced to live.

1:1–36 EXPERIENCING FAILURE

1:1–2 The Opening Scene

The Israelites know that, even after Joshua's death, the task of possessing the land is still far from finished. Territories remain to be claimed and battles need to be fought in order to possess the land fully. Thus, "the Israelites asked the LORD" (1:1a). The Hebrew phrase, "asked the LORD" (literally, "inquired of the Lord"), is a technical term that refers to seeking an oracle from the deity when embarking on a war,[2] although it is also used as a general term for seeking God's guidance in other areas.[3]

---

2. *HALOT* 4:1372. The phrase is used in the context of war in Judg 20:18, 23, 27; 1 Sam 23:2–4; 28:6; 30:8; 2 Sam 5:19–23.
3. See 1 Sam 10:22; 22:10–15; 2 Sam 2:1.

Israel asks, "Who of us is to go up first to fight against the Canaanites?" (1:1b). The verb "go up" presupposes that the Israelites are in a lower location than the Canaanites and are setting out to take possession of the central highlands. However, "go up" may also mean to embark on a military campaign.[4] The "Canaanites" refers to the various peoples of the region, regardless of their ethnic identity.[5]

Israel's question might have arisen out of a desire to know God's-appointed successor after the death of individual leaders, such as Moses and Joshua.[6] God replies by appointing a tribe to start off a renewed military campaign (1:2a), although not necessarily to exercise leadership over Israel. This command is accompanied by a promise. Just as the Lord promised to give the land to Joshua (Josh 1:3), in the same way God promises to give the land to Judah (Judg 1:2). God's declaration, "I have given the land into their hands" (1:2b), accomplishes this deed in the very act of speaking.[7] Thus, it is couched in the form of the Hebrew past tense, even though the realization of the action is still in the immediate future. In these verses, we see a basic rhythm in the divine-human interplay. Human action comes from God's calling, not from one's own presumptions. God's call is a call that accomplishes; God is with people in their acts of obedience. This basic rhythm, however, is ruptured when God's work is done contrary to God's command, or without a call.

1:3–18 Cooperation and Success

Although Joshua has divided the land among the different tribes (Josh 13–22), not all of them have been fully occupied by the designated tribe, since the different tribes are expected to take the initiative in claiming their allocated territory. Yet there is cooperation among the tribes. The tribe of Judah asks the tribe of Simeon to help them with claiming their tribal allocation; in return, Judah promises to help the tribe of Simeon when the time comes for them to claim their own territory (Judg 1:3). The allocated territory of Simeon is

---

4. J. Alberto Soggin, *Judges, A Commentary*, OTL (Philadelphia, PA: Westminster, 1981), 20. This verb is used six times in Judges 1 (vv. 1, 2, 3, 4, 16, 22), five times in connection with engaging in battle.
5. Barnabas Lindars, *Judges 1–5: A New Translation and Commentary*, ed. A. D. H. Mayes (Edinburgh: T & T Clark), 12.
6. Tammi Schneider, *Judges*, 2–3.
7. Other similar phrases are found in other ancient Near Eastern texts, indicating a god's granting of victory over the people's enemies. See Robert Boling, *Judges*, AB, Vol. 6 (Garden City, NY: Doubleday, 1977), 54.

within the territory given to Judah (Josh 19:1–9); hence, it makes sense for them to fight together to possess their respective territories.

In Israel, as in today's world, national identity or communal identity is forged not only by sharing common goals, but also through the hard work of doing things together. This forging of a communal identity is important not only for nations, but also for faith communities. Commonality is built not only through prayer and planning, but also through concerted practical labor.[8] An example is the Filipino *bayanihan* spirit, where neighbors make themselves available to help each other in household undertakings, such as building a house or preparing food for a family celebration, or in times of crisis, such as death in the family.

God blesses the combined efforts of Judah and Simeon with success. Judah wins the battle over the Canaanites and the Perizzites, captures Jerusalem, and expands their reach to encompass the uplands, the Negev, and the lowlands, striking both Hebron and Debir, two cities of the southern regions (Judg 1:4–11; 17). The uplands refer to the hilly country (about 3000 feet) that lies between the eastern mountain ranges and the coastal plain. It is often referred to in English translations as the "hill country." The Negev is the dry land in the southern part of Judah, while the lowlands or the "Shephelah" are the southwestern foothills, which are considered to be the most fertile part of Palestine. Jerusalem and Hebron, on the other hand, are very significant cities in the life of Israel. Jerusalem is a powerful city-state exercising control over many cities even before it becomes the capital of Israel, perhaps because of its almost impregnable location.[9] In Hebron, Judah also strikes down Sheshai, Ahiman, and Talmai, the three sons of Anak (Josh 15:14; Num 13:22; Judg 1:20). The Israelites fear the Anakites because they are taller and bigger than the Israelites (Deut 1:28; 2:10, 21; 9:2).[10]

After this, Judah captures the Philistine cities on the coast – Gaza, Ashkelon, and Ekron, and their territories (Judg 1:18). This is a devastating defeat for the Canaanites and the other peoples of the land. The verb *nakah* (1:4, 5, 8, 10, 12, 17), which can be translated "to strike, defeat, kill, smite, slay," is repeated often in this section, using its military context to

---

8. This is contrary to the interpretation of Matthews, *Judges & Ruth*, 38, who thinks that Judah did wrong in asking Simeon for help.
9. Lindars, *Judges 1–5*, 21.
10. Other references (Judg 1:20; Josh 15:14) show that it was Caleb who killed the sons of Anak, but since Caleb was of the tribe of Judah, it was placed here as part of the account of the successful military campaigns of Judah.

indicate victorious fighting that inflicts heavy losses on the defeated party.[11] Everything seems to go as expected, as if it is only a matter of time before the whole land will be in the hands of the different tribes of Israel.

1:19–26 Partial Success, Partial Failure

Yet verse 19 presents a different picture: "The LORD was with the men of Judah. They took possession of the hill country, but they were unable to drive the people from the plains, because they had chariots fitted with iron." The phrase, "The Lord was with . . . ," is usually a formula for success, but here it is used with mixed results. The text points out that the Lord was with Judah, but God's presence in this case translates only to partial success. Although Judah succeeds in taking possession of the uplands, they fail to take possession of the valley. The reason given is that the inhabitants of the valley have superior military equipment. God, of course, is able to overcome iron chariots (Josh 17:18; Judg 14:15–16), so Judah's lack of success does not imply that Yahweh is weaker than the gods of other nations. However, it does point to the possibility that God's presence may not result in a project's complete success.[12] Thus one should not immediately conclude that God is absent when one encounters failure. In the schema of divine-human interaction, there is nothing completely predictable.

Verses 20–21 present a similar story of partial success. On one hand, Caleb of the tribe of Judah dispossesses the inhabitants of Hebron and the three sons of Anak. On the other hand, the tribe of Benjamin fails altogether to dispossess the Jebusites of Jerusalem. As a result of Benjamin's failure to dispossess the Jebusites, the Benjamites have to share their allocated territory with non-Israelites. This begins to show something of the complexity of Israel's conquest of the land. While there are victories, there are also apparent failures.

The success story is not isolated to Judah. The house of Joseph follows Judah's initiative and goes up against Bethel (formerly, Luz). As God was with Judah, so God is with the house of Joseph, and they are able to take possession of the city. The successful takeover, however, is tempered by an ironic incident. The man whom the spies release goes to another place and rebuilds

---

11. Soggin, *Judges*, 21; Boling, *Judges*, 54.
12. Richard Bowman, "Narrative Criticism: Human Purpose in Conflict with Divine Presence," in *Judges & Method: New Approaches in Biblical Studies;* ed. Gail Yee (Minneapolis, MN: Fortress, 1995), 35.

another city there, giving it the same name (Luz) that the house of Joseph has destroyed (1:22–26).[13]

1:27–36 Failure

The rest of chapter 1 relates the story of the failure of the northern tribes to take possession of their allotted territories.

> 1:27–28 Manasseh "did not dispossess . . ."[14]
> 1:29 Ephraim "did not dispossess . . ."
> 1:30 Zebulun "did not dispossess . . ."
> 1:31–32 Asher "did not dispossess . . ."
> 1:33 Naptali "did not dispossess . . ."

As a consequence of Israel's failure to dislodge the previous inhabitants of the land, the Canaanites continue to live in the midst of the Israelites. In some areas, the Canaanites live as a minority among the tribes of Israel (vv. 21, 27, 29, 30). As the dominant group, the Israelites are sometimes strong enough to compel the Canaanites to forced labor. However, the situation is reversed in some of the tribes, with the Israelites living as a minority among the dominant group of the Canaanites (vv. 32, 33). One tribe, that of Dan is unable to gain a foothold and is restricted to live in less fertile land (v. 34). Thus, we see here a progression from initial success, to partial success, to failure to dispossess, to becoming the minority, and then to being pushed back by the Canaanites into less agriculturally desirable areas. From being proactive and on the offensive, the Israelites are forced to be on the defensive and are unable to move forward.

Three Anecdotes

Interspersed within these stories of the success, partial success, and failure of the different tribes of Israel, there are three small episodes which add human interest to the accounts of possession and dispossession.

1:5–7 The humiliation of Adoni-Bezek

In the ancient Near East, prisoners of war commonly had their thumbs and toes cut off by their captors as a way of humiliating and incapacitating the enemy. Adoni-bezek, however, interprets his fate theologically: "Seventy

---

13. See below under "Three Anecdotes: The Founding of Luz (Judg 1:23–26)."
14. The verb for "dispossess" (*yarash*), which the NIV translates "to drive out," is the same verb used for the meaning "to possess." Thus the act of possessing the land implies the dispossession of the previous inhabitants of the land.

kings with their thumbs and big toes cut off have picked up scraps under my table. Now God has paid me back for what I did to them" (1:7). The use of *Elohim* rather than Yahweh as the name for God shows that Adoni-bezek had a general understanding of the divine, which was common in the ancient Near East. Even non-Israelites recognized that, ultimately, they had to make an account of their actions. Here, divine retribution is at work. Because Adoni-bezek humiliated his prisoners, he himself is also being humiliated as a prisoner. Even though the account is told in a matter-of-fact way and there is no condemnation for Judah's action, Adoni-bezek's statement suggests that Israel is not exempt from retributive justice. If a non-Israelite is accountable, so much more are God's people responsible for their actions.

1:12–15 *The initiative of Aksah*

Richard Bowman provides a simple structure for this section.[15]

| Part I | Judges 1:11–13 | Aksah as Object |
| Part II | Judges 1:14–15 | Aksah as Subject |

In Part I, Aksah is passive throughout, emphasizing her dependent and subordinate role as wife and daughter. Caleb *gives* his daughter as wife to the captor of Kiriath-Sepher (vv. 12, 13). Othniel,[16] the son of Caleb's brother, *takes* the city and *takes* Aksah as well. From the perspective of both Caleb and Othniel, Aksah is a prize, "a viable resource to be bartered"[17] in terms of each one's interest: for Caleb, a military victory; for Othniel, a wife from a prestigious family.

In Part II, however, the focus of the story shifts. Although Aksah is still presented in her role as wife and daughter, she takes initiative in the relationship. "Aksah becomes subject instead of object, active instead of passive, vocal instead of silent."[18] Most English translations reflect the Hebrew Masoretic Text's (MT) account that the subject is Aksah, and she is coming and urging someone to do something (1:14a). It is not clear, however, whom she is trying to persuade. Most logically, Aksah might be entreating Othniel to ask for a bigger dowry from her father. Yet the next scene abruptly shifts to a conversation between Aksah and her father, with Othniel nowhere in sight (1:14b).

---

15. Bowman, "Narrative Criticism," 22.
16. Othniel is the first of all the judge-deliverers. The framework that records his exploits (Judg 3:7–11) is paradigmatic for the rest of the deliverers in the book of Judges.
17. Bowman, "Narrative Criticism," 23.
18. Ibid.

If Aksah is urging Othniel, why does he disappear from the scene and leave Aksah to do her own asking? Perhaps Othniel ignores her request, and so she is forced to ask her father herself. Another explanation is that Othniel has already asked her father for a field, but Aksah wants more – springs to water the field.

The Septuagint (LXX), the Greek translation of the Hebrew text, solves the problem by making Othniel the subject: thus, *he urged her to ask her father for a field*.[19] Yet it is not necessary to follow the Greek translation and change the subject. Grammatically, Aksah can still be the subject if one understands the object in the phrase, "she urged him" (v. 14a), as a reference to Aksah's father and not to Othniel.[20] Thus, the ensuing conversation between Aksah and her father shows in greater detail what transpired in the request.

Aksah's encounter with her father is narrated in the form of a dialogue, which slows down the action and shows that the story is really about the relationship between the father and his daughter. She visits her father and asks, "Do me a special favor. Since you have given me land in the Negev, give me also springs of water" (v. 15). The father responds to her initiative and gives her the upper and lower springs. Because of her initiative, Aksah is able to acquire not only land, but also the means for watering the land and making it productive.

The story of Aksah introduces into the book of Judges a line of women who, in various ways, challenge the stereotypical expectations for women in a patriarchal society.[21] Even though the men around Aksah make decisions for her, which is common in a patriarchal culture, this does not stop Aksah from seizing the initiative. Here, the "woman" is portrayed as an initiator of action, using her role as wife and daughter to gain economic security and well-being for her family. The story suggests that one does not have to be hampered by the limitations imposed by the prescriptive roles of society. Even in a situation where one is treated as an object, it is possible to take the initiative and

---

19. The rendering of the LXX is supported by Boling, *Judges*, 56–57; Soggin, *Judges*, 22.
20. Paul G. Mosca, "Who Seduced Whom? A Note on Joshua 15:18/Judges 1:14," *CBQ* 46 (1984): 21. The infinitive construct is read as a gerund so that 1:14a is translated: "When she came, she urged him, by asking from her father a field." For this use of the infinitive, see GKC §114o; Joüon, § 124o.
21. Danna Nolan Fewell, "Deconstructive Criticism: Achsah and the (E)razed City of Writing," in *Judges & Method: New Approaches in Biblical Studies*, ed. Gail Yee (Minneapolis, MN: Fortress, 1995), 140. On the relationship of Aksah with other women in the book of Judges, see Lilian Klein, "A Spectrum of Female Characters in the Book of Judges," in *A Feminist Companion to Judges*, ed. Athalya Brenner (Sheffield: Sheffield Academic Press, 1993), 24–33.

set the agenda in order to ensure that one is treated as a person and as an agent of one's actions. This may be an important starting point for further reflection, particularly in Asian societies, where the roles of women are often narrowly prescribed. In the book of Judges, various women take the initiative and provide leadership, leading to the blessing of many.

Perhaps there is an implicit contrast here between Aksah and the tribes of Israel. Whereas the tribes do not press on to possess the land fully, Aksah actively seeks not only to get the land, but also to secure the resources needed to make the land fruitful.

1:23–26 The founding of Luz

This incident has several parallels with the story of Rahab and the conquest of Jericho (Josh 2). First, spies are sent to reconnoiter the city preparatory to a military operation. Second, the spies meet an inhabitant of the city (Rahab/the man of Bethel), who provides some form of help. Third, the spies promise to deal fairly with the one who offers help and to spare his or her family from destruction. Lastly, the spies are true to their promise; when the city is taken, the person who offers help and his or her family are given freedom.

Yet in the story of Rahab, she and her family become part of Israel (Josh 6:25), whereas the man of Luz goes to the land of the Hittites and builds another city with the same name. The strategy employed in the conquest of Jericho becomes the means by which Rahab and her family are saved, and so it must have made sense to the Israelites to use the same strategy here. Yet Rahab professes faith in Yahweh even before the offer is made, whereas the man of Luz seems interested only in saving his own skin.

The story seems to illustrate that in real life, good intentions and tested strategies may lead to undesirable outcomes. In some cases, our good actions may lead to unexpected, undesirable results. Hence, we need to look at different angles and think long-term about possible outcomes. For example, a missionary seeking to do some good in a target community may unwittingly introduce something that is detrimental to the local culture. As we seek to do what is best for our project and for others, let us be aware that unanticipated elements may emerge that will thwart our long-term desired goals.

VISION AND REALITY: THE STORY IN ASIAN CHRISTIAN REALITIES

While theories or key ideas or vision statements may be singular and clear, real life tends to be messy, as can be seen in Israel's conquest and settlement in Canaan. The promise of conquest and settlement is clearly set out in the book of Joshua (Josh 1:1–5; 3:9–10). The realization of this promise is summarized towards the end of the book: "So the Lord gave Israel all the land he had sworn to give their ancestors" (Josh 21:43). This realization is framed not only in terms of Yahweh's faithfulness – "Not one of all the Lord's good promises to Israel failed; everyone was fulfilled" (Josh 21:45) – but also in terms of Israel's obedience – "Israel served the Lord throughout the lifetime of Joshua . . ." (Josh 24:31). However, woven throughout this story of seeming victory and success are the threads of difficulty and failure: "Judah could not dislodge the Jebusites. . ." (Josh 15:63). This refrain is reiterated elsewhere in the book of Joshua (Josh 17:12), moving back and forth between "could not" and "did not" (see also Josh 13:13; 16:10; 17:13). As John Goldingay points out, "they take the land, but they do not."[22] While it may be possible to understand this to mean that the main battles have been won and only smaller skirmishes remain, the book of Judges seems to point to another interpretation, which is that much fighting takes place and much of the land still needs to be possessed, as highlighted by the chapter Judges 1:1–3:6 Gappling with Failure.

This then raises all sorts of questions regarding the nature of the conquest and Israel's settlement in the land of promise. Judges 1 clearly demonstrates that Israel did not have or did not follow a single mode of settlement. There is conquest (1:4), there is co-settlement (1:16), there is utter destruction (1:17), there is mutual cooperation (1:24–26), there is separate existence between the Israelites and the Canaanites (1:27), and there is economic exploitation in putting the Canaanites to forced labor (1:28, 33, 35). Thus the process of conquest and settlement is far more complex and finely nuanced. This is no simple policy of "kill and destroy." The seemingly singular vision of the book of Joshua, therefore, becomes more complex in the book of Judges. Reality proves messier than the visionary clarity of Israel's initial settlement in the land.

Scholars, in trying to make sense of this more richly textured picture, have put forward various proposals regarding Israel's settlement in Canaan. While all these proposals have some merits, there are also significant problems.[23] What is clear is that the major note of Joshua (they did possess) and

---

22. John Goldingay, *Old Testament Theology, Vol. 1, Israel's Gospel* (Downers Grove, IL: InterVarsity, 2003), 526.
23. There are four major proposals. First, the military conquest model holds that the land of Canaan was captured in one generation through three campaigns that targeted the center, the south, and the north part of the country. Second, the migration model propounds that over an

the minor note (they were not able to) becomes a complex theme in Judges 1, where settlement takes on many different strategies. Reality is thus more complex than ideology. While the life of faith has visionary dimensions, it has to be lived out in the difficulties of the real world.

The story of the complexity of the Israelites settlement in the land of Canaan suggests some important themes for Asian Christians. The most obvious is that ministry and mission strategies, no matter how carefully thought through and prayed about, need to be open to adjustment in light of realities. Vision statements and plans are important, but these should always be open to flexibility and fine-tuning. Plans that are truly successful are usually plans that have undergone change. Thus, while the movement forward is still in the same direction, revisions may need to occur along the way.

The second implication for Asian Christians is the reality of living with the ambiguities of cultural and religious coexistence. This coexistence usually runs the gamut of radical differentiation, on one hand, and possible syncretism, on the other hand. While the book of Judges calls for radical differentiation, Asian Christians must remain committed to being distinctive in their allegiance to the gospel while at the same time living as an incarnational presence among those of other faiths.

Thirdly, the Judges story suggests the theme of gradualism rather than revolutionary immediacy. Settlement takes a long time. In the story of the ongoing Israelite conquest of the land, we see the call to a long obedience. With no continuous major victories, no magic solutions, and no quick answers, the Israelite tribes were called to a long work, gradual progress, and costly continuance. This is no easy task. It is far easier to mobilize and galvanize people for a task that soon ends, since longer tasks often bring about discouragement and loss of interest and motivation. Thus, faith and courage for the long journey should characterize the people of God. A spirituality of persistence is the fuel for this kind of journey. Such a life of faith and obedience requires constant renewal and revitalization.

We see here the slow march of God. As Asian Christians work for nation building in a post-colonial world, there needs to be a recognition that nothing

---

extended period of time, the Israelites through peaceful occupation, intermarriage, and treaty making, were able to occupy the land by using largely peaceful strategies. This interpretation allows for periodic military conflict due to various rivalries. Third, in the social revolt model, the tribes of Yahweh, together with other people groups, are joined by revolting Canaanite groups to form a new alliance under the banner of Yahweh, who is the God who liberates the oppressed. Lastly, the cultural differentiation model proposes that over a period of many hundreds of years, through both peaceful and conflictual phases, there is the development of important religious differences between the Canaanites and the Israelites, leading eventually to the triumph of social and religious life under Yahweh. See Norman Gottwald, *The Tribes of Yahweh* (Sheffield: Sheffield Academic Press, 1999), 192–219, who also highlights the difficulties in his discussion.

> of great significance happens quickly or easily. Moreover, there are no single answers to complex problems. There are many steps in a long obedience. This holds true not only in nation building, but also in church renewal and the revitalization of religious institutions.
>
> Finally, the book of Judges is about remaining faithful to Yahweh in the midst of life: finding a place, being home, having land, surviving economically, being safe and secure, protecting our families, and having peace and prosperity. Faithfulness to God is as difficult in the midst of peace as it is in the midst of conflict.

2:1–5 LACK OF VIGILANCE

This section acts as a transition between 1:1–31 and 2:6–23. Chapter 1 records how Israel failed to possess the land completely, despite the fact that in some cases "Yahweh was with them." Chapter 2 attempts to articulate theological formulations that make sense of this failure. Why did Israel fail when Yahweh promised to give them the land? As a result of this failure, the tribes of Israel have to reconcile themselves to live with the Canaanites and face the corresponding challenges that arise from this situation.

The form and structure of Judges 2:1–3 has been likened to a prophetic covenant lawsuit, or *rib*, a judgement speech that shows the violations of the covenant followed by an announcement of judgement. The pattern of a covenant lawsuit is as follows: a) historical retrospect, b) accusation, and c) announcement of judgement.[24] Based on this pattern, Judges 2:1–3 has the following structure:

1. Historical Retrospect (1b–2a)
    a. Review of the Exodus (1a)
       "I brought you up from Egypt, and brought you into the land which I had pledged to your ancestors."
    b. Basis of the covenant (1b)
       "I said, 'I will never annul my covenant with you.'"
    c. Content of the covenant (2a)
       "As for you, do not make a covenant with the inhabitants of this land; you shall pull down their altars."

---

24. Lindars, *Judges 1–5*, 74.

2. Accusation (2b)

   "But you did not listen to my voice. How could you have done this?"

3. Announcement of Judgement (3)

   "Furthermore, I said, 'I will not drive them out before you; they shall live side by side with you, and their gods shall become a snare to you'" (trans. mine).

Yahweh's message comes through a messenger (2:1a), the *mal'ak Yahweh*, which is usually translated as "angel of the LORD." This title occurs elsewhere in the book of Judges.[25] The basic meaning is a figure of authority that represents Yahweh, but in some cases is identified with Yahweh. This will be further discussed in Judges 6, but the title "emissary of Yahweh" will be used here. The emissary of Yahweh travels from Gilgal, an important religious site in the time of Joshua, to Bochim, an unknown location, which receives this name because of the reaction of the Israelites to the message of the emissary from Yahweh.

The message starts out with a review of the covenant relationship – its roots, commitments, and obligations. Israel's relationship with Yahweh is rooted in the story of God's promise and God's gracious acts. Yahweh made a pledge to Israel's ancestors, which involved a promise with an oath. Yahweh brought the Israelites out of their lowly state as slaves in Egypt and gave them their own land so that they could have the means to live an economically independent and dignified existence before God. The covenant came not only with a gift, but also with a personal commitment on Yahweh's part. However, it also carried certain obligations on Israel's part. In this case, what is highlighted is that Israel should not make a "covenant" with the inhabitants of the land. Such covenants could take the form of any binding agreements, such as treaties between nations[26] or intermarriage.

The prohibition of covenant-making with the Canaanites is intertwined with the next directive: "pull down their altars." Entering into binding agreements with the Canaanite inhabitants meant being entangled with their gods, since these gods were called as witnesses to any agreements. This

---

25. Judg 2:4; 5:23; 6:11–12, 21–22; 13:3, 13, 15–18, 20–21.
26. See comments on Deut 7:2 by Christopher Wright, *Deuteronomy* NIBC (Peabody, MA: Hendrickson, 1996), 110.

was contrary to God's call for Israel, which was to break the backbone of Canaanite idolatry.²⁷

The pattern of an announcement of judgement in verse 3 fits in with most translations, which take this verse as a conclusion or statement of purpose. The Hebrew phrase *wegam 'amarti* at the beginning of verse 3 is variously translated as, "Therefore, I also said" (NASB), "Therefore, I have resolved" (NJPS), "So now, I say" (NRSV). Such translations identify the statement that follows as a judgement, which is the consequence of the preceding accusation. Based on these translations, the failure of Israel to dispossess the Canaanites is caused by their failure to keep their covenant with God. Because Israel did not fulfill its obligations under the covenant, God is no longer willing to drive out the nations before them.

The picture, however, is more ambiguous than this. The crux of the interpretation lies in the phrase *wegam 'amarti*. The usual sense of the particle *gam* is "also" or "even," and it often has an emphatic or additive force.²⁸ Thus, translating *gam* as "therefore, I say" or "hence" or "so now" gives a different meaning to this particle. A more adequate translation, such as, "And I also said" (NIV), or "Furthermore," or "In addition to," does not identify the phrase that follows as a conclusion, but rather as a reference to a previous warning, which is parallel to the promise outlined in 1b–2a. If translated in this way, the structure of the covenant lawsuit is no longer applicable. The failure to drive out is not a punishment or a consequence of Israel breaking its covenant with God. Rather, verse 3 speaks of a previous word of caution given to the Israelites that the Canaanites will not be wholly driven out of the land, and therefore, the Israelites must be doubly vigilant about not being trapped into the worship of the Canaanite gods. The Israelites will have to cope with the reality of continued Canaanite presence – *They shall live side by side with you* – and learn to be faithful to God, even as they are surrounded by peoples worshipping other gods.²⁹

---

27. See Deut 7:1–5, 25–26.
28. T. Muraoka, *Emphatic Words and Structures in Biblical Hebrew* (Leiden: Brill, 1985), 143–146. If a conclusion is meant, or a statement of a present purpose, it would have been more natural to use other Hebrew particles other than *gam*, like *al-ken* (Lindars, *Judges 1–5*, 78).
29. Literally, the Hebrew reads, "they shall be as sides to you." The meaning of "sides," *tsiddim*, is uncertain. The Septuagint's translation in Greek means "to your distress or anxiety." The NJPS and the NRSV read it as a scribal error for *tsarim* and translate it as "adversaries" or "oppressors." Others derive it from the Akkadian *saddu*, which means "snare." Boling derives it from *tsadah*, which means "to lie in wait." I have chosen an easier reading, referring to the

Thus in verse 2, the accusation of the emissary of Yahweh is about Israel being caught unprepared to live with the challenges of living among the Canaanites. Instead of resisting the Canaanite gods, they are lured into the worship of these gods, because Israel has let down its guard and is not radical enough to change the order of things. As a result, they have been caught unwittingly in a trap and have broken their covenant with Yahweh.[30]

After hearing the emissary's words, the people weep aloud (literally, "they lifted up their voices and wept"), so that the place is called Bochim, which means "weeping" (2:4–5). Why did the people weep in response to the message of the emissary of Yahweh? It could be a sign of repentance; however, the word for repentance (*shub*, "to return") is not used. This may be similar to other instances in the book of Judges, when Israel is said to have cried out, but their crying is not accompanied by a genuine "turning back" to Yahweh (10:10–16).[31] It could also be that they feel sorry for themselves because they failed. Or perhaps they realize that life in Canaan will be more difficult than they anticipated, and they feel sorry that they will have to live in continuous tension and conflict, constantly negotiating the challenges of their situation, instead of living an uncomplicated existence. The sorrow of the Israelites, however, does not translate into something more productive, as we shall see in the rest of the book of Judges.

In many parts of Asia, where Christians are the minority, keeping true to the faith involves constant struggle and continual vigilance so as not be sucked in by the values and beliefs of the dominant culture. However, even in countries where Christians are in the majority, it is still important to be vigilant and not take things for granted. There may be other "snares" that can drag Christians down if they are not prepared to face life's many challenges.

2:6–10 ACKNOWLEDGING YAHWEH

Commentators often consider 2:6–3:5 as a second introduction for several reasons: a) it does not follow chronologically from 2:5, but flashes back again to events just before Joshua's death, thus making the record of Joshua's death

---

fact that the Canaanites would not be completely dispossessed from the land and would live together in the same land with the Israelites; thus the translation, "they shall live side by side with you."
30. The word for "snare" refers to a trap used for catching birds unawares. See *HALOT* (study ed.) 1:558.
31. See discussion on pp. 144–145.

redundant;[32] b) its tone is different from that of 1:1–2:5, being more theological and sermonic;[33] and c) it fits the framework, which introduces the various deliverers in 3:7–16:31.[34] Thus, it is commonly stated that 1:1–2:5 deals with Israel's military failure, while 2:6–3:6 deals with their religious failure.[35] However, as Block points out, the tone of 2:1–5 is also theological and sermonic.[36] Moreover, as noted above, 2:22–3:6 shares in the reportorial quality of 1:1–36. At the same time, 2:22–3:6 gives a different explanation for Israel's failure to possess the land from that of 2:6–21. Thus, instead of considering 2:6–3:5 as a second introduction, it is best to see its various sections as different attempts to explain the dissonance between the ideal of fully taking the land and the reality of failing to do so.

The emphasis of 2:6–10 is to contrast the conduct of the previous generation (that of Joshua and his contemporaries) with that of the current generation (the generation of the judges) in order to explain the apostasy that is expounded in 2:11–19. Joshua and his generation "were gathered to their ancestors" (2:10), a phrase that reflects the custom of burying the family members together in the same burial site or family tombs,[37] which is also practiced widely in Asia. Though the previous generation served Yahweh, the current generation does not. Moreover, though the previous generation knew Yahweh and witnessed to the work that Yahweh did for Israel, the current generation falls short of this knowledge and experience.

What does it mean to serve and know Yahweh (2:7, 10)? The Hebrew word for "serve" (*'abad*) is often used in connection with the worship of other gods and is paralleled with the word for "bowing down."[38] However, *'abad* goes beyond overt actions of worship, such as offering sacrifices and observing ritual acts, as it also involves fearing the Lord, following God's ways, loving God, heeding God's commandments, obeying God, and sticking close

---

32. Lyle Eslinger, *Into the Hands of the Living God* (Sheffield: Almond Press, 1989), 66; Robert Polzin, *Moses and the Deuteronomist: A Literary Study of the Deuteronomistic History* (New York: Seabury Press, 1980), 151; Barry Webb, *The Book of Judges: An Integrated Reading* (Sheffield: JSOT Press, 1987), 106.
33. Webb, *Judges: Integrated Reading*, 119–121; Polzin, *Moses and the Deuteronomist*, 149.
34. K. Lawson Younger Jr., *Judges/Ruth*, NIV Application Commentary (Grand Rapids, MI: Zondervan, 2002), 31.
35. Cheryl Exum, "The Centre Cannot Hold: Thematic and Textual Instabilities in Judges," *CBQ* 52 (1990), 413; Jacobus Marais, *Representation in Old Testament Narrative Texts* (Leiden: Brill, 1998), 71.
36. Block, *Judges*, 76.
37. Ibid., 122, n. 195.
38. Exod 20:5; 23:24, 25; 23:33; Deut 4:19, 28; 5:9; 7:4; 7:16; 8:19; 11:16; 12:2, 20; 13:3, 7, 14; 17:3; 28:14, 36, 64; 29:7, 25; 30:17; 31:20; Josh 23:7, 16; 24:2, 20.

to God in loyalty, affection, and commitment.[39] To serve Yahweh means to be loyal and faithful to Yahweh as this is expressed in acceptable and reverent worship and obedient lifestyle.

On the other hand, the Hebrew word for knowing (*yada'*) Yahweh never means merely theoretical knowledge, but suggests being involved in a relationship that acknowledges Yahweh in one's practical behavior.[40] Thus, the passage does not mean that the current generation is ignorant of who Yahweh is and the works that Yahweh has done for Israel. The usage is similar to Exodus 1:8: "Now a new king arose over Egypt, who did not know Joseph."[41] The phrase "did not know" here does not mean that the new king had no knowledge of Joseph, but that he did not value or honor what Joseph had done for Egypt.[42] In the same way, the current generation is contrasted to the previous generation in that, apart from the fact that they were not eyewitnesses to Yahweh's mighty deeds (see Judg 2:7), they also do not give honor to the one who accomplished those deeds. In their behavior, commitments, and worship, there is no acknowledgement of the role that Yahweh plays in their story.

Indeed, "the great things that the LORD had done for Israel" (v. 7) is related through the form of a story, which tells of God's initiative in calling the patriarchs, bringing Israel out of Egypt by means of awesome deeds, defeating Pharaoh and the Egyptian army in the crossing of the Sea, guiding them in the wilderness, and bringing them to Canaan, where God won their battles and handed over to them the land (Deut 11:1–7; Josh 24: 2–18). To acknowledge Yahweh is to recognize that this story would not have been possible without God. It is to honor God by valuing and appreciating the God who made it all possible. In the same way, we show that we know God by acknowledging the part God has played and is playing in our ongoing story.

The history of religious movements suggests a rhythm of vital beginnings and the eventual need for revitalization. Powerful and revelatory beginnings over time begin to wane and renewal needs to occur. This was no less true in the history of Israel.

The Joshua generation faithfully worshipped and served the Lord (vv. 6–7). The succeeding generation is now facing unique challenges, as it is called to worship faithfully in a different setting, when the initial vision has

---

39. Deut 10:12–13; 11:13; 13:4 [5]; Josh 22:5; 24:24.
40. W. Schottroff, "*yd'*," *TLOT 2*: 517 [508–521].
41. Boling, *Judges*, 72, who sees it as signaling a new era.
42. J. P. Hyatt, *Exodus*, NCB (London: Oliphants, 1971), 58.

begun to fade and the job is far from done. Moreover, unlike Joshua and the elders who outlived him, the new generation did not bear witness to the great deeds that God did for Israel (v. 7b). Thus, out of a spirituality of "absence" rather than a spirituality of "presence," they are called to fulfill similar responsibilities. While they can look back and receive encouragement from what God has done in the past, they are faced with particular temptations. One such temptation has to do with the discouragement that comes from the seeming lack of fulfillment of earlier promises. Another is the temptation to think that God has abandoned them.

There are important insights here. The most basic is that the story of God's action in the past needs to be appropriated by each new generation. The goodness of the past is not automatically credited to the bank account of the new generation. That generation, too, must cry out to God and seek God's deliverance. The encouraging thing is that the God of the past is also faithful in the present. Thus, the next generation cannot live off the grace and goodness that an earlier generation has found. Each generation needs to find fuel for the journey that it must make.

2:11–21 DISOBEDIENCE AND APOSTASY

This section partially introduces the cyclical framework that orients the major part of the book, which was typical of the period of the Judges (see introduction). It develops some of the elements of the framework that are only briefly stated later on. It also explicitly explains that the failure of the Israelites to dispossess the nations of Canaan is a punishment for Israel's violation of its covenant to Yahweh. The section has a moralizing tone, which is similar to 2 Kings 17:7–18. In recounting the Fall of Samaria in 2 Kings 17, the narrator provides a theological interpretation of events by looking backwards to the events that have been narrated; in Judges 2, however, the narrator looks forward to the events that are yet to be narrated. The section can be divided into four parts: a) Israel's infidelity (vv. 11–13), b) God's wrath and discipline (vv. 14–15), c) God's grace and the people's stubbornness (vv. 16–19), and d) God's judgement (vv. 20–21).

2:11–13 Israel's Infidelity

The Hebrew word for evil, *ra'ah*, has a wide range of meanings. It can simply mean what is harmful or disadvantageous or what causes distress or pain. However, in some contexts, it can have a moral-ethical component, and it is used this way in the phrase, "Israel did evil in the eyes of the Lord" (3:7, 12;

4:1; 6:1; 10:6; 13:1). In a chiastic structure, verses 11b–13 describe what this evil consists of:

> A "They served the Baals" (11b)
> B "They abandoned Yahweh the God of their fathers (12a1),
>> the one who brought them out of the land of Egypt" (12a2)
>
> C "They followed after strange gods (12b1)
>> which came from the gods of the peoples around them" (12b2)
>
> C' "They bowed down to them (12c1)
>> and provoked Yahweh to anger" (12c2)
>
> B' "They abandoned Yahweh" (13a)
> A' "They served Baal and the Astartes" (13b) (trans. mine).

In the Canaanite pantheon, Baal is the storm god, while Astarte (in some texts, Asherah) is his consort. The Canaanite gods were understood to be personifications of the powers of nature, and they were seen to have control of natural forces, especially those that affected climate and the annual cycle of rain and drought. As an agricultural society, Israel was dependent on nature for its survival. Thus, the Israelites did not find it hard to adopt the Canaanite nature religion since they wanted to ensure the fertility of their harvest. Sometimes, Baal and Astarte are rendered in plural form (vv. 11b, 13b; see also 2:13, pl. form of Astarte). The plural does not refer to a plurality of gods but to different local manifestations of Baal and Astarte in the various local religious establishments or to the different figurines of Baal and Astarte.[43]

The evil that Israel does, which provokes Yahweh's anger, is that they worship, follow after, and bow down to the gods of the nations around them (see Deut 4:25; 9:18; 17:2). These gods are strange (12b) in the sense that they have no part in the story of Israel. The Hebrew word for strange, *'akhar*, meaning "other," implies that these gods do not belong to Israel; they are outsiders, foreigners, with no significant relationship, investment, or part in the life of Israel. Whereas Israel has a long history with Yahweh, having experienced Yahweh's steadfast love, commitment, and great power on their behalf, they have no history at all with these other gods, who have done nothing for them. However, the Israelites choose them over Yahweh.

---

43. Boling, *Judges*, 74.

In the present-day Christianization of the Western world, we see a similar movement to the one presented in this section. The West has forsaken the Christian God to embrace the gods of covetousness and narcissism. In Asia, except where people have converted from animistic religions, the old gods have remained firmly entrenched, while the Christian God is seen as strange and needing to be resisted. The Christian God is seen as a Western god introduced during colonialism, even though the Bible came from the East and Christianity has been predominantly non-Western for most of its two-thousand-year history. Moreover, seventy percent of contemporary global Christianity is non-Western. Thus, the challenge for the church in Asia is to develop its own theologies, liturgies, art, ecclesiology, spirituality, and missional praxis in order to reflect Asian sensibilities and the contextualization of the gospel in an Asian world.

Israel's adoption of other gods corresponds to its abandonment of Yahweh:

They served the Baals	*They abandoned Yahweh*
	-the God of their fathers
	-the one who brought them
	out of Egypt
They followed after gods	
-strange gods	
-the gods of the peoples	
around them	
They bowed down to them	*They provoked Yahweh to anger*
They served Baal and	*They abandoned Yahweh*
the Astartes	

The verb "to abandon" (*'azb*) commonly means "to leave or depart," which implies a movement from one physical space to another. This passage, however, suggests the betrayal of a relationship. Israel entered into a covenant relationship with Yahweh. Yahweh was to be Israel's God, and Israel was to be Yahweh's people, and they were to serve Yahweh exclusively. Yet Israel shifts its allegiance to other gods that have no part in Israel's covenantal relationship with Yahweh. This does not imply that Israel has ceased to worship Yahweh altogether. In fact, the word *'ahar*, aside from the nuance "what is strange or foreign," can also mean "something that is added to what previously existed."[44] Israel continues to regard Yahweh as their God, but they also add the Canaanite gods to their religious repertoire. However, even though they do not completely cease from being Yahweh worshippers, their adoption of other gods is seen as an abandonment of Yahweh. The covenant between Yahweh and Israel is an exclusive relationship in which other gods cannot have a part. Thus, the adoption of other gods provokes Yahweh to anger because it constitutes a violation of an exclusive covenantal relationship. The evil that Israel commits cannot be described simply as a "wrong action," as it suggests a "violated relationship." Israel violates the relationship by incorporating other gods into its relationship with Yahweh, thus changing its very nature and causing it grave harm.

Religious adherents often want the best of both worlds – they want the God of heaven and the gods of this world. This leads to various forms of syncretism. While this is a problem in many parts of the world, it particularly strikes home in Asia, where many Christians have to live amidst a plurality of religions. Dominant cultural values or elements from other religious traditions can so easily continue to play a part in one's Christian walk. While contextualization needs to be embraced, syncretism needs to be resisted. We cannot have our feet in both camps, for God must be the center out which we live the whole of our lives. Yet God's exclusive claim upon our lives does not spring out of narrow concerns, but out of the wideness of God's mercy that calls us to cling to God's love and grace alone.

2:14–15 God's Wrath and Discipline

With the terms of the covenant violated, "Yahweh's wrath blazed against Israel" (2:14, trans. mine). Yahweh's wrath is expressed in a concrete act (2:14b). Webb shows the balanced structure of this section.[45]

A   He gave them into the hand of plunderers
B   and they plundered them
A'   and he sold them into the hand of their enemies round about
B'   and they could no longer stand before their enemies

Whereas at the beginning of Judges, God gave the Canaanites into the hand of the Israelites (1:2, 4), now God gives Israel into the hand of the nations around them, so that Israel becomes subject to defeat and exploitation.

---

44. S. Erlandsson, "'acher," *TDOT* 1:201–202.
45. Webb, *Judges: Integrated Reading*, 109.

"Wherever they marched out to battle,[46] the hand of the Lord was against them to their detriment" (2:15). Instead of fighting on Israel's behalf, God is now against them. Because they did evil (v. 11), the hand of Yahweh is also against them for evil (v. 15). The Hebrew word for "detriment" is the same word used for evil (*ra'ah*) in 2:11. In verse 11 it means moral evil or wickedness, whereas in verse 15 it means what is detrimental or calamitous. The play on words shows how Yahweh's punishment fits the crime. The punishment is not something arbitrarily given, for Israel has been amply and decisively warned – "just as the Lord said, just as the Lord swore to them" (v. 15b, trans. mine). They are not ignorant of the consequences of their actions. Thus, "they were beleaguered" (v. 15, trans. mine) – the image of the verb *tsarar* for beleaguered is that of being pressed in from all sides, so that they are no longer free to move.

One of the main themes in the book of Judges is that Yahweh is with Israel in their fight with the Canaanites. An Israelite victory is not so much ascribed to the military prowess of the Israelites but to Yahweh's participation (1:4; see also 3:28). In fact, in many battles and skirmishes, Israel's role is minimized and Yahweh's participation is accented (see 4:15; 7:15). Nevertheless, as this section shows, the book of Judges also emphasizes another theme: Yahweh not only fights for his people but also against them (2:15). Yahweh's punishment should not be understood as Yahweh's sudden abandonment of his people. In fact, it reflects the opposite, for it demonstrates Yahweh's active engagement in inflicting pain that leads to repentance and renewal. This is the heavy hand of Yahweh. It is God's brutal work of purgation.

Many of the contemporary forms of Christianity have come to Asia from the Western world. These forms of Christianity seem to emphasize the "sunny side" of God, promoting the idea that God only hands out blessings and never painful discipline. This passage suggests otherwise. God loves his people enough to pursue and purge them. However, God's hard way to the road of repentance is also God's healing discipline for his people. Punishment is not the end of the story. The God who punishes is also the God who delivers. The hand that rebukes and wounds is also the hand that reaches out, as can be seen in the next section.

---

46. Literally, "whenever they go out." The verb *yts'* functions as a technical term for marching out into battle. Block, *Judges*, 127, n. 223; John Gray, *Joshua, Judges, Ruth*, NCB (Grand Rapids, MI: Eerdmans, 1986), 257. See Judg 5:4; 2 Kgs 18:27; Deut 28:7; 2 Sam 11:1.

2:16–19 God's Grace and the People's Stubbornness

As is often the case, God's deliverance comes in the form of human instruments: "So the Lord raised up judges who delivered Israel from the hand of their plunderers" (2:16, trans. mine). The focus on tribal leadership and common undertakings in chapter 1 now gives way to individual figures. These judges, however, are not to be understood as operating in the same way as present-day judges. They were not interpreters of the law, nor did they preside in judicial proceedings. Although judges who render judicial decisions existed in Israel, the judges in the book of Judges functioned differently. None of them were specifically named "judge," although some were described to be judging Israel.[47] It is only in 2:16–19 that they are generally designated "judges." As verses 16 and 18 show, however, the judges' task was not to give a legal judgement but to deliver Israel from its oppressors. Some of these judges are specifically called deliverer or savior – *moshia'* (from the same word as "Messiah") – or are described as delivering Israel in a brief sentence or in an extended narrative account.[48] However, there are passages in which some of these personalities are said to be "judging" Israel for several years, which implies more than performing acts of deliverance, but includes governance or administrative tasks. Thus, the term "judge" broadly encompasses several functions: a) someone who decides legal cases, especially on behalf of the more vulnerable sectors of society; b) a deliverer; c) an administrator or leader. What these have in common is that they all involve the maintenance or restoration of shalom to a community after a period of conflict or strife.[49]

Unlike other references to the cyclical framework of the book of Judges,[50] there is no mention in this section of Israel crying out to Yahweh. Instead, the focus is on Israel's continuous rebellion against Yahweh despite God's pity and merciful actions on their behalf. God's action of deliverance did nothing to change the people's action. It did not lead to repentance or an awareness of wrong: "Yet they would not listen to their judges but prostituted themselves to other gods and worshipped them. They quickly turned from the ways of their ancestors, who had been obedient to the Lord's commands" (2:17). Israel's sin is described in very strong language: "for they prostituted

---

47. See 3:10; 4:4; 10:2, 3; 12:7–9, 11, 13–14; 15:20; 16:31.
48. The designation *moshia'* (deliverer) is used for Othniel (3:9) and Ehud (3:15), while the hiphil form of the verb *yasha'* (to deliver or rescue) is used to describe the activity of Shamgar (3:31), Gideon (6:15; 8:22), Tola (10:1), Jephthah (12:3), and Samson (13:5). See Block, *Judges*, 23, n. 7.
49. T. L. J. Mafico, "Judge, Judging," *ABD* 3:1105. See also *TLOT* 3:1393.
50. Judg 3:9, 15; 4:3; 6:6; 10:10.

themselves to other gods." The verb for "prostituted themselves" (*zanah*) is used to describe sexual relationships outside the formal bonds of a covenant, particularly that of marriage. By bowing down to other gods, Israel has become unfaithful to Yahweh.

Nevertheless, God continues to deliver Israel out of God's pity for their oppression and suffering: "Whenever the Lord raised up judges for their sake, the Lord would be with that judge, and he would deliver them from the hand of their enemies during the judge's lifetime, for the Lord would relent because of their groans caused by the ones who oppressed them and hemmed them in"[51] (2:18, trans. mine). There are echoes here of the exodus. God initiated deliverance upon hearing the groans of the Israelites (Exod 2:24; 6:5) due to the oppression of the Egyptians (Exod 3:9).[52] In the same way in the book of Judges, God is not unmoved by the suffering of the Israelites, even though their hardships are a consequence of their own unfaithfulness, rather than the result of others' harsh policies. Israel has no one but herself to blame for her own miseries, yet God is mindful of her sufferings and seeks to alleviate them. The verb for "relent" (*nikham*) is used in the Old Testament to express pity, regret, repentance, or change of mind. It has both an emotive aspect (regret, sorrow, or pity) and a volitive component (the will to alter the original plan).[53] It is used several times to show how God's mind changes regarding the calamity that God has brought about because of the people's sin. Out of pity for the people's misery, God does not give them the full punishment for their sins.[54] God's discipline is tempered by mercy. Through the judges, God provides the means by which the Israelites can have relief from their distress. Clearly, grace rather than punishment is the dominant note.

Israel's response to God's mercy, however, is a progression of wickedness: "But when the judge died, the people returned to ways even more corrupt than those of their ancestors, following other gods and serving and worshipping them. They refused to give up their evil practices and stubborn ways" (2:19).

---

51. The Hebrew word used for "hem in" (*dhq*) is "rare." Aside from this verse, it is used only in Joel 2:8, referring to how locusts move together without crowding (*dhq*) each other.
52. The same word for groan, *nʿaqah*, and for the verb "to oppress," *lahats*, is used in Judges and Exodus.
53. H.-J. Fabry, "*nhm*," *TDOT* 9:342–343.
54. See Exod 32:12, 14; 2 Sam 24:16; Jer 18:8, 10; 26:3, 13, 19; 42:10; Joel 2:13, 14; Amos 7:3, 6; Jonah 3:9, 10; 4:2.

2:20–21 God's Judgement

The violation of the covenant brings with it certain consequences:

> So the wrath of Yahweh blazed against Israel; he said: "Because this people has violated my covenant which I have commanded their ancestors and they have not obeyed me, I for my part will also no longer dispossess from before them any of the nations that Joshua left when he died." (2:19–20, trans. mine)

The Hebrew word for "violated" (*'abar*) means "to overstep or contravene." Its basic meaning is "to pass or cross over," but it has the extended meaning of breaking the boundaries. Israel has overstepped the bounds of its covenant with Yahweh. Thus, Yahweh is no longer bound to the promise to dispossess the remaining inhabitants of the land. This section clearly shows that complete conquest and settlement will no longer be possible because Israel has been unfaithful to its covenant with Yahweh.

2:22–3:6 FAILURE AND TESTING

Some commentators see 3:1 as the beginning of a new section and separate it from the rest of chapter 2 because the phrase, "These are" (*we'elleh*), begins a new section elsewhere.[55] It is also argued that the shift to a non-sequential narrative sentence indicates the beginning of a new section.[56]

Nevertheless, there are several reasons why 2:22–23 should be linked with 3:1–6. First, there are very clear verbal and thematic connections between the two. The idea of the remaining nations serving as a test for Israel, which is introduced in 2:22, is picked up again in 3:1, 5.[57] The verb "allow to remain" (causative form of the verb *nuakh*) is repeated in both sections, along with the phrase "these nations" (2:23; 3:1).[58] Another parallel construction is the question form in 2:22b (literally, "Would they keep the way of the Lord, walking in them as their ancestors had done or not?") and 3:4b ("Would they

---

55. Block, *Judges*, 77, citing Gen 10:1; 11:27; 25:7; Exod 1:1; 6:16; 21:1; 28:4; Num 1:5; Josh 12:1, 7, etc.
56. Schneider, *Judges*, 36; Block, *Judges*, 136. Temporal sequence in biblical Hebrew is indicated by the consecutive *waw*, a connective with a verb that joins sentences together to indicate temporal progression. When another non-verb element is introduced before the *waw*, the temporal progression is broken and this may indicate (although it may also show other constructions) the beginning of a new section.
57. The same Hebrew phrase is used: *nasot bam et* Israel (to test Israel by means of them).
58. In 2:23 "these nations" (*haggoyim ha'elleh*); in 3:1 "these are the nations" (*'elleh haggoyim*).

keep the commandments of the Lord, which he commanded their ancestors through Moses?").[59]

There are also clear differences in the timeframe and perspective of sections 2:11–22 and 2:22–23, which set them apart. Judges 2:11–21 refers to the nations remaining after Joshua's death (2:21, see also 2:8), whereas 2:22–23 mentions the nations remaining even during Joshua's lifetime (2:23). Moreover, 2:11–21 sees the failure to dispossess the nations as a punishment or consequence of Israel's apostasy, whereas 2:22–23 (along with 3:1–6) sees the failure to drive out the inhabitants of the land as part of God's testing of Israel.

Some translations see 2:22 as a continuation of Yahweh's speech that begins in 2:20 (NJB, NASB, ASV), with 2:23 functioning as the conclusion to the whole section of 2:11–23.

> [20] So the anger of the LORD burned against Israel, and He said, "Because this nation has transgressed My covenant which I commanded their fathers and has not listened to My voice, [21] I also will no longer drive out before them any of the nations which Joshua left when he died, [22] in order to test Israel by them, whether they will keep the way of the LORD to walk in it as their fathers did, or not." [23] So the LORD allowed those nations to remain, not driving them out quickly; and He did not give them into the hand of Joshua. (NASB)

However, other translations (NRSV; NJPS) see a break between verse 21, where Yahweh's speech ends, and verse 22, which is part of the narrator's comments that continue to verse 23. This seems a better option, since verse 22 does not begin with the narrative *waw* (showing continuation with the previous sentence) but with another particle (*al-ken*, "in order that"), which breaks the narrative flow of the speech. Moreover, verse 22 is narrated in the third person rather than in the first person, which would be the case if it were still part of Yahweh's speech.

> [20] So the anger of the LORD was kindled against Israel; and he said, "Because this people have transgressed my covenant that I commanded their ancestors, and have not obeyed my voice, [21] I will

---

59. A smooth reading of these two clauses does not reflect the question construction: whether or not they would keep the way of the Lord, walking in them as their ancestors had done (2:22b); whether or not they would listen to the command, which God commanded their ancestors through Moses (3:4b).

no longer drive out before them any of the nations that Joshua left when he died." ²² In order to test Israel, whether or not they would take care to walk in the way of the LORD as their ancestors did, ²³ the LORD had left those nations, not driving them out at once, and had not handed them over to Joshua. (NRSV)

With a clear break between verses 21 and 22 and with clear verbal and thematic links between 2:22–23 and 3:1–6, it is best to consider 2:22–23 and 3:1–6 as part of one section.

In this last section, we see another reason why God allowed other nations to continue to live among the Israelites. The text says they were for the testing of Israel (2:22; 3:1, 4). In some instances when God tested Israel, it was through a situation of hardship after a great victory, as when Israel experienced thirst and hunger in the wilderness after coming out of Egypt (Exod 15:22–26; 16:1–30; see also Deut 8:2–20). In other instances, the testing involved a false prophet whose prophecies came true, who then enjoined Israel to worship other gods (Deut 13:1–4), or an awesome spectacle of thunder and lightning that terrified the people (Exod 20:18–20). The verb "to test" (*nsh*) is also used in relation to an individual – Abraham – whom God tested by asking him to offer his only son, Isaac, as a sacrifice (Gen 22:1–2). From the above references, a test can involve either a hard and difficult experience or an attractive option that can lead to a positive or negative result. In Israel's case, the purpose of testing can lead to greater fidelity and obedience to and reverence for God, or it can lead to infidelity, disobedience, alienation, and the worship of other gods. Thus, by testing Israel, God is taking a great risk of losing Israel – or the possibility of gaining Israel's allegiance. However, such testing is necessary, for it is only through a situation of adversity or enticement that Israel's true commitments and values are revealed and strengthened. As they keep faith with God when circumstances are not ideal, they learn perseverance; as they see God working in their situation and giving them victory in war, their knowledge of and trust in Yahweh is strengthened; and when they fail, they learn humility (Deut 8:2, 16).

In the context of 2:22–3:6, testing has to do with finding out whether a new generation will follow the example of their ancestors and keep God's ways and obey God's commands (2:22; 3:4). This command has to do specifically with not making a covenant with the inhabitants of the land and thus being lured into the worship of other gods (2:2–3). The mode of testing is through the continued presence of the nations surrounding Israel (2:23–3:1), which Judges 1 has portrayed. Thus, instead of a problem-free life, free from enticement and conflict, Israel has to face constant pressure from the nations around her – not just in terms of the immediate availability of alternative religious options, which take Israel away from Yahweh, but also the prospect of having to fight wars all the time so that Israel can keep its territory and not be subjected to the peoples around her. The reference to war in 3:1–2 should be interpreted within this scenario. Unlike the previous generation of Joshua and his contemporaries, the new generation did not witness God's deeds in the Exodus and the Conquest. They did not experience the hardships of war nor did they see God at work in fighting their battles and giving them victory. The persistent pressure of the different peoples around them acts as a test for Israel, so that the new generation can choose to be faithful to God in the midst of that pressure while also growing in their knowledge and trust of Yahweh as they witness God's mighty deliverance in the midst of war. The phrase, "to teach them about war," does not mean that God wants to teach Israel the art of warfare, thereby allowing the different nations to remain in the land in order to become Israel's sparring partners.[60] Rather, as Israel is plagued by wars on all sides, they can come to appreciate the power and grace of Yahweh as God rescues them and fights on their behalf.

However, a test can also yield the opposite result, as verses 5–6 show. Instead of standing their ground, the Israelites are overcome by the pressure of the other nations. Instead of the other peoples living among the Israelites, the Israelites live among the other nations, which mean that the predominant culture in the land is Canaanite rather than Israelite. As verse 6 shows, Israel is assimilated into the dominant local culture: "They took their daughters in marriage and gave their own daughters to their sons, and served their gods." Thus, Israel fails the test. Instead of remaining separate and influencing others into the adoption of their beliefs, the Israelites capitulate and adopt the Canaanite beliefs.

Theologically, testing has to do with careful and providential activity in which God uses circumstances of both goodness and difficulty as a way of bringing about faith and obedience in God's people. This is often a mysterious work of God that calls for careful discernment. What this highlights is that God can use anything, including life's difficulties and challenges, to bring about God's purposes.

---

60. J. Clinton McCann, *Judges*, IBC (Louisville, KY: Westminster/John Knox, 2002), 38, citing J. P. H. Wessels, "'Postmodern' Rhetoric and the Former Prophetic Literature," in *Rhetoric, Scripture, and Theology: Essays from the 1994 Pretoria Conference*, eds. Stanley E. Porter and Thomas H. Olbricht (Sheffield: Sheffield Academic Press, 1996), 191.

JUDGES 1:1–3:6

Pastorally, a life of faith can only be a tested faith. Spiritually, faith needs to go through a vortex of fire. It needs to be tested. Faith cannot grow in sunshine alone. It also needs to go through the dark night. In order to bring to the fore what is really in our hearts, faith must go through trials and purgation in the process of purification.

COPING WITH FAILURE

A faith community lives in the hope of a final good, rather than a partial good. It is the hope of possessing the land or the hope of new heavens and a new earth. However, the life of faith is never utopian. It is always tempered by realism and sculpted by human inadequacies and failure. The major contours of the stories in the introduction of the book of Judges illustrate this. There are victories and failures. There is obedience and disobedience. Yet life is not only sculpted by the themes of obedience and disobedience but also by the reality of human limitations. Failure is usually a part of any major project, and so we will need to face and make sense of our failures.

The introductory chapters of the book of Judges seek to make sense of such failures while avoiding singular and simplistic answers. After showing in chapter 1 that Israel did not/could not dispossess the inhabitants of the land, the subsequent sections explore multiple reasons for this failure. First, God forewarns the Israelites that this is going to happen, but they are caught unprepared (2:1–5). Second, the next generation, unlike the previous one, forgets what God has done for Israel and fails to acknowledge the role of God in their ongoing story (2:6–10). Third, failure is a form of God's punishment (2:11–21). Fourth, failure is God's way of testing Israel and teaching them the lessons of war (2:22–3:6).

In whatever way we may evaluate these various explanations, one point is clear: simplistic answers are unhelpful in explaining difficulties. Life is complex, and so are human motivations. Things occur in multiple and complex ways. Our failures may stem from the brokenness of the world, human limitation, God's strange providence, or human disobedience, or they may become the setting for further learning.

JUDGES 3:7–31

The Role of Individual Deliverers

In "groupie" cultures, such as those of Asia, it is easy for individual accomplishments to get lost within the identity of the group. On the other hand, within individualistic cultures, leaders with strong personalities can become so elevated that others' contributions are unacknowledged and God's role, even when overtly mentioned, is downplayed. Often, we are oriented to ideal types with a high public profile, and so we may ignore the part played by low-profile individuals whose ways of operating we may find unorthodox and uncomfortable.

In Judges, we move swiftly from the general "Israelites" (1:1), to the tribal "Judah" or "Simeon" (1:2–3), to the role of individuals: Caleb and Aksah (1:11–15, 20), Othniel (3:7–11), Ehud (3:12–30), and Shamgar (3:31).

In the stories of Othniel, Ehud, and Shamgar, we see the uneven nature of the story telling. Othniel, the well-situated and well-qualified deliverer, is acknowledged in a formal and stylized way. The stranger man from the margins, Ehud, is described in graphic detail and with dramatic effect. Yet Shamgar, while an important deliverer, is only mentioned briefly.

Othniel comes from an illustrious family, being the nephew and son-in-law of the famous Caleb, of the tribe of Judah, who had great military exploits in his own right (1:12–13, 3:9). Othniel is presented as the model judge, and this is reflected by the fact that all the elements of the cyclical framework are present in his account. In addition, Othniel's victory is largely attributed to his strength as an individual: "*He* went forth to war and Yahweh gave Cushan-rishathaim, king of Aram into *his* power; *he* overpowered Cushan-rishathaim" (3:10, trans. mine). Othniel is every parent's dream of the perfect husband for their daughter; moreover, he fulfills the prevalent conception of the ideal deliverer.

In contrast, Ehud comes from the small tribe of Benjamin, which by the end of the book of Judges has caused huge problems for the other tribes of Israel. Being skilled in the use of his left hand, Ehud has other resources that ordinary soldiers do not have. Instead of a straightforward conquest of the enemy – in contrast with Othniel, who goes to war (2:10) – Ehud uses stealth and trickery. Although he leads Israel against the Moabites, his victory is attributed to the strength of the collective: "*They* struck Moab at that time . . . Moab was humbled on that day *under the hand of Israel*" (3:29–30, emph. mine).

The reference to Shamgar is very brief and lacks the theological framework that structures the other Judges narratives (3:31). He is briefly mentioned again in the Song of Deborah (5:6), which indicates that his work as a deliverer has made a mark. The name, Shamgar, along with his appellation as "son of Anath" may indicate that he has a non-Israelite origin,[1] but he is nevertheless used by God to relieve Israel from their distress under foreign oppression. The mention of the Philistines foreshadows the work of Samson, while the use of an oxgoad links this story to other deliverer figures, who also use unconventional means and tools to fight the oppressors (Ehud, 3:17; Jael, 4:21; Samson, 15:14).

In spite of their marked differences in background and regardless of how their conquests are described in the narrative, each of these individuals is chosen by God to deliver Israel from the power of its oppressors.

3:7–11 OTHNIEL THE IDEAL DELIVERER

As one reads the book of Judges, one is struck by the focus on the particular. God raises up a particular person (3:9), who makes war against a particular king and defeats him (3:10). This occurs throughout the book. This is no generalizing of a story. The book resounds with particular people and particular events.

However, the book does not allow us to get lost in particulars. The book of Judges echoes with reflective insight. Individual events form a pattern that reveals a bigger picture, which is clearly articulated in the cycle of disobedience and deliverance, which leads to a resurgence of unfaithfulness.

While unfaithfulness and deliverance are the two broad movements of this cycle, the pattern is mapped out in much greater detail, as follows:

Act 1 *People*:   "did evil in the sight of Yahweh" (3:7)
"forgot Yahweh" (3:7)
"served the Baals and Asherahs" (3:7)[2]

---

[1]. Hebrew names typically have three consonantal root while Shamgar has four (s-m-g-r). Anath is a prominent Canaanite goddess of war, so the designation "son of Anath" (ben Anath) may refer to Shamgar's warrior-like qualities. For discussion, see P. C. Craigie, *JBL* 91/ 2 (1972): 239–240; F. Charles Fensham, *JNES* 20/3 (1961): 197–198.

[2]. Scripture quotations in the different acts are from my own translation.

As noted in the previous chapter, the evil that Israel did was identified with the worship of other gods (2:11). Moreover, as in previous verses, Israel's idolatry is tied to the deterioration of their relationship with Yahweh. The current generation does not acknowledge Yahweh (2:10); they abandon the God of their ancestors (2:12, 13). The state of Israel's relationship with Yahweh is further expounded in 3:7: "they forgot Yahweh their God."

Forgetting God suggests that we fail to remember that God is the one who makes it possible for us, our family, or our community to be where we are right now. This often happens when we are in places of comfort, security, or success. Israel forgot God when they were already living a satisfied life in Canaan (Hos 13:6: see also Deut 6:12; 8:12–16; 32:15–18). Having forgotten their humble beginnings and the hardships and difficulties that they had experienced in the past, they also forgot the God who delivered them from these hardships and who provided for them in times of difficulty (Pss 78:11; 106:13). They attributed their success to their own power (Deut 8:17).

Since Yahweh was no longer central to their lives, their thoughts, and their collective story, it became easier to turn to other gods. Thus forgetting God is often related to the worship of other gods (Deut 6:12; 8:19; Pss 44:20; 106:20–21; Jer 2:32; 18:15; 23:27; Ezek 23:35; Hos 2:13) and being unfaithful to one's covenant with God (Jer 3:21–22; Ps 44:18). When we forget what God has done for us in the past, we are apt to look to other sources for our security and hope. This highlights an interesting dimension of human beings–their fundamental religiosity. For the movement of unfaithfulness is often not from God to no God, but from true God to other gods. Forsaking God does not lead to neutrality or to a vacuum but to idolatry.

The second part of the framework that is established in the introduction – of Yahweh's wrath against Israel (see 2:14, 20) – is reiterated in the next act.

Act 2 *Yahweh*: "wrath blazed against Israel" (3:8)
"sold them to the enemy (Cushan-rishathaim), so that the people experienced subjection" (3:8)

Similar to 2:14, the language suggests a commercial transaction. Selling involves the transference of ownership from one person to another.[3] There are many metaphors used for God's relationship with Israel, such as parent-child, husband-wife, shepherd-sheep, king-subject, among others, but

---

3. Block, *Judges*, 147; Soggin, *Judges*, 45–46.

here the primary metaphor is of a lord and vassal. The metaphor underscores Yahweh's ownership of servant Israel. However, it also shows that Yahweh has the responsibility to protect the security and well-being of the servant.

By serving other gods, Israel initiates a change in the relationship by saying that Yahweh is no longer their master, and they are no longer Yahweh's servants. The transference of ownership simply recognizes what has already taken place. However, it also means the removal of Yahweh's protection, which is the master's responsibility towards the vassal. Because Israel is serving foreign gods (3:7), they become subject to the foreign powers (3:8) that worship these others gods.

The one who initiates this change in relationship is not God, but us. Even though our lips may still pay allegiance to God as our lord and master, our actions may actually say otherwise. Thus, when God acts to recognize the change in our relationship, we complain and say that God has abandoned us. Yet it is often we who have abandoned God – instead of the other way around. This shows the faithfulness of God and the often fickle nature of God's people. Instead of blaming God that things are now different, we should first of all acknowledge that we have changed the nature of relationship through our neglect or disobedience.

The third act, the cry of Israel to Yahweh for help, is not mentioned in the introductory framework (2:11–21).

Act 3 *People*: "cried to Yahweh for help" (3:9)

However, this formula is repeated in the introduction to other narrative cycles,[4] except for that of Samson. The verb for "cry" (*za'aq* or the alternative spelling *tsa'aq*) is most often used when a person is in deep distress, anguish, or pain so that the cry takes on the character of a wail, howl, or scream.

The cry can come from an individual or a group and can be triggered by various circumstances. David cried out after the death of his son Absalom (2 Sam 19:4); Tamar cried out after she was raped by Amnon (2 Sam 13:19); Jeremiah cried out upon seeing the violence and destruction of Jerusalem (Jer 20:8); Jehoshaphat cried out when pressed by opponents who were trying to kill him (2 Kgs 22:32). Israel cried out when under oppression, whether experiencing slavery in Egypt (Exod 2:23; 1 Sam 12:8), being besieged by enemies (1 Sam 7:8–10; 12:10), suffering the exploitative practices imposed

---

4. See Judg 3:15; 4:3 (*tsa'aq*); 6:6; 10:10.

by a king (1 Sam 8:11–18), or seeing the destruction of land and people (Jer 11:11).

Sometimes the cry carries with it an appeal for help, which is specifically directed to the one who can alleviate the distress or pain. Thus it may include a call to the deity (1 Sam 7:8; 1 Sam 12:8, 10; Pss 22:5 [6], 107:13, 19; Hab 1:2; 1 Chr 5:20; Neh 9:28). However, the appeal does not mean that the petitioner has repented or has undergone a change in thinking or behavior. The Israelites cry out to God in their distress, and yet they retain their idols (Isa 57:13). They call on Yahweh for help, but they also cry out to their idols, especially when they perceive that Yahweh is not listening to them (Jer 11:11–12). Yahweh indicts Israel for crying out to God while spurning the good (Hos 8:2–3) or for crying out to God, but not from the heart (Hos 7:14). Thus sometimes Israel cries out to God, but God does not respond because the people continue in their sin (Jer 11:11–12; Lam 3:8; Mic 3:4).

For indeed, there are instances when Israel's cry is accompanied by confession of sin. In Judges 10:10 Israel cried and confessed their sin of worshipping the Baals: "We have sinned against you, forsaking our God and serving the Baals because we have abandoned the Lord." This is recounted in 1 Samuel 12:10. Yet rather than being pleased, the Lord refused to be moved by their pleas. Instead God told them, "Go and cry out to the gods you have chosen" (Judg 10:14). This leads one to suspect that the repentance was only skin-deep, dictated by desperation rather than a real recognition of wrong and a deep desire to change. Indeed, the confession in 1 Samuel 12:10 ("we have sinned") is immediately followed by the plea and the promise: "but now deliver us from the hands of our enemies and we will serve you." One gets the impression that the Israelites confessed their sin and pledged their service in order to get God to rescue them. Thus, the repentance was merely utilitarian and was intended to manipulate God into doing what they wanted.[5]

God did not respond because of the people's repentance, but because of their need. This magnifies the compassionate nature of God. The pattern is never: "I will keep you because you have rightly prayed or repented." Instead, the miraculous way of God is: "I will keep you because it is in my heart to do so." So often, pastors wrongly understand the emphasis of the Old Testament – that it is all about law. However, the OT is also all about grace: "I am the Lord your God, who brought you out of Egypt, out of the land of slavery" (Exod 20:2). This is also the story of Judges.

---

5. See pp. 141–145 for further discussion.

JUDGES

In Act 4, God raises up an individual to deliver Israel.

Act 4 *Yahweh*: "raised up a deliverer" (3:9)
"empowered the deliverer" (3:9)

This element is also present in the introductory framework (see 2:16, 19). However, in the introductory passage, the deliverer is referred to as one of the judges (*shofetim*), but in 3:9 Othniel is specifically referred to as a deliverer (*moshia'*).[6] In response to Israel's dire need, Yahweh elevates an individual from among the crowd and entrusts him with the task of rescuing Israel from the cause of its distress – the continued domination and oppression by a foreign power. The reason for designating an individual is not so that this person can then dominate over the rest, but so that she or he can help set God's redemptive activity in motion.

God not only chooses an individual, but also empowers that individual: "The spirit of the LORD came on him" (3:10). The action of the spirit of Yahweh figures prominently in the book of Judges, endowing an individual with strength just before an encounter or a skirmish with the foreign oppressors of Israel (6:34; 11:29; 13:25; 14:6, 19; 15:14). Thus God's action is connected with the judge's task of deliverance, rather than with any moral quality. The spirit does not endow the judge with ethical virtues, but with the power to deliver. Hence, one should not be surprised that some of the judges, like Samson, experience the onrush of the spirit's power while engaging in ethically questionable behavior.[7]

It is clear, however, that the God who chooses is also the God who empowers. God does not elevate an individual to fulfill a certain role and then leave that person to his or her own devices and resources. Rather, God also provides the means by which the individual can carry out the assigned task. In the case of the judges, emotional stamina, fortitude of heart and mind, and sheer physical strength were needed to fight a battle against those who had the psychological and physical advantage, having dominated Israel for many years with superior military force and equipment. The action of the spirit of God provided the emotional and physical equipment needed for the task of deliverance.

This is not to suggest that some of judges were not significant persons, but the focus of the story is not on human effort and courage. Just as Yahweh

---

6. See pp. 33–34 for the meaning of the word "judge."
7. The spirit of Yahweh is discussed further in the Gideon narrative. See pp. 104–105.

won the battle when Judah and Simeon fought (1:4), so also the power of Yahweh enabled the deliverers of Israel to accomplish their task. The story then is about what God continues to do and how God's power brings about significant change.

In Act 5, the judge, who is armed with power from Yahweh, goes forth and delivers the people.

Act 5 *The Deliverer*   "judged and delivered the people" (3:9–10)
"overpowered the enemy" (3:10)
"brought peace to Israel" (3:11)
"died" (3:11)

Just as Yahweh sold Israel into the hands of Cushan-rishathaim, Yahweh now gives Cushan-rishathaim into the hands of Othniel, the judge/deliverer of Israel. After the battle is won and the enemy overcome, there follows a period when the land has rest.

The phrase, "the land had rest," is used to describe a situation where the kingdom or the people are free from war or external threats.[8] This is a refrain that runs through the early chapters of the book of Judges (see also 3:30; 5:31; 8:28). Later in the book, this refrain disappears, as if these seasons of hopefulness and peace fall away.[9]

During the lifetime of the judge, Israel enjoys the blessing of Yahweh by receiving the gifts of political peace and economic well-being. The deliverer's military strength ensures protection from subjugation by a foreign ruler. However, the deliverer's work is temporary – he dies, and the cycle of deterioration begins again (3:12), which necessitates the raising up of a new judge/deliverer (3:15). This raises the question of the correlation between the role of the leader and the faithfulness of the people. Does the text suggest that faithful leaders produce faithful people?

The text is silent about this matter and offers no correlation. It does not say, "because of so and so's outstanding leadership the people remained faithful to Yahweh and enjoyed peace and prosperity." The text simply says, "the land had rest." Whatever the role of the judge/deliverer, it is the Lord's gift. Thus, while we honor the leaders that God raises up and are thankful for the roles they play in the community of faith or in the nation as a whole, we

---

8. See Josh 11:23; 14:15; Isa 14:7; 2 Chr 14:1 [13:23]. In 2 Chr 14:5 [14:4] and 20:30, in which the phrase is used to describe the realm of the king as free from threats. It is interesting that it is the land rather than the people that is described as having "rest" (Block, *Judges*, 155).
9. The phrase "the land had rest" is not present in the Jephthah and Samson narratives.

recognize that they can never be the source of blessing and goodness. At best, our leaders can offer temporary relief through the blessing of God. However, Yahweh alone is the source of any goodness.

In this dramatic cycle of deliverance, the emphasis is clearly on Yahweh, who is the key actor that sets in motion the dynamics of renewal through love and grace. This is no self-recovery program on the part of the people. For Yahweh, the deliverer and healer, sets the people free. Yahweh calls, enables, and empowers the deliverers to be the instruments of Yahweh's purposes.

There are several important implications in this pattern for Asian Christians and leaders. First, the cycle of unfaithfulness and deliverance is not prescriptive but descriptive. There is no suggestion that this *should* happen, but simply a recognition that this *does* happen. Therefore, this is not the iron law of salvation history. There is no fatalism at play here, and there is no suggestion that sin must happen in order for grace to be magnified.

Secondly, the pattern of the people's infidelity and God's work of deliverance alerts us to the fact that no religious activity is beyond the possibility of deterioration. Religious institutions, even with pristine beginnings, can plateau and begin to devolve. This can be equally true of our own faith journeys. Thus we must be alert to the need for revitalization and renewal. In the predominantly face-saving culture of Asia, there can be a temptation to ignore or suppress the poor health of a church or religious organization. However, deliverance can only come when God's people "cry out" (3:9) in acknowledgment of their need for God's intervention. Hope, therefore, does not lie in our faithfulness, steadfastness or spirituality, but rather in the persistent love of God, who seeks to uphold us and who raises us up when we fall and falter.

Thirdly, Yahweh is the primary initiator, and the servant of Yahweh (a judge/deliverer) is a secondary participator. The relationship between Yahweh and Yahweh's servant must be clearly understood and maintained. The judge/deliverer is not the principal actor, for Yahweh initiates the deliverance.

In an Asian culture that is largely characterized by familial headship and older notions of tribal leadership, Christian leaders should not be elevated to approximate societal roles. A pastor is not like a self-determined tribal leader who holds positional power. Instead, the Christian leader cooperates with God, who is the primary source of leadership, power, and wisdom. Yahweh is the key actor, while the pastor, priest, Christian worker is Yahweh's dutiful servant.

3:12–30 EHUD THE UNLIKELY DELIVERER

In contrast to the paradigmatic picture of Othniel, the narrative description of Ehud is full of color and picturesque details. As a Benjamite, Ehud comes from a small tribe squeezed in between the big tribes of Judah in the South and Ephraim in the North. What is peculiar about Ehud, however, is that he is described in the Hebrew text in a roundabout manner: he was "a man whose right hand was crooked" (3:15, trans. mine). This could mean that he had a deformity and was somewhat handicapped. However, the use of the same phrase in Judges 20:16 to describe how the Benjamites "could sling a stone at a hair and not miss" shows that the phrase does not refer to a physical deformity, but rather is an indirect way of referring to someone who has a strong left hand.[10] Far from being a handicap, "a man whose right hand was crooked" actually has a special skill that can be very handy in battle. In biblical narrative, physical descriptions are sparse, so any such description is usually tied to the plot. Later in the story, Ehud's strong left hand proves to be crucial to his ability to carry out his secret plan. Nonetheless, he is described as the one sent by God to be the agent of deliverance in response to Israel's cry. Regardless of how the deliverance is accomplished, God is identified as the principal actor behind the scene.

Many commentators note the highly humorous, satirical nature of the Ehud narrative.[11] An atmosphere of trickery and suspense pervades the story, which makes for an interesting reading – a stark contrast to the almost formulaic presentation of Othniel. Through a combination of comic and satirical devices, such as incongruity, surprise, superiority,[12] and the use of comic

---

10. In 1 Chr 12:2, the Benjamites are described as being able to sling stones and shoot arrows with both hands.
11. Lowell K. Handy, "Uneasy Laughter: Ehud and Eglon as Ethnic Humor," in *SJOT* 6, 2 (1992): 233–246; Marc Zvi Brettler, *The Creation of History in Ancient Israel* (London, New York: Routledge, 1995), 84–85; Robert Alter, *The Art of Biblical Narrative* (New York: Basic, 1981), 38–41; Dennis T. Olson, "Judges," in *NIB*, Vol. 2 (Nashville, TN: Abingdon, 1998), 770.
12. Theories of humor can be broadly categorized into three: (1) the theory of incongruity, (2) the experience of superiority, and (3) the element of surprise. The incongruity theory states that humor arises from the pairing of ill-suited or disjointed ideas or situations. The superiority hypothesis traces the origins of laughter from a sense of superiority over other people and circumstances. Thus, mockery and laughter at the foolish actions of others are central to the humor experience. The last theory, the element of surprise, explains humor as arising from the spontaneous breaking up of routine courses of action. See Jeffrey H. Goldstein and Paul E. McGhee, *The Psychology of Humor: Theoretical Perspectives and Empirical Issues* (New York/London: Academic Press, 1972), 4–10.

types and themes, the narrative portrays the antagonists of Israel, Eglon and the Moabites, as bumbling fools.

The description of Eglon as "a very fat man" (3:17b) contrasts incongruously with an earlier description of him as one who "rallied to himself the Ammonites and the Amalekites; they marched out to war and defeated Israel, then took possession of the city of Palms"[13] (3:13). Eglon then subjugated Israel for eighteen years (3:14). From such a strong military leader, one would expect a physique that would match his reputation. Instead, the description matches the meaning of his name – Eglon, the "fatted calf." Webb notes that the description of the Moabite warriors as *shamen* (3:29), which means "stout," can be taken to mean "robust" or "fat."[14] It seems that the narrator, wanting to break the perception of Moabite superiority, dismisses their robust physical bearing as consisting merely of fat. Name-punning, however, is by no means limited to Eglon and the Moabites. The warriors of Benjamin, "my son (*beni*) of right hand (*yamin*)," were not famous for their right hands, but for their left hands.

The element of surprise is achieved by a disparity of perspectives, in which the characters in the story are placed in a privileged position because they know more than the reader.[15] In this character-elevating device, the narrator is in complicity with the character, since both are privy to what is about to take place, while this information is withheld from the reader. Thus, we see Ehud making a cubit-long double-edged sword and strapping it on his right thigh (3:17). We see him dismissing the people who carried the tribute and returning to the king alone, after having gone past the boundaries around Moab (3:18–19a), and we contemplate what his plan would be. Then we hear his speech to the king: "I have a secret message for you" (3:19b). We wonder what this secret message could be, especially since the king seems so very eager to hear it that he asks everyone to leave, and so the king is left all by himself in the cool upper chamber (3:20). Again Ehud says that he has a message. We see the king arising from his chair, perhaps to hear Ehud's message better, perhaps because he realizes that something is amiss. But the

---

13. Probably Jericho, which is near Moab in the Jordan valley. See 1:16.
14. Webb, *Judges: Integrated Reading*, 130.
15. Meir Sternberg discusses three reading positions in *The Poetics of Biblical Narrative: Ideological Literature and the Drama of Reading* (Bloomington, IN: Indiana University Press, 1987), 163–172. The character-elevating position occurs when a character knows more than the reader, while an evenhanded position is when both reader and character have the same level of knowledge. In a reader-elevating position, the reader knows more than the characters in the story because the narrator shares this prior knowledge with the reader.

moment the king arises, Ehud's left hand quickly shoots out from his right thigh with the double-edged sword and pierces the king's belly, with the fat closing in over the blade (3:21–22). We now realize with a shock the significance of Ehud's left-handed ability as well as the inclusion of the details about the making of the sword and Eglon's obesity. On hindsight, we realize that for all his might, Eglon is really a gullible fool.

The gullibility of Eglon is underscored by a pun on words. In Hebrew the term for "word" (*dabar*) can mean message or thing. Thus there is a double meaning to Ehud's speech to the king: "I have a private word" can mean a secret message or a hidden thing (referring to the sword hidden under the clothes of Ehud's right thigh). Eglon apparently understands it in the sense of the first meaning, for he asks everyone to leave – whereas Ehud is slyly referring to the "thing" on his right thigh. Eglon probably thinks that Ehud is a spy with information to help Moab in its subjugation of Israel. When Ehud is finally alone with the king, he repeats his message, but this time with a twist: "I have a message from God for you" (3:20). From being a spy, Ehud now becomes a seer. Perhaps Eglon thinks that he is going to give an oracle,[16] for when Ehud passed the idol figures in Moab he turned back, allowing others to go ahead of him (3:18–19). When the king arises from his seat to hear the oracle or secret word (*dabar*) better, he gets the secret thing (*dabar*) which is hidden in Ehud's right thigh (3:20b–21).

The narrative also uses a reader-elevating device, wherein the reader knows more than the characters in the story, thus giving the reader a privileged position over the characters. Because readers can clearly see the consequences of a character's actions, they can jeer at the character's "misguided attempts at concealment, plotting, and interpretation."[17] In this story, though readers already know that Eglon is dead and Ehud has escaped, the servants are clueless about what is happening. First of all, they live in such fear before the king that when Eglon says, "Leave us," all of them immediately leave (3:19). Nobody thinks of protecting their king. Secondly, their interpretation of the king's silence and the locked doors is so totally mistaken that it becomes laughable. After seeing Ehud leave, they come back to attend to the king, but the doors are locked. So "they say, 'He must be relieving himself[18] in the inner room of the palace'" (3:24). They think he is in the toilet, perhaps because they can smell the excrement that came out when Ehud pierced the

---

16. Alter, *Art of Biblical Narrative*, 40.
17. Sternberg, *Poetics of Biblical Narrative*, 164.
18. Literally, "covering his feet."

king's belly with the sword (3:22). The servants wait "to the point of embarrassment" (3:25)," and one can imagine them looking at each other, thinking the king must be very constipated to take so long in the toilet! Finally, they have the sense to get the key and open the door, but "Ehud had escaped while they dilly-dallied" (3:26, trans. mine). The combination of toilet humor and the reader's privileged perspective makes the whole incident highly amusing – at the expense of the Moabite attendants and their king.

In contrast to Eglon and his attendants, Ehud is characterized as a slick and wily double-talker and deceiver. Yet the narrative also makes it clear that he has leadership capabilities. First, the Israelites entrust him to lead a retinue of tribute bearers from the hill country of Ephraim to the city of Palms (3:15b). In the ancient Near East, those who were defeated in battle had to pay a tribute to the foreign ruler. This detail indicates that Eglon was not directly ruling over Israelite affairs, but exacting tribute from them. Clearly, the Israelites trust Ehud to get the job done while protecting the tribute from being vandalized by other groups. Secondly, the Israelites willingly respond to Ehud's call to war and follow him in seizing the Jordan crossings and striking down Moab (3:27–29). Thirdly, Ehud is a good strategist. Though it seems as if he plans the whole secret strategy on his own, he also knows the right time to call on the help of others. Finally, Ehud is a careful planner. He makes his weapon so that he can utilize his special left-handed skill, and he ensures the success of his plan by making the sword short enough to hide beneath his clothes, long enough to reach the king,[19] and double-edged to ensure one lethal strike. Despite Ehud's positive leadership qualities, his use of deception is troubling. It is difficult to imagine how God can raise a leader who resorts to trickery to accomplish God's purposes. After all, should there not be some correlation between means and ends? The story raises up all sorts of ethical issues and posits the broader question about whether the good purposes of God can be achieved through deceptive means.

One angle for interpreting the story is to recognize the function of the trickster figure. In the folk literature of many cultures, an amoral and comical mythical figure appears frequently, which scholars refer to as the "trickster."[20]

---

19. A cubit is about the length of the forearm from the elbow to the tip of the middle finger.
20. According to Naomi Steinberg, "Israelite Tricksters, Their Analogues and Cross-Cultural Study," *Semeia* 42 (1988), 2, the term "trickster" was first coined by Daniel Brinton to refer to the chief character of North American Indian stories in *The Myths of the New World: A Treatise on the Symbolism and Mythology of the Red Race of America* (New York: Leypoldt and Holt, 1868). It became part of the academic vocabulary by the end of the nineteenth century, becoming especially popular in the area of folklore studies.

Although there are different manifestations among various cultures, some common general traits define the trickster.[21] Tricksters are adept at fooling others, often embarking on elaborate schemes through the use of deceitful language and wit. They also exhibit a great deal of freedom, often breaking rules unconsciously, behaving as if there were no moral or social norms to guide them.[22] Because of their amoral character, they mock institutions, people, or anything that parades itself as permanent, important, and impermeable. By doing this, they unmask the pretensions of those of who are pompous and arrogant.

The functions of the trickster figure also vary from culture to culture, ranging from "pure entertainment to a psychological steam valve for critiquing social values"[23] or as an outlet for taboo emotions and behavior.[24] Thus, one cannot unilaterally take a trickster figure in one society and then apply its characteristics and functions directly to a similar figure in a different society. Yet across cultures, the trickster figure often appears in the literature of peoples or groups who have been rendered powerless and marginalized. According to Steinberg, "individuals resort to the use of trickery under certain social conditions. In particular, when individuals lack authority – they resort to strategies which allow them to achieve their goals and gain compliance with their wishes."[25]

Thus in the Hebrew Scriptures, because women have a marginalized status, they are often portrayed using trickery and deception to accomplish certain ends. Although not explicitly encouraged, these women's actions are regarded as justifiable, even exemplary, in light of their good intentions and difficult circumstances. These women are willing to undertake risks, even

---

21. The following articles give an overview of the characteristics of the trickster as found in different societies: Lawrence E. Sullivan, "Tricksters: An Overview," in *The Encyclopedia of Religion*, 2nd ed., ed. Lindsay Jones (Detroit, MI: Thomson Gale, 2005), 14: 9350–9352. Victor Turner, "Myth and Symbol," in the *International Encyclopedia of the Social Sciences*, ed. David L. Sills (New York: Macmillan & Free Press, 1968), 10: 576–582; "Trickster" in *Funk and Wagnalls Standard Dictionary of Folklore, Mythology and Legend*, ed. Maria Leach and Jerome Fried (New York: Funk & Wagnalls, 1950), 2:1123–1125. For a seminal work on the trickster, see Paul Radin, *The Trickster: A Study in American Indian Mythology* (New York: Schocken Books, 1956).
22. Turner, "Myth and Symbol," 580.
23. Steinberg, "Israelite Tricksters," 2–3.
24. Tricksters, by exhibiting prohibited behavior and attitudes in a jocular way, are able to represent what everyone would secretly like to do, according to Turner, "Myth and Symbol," 580.
25. Steinberg, "Israelite Tricksters," 6.

sometimes breaking their society's sexual and social codes, in order to accomplish good for themselves, their community, and ultimately for Yahweh.[26]

The appearance of a trickster figure such as Ehud in this story is not surprising, since the Israelites were experiencing oppression from the Moabites. Because of the superior strength of their enemy, Israel cannot use conventional means to gain the upper hand against their foreign rulers. Thus, they have to go around the existing structures and standard operations to catch their enemy by surprise. However, we may evaluate the ethical appropriateness of the use of trickery and deception in this story (and other similar stories in the Bible), it is directed against those who take pride in their own superiority and knowledge.

The undercutting of the pretensions of the powerful and arrogant is reinforced by the use of satirical humor directed against Eglon and his cohorts. Thus Lowell Handy thinks that the story is an ethnic joke, since it is directed against an ethnic group – the Moabites – and caricatures their dull-wittedness.[27] However, there are some reasons why the story cannot be classified as ethnic humor. First of all, the humor is not directed against the Moabites because they are Moabites, but because they hold the power and are oppressing the Israelites. Thus in contrast to ethnic humor, which is directed against the marginal and the powerless, the story ridicules those who are powerful and have superior strength. The presence of the trickster figure underscores the fact that the object of the humor is not the oppressed but rather the oppressor.

There are other similar humorous stories in the Old Testament, which will be discussed further in the Samson narrative.[28] Nevertheless, the commonality among these stories is that they are directed against those who take pride in their superior knowledge and strength – particularly the foreign nations that oppress Israel. The story makes the point that stronger military power is no guarantee of success.

But there is also a more subtle message in this captivating story, which is that humor is a form of survival for the oppressed. The humor of the trickster figure subverts the powerful because it causes a break with the ideology and rhetoric of those in power. Just as God laughs (Ps 2:4) at the pretensions of

---

26. Claudia Camp, "Wise and Strange: An Interpretation of the Female Imagery in Proverbs in Light of Trickster Mythology," *Semeia* 42 (1988): 19. Examples are the midwives in Exodus (Exod 1:15–22), Rahab (Josh 2), Jael (Judg 4:17–22), Naomi and Ruth (Ruth 3), Tamar (Gen 38) and Abigail (1 Sam 25).
27. Handy, "Uneasy Laughter," 233–246.
28. See pp. 187–196.

the wicked who think they are powerful, so the first act in resisting oppressive powers is to relativize them. Because the powerful are not truly powerful, laughing at them – rather than fearing them – is the first act of resistance.

> ## **LIKELY AND UNLIKELY DELIVERERS**
>
> There is much about God's way in human affairs that catches us by surprise. Clearly, God's way does not mirror how we might plan and accomplish things. This reality highlights God's sovereignty and reminds us that God declares: "My thoughts are not your thoughts, neither are your ways, my ways" (Isa 55:8). The above stories highlight that God chooses both typical people, such as Othniel, and odd people, such as Ehud. Scripture never suggests that God prefers the most popular or likely candidates to accomplish God's purposes. "The LORD raised up for them a deliverer . . ." refers both to Othniel and Ehud (3: 9, 15).
>
> God's strange way of selecting people poses a particular challenge for Asian Christians, since many Asian societies continue to have a hierarchical social structure and way of life, which is often reflected in the life of churches. People are invited to play a role in the church due to their social standing. Thus an engineer or a lawyer reads the Scripture in the worship service rather than the house helper or the mother of four children. There is also a tendency to appoint people of social standing as board members of Christian organizations without giving due attention to their wisdom, spirituality, prayerfulness, and discernment. Thus we often work according to the ways of the world rather than in concert with the strange ways of God. The stories of Othniel and Ehud show that God chooses both likely and unlikely leaders – and the challenge for the church is to recognize that God uses both.
>
> The stories in the book of Judges also reveal that, while Yahweh is the God of the people, Yahweh does not only work with people as a collective mass. Individuals play a part. The interplay between a nation, its institutions, and key individuals is not only true of general history, for this is also true of the "story of God." Yet there is a world of difference between the role of the individual in God's story and the issue of individualism, which occurs when a person becomes self-focused and self-preoccupied. When we focus on the role of the individual in the story of God in the world, we emphasize the value of each individual person, and we recognize the unique gifts that each can contribute.
>
> The interplay between the communal and the personal is particularly relevant for Asian Christians. Along with the Asian emphasis on the communal and the familial, we need to place appropriate emphasis on the role of the individual without that leading to an unhealthy individualism. Both the group and the person are important – and so Asian Christians will need to embrace the challenge of fostering both solidarity and individual growth.

JUDGES 4:1–5:31

Partnership and Solidarity in God's Work

While a sense of community and collaboration are ingrained in Asian cultures, the solo leader is often regarded the one who can resolve the community's problems. Typically, this solo leader is a strong, authoritative male with high social status who acts as the patron of the community. Because women are rarely elevated to this position and have been marginalized in both church and society, groups devoted to the rights of women often react by excluding men.

In Judges 4 and 5, women are celebrated for their roles in God's acts of deliverance – but never to the exclusion of men. Instead, both women and men, leaders and people, officials and volunteers, prominent members of the community and low-key housewives, outsiders and insiders – in their various capacities and roles – participate in God's work and bring about God's purposes. While the emphasis of 3:7–31 is on the role of individual deliverers, the focus of chapters 4–5 is on multiple players.

Yet throughout the book of Judges, the role of Yahweh is highlighted and celebrated above all others. For Yahweh calls people to their various roles and tasks and orchestrates both human and cosmic events to bring about the needed deliverance.[1] Nevertheless, Yahweh's role does not cancel out human involvement, as the poem in Judges 5 clearly expresses.

STORY AND THE POEM

The relationship between the story in chapter 4 and the poem in chapter 5 have been construed in various ways.[2] Most commentators consider the

---

[1]. On this theme, see Yairah Amit, *The Book of Judges: The Art of Editing* (Leiden: Brill, 1999), 199. See R. H. O'Connell, *The Rhetoric of the Book of Judges* (Leiden: Brill, 1996), 110, 112–113, 132–134.

[2]. For a summary, see Block, *Judges*, 176–177. K. Lawson Younger, Jr. gives a detailed comparison of the two chapters in "Heads! Tails! Or the whole coin?! Contextual Method & Intertextual Analysis: Judges 4 and 5," in *The Biblical Canon in Comparative Perspective: Scripture in Context IV*, ed. K. Lawson Younger, Jr., et al. (Lewiston, NY: The Edwin Mellen Press, 1991), 127–134.

poem to have an earlier dating.³ Some commentators have tried to reconstruct the sequence of events by using both chapters. For example, Schneider notes that the "two units need each other," but she uses the poem primarily to shed light on the prose account.⁴

However, as two very different literary genres, both accounts can stand by themselves. As a creative enactment, a song or a poem can hardly be subject to the same analysis that one would apply to a narrative. For one does not look *through* a poem in order to discover information,⁵ but one gazes *at* a poem like a stained glass window. Rather than tracing the logical development of the events in a story, a poem focuses on particular scenes and sets them side by side.⁶ Thus the question is not, what does chapter 5 add to chapter 4, but what does the song celebrate?

Nonetheless, the fact that the event was preserved in two ways – as a narrative and as a celebratory poem – reveals the compelling character of this account in the life of Israel. Only one other event warranted both a prose and poetic version – that of the Israelite crossing of the Red Sea (see Exod 14, 15).⁷ Both the Exodus and Judges narratives recount stories of liberation from oppressive powers. Both vividly extol the mighty works of God as manifested in the forces of nature that defeat the enemy. Judges 5, however, puts more stress on the participation of people⁸ – the leaders and the warriors, the different tribes as a whole and specific individual – without detracting from the power of God, who initiated and caused the victory.

In the history of a people, we can often trace the development from an event to a story to a poem or symbol – or vice-versa. The significance and power of a poem or symbol is that it can become paradigmatic for other similar events. A song, poem, or symbol, while finding its genesis in a particular time and setting, can transcend that setting and define other events.

Asian Christianity was born in a world of rich cultural traditions and symbols. Yet the Christianity that came to Asia from the West – particularly Protestant Christianity – is often verbal and propositional, rather than

---

3. For the dating of Judges 5, see Frank Moore Cross and David Noel Freedman, *Studies in Ancient Yahwistic Poetry* (Grand Rapids, MI: Eerdmans, 1975), 3.
4. Schneider, *Judges*, 97; see also O'Connell, *Rhetoric of Judges*, 102.
5. Poetry is not intended primarily to provide historical information. See Michael Coogan, "A Structural and Literary Analysis of the Song of Deborah," *CBQ* 40 (1978): 143–144.
6. Peter Ackroyd, "The Composition of the Song of Deborah," *VT* 2 (1952): 160.
7. On a detailed comparison of Judges 4–5 and Exodus 14–15, see Alan Hauser, "Two Songs of Victory: A Comparison of Exodus 15 and Judges 5," in *Directions in Biblical Poetry*, ed. Elaine R. Follis (Sheffield: JSOT Press), 268; O'Connell, *Rhetoric of Judges*, 134–135.
8. Hauser, "Two Songs of Victory," 268.

poetic, symbolic, and artistic. In order to develop a contextualized theology and faith, the challenge for Asian Christians is to draw from the rich symbolic tradition of Asian cultures in order to tell the story of their church's journey of faith in creative and culturally reflective ways.

4:1–24 CONTOURS OF AN UPSIDE-DOWN WORLD: THE INVERSION OF ROLES

Scripture is never without its surprising themes and nuances. Judges 4 and 5 is no exception, for the narrative subverts common assumptions and expectations.

Judges 4 starts off typically: "Again the Israelites did evil in the eyes of the Lord" – although this time, the nature of the evil is assumed (v. 1). The second part of the cycle also follows a typical pattern: "The LORD sold them" (v. 2). Jabin the king of Canaan is mentioned as the oppressive power (v. 2) while Sisera, the commander of Jabin's army, gets special attention. The narrative emphasizes his military superiority – "he had nine hundred chariots fitted with iron" – and his cruelty – "he cruelly oppressed the Israelites" – and his staying power – "for twenty years" – so that in their suffering, "they [the Israelites] cried to the LORD" (v. 3).

Without the introduction (vv. 1–3) and conclusion (vv. 23–24), chapter 4 can be divided into three scenes, according to the main character pairs and the location of their interaction: Deborah and Barak under the Palm of Deborah (vv. 4–10), Barak and Sisera at the foot of Mt. Tabor (vv. 12–16), and Sisera and Jael at the Tent of Jael (vv. 17–22). The other characters, either directly or indirectly, intrude briefly into each scene, acting as foils to the major players. Verse 11, which refers to Heber the Kenite, stands apart from this structure, but it foreshadows the events of the last scene (vv. 17–22).

4:4–10 Deborah and Barak

If the narrative were following the expected framework, the next element (in response to the people's cry) would be, "he raised up for them a deliverer . . ." (3:9, 15). However, the scene opens with Deborah, which raises the expectation that Deborah is the deliverer. The next verses, however, do not portray her in a military role or with special military skill. Unlike Othniel, who captured Kiriath-sepher and had family connections with the great warrior Caleb (Judg 1:12–13; see also Josh 15:14), and Ehud, who can brandish a sword with his left hand and plan a well-contrived strategy (3:15–16),

Deborah's first appearance has to do with her prominent and authoritative role in society as well as her domestic role: "Now Deborah, a prophet, the wife of Lappidoth . . . (4:4a).

4:4–5 Deborah: A multifaceted leader

The word "prophet" in the NIV actually stands for two words in the Hebrew text, *issha nebi'ah*, which can either be translated literally as "a woman prophetess" or as "a woman, a prophet." Since *nebi'ah* (prophetess) is already in feminine form, the reference to "woman" (*'issha*) is considered extraneous, so the latter translation is often preferred (see ESV, NRSV). In any case, both words emphasize Deborah's gender, especially when seen in parallel to the next description: *'issha nebi'ah* (a woman, a prophetess) with *'issha lapidoth* (the woman or wife of Lappidoth). The fact that Deborah is called prophetess before she is identified as the wife of Lappidoth emphasizes her socio-political-religious role over her domestic role. In the culture of that time, being the "wife of" somebody would define a woman's identity and role. Yet Deborah's identity is cast in very different terms, for her role in the community is given prominence.

The narrative focuses on Deborah's socio-political-religious role without expanding her domestic role. For the next line explains that "she was judging Israel at that time" (4:4b, ESV). The following verses, however, do not expand her prophetic role (although it is prominent in the rest of the narrative), but link her activity with the other judges (3:10; 2:16–18), who functioned as hero-deliverers. Surprisingly, her role as judge does not seem to involve the act of deliverance, for she is not described as "delivering Israel" (see 2:16), nor is she called "deliverer" (see also Othniel, 3:9; Ehud, 3:15). Instead, her task seems to fit our contemporary ideas about the work of a judge: "She was presiding[9] under the palm tree of Deborah, between Ramah and Bethel, in the uplands of Ephraim, and the Israelites went up to her for judgement" (4:5, trans. mine). The verbs "judging" and "presiding" are participles, indicating that they were repeated actions in the past. Thus, when the narrative opens, Deborah is already involved in the ongoing task of presiding over the affairs of Israel.

Deborah's role as a judge is disputed among scholars because, as discussed earlier, the term functions differently within the book of Judges. Of

---

9. The Hebrew verb is *yashab*, meaning "to sit" or "to dwell," but in here has the expanded meaning of exercising a task (Soggin, *Judges*, 64) and a function (Lindars, *Judges 1–5*, 183). The translation "presiding" is from Boling, *Judges*, 95.

the three meanings already discussed for the word "judge,"[10] Deborah seems to be deciding legal cases, especially on behalf of the vulnerable sectors of society. However, Block thinks that the Israelites came to Deborah not "to solve their legal disputes but to give them the divine answer to their cries,"[11] since they were being oppressed by Sisera. A frequentative or continuous sense to the verb "judging," however, challenges this interpretation.[12] Thus, it seems best to see Deborah as fulfilling a well-entrenched role in society, that of arbitrating disputes and administering justice among the members of Israelite society. Nevertheless, her involvement in the war against Sisera, along with Barak, shows that she also shares in the characteristics of a judge as deliverer.

Thus Deborah fulfills the dual role of prophet and judge[13] along with the function of a deliverer. Moreover, the reference to the "palm of Deborah" alludes to a sacred site, since trees were considered places of worship in the ancient Near East,[14] hence giving Deborah a priestly cast. Rather than being cast as a typical woman functioning within her husband's world, Deborah is depicted as a significant force in troubled Israel, who will help to define and mobilize the will and purpose of Yahweh. Not only does she play the role of a judge, who is involved in maintaining the day-by-day affairs of the nation – dealing with issues requiring advice, direction, and arbitration – along with the role of a visionary, who defines the liberating purposes of Yahweh for her time, but she is also a mobilizer who, together with Barak, enters into the fray of battle.

Deborah's multifaceted role parallels that of Samuel, who was called prophet (1 Sam 3:20) and judge (1 Sam 7:6, 15–17) and who performed the task of deliverer (1 Sam 7:10–b14) and the priestly function of offering sacrifices (1 Sam 7:9–10a). Moses also fulfilled these roles. In the chaotic times of transition from the oppression of Egypt to life in Canaan, and from the period of the judges to the monarchy, it seems that an individual could play complex and multifarious roles which, during more stables times, were distributed among several people.

Deborah's complex role reveals the importance of her status in Israel during a time of crisis. To some extent, we could say that in Deborah, kingly

---

10. See p. 33.
11. Block, *Judges*, 197.
12. C. F. Burney, *The Book of Judges with Introduction and Notes and Notes of the Hebrew Text of the Book of Kings with an Introduction and Appendix* (New York: KTAV Publishing House, 1970), 85.
13. Soggin, *Judges*, 71.
14. Ibid., 64.

(kings are tasked with military matters), priestly, and prophetic roles find their integration. Thus, unlike Barak and Jael, whose parts in the overall drama are circumscribed and limited, Deborah's roles are multiple, and it would be difficult to say where one begins and the other ends. Clearly, her prophetic role flows over into her involvement in the military task.

This has important implications. First, in the purposes of Yahweh, people "appear" or "come to the fore" whose roles and tasks are critical during times of difficulty and transition. In times of crises, the concern is about the restoration and stability of the nation as a whole. One needs "big picture" and multi-tasking persons that can help move the nation forward. With Moses and Samuel as the great iconic multi-dimensional leaders in Israel, Deborah forms an appropriate female counterpart.

Secondly, while roles, tasks, and particular institutions, such as the priesthood, were clearly defined in ancient Israel, these roles can be subverted for Yahweh's purposes during times of national crises. When things go radically wrong (4:1), Yahweh calls whomever he wills. And even though there is no traditional call narrative for Deborah in her prophetic role, as is the case with Jeremiah, Gideon, and Moses, she clearly plays the role of a spokesperson for Yahweh (4:6).

Thirdly, although the narrative highlights Deborah's multiple roles, her prophetic role is definitive. For the Word on behalf of Yahweh moves the entire story. This has significant implications for the contemporary mission and ministry of the church. Not only does God raise up unexpected people – and not only are some given crucial and defining tasks and roles, particularly in times of crises – but even more importantly, the Word is generative, creative, and mobilizing, and this power can never be minimized or underplayed.

Fourthly, the Deborah story should not be used to justify solo heroes in the ministry of the church. While God does raise up outstanding leaders in times of crisis and difficulty – individuals such as Martin Luther and Theresa of Avila – the church requires multiple ministries in order to grow into maturity and missional effectiveness.

4:6–10 Divine word to Barak

Consistent with the role of a prophet, Deborah's first communication to Barak is authoritative: "The LORD, the God of Israel, commands you" (4:6). In the Hebrew text, the phrase is constructed as a question: "Has not Yahweh commanded . . . ?" The question, however, is rhetorical, since the answer is well-known to the hearers and is unconditionally admitted by them.[15] This seems to indicate a prior command to Barak, but the question is also a way of introducing the command[16] with an emphatic nuance, hence my translation: "Surely, Yahweh . . . has commanded."

Deborah's initial message from God to Barak includes a promise that uses a pun, which the NIV tries to reproduce: "Go, take with you ten thousand men of Naphtali and Zebulun and lead them up (*mashak*) to Mount Tabor. I will lead (*mashak*) Sisera, the commander of Jabin's army, with his chariots and his troops to the Kishon River and give him into your hands" (4:6b–7). The Hebrew *mashak* literally means "to draw or to drag." As Barak draws the tribes of Naphtali and Zebulun and musters them in Mount Tabor, God also promises to draw Sisera and his army to Wadi[17] Kishon, which is about ten miles from the mountain. As Barak does his part in "drawing" the tribes of Israel to fight in a battle, God does his part in "drawing" Israel's enemies into a trap that will lead to their demise. This highlights the way in which Yahweh seeks to work: divine initiative with human instrumentation.

God's promise, however, is not enough for Barak. He needs Deborah's presence as he fights the battle: "If you go with me, I will go; but if you don't go with me, I won't go" (4:8). The desire for Deborah's presence does not seem to stem from Barak's need for a military leader or strategist, since he seems quite capable of doing the commanding and strategizing himself (4:10, 16). Rather, because he recognizes Deborah's prophetic role, his desire for her presence has to do with his need to be assured that he will be victorious in battle. Indeed, Israel's kings relied on a prophet's word to know whether they would have victory in battle.[18]

Many commentators have criticized Barak's cowardice and reliance on Deborah.[19] Indeed, there seems to be an implicit criticism in Deborah's response to Barak's request: "Certainly I will go with you . . . But because of the course you are taking, the honor will not be yours, for the LORD will deliver

---

15. GKC § 150e.
16. Lindars, *Judges 1–5*, 185.
17. A *wadi* is a small river or rivulet.
18. In 1 Kings 22, King Jehoshaphat of Judah demanded from the King of Israel that they "first seek the counsel of the LORD" before they go to battle (vv. 1–5), so the prophets were consulted. While the false prophets predicted victory (vv. 6, 11–12), Micaiah, the true prophet, prophesied defeat (v. 17).
19. Matthews, *Judges & Ruth*, 66; Block, *Judges*, 224; Cheryl Exum, "Feminist Criticism: Whose Interests are Being Served?" in *Judges & Method: New Approaches in Biblical Studies*, ed. Gale A. Yee (Minneapolis, MN: Fortress, 1995), 71–72; Sternberg, *Poetics of Biblical Narrative*, 274; O'Connell, *Rhetoric of Judges*, 101.

Sisera into the hands of a woman" (4:9). However, the text also reiterates twice that Yahweh will give Sisera into the hand of Barak (4:7, 14). This clearly refers to Sisera's army (4:16), even though Sisera himself falls into the hands of Jael (4:18–22). Moreover, Barak's challenge that Deborah should accompany him (4:8) need not be cast in a framework of doubt and cowardice. Rather, it can be understood as Barak's desire that Yahweh, through Deborah the prophetess, should be present in the conflict (4:8).[20] Furthermore, the text notes Barak's obedience and proactivity. Barak summons the people (4:10), he pursues Sisera's army and defeats them (4:16), and he pursues Sisera himself (4:22). These are all positive qualities and outcomes.

Nevertheless, the implicit criticism may revolve around Barak's insecurity in being able to marshal Israel for battle. Barak knows that Deborah's presence in the battlefield will enhance his status as a military commander, since she is very well known and respected by the Israelites, and he might need her to ensure that the troops will respond to his summons. Barak does not seem to have confidence in his own drawing power and needs Deborah's help in mustering the troops. As a result, however, he will have to forgo a victor's glory, since the prophetic word declares that the glory will go to a woman.

To Barak's credit, he does not have any problems responding to a woman's authority or to a woman's presence in battle, for "Barak summoned Zebulun and Naphtali, and ten thousand men went up under his command. Deborah also went up with him" (4:10). Having been called to the task of leading the forces of Israel against Sisera (4:6), one would expect Barak to take center stage. But while Barak plays a significant role, he does not have a solo hero mentality, for he recognizes his need for Deborah's ongoing presence and involvement. To Barak, gender is not the issue, but rather the person's competence and role. Since God has vested upon Deborah a prophetic gift and role, he is happy to follow her and is not too proud to admit his need for her encouraging presence in the midst of battle. Moreover, Barak does not seem to care whether he gets the glory or not. Nonetheless, God's clear promise of victory (4:7) should have been sufficient to embolden Barak to act without any need for human props.

---

20. Jo Ann Hackett, "In the Days of Jael: Reclaiming the History of Women in Ancient Israel," in *Immaculate and Powerful: The Female in Sacred Image and Social Reality*, eds. Clarissa W. Atkinson, Constance H. Buchanan, and Margaret R. Miles (Boston, MA: Beacon Press, 1985), 27. McCann, *Judges*, 52, suggests that Barak needed the divine presence as it was embodied in Deborah.

For the Asian setting, this chapter – and particularly Deborah's central role in the story – poses some interesting challenges. First, since many Asian societies and churches remain patriarchal, Deborah poses a contrasting paradigm. The key message is not only that God uses women, but also that Yahweh acknowledges the leadership role of women such as Deborah. And if Deborah could be accepted in the patriarchal society of her time, should not women in the present-day church also be allowed to exercise their gifts and play a role beyond the domestic and private sphere? Deborah's role is neither minor nor simple, but is prophetic, religious, and socio-political. In fact, Barak's task is wholly defined by Deborah's prophetic word, including her leadership in sending the troops into battle. Therefore, Barak does well in working willingly within this framework. Can contemporary male workers in the church and in church-related institutions reflect a similar humility and spirit of cooperation?

Secondly, Deborah's role as prophetess, judge, and co-leader in military action is surprising rather than stereotypical. This suggests that being part of the purposes of Yahweh takes precedence over cultural proprieties. This also reinforces the radical and at times subversive nature of God's work in the world. God calls whom he wills for his liberating work. Consequently, neither culture nor social status can define a person's identity and role. Instead, the first priority is to do the work of God in the world.

Thirdly, as a prophetess, Deborah clearly "hears" Yahweh (4:6), but she also acts as judge – giving direction, advice, settling disputes, and dealing with Israel's difficulties. Thus Deborah forms an interesting prototype for how to merge the "spiritual" with the "social," making her a model for a theology of civic life. Because nation-maintenance and nation-building are part of Yahweh's plan, contemporary Asian Christians may be called to these tasks. Thus Deborah challenges those who perceive the church's task as spiritual rather than political to invite the reign of God into the whole of life – both the sacred and the secular.

4:11–16 Sisera and Barak

The section opens with an unrelated and almost inconsequential detail: "Now Heber the Kenite had left the other Kenites, the descendants of Hobab, Moses' brother-in-law, and pitched his tent by the great tree in Zaanannim near Kedesh" (4:11). The Hebrew construction is in inverted word order, with the noun coming before the verb, indicating that there is a pause in the narrative. In this case, the pause serves to insert information that will prove to be important in the development of the plot later on – particularly to the fate of both Sisera and Barak. But at this point in the narrative, no clue is given about its relevance.

Yet there are several details that stand out. First, the verb "had left" refers to one who has isolated himself, who lives alone from, or who is alienated from others.[21] In a culture where people seek to live close together with their kin, Heber's decision to pitch his tent far from his kin group seems peculiar.

Another significant detail is that Heber belongs to the Kenite tribe. Judges 1:16 reports that "the descendants of Moses' father-in-law, the Kenite, went up from the City of Palms with the people of Judah to live among the inhabitants of the Desert of Judah in the Negev near Arad." The repetition of the detail that the Kenites were descendants of the father-in-law of Moses emphasizes the close connection between the Kenites and the Israelites. In fact, they could almost consider each other as extended family. Thus, by living away from his people, Heber has very likely severed his ties with the Israelites.

From the palm tree of Deborah in the hill country of Ephraim, the scene shifts to the vicinity of Wadi Kishon and Mt. Tabor, with the confrontation between Barak and Sisera and their respective armies. As Barak musters troops in Mt. Tabor, Sisera is drawn into the net that eventually leads to his downfall. "When they told Sisera that Barak son of Abinoam had gone up to Mount Tabor, Sisera summoned from Harosheth Haggoyim to the Kishon River all his men and his nine hundred chariots fitted with iron" (4:12–13). Thus as Barak responds to Deborah's prophetic message, God fulfills his promise to lure Sisera to Wadi Kishon.

The charge for battle, however, comes from Deborah: "Go! This is the day the LORD has given Sisera into your hands. Has not the LORD gone ahead of you?" (4:14). At Deborah's prompt, Barak sweeps down the mountain with ten thousand men behind him. But even as Deborah gives the charge, and Barak does the fighting, God clearly causes the victory: "The Lord threw Sisera, all the chariot-riders, and the whole army into a panic before the sword, before Barak . . . All the army of Sisera fell with the edge of the sword; not even one was left" (4:15–16, trans. mine). The verb "throw into panic" (*hamam*), when combined with God as the subject, refers to the confusion that God causes to Israel's enemy.[22]

---

21. The verb form of the Hebrew *paqad* means to "separate oneself." See Jack M. Sasson, *Judges 1–12*, AYB (New Haven, CT: Yale University Press, 2014), 261.
22. Lindars, *Judges 1–5*, 194–195. See Exod 14:24; Josh 10:10; 1 Sam 7:10.

Yet there is one hitch, for as Barak pursues Sisera's army up to Sisera's base in *Harosheth Haggoyim*, Sisera himself escapes: "Sisera got down from his chariot and fled on foot" (4:15b). The inverted word order in verse 16 of the Hebrew text – "Barak pursued the chariots and army as far as Harosheth Haggoyim, and all Sisera's troops fell by the sword; not a man was left" – highlights the sweeping nature of Barak's victory, for "all Sisera's troops fell." But at the same time, the commander – the big fry – is still on the loose. Barak's pursuit of the army up to the base is intended to cut off the power base so that the enemy will not be able to recover. Sisera's escape, however, makes regrouping and rebuilding the army possible.

4:17–22 Sisera and Jael

As Barak pursues the Moabite army up to Sisera's base in Harosheth Haggoyim, Sisera slips out of his chariot and escapes unnoticed to the tent of Jael, wife of Heber. At this moment, Heber's significance in the narrative becomes clear, and another detail emerges: "there was an alliance between Jabin king of Hazor and the family of Heber the Kenite" (4:17), meaning that they have entered into a treaty with each other.[23] This implies that Heber has shifted his loyalties from Israel, his kin by marriage, and has transferred his allegiance to Jabin, further alienating himself from his fellow Kenites, who had a treaty with Israel. Surprisingly, as the narrative unfolds, we learn that Jael does not share her husband's sentiments or allegiances.

The picture of Sisera as he arrives alone at Jael's tent contrasts sharply with the image of him at the beginning of the narrative as a commander with nine hundred iron chariots. The phrase, "Sisera . . . fled on foot" (4:15b, 17a), is repeated twice, perhaps to emphasize that the chariots, which were the principal means by which Sisera oppressed Israel, were no longer around. From a strong, powerful, and violent general, Sisera becomes a desperate fugitive asking for help from a woman.[24] Moreover, he left his army while they were being pursued, which is a dishonorable action for a military commander.

Jael responds to Sisera's presence according to the stereotypical expectations for women. First, she welcomes him as a gracious host.[25] She comes out to meet him and encourages him to turn aside and come into her tent, where

---

23. Lindars, *Judges 1–5*, 197; Block, *Judges*, 206. See also 1 Kgs 5:26, where the same phrase appears.
24. Mieke Bal, *Murder and Difference: Gender, Genre, and Scholarship on Sisera's Death*, trans. Matthew Gumpert (Bloomington, IN: Indiana University Press, 1988), 121.
25. The theme of hospitality is discussed by Mieke Bal, *Death and Dissymmetry*, 212.

she provides him with nourishment (4:18a). However, her encouragement, "don't be afraid" (4:18b), echoes the exhortation that generals give to their army before going to battle[26] and gives a hint of the complete reversal of roles that will occur at the end of the story.

Aside from offering hospitality as a gracious host, Jael takes on the role of a mother.[27] Thus we have the image of Sisera, the mighty general, as a little boy in Jael's hands: "She covered him with a blanket. 'I'm thirsty,' he said. 'Please give me some water.' She opened a skin of milk, gave him a drink, and covered him up" (4:18b–19). The succession of verbs creates an image of a mother putting a babe to sleep after being nursed. The twice-repeated phrase, "she covered him," evokes warmth, security, protection, and nurture.

The stereotype of the woman as protector is exemplified when Sisera commands Jael to shield him from his enemies: "Stand in the doorway of the tent," he tells her. "If someone comes by and asks you, 'Is anyone in there?' say 'No'" (4:20). On the other hand, Sisera uses the masculine rather than feminine form for the command "stand," thus treating Jael like one his troops, ready to do his bidding. In this domineering command, there is a reminder of the old controlling general.[28] The contrast between Sisera as both "a babe" and an "old controlling general" highlights the way in which extreme situations can strip away a person's social persona while some of it still remains.

Aside from host, mother, and protector, the story evokes another stereotype of women as a sexual partner. Many scholars have mentioned the sexual innuendoes present in the narrative.[29] Jael's invitation, "turn aside *to me*," and Sisera's response, "he turned aside *to her*" (4:18, NRSV, ital. mine), can be construed as a sexual invitation and acceptance. Moreover, the phrase, "then she came to him furtively" (4:21, trans. mine), is used in another context to refer to a woman "coming" to a man with a sexual intent.[30]

---

26. Boling, *Judges*, 97, sees a parallel with the divine command and with Moses' instructions to the Israelites as they go out to battle (Deut 1:29; 7:18; 20:1).
27. Bal, *Death and Dissymmetry*, 213; Susan Niditch, *War in the Hebrew Bible* (Oxford: Oxford University Press, 1993), 114; Danna Nolan Fewell and David Gunn, "Controlling Perspectives: Women, Men and the Authority of Violence in Judges 4 and 5," *JAAR* 58 (1990): 393.
28. Bal, *Death and Dissymmetry*, 213.
29. See Alter, *Art of Biblical Narrative*, 43–49; Susan Niditch, "Eroticism and Death in the Tale of Jael," in *Gender and Difference in Ancient Israel*, ed. Peggy Day (Minneapolis, MN: Fortress, 1989), 43–57. Yair Zakovitch, "Sisseras Tod," *ZAW* 93 (1981): 364–374; Fewell and Gunn, "Controlling Perspectives," 392–394.
30. Niditch, *Eroticism and Death*, 45–46; Alter, *Art of Biblical Narrative*. See also Ruth 3:7.

But the conclusion of the narrative hurls the reader into a completely different and unexpected scenario when "Jael, the wife of Heber, took a tent peg and put a hammer in her hand. Then she came to him furtively and drove the peg through his temple, driving it down to the ground – as he was fast asleep and exhausted – and he died" (4:21, trans. mine). This action shatters the stereotypical images of women as host, mother, protector, and lover, for Jael becomes a warrior, a profession traditionally associated with men. "The roles are reversed; here is the woman who controls, who gives – and who kills. She gives life and then she takes it back."[31] Nevertheless, she does not completely shed her domestic role, since her weapon for Sisera's execution is a domestic implement – a tent peg. The death of Sisera – the mighty commander-in-chief of squadrons of chariots and oppressor of Israel – at the "hand of a woman" with a mere tent peg as a weapon is the ultimate humiliation.[32]

The deceptive nature of Jael's killing has generated considerable discussion.[33] Moreover, she is regarded as having violated the rules of hospitality.[34] Matthews seeks to justify Jael's action by claiming that Sisera violated the rules of hospitality first.[35] There are other angles, however, by which one can view Jael's action. The first is to see her in the role of a trickster.[36] As discussed earlier, oppressed and marginalized groups often resort to trickery in order to accomplish certain ends.[37] As a woman, Jael is in a disadvantageous position when Sisera shows up in front of her tent. Although weary and without his implements of war, Sisera is still a dangerous foe, and it would be fatal for Jael to reveal her true sentiments. Thus the trickery is a form of self-protection.

Moreover, as mentioned above, if Heber's household is allied with Jabin, then Heber is not only alienated from the rest of the Kenites, but also from the Israelites. In fact, his alliance with the oppressors of Israel can be seen as a form of betrayal. With the defeat of Sisera's army and Sisera escaping

---

31. Bal, *Murder and Difference*, 21.
32. Arthur E. Cundall and Leon Morris, *Judges and Ruth: An Introduction and Commentary*, TOTC (Leicester: IVP, 1968), 89.
33. See Gale Yee, "By the Hand of the Woman: The Metaphor of the Woman Warrior in Judges 4," *Semeia* 61 (1993): 123–124 and Fewell and Gunn, "Controlling Perspectives," 394–395, for a survey of different views.
34. Soggin, *Judges*, 77.
35. Matthews, *Judges & Ruth*, 68–73; McCann, *Judges*, 53–54. For example, rather than approaching the tent of the male head of the household, Sisera went into Jael's tent instead. Moreover, instead of waiting for the host to offer something, he initiated by asking for a drink. Matthew points out, though, that Jael also violated the rules of hospitality, and Sisera's violations seems to be insufficient for the murder.
36. Niditch, *War in the Hebrew Bible*, 113–117.
37. See the story of Ehud on pp. 52–54.

like a fugitive to Jael's tent, Barak cannot be too far behind. If Jael is caught sheltering Sisera, it will mean death to her and her household, including Heber, her husband. Thus Jael has to act shrewdly and quickly in order to spare her family from certain disaster. By killing Sisera, she proves to Barak that, despite the alliance between Heber and Jabin, the household should not be implicated.[38] This explains the eagerness with which Jael comes out to meet Barak and tells him, "Come . . . I will show you the man you're looking for" (4:22a). "So he went in with her, and there lay Sisera with the tent peg through his temple – dead" (4:22b), demonstrating conclusively the loyalties of her household. This completes the circle. For in the way Jael receives Sisera, she fulfills a woman's stereotypical roles – host, mother, protector, sexual partner – but all these expectations are dashed in her warrior-like killing of Sisera. Furthermore, by taking the risk to protect her own household from dangerous external threats, she establishes a deeper role for women – that of being a savior-figure for their family and community.[39] For Asians, life is not simply about an individual's own survival and well-being. Life is about family and the wider web of social relationships. As individuals, we each bear responsibility for – and can have an impact on – our family's and community's future. Thus we live and think beyond the now by acting with courage and salvific intention for future generations.

One might expect Deborah to accomplish the final act of deliverance, since she has the more public role, but Jael – an outsider, a housewife, a person with no public role – is used by Yahweh to kill Sisera, the symbol of Israel's oppression. As for Barak, although he accomplishes mighty feats in pursuing and decimating Sisera's army, he does not receive the ultimate honor of killing the commander-in-chief himself. So in some sense, he is like Sisera, whose military deeds end in disgrace.

Though Deborah prophesies Sisera's downfall, Barak pursues him, and Jael eliminates him, the last verses of chapter 4 explicitly declare that God provides the ultimate victory:[40] "On that day God subdued Jabin king of Canaan before the Israelites" (4:23). Witnessing God's power at work, however, emboldens the people to use their own power: "And the hand of the

---

38. This was also suggested by Fewell and Gunn, "Controlling Perspectives," 395–396.
39. Her action then is linked to other women savior-figures in the Old Testament: the midwives and Zipporah in Exodus. See Ilana Pardes, "Zipporah and the Struggle for Deliverance," in *Countertraditions in the Bible: A Feminist Approach* (Cambridge, MA: Harvard University Press, 1992), 79–83.
40. Matthews, *Judges & Ruth*, 74.

Israelites pressed harder and harder against Jabin king of Canaan until they destroyed him" (4:24). While the actions of Deborah, Barak, and Jael provide the catalyst for a shift in power so that Israel gains the upper hand over Jabin, it is still up to the persistent, joint, and God-empowered efforts of the Israelites to turn their advantage into eventual and lasting victory.

PLAYING ONE'S PART IN YAHWEH'S PURPOSES

There are many ways to describe the interplay between the three human protagonists in this chapter: Deborah, Barak, and Jael. The main thrust of the text, however, highlights Yahweh's way of deliverance for Israel after many years of cruel oppression (4:3) and the way in which different people play a part. Thus, while Yahweh is central in this act of deliverance (4:15), key figures make their contribution. One of the secondary themes, therefore, is that different people are called to different roles in fulfilling the purposes of Yahweh.

In this story, Barak is neither cast as a solo hero, nor the judge-deliverer, nor the wholly successful military strategist. He is called to a specific task (4:6), but he is also informed about the limitations of his role (4:8), which highlights others' roles and contribution. Were it not for the prophetic call of Deborah, Barak would have no task. As the deliverer, Deborah would have no role if Barak did not play his part. And Jael's role cannot possibly be conceived without Barak's routing of Sisera's forces (4:15), Deborah's prophetic word (4:9), and Jael's marginal and alienated status in the land as a Kenite (4:17).

Important implications may be drawn from the fact that various people contribute to fulfill the prophetic word. First, while the book of Judges does recount stories of the solo hero (such as Othniel), there are also stories with multiple key players. This suggests that cooperating and contributing to an overall task is part of Yahweh's purposes in the world. In the hierarchical structure of many Asian societies, one leader within a community, church, or organization is often elevated and recognized as the one who did all the work, but this leads to the negation of the roles and contributions of others. Gaining inspiration from this episode within the deeply troubled times of Israel's judges helps us to see that the themes of cooperation, making one's contribution, sharing one's gifts, and playing one's part are important in the fulfillment of the purposes of God in our time.

The story also suggests that God works beyond human stereotypes and expectations. God's way is different from social norms. This poses a challenge to the contemporary church, which has made God predictable rather than seeing God as the one who walks new pathways and uses unlikely candidates for his purposes in the world.

5:1–31 CELEBRATING THE MIGHTY DEEDS OF GOD IN PEOPLE'S PARTICIPATION

Judges 5, commonly referred to as the Song of Deborah, has been widely recognized as one of the oldest poems in the Bible. Because of this, scholars have tried to mine it for its historical and linguistic value. However, a song or a poem's primary function is not to provide historical data.[41] Rather, a poem piles up powerful images and scenes, provoking the imagination and affecting the emotions.[42]

One characteristic of Hebrew poetry is parataxis – "the placing side by side of words, images, clauses or scenes without connectives that directly and immediately coordinate the parts with one another."[43] Thus, one should not expect to make logical and complete connections that fit easily onto an outline. In the Song of Deborah, scenes are not completely worked out before they shift; links between scenes are not clearly indicated; and no further explanations are given for names, places, and events. In addition, the poem contains words that are used only once in the OT, or whose basic meaning does not seem to make sense in the context. Thus, different Bible versions and commentaries vary greatly in their translation, drawing from other languages related to Hebrew or from archaeological and historical data in order to shed light on the meaning of the words. In light of these difficulties, one should strive for the overall effect rather than for a complete understanding of the details.

Despite the many challenges of the poem, the overall message is clear: the song functions in the worship life of Israel to celebrate a victory in battle, and the song is directed to Yahweh (5:3). Its purpose is to bless the Lord. God's powerful intention, cosmic cooperation, and mighty deeds dovetail with the deeds of the volunteers, the leaders, the warriors, the tribes, and the outsider who willingly participate in God's work. The dynamic relationship between God's action and human participation moves the poem along through the excitement of battle and its unexpected conclusion.

---

41. See Block, *Judges*, 217: "its value in reconstructing specific historical events of this period is limited."
42. Alan Hauser, "Judges 5: Parataxis in Hebrew Poetry," *JBL* 99 (1980), 26–27.
43. Ibid., 26.

THE SINGERS AND THE STRUCTURE

The poem begins by identifying the singers of the song: Deborah and Barak (5:1). Although the subject is dual, the verb is feminine,[44] showing that the primary singer is Deborah, with Barak playing a supportive role. Nevertheless, "the participants are portrayed as uniting in immediate, voluntary response."[45] It is sung "on that day," a phrase identified with the "day of the Lord," which is seen as a day of salvation for Israel and a day of judgement for Israel's enemies.[46]

In the identity of the singers, we see the coming together of disparate professions – warrior and poet in Barak, judge and poet in Deborah. This raises the possibility of living out one's profession more integrally. Thus, one can speak of a pastor-artist, a theologian-community worker, or a businessperson-preacher.

The song itself can be divided into four stanzas. The first stanza (5:2–9) is framed by an *inclusio* that includes an invocation to "Praise the Lord" (5:2b, 9b).[47] The reason for praising God is that people, especially the leaders, volunteered themselves for the cause of God and of Israel (5:2a, 9a).

The second stanza (5:10–18) recounts the just deeds of the Lord in the warriors of Israel, naming the tribes who participated, while chastising those who chose not to get involved. So while the focus of the first stanza is on those who volunteered themselves, the second stanza contrasts the deeds of those who fought with those who did not.

The third stanza (5:19–22) recounts the actual battle, but moves from the sphere of human participation to actions in the cosmic realm.

The fourth stanza (5:23–30) singles out a specific individual – Jael, the wife of Heber the Kenite. Again, the theme of non-participation is echoed in the curse of the inhabitants of Meroz. Jael is contrasted to the tribes who did not join the battle (5:15b–17) and to the inhabitants of Meroz, who did not come to the aid of the Lord (5:23). Then the scene shifts to another woman, the mother of Sisera, as she anxiously waits for her son to return home. But this poignant scene is shattered by the gloating of Sisera's mother and her ladies over the prospect of their men enjoying the spoils of battle, not realizing

---

44. Schneider, *Judges*, 86.
45. Fewell and Gunn, "Controlling Perspectives," 400.
46. See Richard Hiers, "Day of the Lord," *ABD* 2:82–83.
47. Boling, *Judges*, 110. Some scholars consider v. 9 as an introduction to the second stanza. See Mark Vincent, "The Song of Deborah: A Structural and Literary Consideration," *JBL* 91 (2000), 69–70.

that their men were defeated. The ending of the poem emphasizes the theme of reversal: "So may all your enemies perish, O Lord! But may all who love you be like the sun when it rises in its strength" (5:31).

5:2–9 Praising God for Volunteers

Bible versions differ in their translation of the first part of verse 2, which is translated as, "when locks are long in Israel" in the NRSV,[48] and as, "when the princes in Israel take the lead" in the NIV.[49] The variation has to do with the meaning of the Hebrew root *pr'*, which in other passages refers to hair that hangs loose, or which is set free.[50] The NIV follows Craigie's suggestion of another meaning of *pr'* in Arabic, which is "to dedicate oneself wholly, to lead as leader."[51] This makes sense, especially in parallel with 5:9, which mentions the chiefs of Israel volunteering themselves for the people.

The reason for praise is unusual. Instead of blessing God for creation or for his mighty deeds in Israel's historical experience, such as the Exodus, the focus of praise here is for the eager and dedicated efforts of leaders and people who volunteered themselves for the battle.[52] By highlighting human instruments, the willing attitudes of people and leaders are acknowledged as part of God's handiwork.

Yet even though the focus is on people's contributions, the singer unequivocally portrays "Yahweh as the champion of Israel who is to be praised for his mighty deeds on behalf of his people."[53] In Judges 5:3, kings and princes – presumably the defeated Canaanite kings[54] – are enjoined to listen as the singer extols the attributes and works of Yahweh in order to emphasize who clearly won the victory. In 5:4–5 the battle itself is presented as God's theophany – a divine appearance in the human realm – where God marches

---

48. See NJB and the NJPS.
49. See NASB, ESV, NKJV.
50. Num 3:18; 6:5; Deut 32:42; Ezek 44:20. Those who choose this translation point to the practice in ancient Israel of warriors unloosing their hair in preparation for war (Lindars, *Judges 1–5*, 225–226; Gray, *Judges*, 263; see also Boling, *Judges*, 107).
51. P. C. Craigie, "A Note on Judges V 2," *VT* 18 (1968): 399.
52. The invocation to bless the Lord is used in the Psalms to extol God for various reasons: God's deeds, particularly in the Exodus and his sovereignty over the nations (Ps 66:5–7), his preservation in times of hardships and discipline (66:8–12); God's victory in battle and judgement of Israel's enemies (Ps 68, particularly v. 26); God as the judge of the earth (Ps 96); his mercies and benefits (Ps 103); his creation (Ps 104; 135:7); for being the maker of heaven and earth (Ps 134); and for Israel's history, which includes the Exodus and their gift of the land (Ps 37:8–21).
53. Hauser, "Judges 5," 32.
54. See Hauser, "Judges 5," 28–29.

as a mighty warrior in battle. This is evident in the storm imagery as well as in the reference to Edom (Seir is another name for Edom), which is a common motif in the OT (Isa 63:1; Deut 33:2; Hab 3:3). God as a warrior comes from the southern wilderness and mountains – the site of Edom – in order to aid Israel and judge her enemies.[55] The imagery of earthquakes and rainstorms suggests that the battle is being fought in the heavenly realms. Thus the real character of the battle is not physical (although this may be its visible expression), but cosmic. It is a Yahweh war, and God marches ahead of his people and fights with them.[56]

From this fierce picture of God the warrior, the poem shifts without transition to the earthly realm and human history, as if to ensure that one does not lose sight of the human element in contemplating the awesomeness of God's presence. Moreover, instead of mentioning familiar heroic characters to describe this period in history, the narrative names lesser-known personalities: "In the days of Shamgar son of Anath, in the days of Jael" (5:6). Typically, the phrase, "in the days of . . .", is used to identify a certain historical period associated with a king, a great warrior, or a prominent ancestor.[57] Shamgar is briefly mentioned in Judges 3:31 as killing 600 Philistines with an ox-goad, while Jael, a housewife, is credited with killing Sisera, the commander of Jabin's army in Judges 4 with a tent peg. Both accomplish a great victory, but with the use of domestic implements – an ox-goad, a tent peg – rather than a warrior's armaments.[58] The image of lowly individuals using humble instruments contrasts with the image of God marching as an awesome warrior. Paradoxically, the power of God's theophany is revealed in the humble human act.

Nevertheless, the contrast between the grandeur of God and the vulnerability of human instrumentality is not a strategy that involves the elevation of one through the denigration of the other. Rather, this startling perspective reflects who God is and who we are – a very great God cooperating with

---

55. Jeffrey Tigay, *Deuteronomy*, JPSTC (Philadelphia, PA: The Jewish Publication Society, 1996), 319.
56. Some scholars have adopted the term "Yahweh war" instead of "holy war" because the latter term does not appear in any biblical text. See Gwilym H. Jones, "'Holy War' or 'Yahweh War,'" *VT* 25 (1975), 643–644. Judg 5:4–5 describes the period before the battle and shows its cosmic character (Hauser, "Judges 5," 29). Emphasis is on Yahweh's power over the watery chaos, anticipating later scenes where water is involved (Hauser, "Judges 5," 30–31). The reference to land and sea, being "primordial ingredients of the world," "portray vividly the absolute power of Yahweh over creation" (Hauser, "Judges 5," 31).
57. 1 Sam 17:12; 1 Kgs 10:21; Judg 8:28; Ezra 4:7.
58. This reminds one of David, who killed Goliath with a shepherd's sling and stone.

very ordinary people. God willingly embraces humiliation on our behalf. God not only enters the madness and stupidity of the human fray, but God identifies with and joins with us in fulfilling his purposes. While this should always lead us to wonderment and worship, it often results in humans taking too much of the glory when the praise belongs to God. This is a particular danger in successful ministries when leaders take too much credit for their achievements.

The latter part of verse 6 alludes to the desperate situation in Israel: "Travelers of highways trekked through roundabout paths" (trans. mine). People could not travel freely to transport goods because the roads were blocked,[59] presumably by Israel's oppressors. Possibly, Israel's enemies were seizing the produce that was being transported to the different villages in Israel. This dire economic and oppressive condition continued because "warriors ceased, they ceased in Israel" (5: 7a, trans. mine).[60] There was no one to defend Israel or fight to reclaim the roads and Israel's territory.

But when Deborah arises as a mother of Israel, the situation changes (5:7b). The title "mother" seems to be an official position and speaks of Deborah's role in administering justice.[61] By seeking to do something about the oppressive situation of Israel, Deborah shows herself to be a true mother who will fight for her children when their lives are being threatened by another. In the same way, the church has produced great leaders who acted to bless the church and the nation in times of oppression – such as St. Ambrose and Archbishop Desmond Tutu of South Africa. Just as Deborah was a transformational leader in Israel, the church is challenged to form leaders who

---

59. Gray, *Judges*, 266.
60. An alternative translation for "warriors" (*perazon*) is "village life" (NKJV), "peasantry" (NRSV, NASB) or "villagers" (NIV, ESV). These translations show the effect of the blocked roads: village life ceased because no food could reach the villages located in the uplands where the Israelites lived. However, I have chosen to follow the translation "warriors" by Boling (*Judges*, 109) and Coogan ("Song of Deborah," 147). According to P. C. Craigie, the meaning of "warrior" is derived from the Arabic *faraza* which can mean guidance, leader, bravery or leadership, or warrior ("Some Further Notes on the Song of Deborah," *VT* 22 [1972]: 350), a meaning that fits both v. 7 and v. 11. This is supported by LXX-B *dunatoi* "mighty ones." The meaning "warrior" is also consistent with the theme of the poem, which extols God for those willing to fight in the battle.
61. Dennis Olson, "Introduction, Commentary, and Reflections on the Book of Judges," *NIB*, Vol. 2, eds., Leander Keck and David Petersen (Nashville, TN: Abingdon, 1994), 787; see also McCann, *Judges*, 56. "From this perspective, 'mother in Israel' suggests that it was Deborah's efforts that, in effect, both gave Israel new life and nurtured that conditions that would sustain life" (McCann, *Judges*, 57).

can act decisively in times of injustice and help bring about God's shalom for our world.

The first part of verse 8 is one of the most difficult verses to translate in the whole song. Most versions translate the first part in a similar way, either as passive, "New gods were chosen" (NRSV, ESV, NASB), or active, "they chose new gods" (NJB, NJPS). The next line refers to fighting or war at the city gates,[62] alluding to Israel's apostasy, which resulted in oppression and war with the surrounding nations. Alternatively, one could regard *elohim* (God or gods) as the subject rather than the object, since the verb "to choose" (*bakhar*) is in the singular rather than in the plural. In this case, the plural word *khadashim* ("new"), rather than modifying *elohim*, would be regarded as the object (hence the translation, "new gods"). Craigie translates this verse, "God chooses new men,"[63] referring to the new leaders that God had raised up for the battle. Thus, the latest version of the NIV translation is, "God chose new leaders."[64]

What can be gleaned clearly from verse 8 is the precarious situation of Israel's army. There were hardly any weapons to fight the battle: "If only[65] a shield or lance is to be seen among forty thousand in Israel" (v. 8b, trans. mine). Hence, the willingness of the rulers of Israel who come forward with the people is a reason for blessing God (v. 9). For God has chosen these new dedicated volunteers, who are unfazed by hardships and lack of resources, so long as they can participate in God's liberating work.

In the dynamics of God's initiative and power, human frailty and lack of resources often reveal the power of faith and hope in what God can do. Here, as elsewhere in the book of Judges (e.g. Gideon), the issue is not that God needs "our much," but that God needs our "yielded little." As a consequence, the power of the church does not lie in its multiple resources, but in its obedience and willing service, even when it has little to give.

---

62. Literally, the word for "fighting" or "war" (*lakhem*) sounds like bread, but this does not make sense, so most versions take it as a noun form of the verb "to fight" (*lhm*). The word does not appear as a noun, however, in other contexts.
63. Craigie ("Further Notes," 351) thinks that this makes the syntax easier, although he allows for an alternative reading of "new things" (see Block, *Judges*, 226–227). George F. Moore, *A Critical and Exegetical Commentary on Judges* (Edinburgh: T & T Clark, 1895), 147, however, objects to this translation since the name Yahweh rather than Elohim is consistently used in the poem, but he admits that the alternative "they choose new gods" is equally untenable.
64. See Soggin, *Judges*, 82, 87; Sasson, *Judges 1–12*, 291.
65. The word for "if" (*'im*) here expresses a wish when it is used with an imperfect verb (GKC §151e; Joüon §163c).

5:10–18 Commendation and Reproach

In the first stanza, the command to defeated kings is to "listen" as Deborah praises the victory of Yahweh (v. 3). In the second stanza, the command is "to proclaim" (v. 10; NIV has "consider"; NRSV and ESV "tell of")[66] and is directed to those "who ride on white donkeys, sitting on your saddle blankets, and you who walk along the road" (v. 10). This description may refer to traveling minstrels who sing of the wondrous deeds of famous people (see v. 11) or to various groups who are always on the road, such as dignitaries and merchants.[67] These travelers are to proclaim the song "amidst the song of shepherds,[68] at the watering places" (v. 11a, trans. mine), where people congregate as the shepherds water their flocks, thus providing a natural audience.

The minstrels are to proclaim "the just deeds of the Lord, the just deeds of his warriors in Israel" (v. 11b, trans. mine). The "just deeds" (*tsidqoth*), when used in relation to God, refer to God's acts of justice on behalf of the community and are directed towards the "elimination of anything breaking the peace and preservation of good order."[69] As in the first stanza, there is a connection between God's actions and people's actions in seeking to address an oppressive situation. In this case, Israel is being oppressed by Jabin and Sisera of Canaan. The actions by warriors in freeing the people from oppression are lauded as expressions of the "just deeds of the Lord," since they are trying to address a situation of imbalance.

The key theological notion woven throughout the biblical story and expressed compactly here is that Yahweh and his faithful people are one in the accomplishment of God's liberating work. God acts in what the people do.

---

66. The verb is the imperative form of *sikh*, which is loud, enthusiastic, emotionally laden speech (*HALOT* 3:1320).
67. Sasson, *Judges 1–12*, 292–293.
68. The meaning of the participle *mekhatsetsim* is obscure. It can refer to those who distribute water in the watering troughs (*HALOT* 1:344), hence "shepherds." Other possible meanings are "archers," as those who divide the spoil (*BHS*, 346) or derived from *hts*, the same root as "arrow." The NIV has singers, while ESV and NRSV use "musicians," which is akin to the rendering of the LXX.
69. *HALOT* 2:1006. Parallel verses are 1 Sam 12:7; Pss 11:7, 103:6; Isa 33:15; Isa 45:24; Mic 6:5. In 1 Sam 12:7, the "righteous deeds or acts of the Lord" (ESV, NIV, NASB, NKJB) refer to the times when God saved Israel from the oppression of other peoples. Hence, NRSV translates it as "saving deeds" while NJB translates it as "saving acts." The JPS translation is "kindnesses." In Ps 11:7, the righteous deeds refer to God's acts to judge the wicked, particularly in their acts of violence against the upright. In Ps 103:6, *tsidqoth* is paired with *mishpat* ("justice") and shows how God vindicates those who are oppressed. The context of the use of the word again in Isa 33:15 is that of oppression. Righteous deeds have to do with acts that do not condone oppression. Mic 6:5 also has to do with God's acts that save Israel from foreign kingdoms and nations who are trying to harm and oppress them.

This expresses the amazing synchronicity between the action of God and human work.

The tempo suddenly shifts at the last part of verse 11, which depicts the beginning of the battle that will correct the unjust situation. This line corresponds to verse 13, with a call to arms in between.

> 11e "Then the people of the LORD went down to the city gates."
>
> 12 "Wake up, wake up, Deborah!
> Wake up, wake up, break out in song!
> Arise, Barak!
> Take captive your captives, son of Abinoam."
>
> 13 "The remnant of the nobles came down;
> the people of the LORD came down to me against the mighty."

The phrase, "wake up, wake up," is used in the OT as a call to action and is typical language for a call to arms.[70] In Psalm 7:6, the phrase is used in parallel with "arise" as a call for God to act in a situation of injustice done to the righteous. The same call to God for vindication is found in Psalm 35:23–24a: "Awake, and rise to my defense! Contend for me, my God and Lord. Vindicate me in your righteousness, LORD my God." Here the word for vindicate is from the verb *shapat*, meaning "to judge, to execute judgement." The psalmist calls on God to judge the situation, presumably with the knowledge that God will act to address the imbalance caused by the unfair and unjust actions of others. This same sense is found in Psalm 44:23–24, where "awake" is paired with "arise": "Awake, Lord! Why do you sleep? Rouse yourself! Do not reject us forever. Why do you hide your face and forget our misery and oppression?" Here the antonym for awake is asleep, a metaphor for inactivity and lack of intervention, especially in the face of an intolerable situation.[71]

In Psalm 57:7–9, the imperative "awake" is not addressed to God but to oneself and to human instruments. Here the self is enjoined to sing and make melody to God and to sing praises.[72] In the same way, Deborah enjoins herself to sing. Nevertheless, the call for Deborah to awake and sing is paired with the call for Barak to rise up and take captives – an indication that the context is not merely praise, but war in order to stir up people to act against oppression and injustice.

---

70. Hackett, "In the Days of Jael," 27.
71. See Pss 59:4–5; 80:2; Isa 51:9–11.
72. See Ps 108:1–2.

Verses 11e and 13, which frame the call to arms, name the response to the call: the people march; they join the battle. In verse 13, the people of the Lord who march are called the "remnant" – survivors, escapees, refugees, the ones who are left after a battle or a calamity, which alludes to their harsh or oppressive situation.

After the call to arms and the charge, one would expect an account of the actual battle. Yet the movement slows down as Deborah first gives a roll call of the tribes. She lauds those who are willing to risk their lives and reproves those who hold back at this time of great need (vv. 14–18). This echoes the theme of stanza 1, which praises God for those who volunteered themselves in battle. In stanza 2, the specific participants are named. The list of the tribes who joined in the task (vv. 14–15a; 18) forms an *inclusio* with the list of those who failed to show up (vv. 15b–17).

Thus, Ephraim, Benjamin, Machir (for Manasseh),[73] Zebulun, Issachar, and Naphtali are part of the forces that charge into the valley to rout the forces of the Canaanites. The tribe of Zebulun is mentioned twice (vv. 14, 18) and is honored for being "a people who risked their lives"[74] to free Israel from oppression.

Yet some who could join choose to stay behind. They are pictured as on the brink of coming, but they have second thoughts and hesitate, thus tarrying while the battle wages. Reuben sits among the sheep pens (v. 16). Instead of being galvanized into action by the great need of the other tribes, the different clan divisions think things through, listening to the piping for the flocks, considering whether they should join the battle or not (vv. 15–16). Gilead (for Gad), Dan, Asher – the tribes who live near the Sea – are near the ports, ready to sail, but stay behind.[75]

As part of the same covenant community, the tribes of Israel have an obligation to help each other, particularly in times of distress. In Numbers 32, Moses allowed the tribes of Gad, Reuben, and the half-tribe of Manasseh to have lands beyond the Jordan as long as they agreed to go over to the other side, into the land of Canaan, to fight with their brothers until the other tribes also got their land inheritance (vv. 20–26; see also Josh 1:12–15). The

---

73. Machir is the name of Manasseh's eldest son (Gen 50:23) and functions here as a poetic substitute for the tribe of Manasseh (Block, *Judges*, 232).
74. Literally, "to taunt or scorn life," which means that they were prepared to take risks, even to the point of losing their lives.
75. Judah and Simeon are not mentioned, presumably because they were part of the Southern tribes and are too far away. Those mentioned were the Northern tribes, who were living around the area of the Jezreel valley, the site of the battle.

main assumption of the census in Numbers 1 and 26 is to assess the number of warriors that each tribe can contribute to the war effort. Whenever there is call to war, the assumption is that each tribe will send troops for the battle.[76]

Thus the poem calls the people of Israel to go beyond tribalism for the unity of the nation and the building up of the common good, in cooperation with what Yahweh is already doing in their midst. But as Deborah's rebuke shows, some of the tribes do not participate. This introduces a theme that will be developed further in the book of Judges–the fragmentation of Israel.

5:19–22 When Heaven Fights

After a delay between the charge and the battle with the roll call of the tribes, the poem reaches a crescendo with a report of the actual battle:

> "Kings came, they fought,
>   the kings of Canaan fought.
> At Taanach, by the waters of Megiddo,
>   they took no plunder of silver.
> From the heavens the stars fought,
>   from their courses they fought against Sisera.
> The river Kishon swept them away,
>   the age-old river, the river Kishon.
>   March on, my soul; be strong!
> Then thundered the horses' hooves –
>   galloping, galloping go his mighty steeds." (5:19–22)

Yet after the long roll call of the Israelite tribes, their role in the battle is not even mentioned. Moreover, after commending human participation and reproaching human non-involvement, the poem does not convey how this figured in the actual battle. Instead, the poem portrays how the battle is fought in the cosmic realm. The stars fight (v. 20) and the river Kishon (described as "the age-old river" to emphasize its primordial quality) sweeps away (v. 21) so that the forces of Sisera are routed, and a hint of their panic to escape is shown in the description of galloping horses thumping away (v. 22).[77] Even as the kings of Canaan fight, their defeat is indicated by the fact that they do not get the spoils of battle (v. 19).

---

76. In any major undertaking, whether related to war or not, there was always a representative from each tribe, e.g. the twelve spies (Num 13:1–16; see also Deut 1:22–23); the war against Midian (Num 31:1–6); the division of the land for inheritance (Num 34:16–29; Josh 18:1–10); and the taking of memorial stones at the Jordan River (Josh 4:1–7).
77. Lindars, *Judges 1–5*, 265; Hauser, "Judges 5," 34.

The focus on the cosmic realm underscores the fact that the battle is not just about human troops fighting each other on earthly territory. It is not only the tribes of Israel, under the leadership of Deborah and Barak, who are fighting the battle. God himself unleashes the forces of nature against Sisera and the kings of Canaan. Human participation, although vital and affirmed, is not the decisive factor in the victory.[78] So while the song emphasizes what the people do in routing the enemy, the stars that fight from heaven disable Sisera's mighty forces. Thus, ultimately, it is God's involvement that causes the triumph. However, this does not mean that the tribes can become complacent, for Deborah's battle cry to encourage human participation comes in the middle of the cosmic battle account: "March on, my soul, with might!" (v. 21).[79]

The knowledge that God fights with us and for us should not cause us to slacken off, but should encourage us to continue all the more valiantly with all our abilities. God's intent and power, combined with human participation, is never a fifty-fifty partnership, but requires the totality of God's action and the totality of our participation. We humans are drawn into the will and purposes of God, who is central in the drama. This recognition stirs the poet to use cosmic language in celebrating the power of God.

5:23–30 Blessed Is the Outsider

This stanza is divided into three sections: the curse of Meroz (v. 23), the praise of Jael (vv. 24–27), and the false assumptions of Sisera's mother (vv. 28–30). The structure of the stanza contrasts Jael with both the inhabitants of Meroz and Sisera's mother.

After the account of the cosmic battle, one might expect a hymn of praise extolling God for what he has done, as in Exodus 15:11–12 (following the account of the battle in Exod 15:4–10). But instead of a hymn, there is a curse on Meroz because its inhabitants "did not come to help the LORD" (v. 23). The verse continues the theme of human non-involvement introduced in the second stanza (vv. 10–18), but that theme is interrupted by the intervening account of the cosmic battle (vv. 19–22). Since the curse clearly contrasts the blessing of Jael in verses 24–30, it is better to see verse 23 as part of Stanza 4 (vv. 23–30) rather than as part of Stanza 3 (vv. 19–22). Nevertheless, verse 23 can be connected to the cosmic battle in Stanza 3, because it reiterates that

---

78. Hauser, "Judges 5," 33.
79. The interjection can be considered as a battle cry (Lindars, *Judges 1–5*, 270), which can be regarded as a continuation of the charge in v. 12.

human participation is valued in God's work, despite the cosmic dimensions of the war.

The curse is uttered by the emissary of Yahweh (or "angel of Yahweh"), a reference which seems to be out of place here, since the emissary of Yahweh is not mentioned anywhere else in the poem. However, the emissary or angel is not an unfamiliar presence in the book of Judges, appearing earlier as a bearer of rebuke (2:1–5) and later as a bearer of encouragement (6:11–24; 13:2–21). The fact that the curse is uttered by the emissary of Yahweh gives it weight and reinforces Deborah's rebuke of the tribes who did not participate in the battle.

It is not clear if Meroz is an Israelite or a Canaanite town, since the location is unknown. The contrast between Meroz and Jael and the connection with Sisera's mother in this same stanza may indicate that, like both of them, Meroz is an outsider, meaning that its inhabitants are non-Israelites. On the other hand, the contrast may point the other direction – that unlike Jael, who is an outsider, Meroz, as an insider, is expected to be available and willing when needed for God's work.

The type of help expected of Meroz is suggested by Jael's action, for she finishes the battle by killing Sisera, the commander of Jabin's army – whereas the inhabitants of Meroz do not come to the help of the Lord "with warriors" to capture the fleeing Sisera (v. 23, trans. mine).[80] Perhaps they thought that the battle only involved Israel, and they did not realize that by refusing to give help, they were refusing the Lord himself.

In contrast to Meroz, Jael is pronounced as "blessed."[81] The phrase, in this context, is an expression of praise, admiration, and thanksgiving for a person who does something for the sake of others, with the understanding that God approves of the deed as well.[82]

Jael is said to be "most blessed of tent-dwelling women" (v. 24). According to Genesis 4:20, those who live in tents are herders of cattle and live a semi-nomadic lifestyle. In Genesis 25:7, however, Jacob is described as "content to stay at home among the tents" (Gen 25:27) in contrast to Esau,

---

80. The NIV, with the NASB and ESV, render the last part of v. 23 "against the mighty." NASB has "against the warriors" (see NJPS "among"; NJB "as") since *gibborim*, the word for "mighty," can also be translated "warriors." The preceding preposition *be* can be translated "against," "among," or "with." Since the song celebrates the warriors who volunteered willingly for the battle, a likely translation is "with warriors." See Coogan, "Song of Deborah," 150.
81. Hauser, "Judges 5," 35.
82. Christopher Wright Mitchell, *The Meaning of Brk 'to bless' in the Old Testament*, SBL Dissertation Series 95 (Atlanta, GA: Scholars, 1987), 115–117.

who is a man of the outdoors, implying that Jacob's preoccupations are more domestic in nature. The description of Jael as "a tent-dwelling woman" could mean that she is living a semi-nomadic lifestyle, which is the opposite of the Israelites' and the Canaanites' more settled existence, or it could be a way of focusing on her chief preoccupation, which is the domestic sphere. The latter is more likely, since the next verse (v. 25) portrays her in a domestic role – giving nourishment to a man. Her domestic role is further emphasized in her depiction as the wife of Heber the Kenite (v. 24), though the significant detail about Heber being an ally of Jabin is not mentioned (as it is in ch. 4). Aside from her domestic role, the focus is on the fact that she is an outsider, a non-Israelite who could not have been expected to help in the battle.

The significant point here is that Jael is praised above tent-dwelling women because she is able and willing to move out of her domestic sphere – which she knows and where she is most comfortable – into something that is diametrically opposite to what she has been doing most of her life. Killing a mighty general requires courage, cunning, and strength. Despite Jael's lack of experience, knowledge, and skill in military matters, she unhesitatingly finishes what needs to be done by killing Sisera, the commander, so that the army will not be able to reposition itself for another attack. Jael's readiness to complete a difficult task, despite her inexperience and lack of obligation as an outsider, is contrasted to the half-heartedness of some of the Israelite tribes.[83] Whereas some insiders vacillate in helping their fellow Israelites, Jael, as an outsider, responds quickly and decisively.

In contrast to the prose account, the poetic version omits the details of Jael's encounter with Sisera, emphasizing instead how Jael treats her visitor like a king – "he asked for water, and she gave him milk; in a bowl fit for nobles she brought him curdled milk" (v. 25). She serves Sisera richly and with honor, but those gentle hands that give so generously are the same hands that forcefully hammer him to death. The poem graphically depicts Sisera's violent death and fall, using verbs that convey the sound of hammering.[84]

> "Then she *struck* Sisera, she *shattered* his head
>   She *smashed* and *pierced* his temple." (v. 26, trans. and emph. mine)

---

83. O'Connell, *Rhetoric of Judges*, 125.
84. Hauser, "Judges 5," 37, comments on the repetitive sound pattern of the Hebrew verbs so that the effect of hammering is produced.

Similar to the prose account, the poem also uses sexual allusions in portraying Sisera's defeat. Twice, Sisera is described as kneeling "between her [Jael's] legs" (v. 27).[85]

> "Between her legs he knelt, he fell; he lay.
> Between her legs he knelt, he fell
>   Where he knelt, there he fell – destroyed!" (trans. mine).

Yet in chapter 4, the sexual hints evoke seduction, whereas in chapter 5, the sexual references conjure up images of rape – violent, lusty, forced, with the sexual conquest intended as a metaphor for military defeat.[86] These images suggest Sisera's complete humiliation and subjugation, which is emphasized by the repetition of the verbs "he knelt" and "he lay." The mighty warrior Sisera has been "unmanned" and is under the complete control of a woman.

From the scene of a decimated Sisera, lying dead at Jael's feet, the scene suddenly shifts to a worried mother, wondering at her son's delay in coming home (v. 28). Every mother can identify with the experience of looking out of the window now and then to check for child who is past the time for coming home, and so the figure of Sisera's mother waiting anxiously for her son invites sympathy. This contrasts so starkly with the provocative and graphic language used to recount the death of Sisera that one wonders about its function in the poem. The mother of Sisera comes into view as a person of status and power whose future will be negatively impacted by her son's death.

However, the next verses (vv. 29–30) shatter whatever pity one might feel for a grief-stricken mother once she hears about the death of her son.[87] Sisera's mother and the ladies of the palace (in contrast to Jael, a woman of the tent)[88] try to assure themselves that, despite the delay, their men are safe because the warriors are merely enjoying the spoils of battle. The Canaanite women, in their imaginations, relish the thought of the men "dividing the spoils, a *womb* or two for each man" (v. 30a, emph. mine). Instead of "woman" or "female," the ladies' speech uses a term for an intimate part of a woman's body, "womb," showing how they revel at the thought of the captured Israelite

---

85. The NIV and NRSV has "at her feet," but most translations have "between her feet" (ESV, NASB). The Hebrew word for "feet," *regel*, can also refer to the legs or to the sexual parts. The preposition *ben* ("between") before *regel*, occurs only one other time in Deut 28:57, referring to the issue of blood that comes out between the legs of a woman after giving birth (Lindars, *Judges 1–5*, 279).
86. Adrien Janis Bledstein, "Is Judges a Woman's Satire of Men Who Play God?," in *A Feminist Companion to Judges*, ed. Athalya Brenner (Sheffield: Sheffield Academic Press, 1993), 41.
87. O'Connell, *Rhetoric of Judges*, 131–132.
88. Bledstein, "Judges a Woman's Satire," 41.

women being raped by their men. Moreover, the Canaanite women gloat in anticipation of the luxurious feel of the richly woven cloth that their men will get from the fallen Israelites (v. 30b) without a thought for the Israelite women to whom those pieces of cloth belong. Thus, Sisera's mother and her noble ladies reduce a living, breathing Israelite woman into a body part or a piece of accessory.

Ironically, the reality is completely opposite to the scene that the women are anticipating. Instead of spoils being laid at the feet of Sisera's mother, her son lays spoiled at the feet of the hoped-for protector. Instead of gloating over the rich spoils of battle, Sisera is himself despoiled. Instead of the captive Israelite women being raped, "it is Sisera who was in a sense the victim of rape."[89] Thus, the song ends appropriately:

> "So may all your enemies perish, LORD!
> But may all who love you be like the sun
>   when it rises in its strength." (v. 31)

In this last verse, an antithesis is made between God's enemies and those who love him. Love here is not just an expression of an emotional sentiment, but is demonstrated in covenant loyalty.[90] Those who are loyal to Yahweh – who cooperate with him and aid him in his purposes and plans and who are in solidarity with those who do so – are like the sun when it is fiercest and most powerful. On the other hand, those who gloat at the misfortune of others are warned to beware since the tables can easily turn against them.

Those who have the upper hand or are in a privileged position can easily gloat over or be indifferent to the misfortune of others. It may begin as a secret self-congratulation that we are not in the same place as those "poor people," but it can progress to a perverse delight at other people's pitiful state. This is especially true in war situations, where it is easy to demonize the enemy and focus only on the suffering of one's own troops. For example, during the height of the recent Iraq war, media reports about the struggles and heroism of the invading army aroused sympathy for the troops, whereas there was general indifference about the growing number of Iraqi casualties, especially among civilians. Even Christians on the side of the invading troops directed their prayers of protection for their own troops while ignoring the suffering of the other side.

---

89. Lindars, *Judges 1–5*, 280.
90. Ibid., 287; Block, *Judges*, 244.

Judges 4:1–5:31

The poetic song of deliverance from Judges 5 celebrates the mobilization of the tribes and key individual players (Deborah, Barak, and Jael) in the drama of Yahweh. Yet it also provides various critiques: first, towards those who did not join Yahweh's call through Deborah and therefore did not support the Lord's work; second, towards those who gloat over the sufferings of others while enjoying the spoils of war. The poem not only identifies God's initiative and human instrumentality, but also couches Yahweh's work in cosmic terms. Because other factors are at work than we can see in the human sphere, we need to preserve a sacral view of life and avoid centralizing the human role in deliverance and restoration.

COOPERATING IN GOD'S WORK

The song of Deborah points to several theological truths. First, God acts in times of conflict and oppression – and God also takes sides. Secondly, God acts not just *for* his people, but *with* his people. God invites participation and welcomes all to join him in accomplishing his purposes. Thus, God is an empowering God.

Thirdly, God is willing to use all who make themselves available – leaders and ordinary people, women and men, outsiders and insiders, judges and housewives, warriors and civilians. This vision must come to expression in the body of Christ, where all play their part in building up the kingdom of God. While the song clearly celebrates the instrumental roles of Deborah (5:7, 15), Barak (5:12, 15), and Jael (5:24), it focuses on the leaders and people who volunteer to join Yahweh in his liberating activity (5: 2, 9). Yahweh draws his people into his purposes and this forms a powerful unity – a people in harmony and cooperation with their covenant God. But this sense of unity is so often under threat at both the vertical and horizontal levels. The vertical level is eroded when the people as a whole are resistant to God's call. The horizontal level is threatened when only some of God's people respond to God's command. So often, fragmentation is the story, rather than unity and cooperation.

The poem has important implications for the church in Asia, which still carries the DNA of Western mission efforts with their fragmented denominational priorities. Guarding one's ecclesiastical niche and championing one's often minor theological distinctive is often a higher priority than seeking strategies of cooperation in order to be a witnessing, serving, and healing presence in our world. Rather than reflecting the "Beloved Community" and working to be God's agents of renewal and change in our society, many Protestant and Evangelical churches seek to gain the market edge by pursuing the vision of growing their own church. This form of "tribalism" needs to be challenged

> by embracing a cooperative vision of the kingdom of God and by working together to see men and women come to faith, neighborhoods transformed, and the shalom of God spread into the human community.

JUDGES 6:1–8:29

The Use of Power: Empowerment, Abuse, and Violence

Lack of resources, family background, and our inherent insecurities can often hinder us from accomplishing God's good purposes for our lives – particularly if we are poor or belong to a marginalized group. The lack of opportunities in education or employment and the low regard of others can create apathy and hopelessness. Moreover, if one is caught up in the daily grind of survival, it is difficult to imagine other possibilities in life.

The term "empowerment" has become fashionable nowadays, both in church and society. Along with the word "transformation," this emotionally laden word has come to mean different things to various people. It is important to emphasize, however, that at the root of the term "empowerment" is the belief that marginalized groups – no matter how poor, disadvantaged, or oppressed – have both the individual and collective capacity to identify and analyze their own needs and problems, creatively propose solutions, and actively carry out successful plans and projects.[1]

In the book of Judges, the richly textured story of Gideon gives us a detailed account of the difficulties facing Israel at that time, the particular setting for Gideon and his family, and Gideon's gradual transformation into an empowered leader – even though that transformation leaves much to be desired.

The extended story opens up possibilities for reflection on a range of topics, including: a) the disempowerment of Israel due to the economic nature of its difficulties; b) the gradual emergence and development of Gideon as a liberating leader, relating to issues of empowerment and transformation; c) the flaws and difficulties evident in the liberating process and the implicit message that significant transformation requires deeper and more radical

---

[1]. For a discussion of empowerment as an approach to community development in the Philippine context, see Rex Linao, *Community Immersion; Toward Becoming Agents of Community Empowerment* (Quezon City: Great Books Trading, 2004); Joel Maribao, *Strategies for Empowerment: A Filipino-Christian Perspective* (Logos Publications, Society of the Divine Word, 1996); Camela D. Ortigas, *Training for Empowerment* (Quezon City: Office of Research and Publications, Ateneo de Manila University, 1992).

processes, and d) the ways in which power can be abused, leading to violence. The theme of power runs like a thread through Judges 6:1–9:57.

STRUCTURE OF THE GIDEON-ABIMELECH CYCLE

The first element of the cyclical framework, "the Israelites did evil in the eyes of the LORD . . ." is mentioned in 6:1 to introduce the Gideon narrative (6:1–8:32). However, the Abimelech narrative (8:33–9:57) is not introduced by this phrase, which does not occur again until the introduction to the Jephthah narrative cycle (10:6). The omission of this phrase, along with several other factors, suggests that the Gideon and Abimelech narratives actually belong together.

First, Abimelech is a son of Gideon, and the story of Abimelech's rise is inextricably related to the fate of Gideon's sons. Second, Abimelech is neither a judge nor a deliverer. Although Abimelech ruled over Israel, he was not involved in saving Israel from its enemies. The formula for the choosing of a judge – "the LORD raised up . . ." (2:16, 18; Othniel, 3:9; Ehud, 3:15) – is not used regarding Abimelech. There is no divine commissioning through a prophet (as when Deborah commissions Barak) or through a messenger of Yahweh (as with Gideon and Samson). Other prominent phrases in the other judge's stories that show God's involvement in the act of deliverance are not present in the story of Abimelech.[2] Thus it is best to see the Gideon and Abimelech narratives as comprising one overarching unit.[3]

However, there is a clear distinction between the Gideon narrative cycle and the Abimelech story so that the whole can be divided into two broad divisions: Gideon (6:1–8:32) and Abimelech (8:33–9:57), although 8:22–32 impinges on the Abimelech narrative with its reference to kingship and the birth of Abimelech. Based on the theme of power, however, the narrative can be sub-divided into the following smaller units.

6:1–10	The Disempowerment of the Israelites
6:11–7:24	The Empowerment of Gideon
8:1–29	Gideon's Abuse of Power
8:30–9:57	Power and Violence in Abimelech's Regime

---

2. These phrase are: "the Spirit of the LORD came powerfully upon him" (14:6, 19; 15:14) or "on him" (3:9; 6:34; 11:29) or "began to stir in him" (13:25); "the LORD has/I have given (your enemies) into his/your hand" (3:10; 3:28; 4:7, 14; 7:9).
3. O'Connell (*The Rhetoric of the Book of Judges*, 139–171) sees three plot-levels in the plot structure of Judges 6–9 (See also Block, *Judges, Ruth*, 249–250).

JUDGES 6:1–8:29

The narrative introduction (6:1–10) establishes the need for a deliverer. The next section (6:11–7:24) traces the choosing and empowering of a deliverer. Instead of following Gideon's maturation process, however, the next section (8:1–29) traces Gideon's deterioration as a deliverer and his abuse of power, leading to excessive violence and idolatry until his death. In Judges 9, this violence becomes systemic, where Gideon's son, Abimelech, and the Shechemites engage in brutal acts against each other. Only God's intervention stops the cycle of violence and abuse, although the theme of violence runs through the rest of the book of Judges. Because of the length of the Gideon narrative, we have set off the Abimelech narrative separately.

6:1–10 DISEMPOWERMENT: THE ECONOMIC PLUNDER OF ISRAEL

As in other cycles, the narrative begins: "The Israelites did evil in the eyes of the LORD, and for seven years he gave them into the hands of the Midianites" (6:1). The enemy, while it involved the combination of several people groups (6:3), were primarily the Midianites (6:7, 16; 7:2, 14, 25; 8:1, 28), with whom the Israelites had a mixed and complex relationship.[4] In this story, the Midianites were involved in the economic plunder of their neighboring nation, Israel.

The narrative provides specific details about the severe economic nature of Israel's oppression under Midian. Earlier accounts in Judges describe Israel's oppression in more general terms – how the Israelites served a foreign power for a certain number of years (3:8, 14), or how they were cruelly oppressed by their enemies (4:3) – whose military forces had superior technology (4:3) – or how they had to pay foreign tribute (3:15–18), such as gold, silver, livestock, or produce.[5] The Midianite domination, however, was more harsh and acute, since the Midianites did not wait for tribute to be brought to them, but ransacked and pillaged the land and stripped it of its produce and livestock so that nothing was left for Israel to live on (6:3–5). This occurred

---
4. The OT perspective regarding the Midianites is complex, with both positive and negative views. The book of Exodus gives a favorable view of the Midianites, particularly in their relationship to Moses (Exod 2:15, 21; 18:9–27), but other parts of the Pentateuch portray the Midianites as being antagonistic to Israel (Num 22, 25, 31). See Goldingay, *Old Testament Theology, Vol. 1: Israel's Gospel*, 503–504; George W. Coats, *Moses: Heroic Man of God* (Sheffield: JSOT Press, 1988), 55–56.
5. 2 Chr 17:11. Defeated nations and groups paid tribute to their conquerors (2 Sam 8:2; 2 Chr 18:2, 6, 11).

repeatedly,[6] so that every time the Israelites would begin from scratch and produce food again, the Midianites and their cohorts – the Amalekites and the people of the east[7] – would plunder them again "like swarms of locusts" (6:5), so that they never recovered economically.

Under this economic exploitation, "Israel became greatly impoverished because of Midian" (6:6a, trans. mine). The Hebrew verb for "impoverished" (*dll*) means "to be brought low, diminished."[8] The economic exploitation brought not only poverty, but also powerlessness and feelings of insignificance. This form of powerlessness arose not only from economic need, but also from having their economic and political capacity cut off.

This experience of economic plunder is familiar to those who have been colonized. Sadly, such plundering continues even in our contemporary world through loan and trade agreements that favor the former colonizer nations and marginalize the former colonies. In many Asian economies, these unequal and exploitive arrangements continue, sapping the will of governments, development and welfare groups, and the people, since no matter how hard they work, the odds are still stacked against them. Moreover, in many parts of Asia, the regular cycle of typhoons destroys crops and infrastructure so that people have to start all over again each year while earthquakes kill thousands and destroy entire cities.

As people who seek to live in Yahweh's shalom and in the way of Jesus, who embodies good news for the poor, those who have power and resources must never exploit others but must find ways to help and empower the least. Moreover, those who live in difficult circumstances due to war, earthquake, and other natural disasters must find ways to keep hope alive, build community, and work in solidarity for the common good.

As in previous narratives, "the Israelites cried out to the LORD" (6:7), and the Lord sends a prophet to deliver an indictment speech. The speech follows the pattern of a covenant lawsuit,[9] except that the final announcement of

---

6. The NRSV shows the frequentative meaning of the verbs (all in inverted perfects) in 6:3–6: "For whenever the Israelites put in seed, the Midianites and the Amalekites and the people of the east *would come up* against them. They *would encamp* against them and destroy the produce of the land . . . For they and their livestock *would come up*, and they *would even bring* their tents, as thick as locusts . . ." (ital. mine).
7. The "people of the east" is a general term used for groups from the east side of Jordan, perhaps referring to nomadic tribes from this region. See Soggin, *Judges*,110; Block, *Judges*, 252.
8. *DCH* 2:440.
9. Discussed on pp. 22–23.

judgement is omitted.[10] Presumably, the economic plunder of the Israelites is the judgement, so the function of the indictment speech is to explain, rather than predict, the judgement. Following is a structural outline for verses 8–10 (trans. mine):

1. Historical Retrospect (8b–10b)
    a. Review of the Exodus (8b–9)
        "I myself[11] brought you up from Egypt and brought you out of the house of bondage. I delivered you from the power of Egypt and from the power of all those oppressing you. I drove them out before you and gave you their land."
    b. Basis of the covenant (10a)
        "I am the Lord your God"
    c. Content of the covenant (10b)
        "You shall not fear (reverence) the gods of the Amorites with whom you are living in the land"
2. Accusation (10c)
    "but you have not obeyed me."
3. Announcement of Judgement (omitted)

The historical review of Yahweh's liberating action in the Exodus reminds the people that oppression is not God's desire. For Yahweh delivered them from their bondage in Egypt and from the power of their oppressors, and God gave them a land of their own, where they could live in freedom. Thus, the people are not oppressed because of Yahweh's lack of concern or lack of power. Moreover, Yahweh is personally committed to them: "I am the LORD your God" (6:10a). However, this personal commitment with Yahweh includes a claim of ownership and a demand for loyalty: "You shall not pay reverence[12] to the gods of the Amorites with whom you are living in the land" (6:10b). Because Israel failed to keep its part of the covenant – "but you have not obeyed me" – they continue to be oppressed. Yet, as in the Exodus

---

10. In 2:1–5, there is also no announcement of judgement, but there is an additional warning. Moreover, in 2:1–5, the speech is delivered by the angel of Yahweh while in 6:8–10, the indictment speech is given by an anonymous prophet.
11. The sentence is not in the normal narrative word order with the verb before the subject. Here the subject comes first, which shows that the focus of the sentence is God, who initiated Israel's deliverance from oppression and therefore rightfully demands Israel's loyalty.
12. The translation "pay reverence" is from the NRSV. The Hebrew word literally means "to fear" (see NASB, NJB, NKJV), in the sense of paying homage to the gods of the nations surrounding Israel.

(Exod 2:23–25), Yahweh hears the cry of Israel and responds by empowering a leader.

6:11–7:25 THE GROWING OF A LEADER: ISSUES IN EMPOWERMENT

In the Gideon story, the mighty deliverer called by Yahweh does not appear suddenly, ready for the task. Instead, a deliverer is gradually formed at a painstakingly slow pace while Yahweh shows great patience.

The phases in Gideon's mobilization and empowerment are somewhat surprising, since this ancient story traces a contemporary understanding about leadership formation, based on psychological and sociological sources. The Gideon cycle is also instructive, since it outlines important principles for growing leaders in the life of the church and other Christian institutions. Implicit to the story is the theme of empowerment, which describes the processes by which a person or a people are moved from a position of disempowerment, hopelessness, and oppression to a place of action and initiative, leading not only to individual transformation, but also to the transformation of communities.

6:11–24 Empowering Speech: Convergence of Perspectives

The story of Gideon begins when a traveler comes and sits under an oak tree on the land of Gideon's father. In the ancient Near East, people who traveled by foot over the dry, dusty paths often stopped to rest under the shade of a tree on someone else's property – so it is not surprising that the traveler is resting there.[13] But the stranger's identity is a surprise to the reader, for he is described as "the emissary of the LORD."[14] The fact that he appears while Gideon is "threshing wheat in a winepress to keep it from the Midianites" (6:11) conveys the difficulty of the Israelite circumstances, for Gideon is beating the wheat in a hollow carved out of a rock that is commonly used to tread grapes, with the juice running down to a lower receptacle. Normally, threshing would be done by oxen in a public place, but the marauding bands of Midianites make it impossible to thresh grain openly, and so Gideon has to do it furtively.

---

13. Abraham's visitors also rested under a tree (Gen 18:1–8).
14. "Angel of Yahweh" in most English translations. See pp. 22–23 for the translation "emissary of Yahweh."

Judges 6:1–8:29

Unaware that someone is watching him, Gideon continues threshing grain when the emissary of Yahweh addresses him: "The Lord is with you, mighty warrior" (6:12b). This speech from the divine messenger is prefaced by the phrase, "the angel of the Lord appeared to Gideon" (6:12a). The Hebrew form of the verb "appeared," *ra'ah* (niphal), occurs only in relation to a divine manifestation or theophany.[15] Hence, instead of the marauding Midianites confronting Gideon and reinforcing his powerlessness, we see the emissary of Yahweh (which later in the narrative is identified as Yahweh) in a revelatory appearance, speaking to Gideon about a new reality that starts with a redefinition of who Gideon is – a "mighty warrior."

Gideon, however, thinks the visitor is only a human being, and so he addresses him as *bi adoni*, an idiomatic expression that is literally translated, "upon me, my lord," but means, "pardon me, lord" or "excuse me, lord."[16] The expression is used to precede an entreaty or an explanation from an inferior to a superior.[17] In some passages, the phrase may express a courteous but firm disagreement with a superior, which seems to be the case here.[18] Gideon is polite, but he shows through his address that he does not really share the perspective of the visitor or the narrator. For example, Gideon does not call the visitor *adonay*, a name used for God,[19] but rather *adoni* ("my lord"), which is a simple title of respect for human persons, similar to the English "sir."

The visitor's greeting, "The Lord is with you, mighty warrior" (6:12), can be interpreted in different ways. First, it can be an ordinary form of greeting, such as "good day." On the other hand, it can be read as a wish – "May the Lord be with you" – or a promise of salvation[20] – "The Lord is going to be with you." The phrase in the Hebrew, however, is not couched in the form of a wish, but is a statement of the current state of affairs – "The Lord *is* with you." Apparently, Gideon thinks that the visitor is describing what is true about Israel's situation, for he politely but strongly objects, "Excuse me, sir, if Yahweh is with us, then why has all this happened to us? Where are all his wonders that our ancestors recounted to us, saying, 'Surely, Yahweh has

---

15. Soggin, *Judges*, 115, citing Gen 12:7; 17:1; 18:1; 26:2, 24; 35:9; Exod 3:2; Lev 9:23; Num 16:19; 17:7; 20:6; Deut 31:15; Judg 13:3; 1 Kgs 9:2.
16. Joüon § 105c.
17. Gen 43:20; 44:18; Num 12:11; 1 Sam 1:26; 1 Kgs 3:17, 26.
18. Exod 4:10, 13; Josh 7:8. The expression is used by Moses in Exod 4:10.
19. The plural form *adonay* in Hebrew shows a plurality of majesty and is used to address God.
20. Soggin, *Judges*, 118.

brought us up from Egypt?' But now, Yahweh has forsaken us and has handed us over into the control of Midian" (6:13, trans. mine).

There are several differences in perspective between the divine visitor and Gideon. First, Gideon does not immediately recognize the visitor as the emissary of Yahweh, since he keeps calling him, "sir," while the narrator clearly states that the "emissary of Yahweh" "appeared" to Gideon, clearly indicating a divine personality. Secondly, the emissary of Yahweh uses the second person singular in his address to Gideon: "The LORD is with *you* (singular), mighty warrior" (6:12); whereas Gideon's response is in the first person plural: "if the LORD is with *us*, then why has all this happened to *us*?" (6:13). Thirdly, Gideon disagrees with the visitor's comment that God is "with you." Apparently, he cannot believe that God is present with him personally and that he is considered a mighty warrior.[21]

Gideon's questions are similar to the questions in the Psalms of lament: "*Why* has all this happened to us? *Where* are all his wonders . . . ?" (6:13, emph. mine). In the psalms of lament, an appeal to God is made for deliverance in a time of individual or communal crisis. The appeal, however, is preceded by questions that ask God why the crisis is happening.[22] Gideon's lament highlights the contrast between God's dealings with Israel in the past and its current situation of oppression. Again, there is a reference to the Exodus: "Surely, Yahweh has brought us up from Egypt" (6:13).[23] Gideon knew of God's mighty deliverance of Israel from the oppression in Egypt, since his "ancestors recounted" the story to the next generation. In Gideon's view, the present circumstances are inconsistent with God's dealings with Israel in the past, and this is emphasized in the next sentence: "But now, Yahweh has abandoned us and has handed us over into the control of Midian" (6:13b).[24]

Gideon uses the Hebrew verb *natash* for "abandon," which implies "giving up something, not wanting to be bothered with it anymore," as when a farmer lets the land lie fallow and no longer does anything to make the land productive (Exod 23:11), or when a person permits things to happen (Gen

---

21. See Block, *Judges*, 260.
22. Claus Westermann, *Praise and Lament in the Psalms* (Atlanta, GA: John Knox, 1981), 176–178.
23. The Hebrew construction is in question form, "Has not Yahweh brought us up from Egypt?" (see NRSV and NIV), but the question is rhetorical and is expected to be answered by "yes, indeed."
24. The Hebrew starts with the particle *'attah*, which means "now," but the inverted order (with the subject coming before the verb instead of the usual narrative order of a verb followed by a subject) shows a contrast, hence the translation "but now" (see NRSV, NIV, ESV).

31:28). Another verb for abandon is *'azab,* but it has the sense of betrayal, or leaving something or someone behind, as when Israel forsakes the Lord.[25] Gideon's use of *natash* shows that his complaint has to do with his perception that God is no longer exerting effort on Israel's behalf, but is allowing things to remain as they are. Israel's hardships under foreign domination demonstrate a discontinuity between God's presence (God is with us, yet we are experiencing oppression), God's wonders and actions in the past (God delivered us in the Exodus, but no mighty deliverance is currently happening), and God's promises to the ancestors of a good land (the land is ravaged by the foreign raiders). Thus, Gideon thinks that God has abandoned them.

As if uninterrupted by Gideon's objections, the divine visitor continues his affirmation of Gideon by sending him on a mission: "Go in the strength you have and save Israel out of Midian's hand (6:14). The construction, "Go, in the strength you have," stresses that Gideon already has the strength to deliver Israel. Thus once more, the visitor emphasizes Gideon's strength. The visitor concludes his missional message with a question: "Am I not sending you?" (6:14b). But in Hebrew the question is rhetorical, functioning in a performative way as both a question and an emphatic command: "Indeed, I hereby send you."[26]

Interestingly, at this point in the narrative, the identity of the visitor changes from *mal'ak adonai,* which means the "emissary of Yahweh" (or "angel of Yahweh" in the NIV) (6:11) to Yahweh (6:14). The identity of the *mal'ak adonai* in the OT is fluid, with the *mal'ak* always having a human form. In Judges 2:1, the *mal'ak adonai* travels from Gilgal to Bochim; in 6:1, he sits under a tree; in 13:2–5, 8–18, he converses with Manoah and his wife and is perceived by the couple as a "man" or a "man of God." In Genesis 16:8, the *mal'ak* finds Hagar by a spring of water. The fact that Gideon, Manoah, and Hagar do not immediately recognize the supernatural character of their visitor reveals that the *mal'ak* appears as an ordinary human being. In some passages, the *mal'ak adonai* is seen as a representative and emissary of God, subordinate to God and functioning as God's aid.[27] In other passages, the *mal'ak adonai* plays the role of God's spokesperson, bringing a word from

---

25. Judg 2:12, 13; 10: 6, 10, 13.
26. See discussion on Judges 4:6.
27. The *mal'ak* revealed God's will to Balaam by blocking his path (Num 22:22–35), took care of Elijah's needs (1 Kgs 19:7), and acted as an instrument of God's judgement (2 Kgs 19:35; 1 Chr 21:16).

God and functioning as a prophet.[28] However, in some passages (Hagar in Gen 16:7–14; Gideon in Judg 6:22–23; Manoah and his wife in Judg 13:21–22), the *mal'ak adonai* shifts from an emissary of Yahweh to Yahweh himself.

From a literary perspective, the shift in naming and identity might serve to delineate various points of view in the Gideon narrative: the narrator's, or Gideon's, or the divine messenger himself. While the narrator designates the visitor as the *mal'ak adonai*, Gideon calls him *adoni* ("my lord"), showing the divergence in perspectives.

On a theological level, Fretheim explains the phenomenon as a way of preserving both the idea that God appears in human form (and thus corporeal like any human being) and, at the same time, that God cannot be captured in a human body (and thus unlike any human being). The fluidity in the text captures both these ideas at the same time. "The human form is the form of divine self-manifestation,"[29] yet the manifestation of God cannot be fully contained in the human form. Hence, there is both identification and distance in the association of the *mal'ak adonai* and Yahweh.

In Gideon's next response, once again he politely contradicts what is said about him: "Pardon me, my lord, but how can I save Israel? My clan is the weakest in Manasseh, and I am the least in my family." The Hebrew word for clan in this verse, *'eleph*, means "thousands" or "a group of thousand." In contrast to *mishpakhah,* another Hebrew word for clan, *'eleph* has a military sense in that it refers to the fighting group mustered from a clan.[30] Thus, Gideon is saying that his clan can only supply a very small contingent for the army. The adjective "weakest" (*dal*) echoes the root of the verb previously used for Israel's impoverishment (*dll*, see 6:6). Israel has become poor and lowly because of the military raids, and Gideon's clan, according to him, is the poorest among the already poor Israel. This suggests not only poverty, but also "paucity of numbers and lack of influence in the affairs of the tribe as a whole."[31] However, not only is Gideon's clan the weakest, Gideon himself is also the least, which might refer to his being the youngest. In

---

28. Gen 22:15; 2 Kgs 1:15.
29. Terence Fretheim, *The Suffering of God: An Old Testament Perspective* (Philadelphia, PA: Fortress, 1984), 103.
30. According to Boling, *'eleph* originally refers to a village or population unit in an agricultural society, then to the quota supplied by one village for the military muster, then to the military unit itself; hence it is better translated by the word "contingent" (*Judges*, 55). Nevertheless, even though the word "contingent" puts into the forefront the military nature of the *'eleph*, it misses its nature as a clan unit; hence, most English translations opt for "clan."
31. Burney, *Judges*, 189.

ancient Israel, the youngest had the least status, and therefore was less likely to lead.[32] Thus Gideon sees himself as doubly disadvantaged to take up the reins of leadership.

Yahweh's reply to Gideon is similar to his response to Moses' objections of inadequacy: "Surely, I will be with you" (6:16a; see also Exod 3:11–12).[33] As with Moses, God does not address Gideon's fears by contradicting what he thinks about himself, but by assuring him of the divine presence. The form in Hebrew alludes to the divine name:[34] "*Ehyeh*[35] shall be with you" or "*I am* shall be with you." The promise of presence also involves the promise of victory over Israel's oppressors: "Thus, you shall smite Midian as one man" (6:16b, trans. mine), meaning that Gideon will smite the Midianites altogether.[36]

At this stage, there seems to be a growing recognition within Gideon that the one he is speaking with is more than just an ordinary human being, for he replies: "If now I have found favor in your eyes, give me a sign that it is really you talking to me" (6:17). Signs function to confirm God's call, as in Moses (3:12; 4:1–9). The reference to a sign indicates that Gideon is not only trying to ascertain the exact import of what the visitor is saying, but also to verify his identity. The phrase, "If I have found favor in your sight," usually means "if it pleases you" or "if you want to" (see Gen 18:3), but there seems to be something more than politeness in this request. "Favor" (*hen*) can also imply help or assistance, so Gideon's request can also mean: "If you are going to help us, as you said you would, then please show me a sign."

Gideon asks the visitor to stay until he is able to prepare a present (*minkhah*). As Gideon prepares food (6:19), one is left wondering which of the two meanings of *minkhah* he is preparing: a) a simple present to honor the guest without any sacral meaning, or b) an offering to the deity in the form of food.[37] The inverted narrative form may indicate simultaneity of action[38] – while Gideon is preparing the *minkhah*, the *mal'ak adonai* is waiting

---

32. Note how David was also ridiculed by his older brother Eliab for wanting to join the war (1 Sam 17:28).
33. Klein, *Triumph of Irony*, 51.
34. Boling, *Judges*, 132; Burney, *Judges*, 189.
35. *'ehyeh* is the first person, singular form of *hayah*, while the divine name *Yhwh* recalls the third person, masculine, singular form of the same verb.
36. See parallel expression in Num 14:15; Judg 20: 1, 8, 11; 1 Sam 11:7; 2 Sam 19:15; Ezra 3:1; Neh 8:1. See also translation of NIV: "you will strike down all the Midianites together."
37. *HALOT* 2:601. Another meaning of *minkhah* is tribute, which is used in 3:15–18.
38. See Christo H. J. van der Merwe, Jackie A. Naudéa, and Jan H. Kroeze, *A Biblical Hebrew Reference Grammar* (Sheffield: Sheffield Academic Press, 1999), 336ff.

under the Terebinth tree. This inverted form, along with the ambiguity in the two meanings of *minkhah*, creates suspense: Will Gideon finally recognize the visitor's identity?

Upon the instructions of the visitor, who is referred to once again by the narrator as *mal'ak adonai* instead of Yahweh, Gideon places the food on the rock and pours the broth on the ground. "Then the emissary of Yahweh stretched out the tip of the staff in his hand and touched the meat and the unleavened cakes and fire leaped up from the rock and consumed the meat and the unleavened cakes. Then the emissary of Yahweh disappeared[39] from his sight" (6:21, trans. mine). Ironically, when the emissary of Yahweh disappears, and Gideon can no longer see him physically, Gideon is finally able to "see"[40] the visitor's divine nature. Upon realizing that the visitor is the emissary of Yahweh, Gideon cries out for fear of his life (6:22).[41]

Quickly, Yahweh (no longer the *mal'ak adonai*, since Gideon now knows who his visitor is) assures Gideon: "Peace! Do not be afraid. You are not going to die" (6:23). The word for peace, shalom, is a comprehensive term used to indicate harmonious relationships, but in this context, there is the sense of "to be safe." Hence, Boling's translation is: "You are safe. Do not panic. You will not die."[42]

Gideon's recognition of the messenger's identity leads to a new understanding of what God can do for Israel. He builds an altar and names it "The Lord is shalom," indicating his belief that Yahweh is Israel's safety and well-being. Thus, the initial doubts about God's presence, promises, and ability to save Israel are resolved as Gideon encounters and recognizes the presence of God. Gideon also sees himself as the *mal'ak adonai* sees him, though insecurities linger (as the following episodes show). With a vision of Yahweh and a transformed perception of himself, Gideon has enough confidence to take the first steps in carrying out God's command.

One form of empowerment that leads to change involves a redefining of one's circumstances and one's inner world or self-identity. The basis of this new identity is the power and word of Yahweh, which asserts itself in the midst of economic deprivation, oppression, and a tired religion that brings no hope or deliverance. For oppressed peoples, change does not begin with

---

39. Literally, "went out."
40. The Hebrew verb *ra'ah* can also have the meaning of inner perception and recognition (*TLOT* 3:1178).
41. Death follows those who see the deity face to face.
42. Boling, *Judges*, 129.

a change of circumstances, but with a revelation that change is possible. The key to this revelation is the promise, "The Lord is with you." Gideon begins to share the divine perspective when he recognizes the identity of the one who confronts him and begins to trust that Yahweh is committed to journeying with him.

However, few of us will immediately embrace a revelatory word that challenges us to a radical reorientation. Such change is usually resisted, and the most common objection is one of self-deprecation. This is the case with both Moses and Gideon. Nevertheless, there are important elements that help Gideon in embracing Yahweh's call and move him towards deeper levels of engagement.

First, there is a specific call to deliver Israel from her enemies. From the broad affirmation of "mighty warrior," Gideon is given a specific task, a promise of victory, God's presence, and an assurance of inner resources – "go in the strength you have" (6:14). Secondly, Gideon becomes more engaged as he tries to discern the identity of the visitor by asking for a sign and offering to prepare food. Lastly, Gideon's commitment is deepened by an awareness of his own need (6:22) and God's assurance of safety (6:23), leading to an act of religious dedication as he builds an altar to the Lord (6:24). Through these steps, Gideon gains a new identity that results in significant religious re-orientation.

At the beginning of the story, Gideon feels helpless and disempowered. He feels insecure in many areas: a) the influence his family can wield; b) his own status within the family; c) his own strength and ability to lead; d) his ability to discern what God wants; and e) Israel's capacity to overcome Midian through his leadership.

The process of empowerment begins with an affirmative speech from the deity. At first, Gideon is cynical and despondent. As the *mal'ak adonai* repeatedly affirms Gideon, Gideon starts to see beyond the narrow confines of his circumstances and self-definition, and he begins to glimpse possibilities about what life can and should be for himself, his family, and Israel. As he becomes engaged, he embarks on a series of small steps that lead to greater involvement and commitment. Thus, the empowering process that begins with Yahweh is sustained as Gideon participates in his own empowerment. The crucial point is reached when Gideon gains a vision of Yahweh that gives him the confidence to keep moving forward.

> ## GOD WITH US – KEY TO TRANSFORMATION
>
> Sometimes, there is a cognitive dissonance between how God views us and how we view ourselves. Because of our family background or society's perception about the value of our appearance, socio-economic status, and abilities, we may have developed a low self-image that does not coincide with how God views us. Moreover, our government's actions and policies may have disempowered us and made us cynical regarding our own abilities to effect change. Nevertheless, God's word continues to affirm us; God's presence and power remain with us; and God invites us to participate in the transformation process within ourselves, in our community, and in our nation. Hence, we can go forward with confidence in doing God's work, knowing that the Lord – our shalom – is with us.

6:25–32 Empowering Actions: Taking Risks

Immediately after Gideon affirms that the Lord is his safety and well-being, the Lord asks him to do something risky.

> Now on the same night the LORD said to him, "Take your father's bull and a second bull seven years old, and pull down the altar of Baal which belongs to your father, and cut down the Asherah that is beside it;[43] and build an altar to the LORD your God on the top of this stronghold in an orderly manner, and take a second bull and offer a burnt offering with the wood of the Asherah which you shall cut down" (6:25–26)

Here, we are surprised that the entire household of Gideon – and the whole town for that matter – are Baal-worshippers. Gideon's father has his own backyard shrine, and Gideon's task is not just to be a mighty regional deliverer, but also to break the backbone of Baal worship right in the midst of his own family. The fact that his household has its own Baal altar and Asherah pole shows how deeply entrenched the worship of the Canaanite gods has

---

43. It is not clear whether one or two bulls are involved in the story. Judg 6:25 seems to refer to two bulls because of the reference to the second bull. However, after this verse, only the second bull is mentioned (see 6:26, 28), which leads many commentators to think that only one bull is involved (Burney, *Judges*, 194; Block, *Judges*, 266; Boling, 134; see also NIV, NJB). Block follows Emerton in translating *par hashani* "the second bull" (see NRSV, NASB) as "the prize bull," using a different root. See "Emerton, 'The 'Second Bull' in Judges 6:25–28," *Eretz Israel* 14 (1978).

become in the life of the people of Yahweh (see Judg 17:10–13; 18:3–6, 14–20). Instead of fearing Yahweh, the Israelites are more afraid of what Baal will do to them. Yahweh no longer seems to hold a place in their lives, for they prefer the altar of Baal. Yet ironically, Israel never attributes their political and economic suffering to the ineffectual nature of their Canaanite gods. Even so, their submerged "memory" of Yahweh is stronger, for they are disappointed with Yahweh rather than Baal.

Yahweh's command to Gideon suggests that those who are being formed and empowered as leaders must be willing to live with the consequences of their new identity and calling. This will require them to dissociate from old patterns and ideas while identifying with new ones. By engaging in this important transition, transformational leaders help their kinfolk and others in the community embrace the new direction. But this process also requires leaders to take risks and suffer the disapproval and threats of those who are still committed to the old.

Because Gideon knows that the townspeople will see his action as a capital offense (6:30), he carries out God's command in the night so that the townspeople will not immediately see who did the crime and kill him (6:27). Many commentators have criticized Gideon for being cowardly,[44] yet his fear was understandable since he faced the very real threat of death from his community, who were entrenched in Baal worship. Similarly, in many Asian societies, going against the faith of one's family and community not only means being ostracized and rejected, but may also involve suffering to the point of death. Even though Gideon's bold act was done in the secrecy of night, the narrative does not condemn him for doing so.

Because Gideon takes ten servants with him, the townspeople soon discover that the perpetrator of the crime was Gideon, the son of Joash, the owner of the Baal shrine. Seeing Gideon's act as sacrilegious, the people confront his father and demand that he hands over Gideon to be killed by them.

Surprisingly, Joash is not incensed with Gideon for destroying his shrine, killing his bull, and ruining his reputation with his neighbors. Instead, Joash responds to the townspeople who want to kill his son with skepticism: "Are you going to plead (*rib*) Baal's cause? Are you trying to save him? Whoever fights (*rib*) for him shall be put to death by morning! If Baal really is a god,

---

44. Block, *Judges*, 267; McCann, *Judges*, 64–65; Matthews, *Judges & Ruth*, 87; Klein, *Triumph of Irony*, 54.

he can defend [*rib*] himself when someone breaks down his altar" (6:31, insertions mine).

Joash's speech plays on the verb *rib,* which can mean "to plead for the cause of" or "defend," but it can also mean "to fight," "contend," or "quarrel with." The townspeople are trying to defend (*rib*) and save Baal's honor, since Gideon's actions dishonored their deity. However, according to Joash, if Baal is a real god, he will be able to defend (*rib*) himself by killing those who quarrel (*rib*) with him. In other words, Baal can take care of himself, and he does not need his followers to defend him. If Gideon did wrong in pulling down Baal's altar, then Baal himself will get angry and strike Gideon dead. The fact that this did not happen casts doubts on Baal's power and reality.

Thus Gideon's actions, though carried out with trepidation, are instrumental to his father's conversion,[45] since his father witnesses for himself that Baal is not as powerful as he once thought him to be. In turn, Gideon is saved through the "conversion" and practical wisdom of his father (6:31–32), whom he has won over to his side. Moreover, Gideon is given another name: "Jerubaal" ("let Baal fight with him"), which mocks Baal for being ineffectual, since Gideon was not harmed after insulting Baal by pulling down his altar and building a rival altar in its place.

In this section, Yahweh challenges Gideon to initiate a risk-taking action that puts him on a collision course with his own family and community (6:28–29). Even though Gideon accepts the challenge with fear, the positive outcome of his action builds his confidence, empowering him to take on the bigger project of defeating Midian and liberating the Israelites. At the same time, he removes the religious blockage of Baal worship and wins over the cooperation of his father – and eventually his community.

6:33–40 Empowering Presence: Spirit, Sign, and People

The scene opens with the Midianites, Amalekites, and the people of the east swooping down on the land for their regular raids. Having already been empowered by the emissary of Yahweh's affirmative words and Yahweh's challenge, Gideon now experiences another form of empowerment: "the Spirit of the LORD clothed Gideon" (6:34, ESV). In the Othniel and Jephthah narratives, the language used for the spirit's empowerment is "the Spirit of the LORD came on (*hayah al-*) . . ." (3:10; 11:29), but the verb used here is *labash*, which refers to putting on garments. Drawing from the battle reports

---

45. McCann, *Judges,* 65.

of Assyrian kings, Waldman parallels the spirit's action on Gideon with the awesome radiance (*melammu*) from the gods that enveloped the Assyrian kings in battle so that their enemies become overwhelmed with terror. In other contexts, however, "to be clothed" in a figurative sense means to be "a wearer of positive enhancing qualities" that are added to one's basic nature.[46]

Through the spirit's energizing power, Gideon overcomes his natural timidity and insecurity and gains enough confidence to summon Israel to war. From his narrow circle of family and neighborhood, Gideon expands his circle of influence to his own clan of the Abiezirites, then to his own tribe of Manasseh, and then beyond to the tribes of Asher, Zebulun, and Naphtali.

In spite of Gideon's growing confidence, however, the spirit does not negate his natural personality, which is reflected in Gideon's lingering doubts about the success of the venture and his need for ongoing confirmation and certainty (6:36–40). The call narrative of Gideon (or vocation narrative) follows the standard plot line of some call narratives in the OT, whose main elements are: (1) divine appearance or confrontation; (2) introductory word; (3) commission; (4) objection; (5) reassurance; and (6) sign.[47] In the Gideon account, however, the assurance and sign elements are extended, while the objection portion is short. Twice, Gideon asks God for a confirmation, "if you will save Israel by my hand as you have promised" (6:36; see also 6:39) – first through wet fleece and dry ground, and then the reverse, through dry fleece and wet ground – even as he pleads with God not to be angry with him.

Yet the Lord does not rebuke Gideon for his insecurity, but patiently provides one confirming "fleece" after another. This contrasts with God's interaction with Moses, for in the account of Moses' call, the narrative focuses on Moses' objections. But with Gideon, the narrative focuses on the signs. Moreover, God gets angry at Moses for his repeated objections, but not at Gideon for his need for confirmation. This may stem from the fact that Moses was situated in a comfortable place, insulated from the degradations and humiliations of his fellow Israelites in Egypt, whereas Gideon is living

---

46. N. M. Waldman, "The Imagery of Clothing, Covering, and Overpowering," *JNES* 19 (1989): 162–163. See also Block, *Judges*, 272 n. 576. Thus, "the Spirit of Yahweh, as the clothing of Gideon, protects him, empowers him, and identifies him as Yahweh's chosen judge who will lead the Israelites to freedom" (Lee Roy Martin, "Power to Save!?: The Role of the Spirit of the Lord in the Book of Judges," *JPT* 16 [2008]: 36).
47. Terence E. Fretheim, *Exodus*, IBC (Louisville, KY: John Knox, 1991), 51; George Coats, *Exodus 1–18*, FOTL IIA (Grand Rapids, MI: Eerdmans, 1999), 34–42; Norman Habel, "The Form and Significance of the Call Narrative," *ZAW* 77 (1965): 298–301. See the call narratives of the following: Moses (Exod 3:1–4); Jeremiah (Jer 1:1–19).

in the midst of poverty, oppression, powerlessness, and insecurity. Gideon seems to need encouragement rather than rebuke, which God amply and patiently provides as he empowers Gideon to lead Israel to victory.

Evangelical Christianity often "packages" religious ideas, strategies, worship, and service. In the Moses and Gideon narratives and through the entire biblical witness, we see the wideness – rather than narrowness – of God's mercy. For God interacts with people in different ways in various contexts, and so we cannot expect the call experience of one to fit the call experience of another, nor God's dealings with one to be replicated with another. Thus we need to discern what story or stories in the Bible can provide points of reflection for our own specific contexts. However, there is not one way to have meaningful prayer, nor one way to do effective evangelism, nor one way to do church, even though the dimensions of worship, word, sacrament, fellowship, and service should all be present.

7:1–8 The Limits of Empowerment

After affirming and encouraging Gideon through encounters with the divine presence and confirmations from the spirit through signs, God issues a surprising command to Gideon as he is camped with all the people who have rallied to follow him in the battle against the Midianites. But instead of taking advantage of the momentum that Gideon's summons has created among the Israelites and using the formidable force he has amassed to fashion an army that can deal a decisive blow against the Midianites, God orders Gideon to cut down the size of the army. Apparently, the building up the army is not one of God's confidence-building measures. However, since the raiding army is like locusts in their number (6:5; 7:12), God's command does not make sense from a practical point of view. Moreover, from a sociological perspective, in which change is brought about by creating greater spheres of influence through networking and increased people participation, the instruction to downsize the army is a reversal of the community-organizing process. This shows that although community-organizing principles are reflected in God's transformation process, God may also choose other ways of operating.

God explains that the troops need to be scaled back so that Israel won't take the glory for itself, saying, "My own strength has saved me"(7:2). The focus here is on what God can do through Gideon rather than the strength of the Israelite army. As mentioned earlier, one of the great sins of Israel is that they "forgot the LORD their God" (3:7), and this often occurred when Israel was experiencing security, comfort, and success. Moreover, during these times of forgetfulness, Israel became susceptible to worshipping other gods. Throughout Judges, in each repeated cycle of sin-oppression-deliverance-rest, God delivered Israel from their distress when they cried out, despite the fact that they did not fully repent – and yet Israel never understood God's grace, and so they continued "to do evil in the sight of Yahweh." Thus Yahweh's goal is not to empower Gideon so that he and his followers can topple the oppressors of Israel, but rather to instill in Israel an appreciation of the grace of God in delivering them from their oppressors so that they might turn to Yahweh with confidence and serve him without relying on other gods.

God instructs Gideon to weed out the troops using two criteria. The first – "anyone who trembles with fear may turn back" (7:3) – seems to be a concession to those who are too scared to fight and may be demoralized by fighting with a small army. The second is more arbitrary: "those who lap the water with their tongues as a dog laps" are separated from "those who kneel down to drink" (7:5), and the ones who lap are chosen to fight the battle. However, one might interpret the strategic difference between the two groups, the point is that the victory does not ultimately depend on the characteristics of the ones who are directly involved in the battle. While some think that the test is one of alertness, there may be no significant difference in the character of the two groups, other than the test serves to limit the number of fighters.[48] For after most of the troops have left, God promises: "With the three hundred men . . . I will save you and give the Midianites into your hands" (7:7). There is not even a contingency plan, since the rest of the troops are sent home as reservists, although their provisions and trumpets are given to the ones who are left to fight (7:8).

When we become empowered, it is easy to think that we are able to accomplish things by our own capacity and the concerted efforts of our community. This passage, however, emphasizes that the real source of change is God, who delivers and gives victory by empowering individuals and communities. Thus when we see change taking place, let us not forget that the power is not in us, but is a gift from the gracious hand of God.

7:9–25 Gideon's Transformation: From Hesitancy to Leadership

After the culling of the troops, the only thing left to do is to attack the Midianite camp. Indeed, God gives the battle charge that night: "Get up,

---

48. Boling, *Judges*, 145; see also Cundall and Morris, *Judges & Ruth*, 110.

go down against the camp, because I am going to give it into your hands" (7:9). However, before the actual battle, God embarks on another confidence-building measure, perhaps to assuage Gideon's fear after whittling down the size of his army. Interestingly, God's plan for assurance involves another big risk, for after issuing the battle charge, God instructs Gideon to go down to the outskirts of the enemy camp with only a servant to attend to him (7:10–11). Though God has already provided plenty of opportunities for Gideon to overcome his apprehensions, God continues to push Gideon to take greater risks. The risk pays off, however, when Gideon hears the interpretation of a Midianite's dream by one of his comrades (7:13–14). Ironically, the dream depicts Gideon as a cake of barley bread crushing the tent of the Midianites (7:13). This image reverses the hunger that Gideon and his fellow Israelites experienced at the hands of the marauding Midianites when they plundered the land and its produce – for the source of plundered food for the Midianites and their cohorts becomes a catapult that will destroy them.

The victory formula is repeated the third time – "God has given the Midianites and the whole camp into his [Gideon's] hands" (7:14) – but here it is coming from the mouth of the enemy instead of Yahweh (see also 7:7, 9). Ironically, after hearing the word of victory from a Midianite, Gideon finally believes that he will defeat the Midianites. The oppression of the Midianites has become such an overpowering and overwhelming reality in his life that he can no longer imagine another possibility. With this strange assurance, Gideon mobilizes his men, saying: "Get up! The LORD has given the Midianite camp into your hands" (7:15).

After dividing the three hundred men into three divisions, Gideon embarks on an ingenious strategy, a "sound-and-light show"[49] that involves trumpets, jars, and torches (7:16). The smashing jars, the lit torches, the sound of the trumpets, and all the shouting causes confusion among the Midianite army, throwing them into a panic so that they begin to kill each other. Although Gideon's strategy creates these effects, the Lord routs the army and brings victory to Israel, for the narrative continues: "The LORD caused the men throughout the camp to turn on each other with their swords. The army fled . . ." (7:22).

With the initial rout of the enemy in place (7:22), Gideon moves to call others into the fray, including the Ephraimites, to help in pursuing the

---

49. Klein, *Triumph of Irony*, 55.

enemy (7:23–24). We thus see Gideon exhibiting a capacity for leadership and a confidence that were not evident in the initial stages of the narrative.

However, in the midst of this victory over the Midianites, a disquieting feature of Gideon's call to arms diminishes God's role in the whole process.[50] For while the men blow their trumpets and break their jars, they cry out: "A sword for the LORD and for Gideon!" (7:20; see also 7:18). Since the narrative clearly indicates that Yahweh has given the victory (7:9, 22), the sole rallying call should have been for Yahweh. Apparently, Gideon now sees himself as God's equal partner in the enterprise – rather than God's deliverer.[51] Moreover, his call emphasizes the human instrument of victory – the sword – rather than focusing on the power of God.[52]

This implies that the Israelites perceive both Gideon and the Lord as the ones responsible for the victory, which directly opposes Yahweh's intentions when he instructed Gideon to cut back on the number of troops. Thus Gideon fails to provide the Israelites with a learning opportunity about how God is at work in their own situation.[53] Despite the fact that God called, challenged, encouraged, and empowered Gideon – even when Gideon had no confidence in himself – God does not get the full credit for the victory. At this point in the story, we are introduced to the theme of the marginalization of Yahweh, which is developed later in the book of Judges.

EMPOWERING ASIAN LEADERS

Gideon's formation as a leader follows the pattern of Yahweh using unlikely people (Ehud, 3:15; Deborah and Jael, 4:4–7, 17–22). Gideon is hiding (6:11), his family is religiously compromised (6:25), he is constantly looking for signs and affirmation (6:36–40), and he believes the interpretation of a Midianite soldier about Israel's victory (7:15) more than Yahweh's own word regarding a definitive victory (7:9). None of this indicates a person poised to become an effective deliverer.

---

50. McCann, *Judges*, 65.
51. L. Juliana Claassens, "The Character of God in Judges 6–8: The Gideon Narrative as Theological and Moral Resource," *HBT* 22 (2001): 61; Dennis T. Olson, "Judges," Vol. 2, *NIB* (Nashville, TN: Abingdon, 1998), 803; Ellie Assis, *Self-Interest or Communal Interest: An Ideology of Leadership in the Gideon, Abimelech and Jephthah Narratives (Judg 6–12)* (Leiden: Brill, 2005), 77.
52. Marais, *Representation*, 112.
53. Gideon's role was to mediate between God and people, directing the people to recognize God's power at work in defeating the ones who were oppressing them. Gideon, however, failed in fulfilling this function. See Claassens, "Character of God in Judges 6–8," 60.

However, in this rich and complex story, we gain a mixed picture of the growing of a leader and the issues related to empowerment. By way of summary, several themes are prominent.

First, Gideon's growth and development from an oppressed and fearful person to an empowered and liberating leader is a slow and difficult journey. Gideon is gradually formed into his God-given task.

Secondly, Gideon's encounters with Yahweh are central to his transformation. These encounters lead to a change in Gideon's identity and his ability to accept the role and task of leadership.

Thirdly, Gideon's significant revelatory encounters are consolidated over time. This story highlights that leaders are not formed overnight, but grow by negotiating transitions and difficulties.

Fourthly, a leader is only a leader when his or her self-understanding, calling, and identity become evident in the public arena and others respond. With Gideon, this involves confronting the idolatry within his own family and making a public stand for Yahweh. Yahweh's cause is the vision that Gideon symbolizes, enacts, and into which he calls the Israelite community.

Fifthly, after Gideon receives multiple assurances that Yahweh will make Gideon victorious, Gideon acts competently and decisively. In this sense, Gideon is a competent and successful leader. But he is flawed, for his transformation is related to Yahweh's cause to free his oppressed people, and it does not go deep enough to produce long-lasting ethical qualities.

Thus Gideon is successfully task-oriented, but he lacks character virtues. His weaknesses and failures eventually play themselves out in Israel as a whole. This highlights the connection between a leader's ongoing personal transformation and the depth of work that the leader can accomplish in society.

In more hierarchical societies, such as many Asian cultures, capable leaders are often elevated and idealized, which places them beyond the need for personal growth and development. Though much may be expected of these leaders, there is no system in place for nurturing them. This is particularly true of church leaders – for no one seems to pastor the pastors. Capable leaders are still human, with shadow sides, weaknesses, and struggles. Yet this reality is seldom acknowledged, particularly in shame-based hierarchical cultures. Thus the entire operation of a church, ministry, or institution can be over-identified with the leader – as when we speak of a particular person's church or Bible college.

This problem becomes further complicated when leaders assume roles that leave them open to temptation, yet they have no accountability. This happens to Gideon. Rather than being characterized by humility, in light of all that Yahweh has done, he allows himself to be sucked into his society's elevation of leaders – and so begins the downward spiral that will reveal his internal weaknesses and result in disastrous consequences.

JUDGES 6:1–8:29

8:1–35 DIFFICULTIES AND RESISTANCES IN THE TRANSFORMATION PROCESS

In contemporary Christian circles, some promote visionary projects with simplistic catch phrases, such as "changed individuals change the world" or "all we need is a good Christian leader to change society." Yet religious and social transformation can never be thought of in such simplistic terms. The complex narrative in the Gideon cycle not only reflects the formation and development of a liberating leader in Israel and the inherent problems in this process, but it also invites further reflection about the transformation process as a whole.

Moreover, the narrative highlights how internal and external counter-forces work within a particular setting. In the Gideon narrative, we see external counter-processes in the disunity of the Israelite community after the glorious victory, and we see internal counter-processes in Gideon's self-focus in the process of delivering Israel. Though liberating leaders may set the forces for social good in motion, they may also become counterproductive.

8:1–3 Disunity in the Israelite Ranks

In Judges 8:1–3, the Ephraimites furiously upbraid Gideon for not including them in the first attack. Gideon demonstrates diplomatic leadership skills in settling their complaints by helping them feel good about their contribution: "God gave Oreb and Zeeb, the Midianite leaders, into your hands. What was I able to do compared to you?" (8:3). Since the Ephraimites were called upon to do the mopping up operations at the end rather than join in the decisive strike (7:24), they now want a share in the credit. Similarly, in our contemporary world, those who get fewer sound bites often feel that they have been sidelined in a project.

The scene with the Ephraimites brings narrative focus to Israel's fragmentation, a theme that runs throughout the book of Judges. In Judges 1, the tribes of Judah and Simeon cooperate with each other to possess their allocated territories (v. 3). In Judges 5, the narrative highlights the tribes who do not respond to the summons for battle – but wait it out in comfort – while the rest join in the fray with Deborah and Barak (vv. 15b–17, 23). The Ephraimites display "attention-seeking behavior," constantly peeved for not being given the starring role (8:1; 12:1). Thus instead of rejoicing in God's victory, they detract from it by focusing on themselves. The attitude of non-cooperation, however, turns into downright treachery when the Judahites hand Samson, their fellow Israelite, over to the Philistines (15:11–13). The disintegration of relationships among the tribes of Israel reaches its climax in the inter-tribal wars in Judges 20.

The Israelite settlement in the land of Canaan was built upon extended families that saw themselves as part of the wider tribal configuration. Thus throughout the book of Judges, references are made to the various tribes. At the same time, the more general terms "Israel" and "Israelites" are also used. This raises questions about the possible differences and tensions regarding one's fundamental identity. Does one see oneself in terms of one's extended family, or one's tribal affiliation, or within the broader designation of nationality?

As noted above, the book of Judges traces stories of tribal cooperation, but also stories of disunity and – even more glaringly – Israelites fighting Israelites. For Asian Christians, whose culture is strongly familial, this raises several important questions. The family not only forms one's primary social identity, but also spills over into one's social relationships, marriage choices, economic concerns, and alliances. Thus strengthening the extended family – and, in some cases, one's tribal or regional group – is a primary social value. Asian culture is incredibly diverse, and regionalism characterizes many Asian communities. Thus one may have particular loyalties that do not reflect those of the more centralized government.

Both sets of loyalties, while good in themselves, may have some negative outcomes. For example, a church may consist of extended families that prioritize "their own" over the whole community of faith. Tribalism and regionalism may hamper Christian participation in nation-building. Moreover, "religious tribalism" characterizes much of Christianity, including the church in Asia. Lack of grassroots ecumenism or church networking and cooperation may affect the church's mission as it seeks to accomplish God's purposes in a divided and wounded world.

Having inherited a divided Christianity from the West and having been marked by ethnic diversity in their own countries, Asian Christians have a tendency to work in oppositional rather than cooperative modes. This oppositional tendency is reflected in the sheer concentration of independent churches and Bible Schools in just one part of a major city in many Asian countries. Instead of strategies of cooperation, many churches, Christian organizations, and Bible Schools replicate ministries and training programs. This leads to competition instead of collaboration – and an overall diminishment of God's work in a particular place.

In the Gideon cycle, Yahweh expresses concern that a large army will lead Israel to take the credit for its own capabilities and military strength instead of recognizing the victory as a gift from God (7:2). As the incident with the Ephraimites suggests, the concern is not to glorify God, but to make sure that they are given some of the credit.

Similarly, many Christians and Christian groups feel slighted when their contributions are not acknowledged, or when they are unintentionally excluded from a major Christian undertaking. This is especially true in Asia, where honor and inclusion are central values of the culture. Yet we may need to be content with less honor and accept some exclusion in order to see God's kingdom advanced and God's glory magnified.

8:4–35 The Dark Side of Gideon

As noted previously, though Gideon slowly comes to the point of doing what Yahweh asks him to do, several counter-forces remain within him. First, Yahweh's accusation that Israel will take the credit for routing the enemy suggests an implicit criticism of Gideon (7:2). For if the people are thinking about their own glory, then Gideon stands co-accused as their leader. Secondly, Gideon is more willing to believe an enemy soldier than Yahweh regarding the victory over the Midianites (7:15). This implies that Gideon does not fully trust Yahweh. Thirdly, as discussed earlier, the Israelites rally around the disconcerting cry, "for the LORD and for Gideon," which puts Gideon alongside Yahweh in the liberating action.

As the narrative progresses, Gideon acts more autocratically and vindictively, devolving from a fearful warrior into a despot. "The coward becomes the bully."[54] After crossing the Jordan in pursuit of the Midianite kings, he comes to the towns of Succoth and Penuel in the east, where Gideon demands support since his troops are weary and famished (8:4–9). The people of Succoth and Penuel, however, do not want to cast their lot in with Gideon until they are certain that the Israelite leader already has the victory: "Are Zebah and Zalmunnah now already in your hands that we should give bread to your troops?" (8:6, trans. mine). After appraising the weakness of Gideon's three hundred weary men, perhaps they are skeptical that he will overcome the might of the two kings.

Gideon's responses to the leaders of Succoth and Penuel express his new-found confidence – "when the LORD has given Zebah and Zalmunnah into

---

54. Klein, *Triumph of Irony*, 61. The battle becomes Gideon's vendetta because of a personal affront. See Schneider, *Judges*, 123–124; Assis, *Self-Interest or Communal Interest*, 77.

my hand" (8:7) and "when I return in triumph" (8:9) – but they also carry excessive and cruel threats of retribution. After gaining victory, Gideon brutally carries out these threats: "He took the elders of the town and taught the men of Sukkoth a lesson by punishing them with desert thorns and briers. He also pulled down the tower of Peniel and killed the men of the town" (8:16–17). Gideon's impatience with these men who were afraid to risk themselves contrasts sharply with Yahweh, who patiently encouraged Gideon in his fear, skepticism, and indecision.[55]

As the narrative progresses, Yahweh's marginalization becomes more evident. The narrative formula for divine assistance ("The Lord gave . . . into their hands"; "The Lord was with . . ."; "The Lord caused confusion . . .") is no longer present, except from Gideon's lips (8:7). Thus there is nothing from the narrator to indicate that the Lord is involved in Gideon's actions.[56] From "*the Lord* set each man's sword against another and against all the army" (7:22, emph. mine), the description shifts to "*he* [Gideon] . . . threw the whole army into a rout" (8:12, emph., trans. mine). Moreover, Gideon's speeches predominantly use first-person singular verbs: "*I* am pursuing" (8:5); "*I* will thresh" (8:7); "*I* will pull down" (8:9) (trans. mine).[57]

Furthermore, Gideon's killing of Zebah and Zalmunnah, the kings of Midian, is motivated by his desire to avenge the killing of his family (8:18–19) rather than by a desire to carry out God's commands.[58] His dialogue with the kings is surprisingly civil, in contrast to the harsh retorts he delivered against the people of Succoth and Penuel. Nevertheless, he wants to humiliate the kings by asking his firstborn to kill them, since it is a badge of honor for kings to be killed by a mighty warrior.[59] The young boy, however, is afraid (8:20), an attitude reminiscent of the former Gideon,[60] but which acts now as a foil to Gideon's cruelty and violence. However, "Gideon could not see his former self in his son, because he had changed too much."[61]

Given Gideon's increasingly despotic actions, it is not surprising that the people ask him to rule over them: "Rule over us – you, your son and your grandson – because you have saved us from the hand of Midian" (8:22). The people use the verb "to rule" (*mashal*) rather than "to be king" (*malak*),

---

55. Klein, *Triumph of Irony*, 62.
56. Claassens, "Character of God," 64; Olson, "Judges," 807.
57. Claassens, "Character of God," 62–63; McCann, *Judges*, 68–69.
58. Webb, *Judges: Integrated Reading*, 151.
59. Matthews, *Judges & Ruth*, 96.
60. Marais, *Representation*, 113.
61. Ibid.

which may indicate an avoidance of any reference to the monarchy, since that was not Israel's system of government at that time. Nonetheless, the people clearly have something akin to a monarchy in mind, since they request dynastic succession.

The Israelites ask Gideon to rule over them using the troubling phrase, "for you have saved us from the hands of Midian." In God's work, there is certainly room for proper appreciation of those who are willing to pay a high personal cost for the sake of the community. Yet God explicitly warned Gideon about the people's temptation to attribute success to their efforts: "lest Israel take the glory for itself, in disregard of me, saying, 'My own power has delivered me'" (7:2, trans. mine). Though Gideon succeeded in shifting Israel's focus away from the Canaanite gods, Israel's attention is now riveted on Gideon's achievements rather than on Yahweh's grace and power. Thus Gideon fails to accomplish the fuller work that he is called to do, which began in his father's house when he replaced false worship with a renewed faith in Yahweh. Though the enemy without has been routed, the enemy within is still present.

Even so, Gideon refuses to be ruler: "I will not rule over you, nor will my son rule over you. The LORD will rule over you" (8:23). Gideon's response seems to be noble, full of the appropriate humility and piety in the face of great victory. However, there are several disturbing things about Gideon's reply, along with his actions afterwards.

First, even though Gideon refuses to be ruler, pointing to Yahweh as the true ruler of Israel, he does not disabuse Israel's notion that he is responsible for the victory against the Midianites.[62] Thus Israel's pronouncement, "because you have saved us from the hand of Midian" (8:22), and Gideon's failure to object to this statement, wholly disregard Yahweh's role and power.

Secondly, Gideon's prior and subsequent actions evoke the privileges exercised by ancient Near Eastern kings. He harshly treats those who oppose him (8:4–9, 13–17); he appropriates for himself the royal symbols of power worn by the Midianite kings (8:21, 26); he asks for a share of the spoils of battle and accumulates a treasure fit for a king (8:24–26); he establishes a religious oracular site often maintained by kings (8:27); he keeps a harem (8:30); he names one of his sons Abimelech, which means "my father is king" (8:31);

---

62. Block, *Judges*, 299; Claassens, "Character of God," 65.

and he does not sufficiently challenge the notion of dynastic succession, since his sons still rule after him (9:2).[63]

Gideon's making of an ephod (8:27) seems to be an aberration, given his earlier decisive dismantling of Baal's altar and the symbols of the Canaanite cult (6:25–27). An ephod is an elaborate garment worn or carried by the priest (see Exod 28:3–14, 31–35). In some verses, it functions as an oracular device to ascertain the will of God (1 Sam 23:6–11), since it bore the Urim and the Thummin (Exod 28:6–30), sacred lots that were used to inquire of the Lord. One may interpret Gideon's action as a simple return to Canaanite idolatry, but this does not fully account for the nuances of Gideon's position. Perhaps Gideon wants to make an ephod so that it will be easier for him and for Israel to know the Lord's will in specific situations and circumstances.

Another possibility is that Gideon sees himself as Yahweh's helper (7:18, 20). As the man who pulled down the symbols of Baal and led the people back to Yahweh, Gideon may want to draw all the people together by having them contribute to the effort (8:24–25) and then collectively create a powerful Yahwistic religious icon that will encourage devotion and loyalty to Yahweh. By placing the ephod in his own town (8:27), Gideon may be consolidating the end of the power of Baal and establishing the reign of Yahweh's power.

A more likely position is that Gideon wants to establish a site that will ostensibly remind people of the great victory that Yahweh has accomplished for Israel. But in doing so, he also reminds people that he is the main instrument of that victory. In the first place, Gideon does not ask the people to give a share of the spoils of battle on Yahweh's behalf. Rather, the people give gratefully to Gideon because they think that he brought them out of their situation of oppression. The fact that Gideon places the ephod in his own town reinforces his central role in the deliverance of Israel from Midian.[64]

Thus the ephod functions as a memorial to what Gideon has accomplished and what the Israelites themselves have contributed.[65] In this way, it "became a snare to Gideon and his family" (8:27). A snare (*moqesh*) is a trap that catches prey by surprise because they unknowingly walk into it. If the creation of the ephod were just a return to Canaanite worship, it would not have been a trap. The ephod becomes a trap in the sense that it is supposed

---

63. Cundall and Morris, *Judges*, 121; Block, *Judges*, 299–301.
64. Assis thinks that the ephod was a victory monument for Gideon (*Self-Interest or Communal Interest*, 106–107).
65. Wolfgang Bluedorn, *Yahweh versus Baalism: a Theological Reading of the Gideon-Abimelech Narrative* (Sheffield: Sheffield Academic Press, 2001), 174.

to promote Yahweh worship, but it results in the marginalization of Yahweh and the glorification of Gideon. Thus, the narrative uses the language of prostitution (8:27; see also 2:17), since Israel turns away from right worship of Yahweh, substituting a pseudo-worship that minimizes Yahweh's role in their lives.

TAKING THE SPOTLIGHT AWAY FROM YAHWEH

The Gideon narrative is a story of great beauty and great pain. The beautiful aspects of the narrative are captured in Yahweh's thoughtfulness and gentleness in empowering the powerless, victimized, and oppressed Gideon to a place of decisive leadership, paving the way for spiritual renewal within his family and community and liberation from economic oppression for his tribal group. This captivating story traces a wonderful picture of integral or holistic liberation, in which many elements play a part to make a whole. Yahweh is depicted as the great life coach, personal trainer, mentor, personal and vocational formator who brings about a great, gentle, and decisive work.

Yet even though Yahweh is completely for Gideon in wanting to work God's purposes through him, Gideon is not completely for Yahweh. Gideon's initial deviation appears to be minor: he takes credit for the rout of the Midianites when that credit, in the light of the whole tale, should only be given to Yahweh. Thus Gideon falls into the temptation of attributing something of God's work to himself. Because this deviation is not corrected at its genesis, one thing leads to another, and the deviation ends in senseless violence and idolatry. The fearful, disempowered, and unskilled young man at the beginning becomes an empowered leader, yet he is not able to cope with his new position of power.

What is tragic and disturbing in this story is that Yahweh is marginalized when Yahweh should have become more central in the hearts and minds of God's people. Sadly, the displacement of God leads people to replace God with something else–and in this story (and in many other stories of faith), idolatry and chaos take the place of God.

The displacement of Yahweh is not limited to the Gideon story. As the book of Judges progresses (or rather devolves), Yahweh, the covenant God, who initiates redemption and shalom, is increasingly pushed to the margins, while chaos and madness take center stage.

JUDGES 8:30–9:57

The Pitfalls of Power

At election time, questions arise about whether or not Christians should run for political positions. Some argue that in order for change to take place, Christians should be involved in politics. Others feel that the corrosive effects of power, the corrupt political system, and the often naïve perspectives of Christian politicians make it unlikely that Christians will ever be able to introduce real change. Thus many opt to be involved in grassroots community efforts rather than positions of governance.

This ambivalence towards power, politics, and governance is not new – as we see from church history. Christian churches have understood their role differently vis-à-vis the state. Traditionally, the Anabaptists have been more critical of the state and its use of force and power.[1] On the other hand, the descendants of the Calvinist tradition see the state and its power in a more positive light – as the guardian of order, the source of protection, the administrator of justice, and creator of a framework for human and social well-being to flourish.[2] This highlights both the ambiguity and the struggle that Christians have in affirming the radical qualitative difference of what it means to be the people of God in Christ, along with what it means to affirm what is good in society, including its political structures and the power they exercise.

The biblical account reflects this ambivalence as well. For example, from the book of Joshua through Kings, there are positive evaluations of kingship, as revealed in God's establishment of an eternal covenant with David. On the other hand, there is also a critique of the monarchy because of the way that kings abrogate for themselves what belongs to God and fail to carry out their covenantal responsibilities. Judges 9 offers one such critique about the negative effects of centralized power and how it can lead not only to abuse, but also to violence and murder. Abetted by kinship ties, wealth, and the claim of religious legitimacy, Abimelek's power-grab created political structures that led to the perpetuation of violence.

---

1. J. H. Yoder, *For the Nations: Essays Evangelical and Public* (Eugene, OR: Wipf and Stock, 2002).
2. See R. E. Webber, *The Church and the World* (Grand Rapids, MI: Academie Books), 124–142.

As discussed in the previous chapter, the Abimelek narrative is part of the Gideon narrative, but it is treated separately here because of the overall length of these narratives.

8:30–35 TRANSITIONS: HONORING LEADERS RIGHTLY

The text transitions from the Gideon narrative into the Abimelek narrative by tracing the generational changeover through the birth of Gideon's sons. We are told that Gideon had seventy sons from many wives (8:30),[3] which reflects his monarch-like status, since kings then maintained large harems. Of Gideon's sons, only Abimelek – whose name means "my father is king" – is mentioned. We are told that his mother is Gideon's concubine in Shechem. The narrative says that Gideon died at "a good old age" and was buried in his father's grave (8:32; see also Samson, 16:31) – an honorable end to a long life. Yet the events that unfold after his death negate any honor that was accorded to him during his lifetime.

Shortly after Gideon's death, the narrative states that the "Israelites again prostituted themselves to the Baals" (8:33). The fact that the Israelites had already prostituted themselves to the ephod that Gideon had made (8:27) seems to confirm that the installation of the ephod in Gideon's hometown did not signify a return to Canaanite worship at that time, but was a form of prostitution, since it shifted the spotlight away from Yahweh by focusing it on Gideon.

Having diminished Yahweh as the source of security and hope and elevated Gideon as the human instrument of liberation, the Israelites return to Baal worship as soon as Gideon dies. Verse 34 says that the Israelites "did not remember the LORD their God, who had rescued them from the hands of all their enemies on every side." This forgetfulness (see 3:7) was already evident during Gideon's lifetime, when Israel attributed victory to him instead of Yahweh. Thus when people focus their attention on human accomplishments and deeds, they become susceptible to searching for substitutes as soon as the leader is gone, because they have not been trained to put their hope and dependence on Yahweh alone.

---

3. The number seventy seems to be an idealized number. See the seventy kings that Adoni-bezek vanquished (1:7); seventy sons of the judge Abdon (12:14); the seventy sons of Ahab (2 Kgs 10:1–7); the seventy persons of Jacob's family who went to Egypt (Gen 46:27). See Boling, *Judges*, 162; Block, *Judges*, 303, n. 713.

Nevertheless, the narrative does not minimize the importance of honoring those who have willingly taken on the mantle of leadership and courageously risked themselves on behalf of others. Indeed, part of Israel's failure is that they "failed to show any loyalty to the family of Jerubaal (Gideon), in spite of all the good things he had done for them" (8:35). The word used for *hesed*, "loyalty," cannot be captured fully by English translations.[4] The word has to do with obligations and commitments that are expected in certain relationships, as between relatives or friends, or between host and guests, master and servants, husband and wife, king and subjects, or those who mutually help one another. This commitment goes beyond legal duties, since it is motivated by genuine goodwill towards the other.[5] Since Gideon risked his life on behalf of his fellow Israelites as part of his expression of *hesed*, he and his family deserve to be treated with gratitude and loyalty, with acts that will honor his memory and lineage. The Israelites, however, fail to fulfill the requirements of *hesed*.

At first, the Israelites went overboard, attributing to Gideon what properly belonged to God. Their offer of kingship and the surrendering of their spoils of battle were not part of what was due to Gideon (8:22–26). However, after Gideon dies, they violate his memory by murdering his family. This is a clear violation of *hesed*, as shown in 9:16–19. Although the word *hesed* is not mentioned in these verses, the word *'emet* (variously translated as "faithfulness," "good faith," "honorably," "in sincerity," 'in truth") is often paired with *hesed*.[6] The *hesed-'emet* word pair, when used for human relationships, deals with obligations and responsibilities that arise from a certain relationship, or in return for an action done by another person. Because Gideon risked his life for the sake of Israel, it is Israel's obligation to honor Gideon's name and legacy by treating his progeny well. Instead, they massacre nearly all his sons.

---

4. Other translations are "steadfast love" (ESV), "faithful gratitude" (NJB), "kindness" (NASB, NJKV).
5. Robin Routledge, "*Hesed* as Obligation: A Re-examination," *TynBul* 46/1 (1995): 181, 185.
6. H. J. Stoebe, "*Hesed*," *TLOT* 2:450. See Gen 24:49 (the servant to Abraham's relatives–to give Rebekah for Isaac's wife–is considered to be dealing kindly and in truth); Josh 2:14 (the spies promise to deal kindly and faithfully with Rahab after she hid them); Prov 3:3 (exhortation not to let steadfastness and loyalty leave a person); Prov 14:22 (those who plan good will find steadfastness and loyalty); Prov 20:28 (these qualities preserve the king). On the human level, these qualities are found to be important. They seem to have to do with the fulfillment of obligations or responsibilities that arise from a relationship or an action done by another. The word pair is also applied to God's qualities (Gen 24:27; Exod 34:6; 2 Sam 2:6, 15:20; Pss 25:10; 40:11).

In Filipino society, those who render us a favor – such as hospitality, financial resources in times of need, a connection to a steady job, or risking their lives on our behalf – deserve gratitude, respect, and some return for their good service. In Filipino culture, we refer to this sense of appreciation for those who stand with us in solidarity as *utang na loob*.[7] Sadly, utilitarianism has eroded traditional Filipino values so that those who are productive and successful are honored, while those who are no longer deemed "useful" are often relegated to the sidelines, even though they may have contributed much before.

Yet *utang na loob* can be abused, as when people do "kind deeds" in order to manipulate others to support their agendas out of a sense of obligation, rather than a sense of common humanity and shared solidarity. *Utang na loob* can also be abused when recipients look to the one who responded to their needs as a patron or as the source of their security and hope, rather than looking to God as the provider, deliverer, and sustainer of life. Both of these abuses of *utang na loob* occur in the Gideon story. Gideon used his deed of delivering Israel to incur favors from the Israelites that would enable him to live as king. On the other hand, Israel looked to Gideon instead of Yahweh as the source of their deliverance, thus putting themselves in a position where Gideon could exploit their sense of obligation.

9:1–6 THE DESTRUCTIVE SIDE OF FAMILY TIES

The Gideon narrative traces the slow, painful, and exciting transformation of a hesitant young man into an important leader, but his death leads to the beginning of a political religious dynasty, with the seventy sons ruling after him (9:2). However, because Gideon's sons do not go through the prism of Gideon's formative process, they do not automatically inherit his leadership capabilities. The text does not convey how the sons of Gideon ruled over Israel. The verb "to rule," or *mashal* in Hebrew, can have a political sense and often coincides with *malak,* which means "to rule as king."[8] However, it would have been impossible for all seventy sons of Gideon to rule as king at the same time, so their rule must have been exercised in a more general

---

7. Virgilio Enriquez, *From Colonial to Liberation Psychology: The Philippine Experience* (Manila: De La Salle University Press, 1994), 68–70. This understanding of *utang na loob* goes beyond common definitions that have to do with reciprocity or the mere returning of favor.
8. J. A. Soggin, "*msl*," *TLOT* 2:690.

political sense of having some control over Shechem, but not necessarily having direct governance over its affairs.⁹

The text tells us that Abimelek goes to his relatives on his mother's side in Shechem to solicit their support for a power-grab. He bases his appeal on the following arguments. First, he says that it is better for one man to rule over the people than all the seventy sons of Jerubaal (9:2). Thus in the interest of effective leadership, he argues that he should be installed as the absolute decision-maker over all the others. However, when Abimelek speaks of "one man to rule over you," he is referring to ruling as king, not just in the sense of general oversight. The Shechemites must understand this, for later in the story they crown Abimelek as king (9:6).

Abimelek's second argument emphasizes his blood ties with the people of Shechem: "for I am your flesh and blood" (9:2).¹⁰ He is referring, of course, to his mother's relatives who are living in Shechem – not to all the inhabitants of the city. But he asks his relatives to appeal to the lords of Shechem¹¹ on his behalf. And the lords of Shechem, apparently proud of their native boy, support his bid for power and treat him as extended family, saying: "'He is related to us'" (9:3). Having a relation in a position of power would be to their advantage, since they would be able to push their agendas and glean the benefits of being a near relation of the king. Thus Abimelek uses his family ties to seize power for himself, remove any threats to his plan to become the absolute ruler, and consolidate his power.

> **NEPOTISM IN ASIAN SOCIETIES**
>
> The Asian political system is riddled with the problem of nepotism, where people entrusted with political power use their position to grant favors to their family and relatives instead of using it on behalf of all the people. Moreover, family dynasties abound even in so-called democracies because people tend to elect one of their relatives or someone from their hometown, even if the person is not qualified. One chronic feature of Philippine politics, which is

---

9. The rulership could have been manifested through some form of tribute or tax. See Philistine rule over the Israelites (Judg 14:4, 15:11).
10. The idiom in Hebrew reads, "I am your flesh and bone," a formula used to refer to kinship ties (see Gen 2:23, 29:14; 2 Sam 5:1). See Gordon J. Wenham, *Genesis 1–15*, WBC (Waco, TX: 1987), 70.
11. The NIV translates *ba'ale Shekem* as "citizens of Shechem," but it is more likely that the phrase refers to the leaders of the city, rather than the citizens at large.

> also seen in other Asian democracies, is the presence of political dynasties. Husbands and wives, siblings, uncles and aunties, as well as their sons and daughters all jostle together for a political position, whether as part of the same political party or as opposition. In the Philippines, it is not uncommon to see the husband as governor, the wife as mayor, and the children as members of congress. On top of this, non-elective administrative positions are often occupied by people who are related by blood or by marriage.
>
> The persistence of political dynasties, despite efforts to combat them, may be attributed to family influence – "politics run in the blood," so to speak. But more to the point, running for an elective position is an expensive enterprise and having a wealthy family to back one's political ambitions is a definite advantage. Hence, those who run for public office tend to come from more affluent families. Moreover, only the rich can afford to send their children to the best schools, which prepare them for positions in government or the private sector that become springboards for elective office. This perpetuates a system in which wealth breeds power and power breeds wealth.
>
> Because nepotism and political dynasties concentrate power in the hands of a few families for generations, the power base is never broadened – and this is the goal of true democracy. In the same way, Abimelek's story shows how religious dynasties can also go awry. Asian Christians can learn from this story about the dangers of supporting the relations of a successful and competent political leader, pastor, or head of a Christian organization when they do not possess the necessary gifts and qualities for the task.
>
> The concentration of power in the hands of a few not only excludes many people from making decisions about affairs that concern their lives, but it also opens up a path for abuse. When the normal systems of accountability are short-circuited by family ties, those whose positions should uphold the common good often promote their own vested interests instead. The unbridled exercise of power, along with a lack of accountability, makes the system vulnerable to the use of violence, especially against those who might threaten the interests of the family and its cronies. Hence, Philippine politics is riddled by assassinations and political killings – of both politicians as well as journalists who try to expose the truth.

Abimelek's road to kingship is messy and requires the elimination of those who might possibly prevent him from being crowned king. There are still seventy living sons of Gideon, and each has a claim to kingship, and all are enjoying the benefits of rulership. Moreover, Abimelek is the son of a concubine (9:31), so it is inconceivable for him to be elevated above his siblings.

Thus Abimelek's first step is to kill his brothers, but he cannot do it on his own, so he hires hatchet men – "reckless scoundrels"– to help him. The lords of Shechem supply the cash for the gruesome task, giving "him seventy shekels of silver from the temple of Baal-berith" (9:4). We learn earlier in the narrative that the Israelites installed Baal-berith (literally, "Baal of the covenant") as their god after Gideon died (8:33).[12] Apparently, the aristocracy of Shechem feels comfortable with getting money from the treasury of their god (presumably from the accumulated offerings of worshippers) to achieve their objective of putting someone in power who will work for their own interests. Since they obviously have no problem disregarding the interests of their god for their own political interests, religion has become a mere tool rather than a way of life.

It is worth noting here that the first king of Israel (apparently an aberrant one) was installed through the combined efforts of a despot who claimed to have a legitimate right to the kingship, the support of the aristocracy, and the use of religious wealth. In Asia, the perpetuation of despotic rulers comes about as a confluence of several factors: a claim to some sort of legitimacy by reason of military accomplishment, legal support or kinship, the support of the religious establishment, and the complicity of the wealthy aristocrats and the military elite. With such deep-seated support, it is very difficult to remove an oppressive leader.

With the elimination of the threat, Abimelek is crowned king by "all the lords of Shechem and all the household of Millo beside the oak, the pillar in Shechem" (9:6, trans. mine). However, Abimelek's ascendancy to kingship is an aberration that is not only ahead of its time, but also ahead of Yahweh's purposes (see 1 Sam 8). Abimelek clearly introduces something new in Israel, although it is not new for the nations surrounding Israel (1 Sam 8:5). His plan seems efficient – one person making a decision is better than seventy people all voicing their opinions. Yet to implement his new plan, he has to remove all threats that will challenge his position. This requires not only the consolidation of his political base, but also an explosion of violence that silences all dissenting voices.

For the sake of efficiency, some leaders argue that it is necessary to eliminate all threats and silence all voices. While efficiency and effectiveness are important, the essential heartbeat of the Christian life is to be a follower of

---

12. Baal worship was widespread in the Canaanite region, although there were many local manifestations. See Karel van der Toorn et al., *Dictionary of Deities and Demons in the Bible*, 133, 136. *Berith* may refer to the function of the Baal as the witness or guarantor of the covenant (Toorn, *Dictionary of Deities and Demons*), 272.

God's ways. This means eschewing all forms of manipulation and control in bringing about the fulfillment of one's project.

9:7–15 THE PERILS OF KINGSHIP

In many stories, when a king's son escapes murder by an evil usurper, he usually ascends to kingship at the end of the story, after undergoing severe trials and accomplishing mighty deeds on behalf of the people. Yet Jotham is a strange figure. His appearance shortly after the crowning of Abimelek raises expectations that he will later rescue the people from Abimelek's despotic leadership and then become a wise and benevolent ruler. However, apart from delivering a speech that indicts both Abimelek and the aristocracy of Shechem, Jotham has no other significant role in the story. He does not lead an army or fight battles, nor does he assume leadership after Abimelek's demise. In fact, he disappears after giving his speech, and the story unfolds without him. Perhaps this story emphasizes the fact that true liberation will not come through any human king or instrument. Nevertheless, Jotham's words continue to reverberate throughout the rest of the story. In this way, he serves as a prophet, whose efficacious words in the historical books from Judges to Kings pronounce what is going to take place.

The setting of Jotham's speech at the top of Mt. Gerizim is curious (9:7). Most likely, this does not mean the very top, since Mt. Gerizim rises about a thousand feet from the floor of the valley, and his message would be wasted on the winds. Rather, it might refer to a low overhanging cliff that overlooks the city.[13]

Jotham's speech consists of two parts: the first part is a fable about the trees (9:8–15), and the second part takes the fable and applies it as a judgement to the actions of Abimelek and the aristocrats of Shechem (9:16–20). Jotham introduces the parable with an admonition to the people of Shechem to listen: "Listen to me, lords of Shechem, so that God may listen to you" (9:7, trans. mine). The play on the words "listen" underscores the prophetic quality of Jotham's speech. Heeding the warning in Jotham's speech will result in God's favor towards the leaders of Shechem.

The parable starts with a weak emphatic nuance:[14] "One day the trees went out to anoint a king for themselves" (9:8). The trees approach the olive tree, the fig tree, and the grape vine respectively. The olive and fig trees, along

---

13. Boling, *Judges*, 172.
14. This is indicated by the infinitive absolute in Hebrew (Joüon § 123k).

with the grape vine, play a huge role in the economy and daily life of both ancient and modern Israel. The oil from the fruit of the olive tree is used for culinary and medicinal purposes and for ceremonial anointing, while the fruit is used for food, and the leaves are used for herbal infusions. Raw or dried figs are eaten by themselves and used in desserts, since they are not only delicious, but also believed to strengthen and restore the body. The grapes from the vine are eaten raw, but mostly they are made into wine. The trees and vine respond in similar ways to the offer of kingship, each responding that they are already involved in producing something beneficial and satisfying for human beings. This implies that accepting the position of a king would merely distract them from their primary purposes.

The meaning of the phrase, "sway over the trees," is unclear (9:9, 11, 13). Many commentators take the phrase to have the sense of "to influence, to control, wield authority."[15] However, the usages of the underlying Hebrew word for "sway" (*nua'*) do not seem to support this view. Its basic meaning refers to the motion of moving back and forth, whether this refers to the shaking of a body part (head, hand, lips)[16] or the whole body, as when one trembles in fear or swaggers around like a drunkard.[17] Less common usages refer to the shaking of the doorposts, ripe fruit, and moving the bones of the dead from one place to another.[18] In one instance, the swaying (*nua'*) trees in the wind are compared metaphorically to the shaking of the heart of King Ahaz and the people because of the alliance of Syria and Israel against Judah (Isa 7:1). Literally, "to sway" is an action common in trees. To "sway over the trees" may evoke the image of lording it over them. However, "to sway," as the following section shows, does not connote purposeful action.

Another usage of *nw'* when referring to people is "to wander," that is, to roam back and forth in the land.[19] This meaning of "sway" connotes a futile movement rather than a deliberate action. This is reinforced further by the word pair *nwd*, which is used in connection with *nua'*, and which means "to sway, to be aimless, and homeless."[20] The refusal of the olive, fig, and grape-

---

15. Boling, *Judges*, 173: "The picture is that of the king who nods, sitting above his subjects" (173). According to Burney (273–274), the swaying motion of the tree is "represented as a gesture of authority."
16. 1 Sam 1:13; 2 Kgs 19:21; Job 16:4; Pss 22:7 [8]; 109:25; Isa 37:22; Lam 2:15; Dan 10:10.
17. Exod 20:18. Isa 19:1 (fear); Ps 107:27; Isa 24:20, 29:9 (being drunk).
18. Isa 6:4 (doorposts); Nah 3:12 (fruit); 2 Kgs 23:18 (bones).
19. Gen 4: 12, 14; Num 32:13; 2 Sam 15:20; Pss 59:15; 109:10; Prov 5:6; Jer 14:10; Lam 4:14, 15; Amos 4:8, 8:12.
20. *HALOT* 2:681.

vine to sway over the trees because they are already doing good work further supports the view that the sense of "to sway" (*nua'*) in this passage has to do with the motion of going back and forth without any clear purpose. Such an image would accurately reflect an organization where there are many top-level supervisory roles, but very little is being done on the ground. Outwardly, things appear to be busy, even hectic – the trappings of management and control – but in reality, goals are not being reached, the mission of the organization is not being effectively carried out, and there is very little fruit that will benefit the organization or the community.

While the fable can be regarded as an anti-monarchical "prophecy," it has very important pastoral elements. The fable implies that just as certain trees/vines "know" their task and what they are good at, this also ought to be true of people. In Asian Christianity, the role of the pastor is often elevated, even though there are other roles and gifts within the community of faith, such as healers, administrators, teachers, evangelists, among others. Moreover, there are lay people who have the gifts of the spirit and minister within their families, workplaces, and neighborhoods. The fable seems to suggest that we should know our capacities and gifts and be productive within those possibilities rather than trying to be something we are not. Most importantly, we should not lord our gifts or capacities over others.

On the other hand, some of us may be offered positions of power and authority at some point in our ministry that will require us to leave the work that we are effectively doing. In this case, accepting an administrative position may detract us from doing work that serves the real needs of people. This is not to say that administrative positions and management roles do not benefit the community, but we need to exercise careful discernment before accepting those roles. We need to ask ourselves whether doing so will enhance what we believe God has called us to do rather than just taking us away from it.

The parable, which is couched in a poetic pattern, can be divided into four subsections. In the first three sections, the olive tree, the fig tree, and the vine each refuse the trees' invitation to be king through a rhetorical question:[21]

> Olive Tree: "Should I give up my oil, by which both gods and humans are honored, to hold sway over the trees?" (9:9).
>
> Fig Tree: "Should I give up my fruit, so good and sweet, to hold sway over the trees?" (9:11).

---

21. Graham S. Ogden, "Jotham's Fable: Its Structure and Function in Judges 9," *The Bible Translator* 46, no. 3 (1995): 301–308.

Vine: "Should I give up my wine, which cheers both gods and humans, to hold sway over the trees?" (9:13).

Each question reflects that plant's unwillingness to cease from the good that they are already doing.

This poetic pattern is broken in the fourth subsection, when the trees extend the offer to the thornbush (9:14–15).[22] Although this section begins with the same pattern, the ending is different. This signifies the climax of the parable,[23] which is "calculated to jar the listeners out of the complacency induced by the familiar and rhythmical."[24] The thornbush, rather than refusing to be king, invites the trees to come and take refuge in its shade – if the trees are sincere in making him king. However, if the trees are not acting in good faith, then fire will come out of the thornbush to consume the trees.

The thornbush's response is ironic, for the expression "to be in one's shadow or shade" was a popular expression at that time associated with those who enjoyed the special protection of the king.[25] Though the thornbush claims to offer kingly protection to the trees, in reality it is only a spindly and prickly bramble, with beautiful blossoms but few leaves – thus it cannot offer any shade, and its wood is good only for fires. Even more ironically, the thornbush offers to protect the "cedars of Lebanon," a metaphor used for powerful monarchs.[26] Clearly, the thornbush is claiming more than it can actually deliver, pointing to the pretensions of those in power[27] who project a good image, but do not serve the real needs of people.

Moreover, despite the fact that the thornbush cannot offer the protection it promises, it is capable of issuing a threat. And indeed, although it cannot offer shade, its dry wood and lack of foliage can start a forest fire that can consume the most majestic of trees. So although it cannot deliver on its promises, it has the ability to carry out its threat.

Jotham's fable clearly has an anti-monarchical character. First, it mocks the trees in their desire for a king because they are willing to settle for someone who is not fit to rule them, just to satisfy their desire for a king. This echoes 1 Samuel 8, in which Israel demands that Samuel give them a king "like all the other nations" (1 Sam 8:20). The trees are foolishly putting themselves in

---

22. The *attad* tree.
23. Ogden, "Jotham's Fable," 303. See also Matthews, *Judges & Ruth*, 106.
24. Boling, *Judges*, 174.
25. Ibid.
26. Ibid.; see also Soggin, *Judges*, 176.
27. Ibid.

a position where somebody can threaten them with destruction. The thornbush does not care about the trees' welfare; it just wants to exercise its power. Secondly, the fable mocks the thornbush for being so presumptuous in accepting the kingship when it can only offer wild boasts. Thus the fable mocks those who desire a king as well as those who think they can be king.

Some argue that the fable is not against the institution of kingship, but serves to rebuke the members of the community who are not willing to take up leadership responsibilities, leaving the position to irresponsible members to the detriment of the community.[28] Eugene Maly supports this interpretation: "The meaning of the original fable, therefore, was clearly not directed against kingship itself, but against those who refused, for insufficient reasons, the burden of leadership."[29] There is nothing in the text, however, to indicate that the positions taken by the olive tree, the fig tree, and the vine are not desirable. The ironic tone is directed wholly towards the trees who desire a king and the thornbush, which suggests a strong anti-kingship polemic.

The fable probably emerged early in Israel's history, as it was transitioning to the monarchy, from groups that did not see any positive function in the institution of kingship.[30] It likely existed before the narrative in Judges[31] and would have been known by Jotham's audience, but Jotham gives it a twist that applies specifically to the power-grab of Abimelek and the elders of Shechem.

The twist relies on the common phrase, *be'emeth*, which literally means "in truth," and which was used in covenants to signify fidelity to an agreement[32] (9:19, 15, 16).[33] This phrase can refer to lack of falsehood, being sincere or fair, and sometimes is translated "surely" or "truly," but in many instances, it is used to express Israel's or individuals' faithfulness to their covenant with God (Josh 24:14; 1 Sam 12:24; 1 Kgs 2:4; 3:6; 2 Kgs 20:3; Isa 38:3). It is also used in God's promise of faithfulness to Israel (Jer 32:41; Zec 8:8). Since Jotham makes the speech on top of Mt. Gerizim – the site in which the Israelites were reminded of the demands of the covenant and the

---

28. Gerald Edie Gerbrandt, *Kingship according to the Deuteronomistic History* (Atlanta, GA: Scholars Press, 1986), 129.
29. Eugene Maly, "The Jotham Fable – Anti-Monarchical?" *CBQ* 22 (1960): 303. Barnabas Lindars agrees ("Jotham's Fable – A New Form Critical Analysis," *JTS* 24 [1973]: 355–366).
30. Gerbrandt, 130; F. Crüsemann, *Der Widerstand gegen das Königtum* (Wissenschaftliche Monographien zum Alten und Neuen Testament, 49; Neukirchen: Neukirchener Verlag, 1978), 19–32; Soggin, *Judges*, 175.
31. Soggin, *Judges*, 174–175.
32. Boling, *Judges*, 173.
33. NIV translates this as "really," but this phrase is too weak to convey the full sense of the term.

blessings that come from obeying it (Deut 11:29; 27:12; Josh 8:33)[34] – the allusion to the covenant becomes clear.

By alluding to the covenant through the speech of the thornbush, Jotham directly reminds his audience of the covenant they made with Abimelek to crown Abimelek king. He also suggests that the Shechemites' motive was insincere because they crowned Abimelek to use him for their own advantage – and not because they think he is fit to rule them. The lack of good faith on the part of the Shechemites will only lead to their destruction by the very person they crowned as king. This unexpected twist makes the impact of the fable that much greater on the listeners.

According to Rainer Albertz, the decentralized power structure in the period of the judges expresses a deliberate political concern:

> The tribal alliance of Israel derives from a political option which is opposed to domination, and which by deliberately standing apart from the monarchical Canaanite city-states allows the institutionalization of political power only to the degree that is absolutely necessary for safeguard[ing] the survival of families and clans.[35]

But even more important than safeguarding the freedom of families is the understanding that Yahweh is king – and the only political authority that can unite the tribal alliance. "Yahweh was experienced as the one who created social solidarity beyond the limits of clan and tribe."[36]

Thus, the advent of the monarchy brought with it conflicts, especially since the king in other ancient Near Eastern nations had divine status and therefore could be seen as a human rival power to Yahweh.[37] The king could arrogate for himself the power and roles that the ancient Israelites were to give to Yahweh alone. He could see himself as the interpreter of the divine will and could silence those whose authority was derived from the action of the spirit (e.g. the prophets), even though the authority of the king himself may not have derived from the endowment of the spirit, but from hereditary succession.[38]

---

34. McCann, *Judges*, 73.
35. Rainer Albertz, *A History of Israelite Religion in the Old Testament Period*, Vol. 1: From the Beginnings to the End of the Monarchy (Louisville, KY: Westminster/John Knox, 1994), 75.
36. Ibid., 78.
37. Walther Eichrodt, *Theology of the Old Testament* (Philadelphia, PA: Westminster, 1961), 439–440.
38. Eichrodt, 1:441–442.

While the kings in Israel were to be faithful shepherds and guardians of the people under Yahweh, the books of Judges through Kings reveals that the kings tended to take more from people than they gave (see 1 Sam 8:11–17). This taking enhanced the power of the king, developing a social and political hierarchy that further entrenched the king's power.

This is a familiar tale in the history of the church and society. Too often, those who have power become self-serving. Pastors of churches and leaders of parachurch organizations, as well as politicians, can build little empires on the backs of the faith and gifts of the people who support them. While Yahweh wants servant-kings, self-servings kings are often the sad reality.

9:16–20 DEALING WITH INTEGRITY

After concluding the fable, Jotham addresses his audience directly, using the language of the thornbush to unmask the Shechemites' lack of integrity. Jotham's speech begins with the conditional *if*, which he repeats three times:[39]

- *if* you have acted (*'asah*) in good faith (*'emeth*) and integrity (*tamim*) when you made Abimelek king, and
- *if* you have acted (*'asah*) fairly (*tob*) in relation to Jerubaal and his sons, and
- *if* you have done (*'asah*) to him according to what he deserves (literally, "according to his hand") (9:16, trans. mine).

The *if* in these clauses does not mean "if . . . and you have," but rather "if . . . and you have not." The parallel structure implies that their actions in supporting Abimelek's power bid and in eliminating Jerubaaal's sons spring from the same source: a lack of good faith, integrity, and fairness in dealing with others. If their evil intentions towards Jerubaal and his sons are reflected in their evil motives to make Abimelek king, this suggests that integrity is expressed in one's dealings with everybody rather than in one particular relationship.

The immorality of the actions of the Shechemites is further emphasized through the repeated use of the Hebrew root word *'asah*, which means "to do" or "to act." The first conditional clause applies to their actions in installing Abimelek as king. In this clause, *tamim* (integrity) forms a word pair with *'emeth* (good faith), which reinforces the meaning of "integrity, honesty, sincerity, or good faith." The second and third conditional clauses have to do with the Shechemites' dealings with Jerubaal and his sons. The two clauses

---

39. Ogden, "Jotham's Fable," 305.

form a pair: to act fairly means to deal with someone according to what he or she deserves.

And what did Gideon deserve? Jotham points out that his father risked his life[40] in order to rescue them from the control of Midian (9:17), and so the least Gideon deserves is kindness for his progeny. In several instances in Scripture, the kindness of the father is rewarded by a similar kindness to his offspring.[41] Whereas Gideon acted in accordance with the kindness demanded from co-sharers of Yahweh's covenant with the Israelites, the Shechemites killed all of Gideon's offspring, except the one they could exploit for their own advantage. In doing so, they show a total disregard for covenant relationships and a total disrespect for Gideon's memory and the good he did for Israel.

Interestingly, Jotham's indictment is directed against the Shechemites rather than Abimelek. Perhaps this suggests that the despotic actions of an individual can only be possible if there are others who are willing to support him, especially those who can gain power through the arrangement.

The Shechemites might argue that their actions were demanded by covenant loyalty to their own kin. However, Jotham's argument shows that their actions towards Jerubaal and his family show a lack of respect for covenant obligations, and so their favorable actions towards their own kin cannot be regarded as a faithful expression of covenant obligations. Some people may justify wrongdoing by saying, "I did it for the sake of my family." The flaw in this argument is that one cannot act with integrity in relation to one's family if one does not act with integrity towards others in the community, especially towards those who have sacrificed themselves for the sake of the community.

In verse 19, Jotham repeats the condition stated in verse 16, combining phrases from the first condition (regarding the crowning of Abimelek) and the second condition (pertaining to Jerubaal and his sons), followed by the logical conclusion of the condition: "So have you acted honorably and in good faith towards Jerubaal and his family today? If you have, may Abimelek

---

40. The literal translation is "he threw his life in front," indicating Gideon's willingness to rescue the Israelites from Midianite oppression without any reservations and "without a thought of personal safety" (Burney, 176).

41. David treated Jonathan's descendants well because of his covenant with Jonathan (2 Sam 9:1–8). On the other hand, David wanted to treat Hanun, the heir of Nahash, the king of the Ammonites, with kindness since Nahash had shown kindness to him. The son, however, mistrusted David and humiliated David's men (2 Sam 10:1–5). The word for kindness used here is *hesed*, which means covenant loyalty. Although the word *hesed* is not used in relation to Gideon and the Israelites, Gideon's action show *hesed* or covenant loyalty by virtue of the fact that the Israelites, including the Shechemites, were bonded together by the same covenant.

be your joy, and may you be his, too!" (9:19). The tone is obviously ironic,[42] since the nobles of Shechem did not act with integrity in relation to Jerubaal and his family, and so the "rejoicing" will not take place. Instead, the "curse" of Jotham (see v. 57) is that Abimelek and the Shechemites, having acted in bad faith, will seek to destroy each other.

One important dimension of the prophetic task is to call God's people back into covenant faithfulness with Yahweh. We see this in Jotham's fable. However, the story also highlights the vulnerability of such a task and ministry. Jotham assumes no religious position. He has no institutional power. He is the bearer of the prophetic word, and he disappears afterwards. Thus his word of intervention and correction is marginalized in the story. This is often the case in Christian groups when leaders with new plans are readily followed. Abimelek had a new plan –the kingship. However, those who offer correctives to the new plan are seldom understood and are frequently marginalized. Hence a "prophet" often walks a lonely road.

9:21–56 RETRIBUTIVE JUSTICE

Subsequent events in the narrative depict the fallout of Jotham's predictions. For three years, Abimelek reigns over Israel, while his brother Jotham disappears from the scene.

The turn of events is preceded by a theological explanation from the narrator:

> The Lord sent an evil spirit[43] between Abimelek and the lords of Shechem, so that the lords of Shechem dealt treacherously with Abimelek, in order to repay the violence done to the seventy sons of Jerubaal and to lay the guilt for their blood on their brother Abimelek who killed them, and on the lords of Shechem, who abetted Abimelek to kill his brothers. (9:23–24, trans. mine)

For many Christians, an evil spirit is a supernatural personal being originating from Satan, whose purpose is to afflict both believers and non-believers and keep them from the knowledge of God. Yet the above verses show that in this particular situation, the source of the evil spirit is God, who sent it to create dissention between Abimelek and the Shechemites. Its ultimate purpose

---

42. Ogden, "Jotham's Fable," 306.
43. Most translations (NRSV, ESV, NAB) render the phrase *ruakh ra'ah* literally as "evil spirit," as did the older versions of NIV. But the 2011 NIV translates the phrase as "animosity." The NJPS and NJB retain the "spirit," but qualify it as "spirit of discord."

is to bring Abimelek and the lords of Shechem to justice[44] by causing them to experience in their own persons the evil they did to others. This exemplifies a clear case of retribution.[45]

In Hebrew, the phrase for "evil spirit" is *ruakh ra'ah*, which is used only once more in the Old Testament in the story of Saul.[46] In both stories, the evil spirit comes from God: "God sent an evil spirit . . ." (Judg 9:23, NASB, ESV); "an evil spirit from the LORD" (1 Sam 16:14). In other instances in the Saul narrative, the evil spirit is described as *ruakh elohim ra'ah*, which literally means "an evil spirit from God," with the genitive functioning in the sense of source.

The phrase is less troubling if one understands the nuances of the words *ruakh* (spirit) and *ra'ah* (evil) in the Old Testament. *Ruakh* can mean wind, breeze, and breath, with emphasis on its dynamic nature that set things into motion.[47] It is also used to describe a disposition, frame of mind, or characteristic, such as "a spirit of wisdom" (Exod 31:3: Isa 11:2), or a psychological or mental state, such as "a spirit of jealousy" (Num 5:14, KJV) or "a spirit of prostitution" (Hos 4:12; 5:4). In the OT, "spirit" is often understood as an impersonal force of power rather than a personal being. On the other hand, *ra'ah* does not necessarily mean evil in the sense of demonic or of the devil, but can simply mean bad, calamitous, or destructive. Thus *ruakh ra'ah* can refer to a *power* that can govern a person's actions and emotional state, leading to destructive results. The *ruakh ra'ah* that Yahweh sends sours the fragile relationship between Abimelek and the Shechemites, which was already based on self-interest. As a result, mistrust and sinister plots erupt between them. The translation "spirit of discord" (NJPS, NJB) or "spirit of ill will" (NKJV) captures this meaning well.

Theologically, the narrator's statement, "God sent an evil spirit . . ." helps to express the theme of retribution. This is reiterated in 9:56–57 through a summary statement with a chiastic structure:

A "And God caused to return
   B the evil of Abimelek – which he did to his father in killing
   his seventy brothers –
   B' and the evil of the men of Shechem
A' God caused to return upon their heads . . ."[48]

---

44. Ogden, "Jotham's Fable," 306–307.
45. See T. A. Boogart, "Stone for Stone: Retribution in the Story of Abimelech and Shechem," *JSOT* 32 (1985): 45–56.
46. See 1 Sam 16:14–16, 23; 18:10.
47. R. Albertz, C. Westermann, "*rûaḥ*, spirit," *TLOT* 3:1204.
48. The translation is from Boogart, "Stone for Stone," 49.

Among Filipinos, there is a popular belief that any evil deed will return to the doers later in life, so that whatever they do to others will also happen to them. Filipinos call this *karma*, where retributive justice acts like an impersonal force that corrects imbalances in the universe. In contrast, the Bible attributes retribution to a divine being who calls people to accountability for their deeds. In this way, retribution is a form of judgement for acts of violence and injustice. This is clearly stressed in the last verse of Judges 9: "The curse of Jotham son of Jerubaal came on them" (v. 57). In the OT, curses fall upon those who are unfaithful to the covenant. The lack of covenant faithfulness expressed by Abimelek and the Shechemites towards Jerubaal and his family is recompensed when they experience the same lack of covenant faithfulness, integrity, and good faith in their relationships with each other.

This tragic story is particularly pertinent for Asian Christians, who often encounter various religious views regarding retribution and justice in the world. For some, the bad deeds of this lifetime play themselves out in a lower form of existence in one's next earthly life. For those who hold a reciprocal fatalism, any evil people do will rebound upon their heads in this lifetime. In the Abimelek story, Yahweh is the God of justice. While God's justice is primarily restorative, so that through grace there is the possibility of change by heeding the words of a prophet, God's justice can also be retributive. Wrongdoing may be healed and restored through repentance, faith, and obedience. However, God's "severe" way may also come into play. This does not suggest a vindictive God, but a God who, for the sake of the community as a whole, will bring someone's misuse of power to an end so that a new beginning can be made in harmony with Yahweh's purposes.

Boogart traces the unfolding theme of retribution in the rest of the narrative.[49] Just as Abimelek went to Shechem and got help from his kin to conspire against the sons of Jerubaal (vv. 1–3), Gaal goes to Shechem with his brothers to conspire against Abimelek (vv. 26–27). In the same way that Abimelek emphasized blood ties to gain the support of the Shechemites (v. 2), Gaal also emphasizes the importance of blood ties – for as a Shechemite, he is a closer blood relative than Abimelek (v. 28). Moreover, just as the Shechemites trusted Abimelek (v. 3), they quickly shift their loyalties to Gaal (v. 39).

However, though Jerubaal's sons were unsuspecting of their brother and seemed to offer no resistance to his plots, Abimelek, wizened by his own

---

49. Boogart, "Stone for Stone," 50–53.

schemes, has informants among the Shechemites. Upon learning of the conspiracy, he does not hesitate to wage a surprise and violent attack against Gaal and his men, successfully driving them out of Shechem (vv. 30–41). While the people of the city suffer under Abimelek's attack, the conspirators themselves – the lords of Shechem – flee to the city's underground stronghold, the temple of Baal-berith. Ironically, they used the money from the temple of Baal-berith to support Abimelek's murderous plot against his brothers, and yet now they appeal to the same god as they flee from Abimelek as he massacres the city's inhabitants (vv. 42–45). With wrathful vengeance, Abimelek and his men then burn the tower, along with the thousand men and women hiding inside it (vv. 46–49). Thus in the same way that the Shechemites helped Abimelek to murder his brothers (vv. 4–5), they themselves are murdered brutally by Abimelek (vv. 34–40). Abimelek's actions also mirror those of his father, Gideon, who acted with cruel brutality towards those who spurned him (see 8:16–17).

The killing spree so energizes Abimelek that he goes on to capture another city, Thebes, whose inhabitants have nothing to do at all with the conspiracy (vv. 50–52). The lust for killing and the experience of having unrestrained power over people's lives can desensitize people until they no longer feel remorse about killing, even if their victims are innocent. Perhaps this explains the despotic regimes that kill people without any compunction, such as the horrors of Auschwitz, or the killing fields of Cambodia, or the genocide in Darfur. Such events remind us that the decision between life and death is seductive and must be exercised with caution and constrained by law and judicial authority. They also reveal how violent streaks in human nature can be worked into frenzy in the heat of a moment.

Mercifully, Abimelek is killed before he can cause more harm – especially against the innocent (vv. 52–54). Ironically, Abimelek killed his brothers on one stone (v. 5), while he himself is killed by a single stone when a woman drops a millstone out of a tower on his head (v. 53). Abimelek is so ashamed that he would rather die quickly in the hands of his armor-bearer than be humiliated by the thought that he has been killed by a woman (v. 54).

This story offers a sad commentary about how abuses of power can be abetted by family ties, particularly when there is lack of integrity and covenant faithfulness. Such unchecked power can unleash horrific violence – not only against former allies and friends, but also against innocent victims.

THE AMBIGUITY OF POWER

The Abimelek passage highlights the frequent move in history towards the centralization of power – both in church and in society. More communal forms of power are often seen as too messy, slow, and cumbersome. Thus one king makes more sense than the communal power of many. One bishop makes more sense than a group of elders in the governance of the church. One executive director for a Christian organization is more efficient than a plurality of leadership. Such views reiterate the rationalization processes that mark the modern world. However, more communal forms of power may help forestall movements towards holocausts.

Another message we learn from the Abimelek narrative is that the quest for centralized power typically involves the disempowerment of others – and in this case, the perpetration of brutal murders. In order to attain centralized power, all forms of opposition and threat may need to be eliminated or kept at bay. This is also true in the history of the church, where the voice of laity has been kept at bay so that the clergy could maintain control.

One inherent danger in taking positions of power and governance is that we might be tempted to misuse power to eliminate all opposition in order to gain what we perceive as good. For example, we may have a good vision for church, organization, or society, yet become impatient with the slow process of decision-making. Then we may become tempted to use our power to impose our will on others by excluding them in the decision-making process. In the political arena, this often leads to more violent forms of imposition – even to the point of silencing all opposition through murder. These narratives reveal that any form of governance that is unjustly established cannot bear good fruit. It cannot deliver on its promises for creating a peaceful and flourishing society. It can only carry out self-protective threats.

Nevertheless, other parts of the OT show a positive evaluation of kingship, as revealed by God's establishment of an eternal covenant with David and God's approval of Josiah and Hezekiah, kings of Judah. The God of the Bible is not opposed to social and political structures and forms of organizing life, for Yahweh delegates his power and authority to authorized leaders, such as prophet, priest, and king. Thus political forms of life are seen as possible and even necessary for a society to flourish.

Still, this narrative warns that any human form of governance – whether kingship or democracy – that loses sight of God's lordship will become subject to deviance. While contemporary Christians can and should serve in society, government, and other social institutions, they will have to live in the tension of being loyal to God amidst their social and political responsibilities.

JUDGES 10:6–12:7

The Marginalization of Yahweh

The words "marginalization" or "marginalized" suggest groups of people or sectors in society from the peripheries. Politically, the marginalized do not have a part or voice in decision-making. Socially, they are excluded from the mainstream of life and become almost invisible. Economically, they do not have access to resources. If we have experienced marginalization at some point in our lives, we know how it feels to be excluded.

With the Gideon narrative, the theme of marginalization becomes stronger in the book of Judges; yet it does not depict the marginalization of people, but of God. Despite the role that Yahweh played in Israel's victory against the Midianites, Yahweh becomes marginalized as Gideon magnifies his own contributions to the liberating process and minimizes Yahweh's role and power. In the account of Abimelech's rulership, Abimelech takes center stage, further marginalizing Yahweh, who enters the story only as a troubler (9:23) and the bringer of retribution (9:56–57). In the Jephthah narrative, Yahweh's name is constantly on Jephthah's lips, but Jephthah thinks that the victory is brought about by his own political skills and bargaining power, thereby diminishing Yahweh's presence in this story.

In some sense, to speak of God's marginalization is a contradiction, since God always has access to resources and power. But as the Jephthah narrative shows, God's name can be at the forefront of people's speech, even while God is at the periphery of their decisions and actions. Such marginalization happens when characters use the name of God to preserve and advance their own interests.

Utilitarianism, which makes use of things and people in order to achieve certain outcomes, is a characteristic of the global modern world – even in the Asian setting, where the traditional values are marked by relationships and honor. Christians bring a utilitarian attitude into their relationship with God when God becomes a tool to achieve certain desired outcomes. Such utilitarianism can lead to tragic results, as we see in the Jephthah story.

The Jephthah narrative cycle can be divided into five episodes, according to the characters that appear in each episode. At the heart of each episode is a dialogue between two characters, whether the character is an individual or a group.[1] In the dialogue portion of each episode, the characters are involved in some form of negotiation or confrontation.

Episode One (10:6–16)	Israel and Yahweh
Episode Two (10:17–11:11)	Jephthah and the Gileadites
Episode Three (11:12–28)	Jephthah and the Ammonite King
Episode Four (11:29–40)	Jephthah and his Daughter
Episode Five (12:1–6)	Jephthah and the Ephraimites[2]

10:6–16 THE DIMINISHMENT OF YAHWEH

The literary setting for the dialogue between Israel and Yahweh repeats the deuteronomistic framework, which is similar to the introduction to other narrative cycles in the book. However, there are some indications that a shift in the recurrent framework is taking place. First, instead of using the formulaic phrase, "Israel did evil in the eyes of the LORD," the narrative gives a detailed list of the gods that the Israelites served (10:6), emphasizing the extent to which they have followed other gods. Not only did the Israelites serve the Canaanites gods – the Baals and the Astartes – but they also adopted the gods of the other nations around them, including those of Syria (Aram), Phoenecia (Sidon), Moab, Ammon, and Philistia.

The next phrase follows the typical cyclical formula: "So the anger of the LORD was kindled against Israel, and he sold them into the hand of the Philistines and into the hand of the Ammonites" (10:7, ESV). As in the other cycles, the narrative emphasizes the severity of the oppression: "who [the Ammonites] that year shattered and crushed them [the Israelites]" (10:8; see also 4:3; 6:6). The verb "to shatter," which is used previously in Exodus to describe God's actions against the Egyptian army (Exod 15:6), is utilized here to describe the enemy's actions against the Israelites. The verb parallels a similar verb, "to crush," which is also used to describe the stone that cracked open Abimelech's head (9:53).[3] The physical metaphor of "shattering" and "crushing" stresses the brutality of Israel's subjugated existence. The oppression is located within the Transjordan tribes in Gilead, but the strength of the

---

1. Polzin, *Moses and the Deuteronomist*, 177.
2. This structure is modified from Webb, *Judges: Integrated Reading*, 42–73. See also Webb, *Book of Judges*, 302.
3. See McCann, *Judges*, 78.

oppression is so great that the Ammonites can cross the Jordan and fight the tribes on the other side–Judah, Benjamin, and Ephraim. Thus the Israelite tribes from the central regions cannot be called upon for aid since they have to defend their own borders as well.

Secondly, phrases from the programmatic framework at the beginning of the book of Judges (2:11–21) are repeated here. The accusation, "they forsook the LORD," is repeated (10:6; see also 2:12, 13), highlighting the relational character of the "evil" that Israel did in the sight of the Lord. Another reiterated phrase, "they were pressed hard" (10:9 trans. mine; see also 2:15), shows the effect of the oppression on the spirit of the Israelites. This echoing of the programmatic framework, which establishes the theological lens through which the rest of the narratives can be seen, reveals the pivotal character of the Jephthah narrative. As a turning point, the events that transpire in this narrative provide clues to understanding the deterioration that occurs in the last part of the book of Judges.[4]

Utilitarian Confession

The most significant departure from the cyclical framework, however, is that for the first time, Israel's cry is accompanied by a confession of sin (10:10). This confession introduces the dialogue between Israel and Yahweh, which forms the heart of episode one (10:10–16).

> The Israelites cried to the Lord: "We have sinned against you for we have abandoned the Lord and have served the Baals." (10)

The Lord said to the Israelites: "Did I not deliver you from the control of the Egyptians, the Amorites, the Ammonites, the Philistines – the Sidonians, the Amalekites, the Maon who oppressed you; you cried out to me and I delivered you from their control? Yet you have abandoned me and have served other gods. Therefore, I will no longer deliver you. Go and cry out to the gods that you have chosen. Let them save you at the time of your distress" (11–14).

> The Israelites cried to the Lord: "We have sinned. Do to us according to what is good in your sight. Only rescue us today." (15)

> So they put aside their foreign gods from their midst and they served the Lord. And he became impatient because of the hardship of Israel. (16, trans. mine)

---

4. Webb sees the Jephthah narrative as crucial to understanding Judges – so much so that he begins *Judges: Integrated Reading* by analyzing it (41–78). See also David Janzen, "Why the Deuteronomist Told about the Sacrifice of Jephthah's Daughter," *JSOT* 29 (2005): 346.

Israel's confession of sin begins with a formulaic phrase used to admit wrong: "I have sinned" or "We have sinned." The content of Israel's confession echoes the very sin for which they are indicted: "We have abandoned the LORD. We have served the Baals" (see also 2:11–13; 10:6). The confession seems to indicate a turn for the better, as if Israel finally realizes its culpability and genuinely repents, which will lead to a break in the repetitive cycle of sin-oppression-deliverance-rest. After failing for so long, Israel finally gets the message that God has been trying to communicate through this repetitive cycle of events.

But Yahweh's response (10:11–14) comes as a total surprise. Instead of embracing the Israelites and proclaiming forgiveness and restoration, Yahweh repeats the pattern of an indictment speech, echoing the message delivered by the messenger of the Lord in 2:1–3 and by a prophet in 6:8–10. Yet this time, the messenger of judgement is Yahweh himself.

1) Historical Retrospect (11b–12)

   "Did I not deliver you from the control of the Egyptians, the Amorites, the Ammonites, the Philistines – the Sidonians, the Amalekites, the Maon who oppressed you; you cried out to me and I delivered you from their control?"

2) Accusation (13a)

   "But as for you, you have abandoned me and have served other gods."

3) Judgement (13b)

   "Therefore, I will no longer deliver you."

4) Ending Comments (14)

   "Go and cry out to the gods that you have chosen. Let them save you at the time of your distress." (trans. mine)

Compared with the indictment speeches of 2:1–3 and 6:8–10, the historical retrospect in this passage focuses not only on Yahweh's deliverance in the Exodus, but also on God's subsequent deliverance from all the peoples that have oppressed Israel. God seems to be drawing attention to the circular pattern of events in which God and Israel are caught: foreign peoples oppress Israel, Israel cries out to God, and God delivers them.

Moreover, the long list of peoples from which Yahweh has delivered Israel corresponds with the long list of gods that Israel has served (10:6), revealing the direct relationship between Israel's situation of oppression and her idolatry. Yet Israel cannot see this connection. They cry out to God in their suffering, but they are not self-reflective enough to go beyond their physical, emotional, and psychological pain to consider the causes and effects of their own behavior.

> **THE FALSE GODS OF ASIAN SOCIETY**
>
> We often cannot see the connection between the gods we serve and the suffering and distress that we experience in our daily lives. But if we examine the anxieties and fears that oppress us, we might discover that some are caused by gods that we have chosen. For example, we may cry out to God for rest, but we remain compulsive in our work habits. Or, we may cry to God for health, but we are irresponsible about what we eat.
>
> Moreover, Asian societies, which have deep and differing religious systems, tend to emphasize the honoring of cultural and family traditions, social conformity, and the maintenance of a group ethos. In honoring these values, we may indirectly honor the false "gods" of excessive filial piety, disproportionate commitment to a family business, conformity to corrupt practices in the workplace, or the elevation of persons with social and economic status above the general needs of the Christian community. These powerful and systemic pressures can lead to shallow conformity to the way of the gospel and a subsequent shallow repentance, leaving these "gods" intact in our lives, even when we go through the motions of outward renunciation. The challenge is for us to recognize that social and cultural conformity may go a lot deeper than we think, particularly if our churches do not provide Christian formation and discipleship.

God's indictment contrasts what God has done for Israel by continually intervening to bring them out of their oppression with Israel's response – "But as for you, you have abandoned me and have served other gods" (v. 13a, trans. mine). The accusation contains a hint of exasperation and a sense of betrayal, which is clearly expressed in the judgement: "Therefore, I will no longer deliver you" (v.13b, trans. mine). God is ending the cycle by ceasing to be part of Israel's habit-forming negative behavior.[5]

God's speech concludes with an angry comment: "Go and cry out to the gods you have chosen. Let them save you in the time of your distress" (v. 14, trans. mine). The sarcastic tone suggests that God has been aggrieved and pushed to the limits. Yet it also acknowledges that since the Israelites

---

5. Boling, *Judges*, 193.

have abandoned Yahweh for other gods, it is presumptuous and impudent of them to expect help from Yahweh. If the other gods that the Israelites serve are true, then Israel should turn to them for intervention in their distress. Here we see God's profound engagement with humanity – even to the point of frustration. Clearly, the frustration is not arbitrary, for Yahweh has helped Israel again and again. But God can also feel disappointment, which reflects the pain of a God who loves so deeply.

In response, the Israelites reiterate their confession of sin, and their repentance seems to be genuine. First, the confession of sin is followed by an acceptance of responsibility and consequences: "We have sinned; do to us what seems good in your sight" (v. 15a, trans. mine). Secondly, it is followed by acts of repentance: "And they removed the foreign gods from their midst and they served the Lord" (v. 16a, trans. mine). Ironically, God rescued them when they did not turn away from their sin, and yet now that they have repented, God no longer seems interested in helping them.

This raises a question about whether Israel's confession of sin, along with the removal of foreign gods from their midst, signifies a true change of heart. As the rest of the book of Judges shows, their repentance is not genuine. In the first place, the phrase "do to us what seems good in your sight" (v. 15a, trans. mine) can be interpreted to mean that the people cast themselves on providence rather than on the mercy of God.

Moreover, in several instances in the OT, the confession, "We have sinned" or "I have sinned," does not indicate a genuine change of heart and life. In Exodus 9:27–35 (see also Exod 10:16–20), Pharaoh uttered the very same words as a plague ravaged his land, but as soon as the plague was lifted, he continued "to harden his heart." In Numbers 14:40–45 (see also Deut 1:41–45), the Israelites tried to push through with their original plan of occupying the land by overcoming the inhabitants, even though God had explicitly told them not to do so. In this case, Israel's confession of sin did not indicate a willing acknowledgement of wrong, but rather a desire to reverse the consequences of their unbelief and rebellion, which was that they would not be able to enter the land that God had promised. In 1 Samuel 15:24–31, Saul's confession of sin was an attempt to manipulate Samuel to worship with him so that Saul would not lose face before the people, since their approval was very important to Saul. Thus a mere confession of sin may not reveal a heart fully submitted to God, but may be self-serving in order to escape the consequences of sin.[6]

The narrative suggests that Israel confesses their sins and puts away their foreign gods in order to find immediate relief from their suffering. This attitude is revealed by an added line in their confession of sin: "We have sinned . . . rescue us now" (v. 15). Their desire is to gain an instant, short-term solution to the problem of oppression. They do not process their situation, nor search their souls, nor scrutinize their actions to understand the root of their problem. God refuses to be used by Israel in this way. As Polzin comments, "What comes through quite forcefully in this dialogue are both Israel's rather self-serving conversion as an apparent attempt once more to use Yahweh to insure their peace and tranquility, and Yahweh's argument that a slighted and rejected God will be used no longer."[7]

The last line in this episode (10:16b) introduces a painful ambiguity that is not evident in the earlier stories. This ambiguity, while textual, reflects Yahweh's growing ambivalence towards Israel. Most translations render this passage in relation to Yahweh's ongoing concern for Israel's affliction, but others suggest a growing frustration within Yahweh. The Hebrew itself invites this ambiguity. The crux of interpretation lies in two expressions – *qatsar nefesh*, which is translated as "could no longer bear" or "became impatient" or "intolerable" and *'amal*, which is translated as "misery," "suffering," "plight," or "troubled efforts." While Soggin prefers, "his heart felt sorry for Israel," he points out that the text can also be translated, "his spirit was impatient."[8] Consider the following translations:

> NRSV: "he could no longer bear to see Israel suffer."
> NIV: "he could bear Israel's misery no longer."
> Boling:[9] "the plight of Israel became intolerable to him."
> ESV: "he became impatient over the misery of Israel."
> Polzin:[10] "he grew annoyed (or impatient) with the troubled efforts of Israel."

---

6. Other examples of the same attitude can be found in Num 21:7 (Israel); 1 Sam 12:10 (Israel); 1 Sam 26:21 (Saul).
7. Polzin, *Moses and the Deuteronomist*, 178.
8. Soggin, *Judges*, 202.
9. Boling, *Judges*, 190.
10. Polzin, *Moses and the Deuteronomist*, 177.

The verb *qatsar* can mean "to be short, shortened,"[11] but when paired with *nefesh* (soul) or *ruakh* (spirit), it takes on the meaning of "to be impatient."[12] For example, the phrase is used to describe Samson's exasperation about Delilah's constant nagging to get him to reveal the secret of his strength (Judg 16:16).[13] This suggests that "to be impatient" is a better translation.[14] Nevertheless, there is sufficient ambiguity in the phrase to warrant the translation, "he could no longer bear," since the impatience could provoke God to do something about Israel's miserable situation, which he eventually does by using Jephthah to deliver Israel.

The meaning of *'amal* in this passage is also ambiguous. The more obvious meaning is suffering, hardship, trouble,[15] which refers to the afflictions of the Israelites under the persistent raids and attacks of the Ammonites. However, *'amal* can also suggest an extended sense of trouble or harm done to others, that of mischief. If *qatsar nefesh* means impatient, perhaps *'amal* refers to Israel's mischief, since their repeated sin causes harm to themselves and frustration to God.

One further nuance of *qatsar nefesh*, which is ignored in the different translations, is "his soul is diminished." McCann makes the point that the phrase literally means, God's "life is shortened," in the sense that God's quality of life is diminished. Drawing from the work of Terence Fretheim, McCann interprets this diminishment in terms of God suffering not only *with* his people but *because* of his people.[16] Indeed, God both delivers and suffers. God not only grieves for and on behalf of his people, but also because of his people. The depth and breadth of God's love and relationship places a responsibility of grace on his people – a responsibility exercised in love, worship, obedience, and service.

However, the diminishment may also have something to do with a reduction or ineffectuality in God's ability to act on Israel's behalf. As the Jephthah narrative and subsequent stories in Judges reveal, Yahweh seems to become a marginalized and diminished figure. In the face of Israel's foolishness, God seems to fall silent and leave his people to their own devices. This does not mean that God's actual power diminishes, but that Israel's continued

---

11. *HALOT* 3:1126.
12. *DCH* 7: 286. See Num 21:4; Judg 16:16; Zech 11:8; Mic 2:7; Job 21:4.
13. See Webb, *Judges: Integrated Reading*, 46–47.
14. See McCann, *Judges*, 79.
15. In English translations, *'amal* is translated as misery/ies (NIV, NJPS, ESV); suffering, suffer (NJB, NRSV).
16. McCann, *Judges*, 79. See Terence Fretheim, *The Suffering of God*, 107–187.

disobedience, betrayal, and apostasy push Yahweh to the periphery, where God is rendered "powerless" to do something about their situation.

To understand the apparent contradiction between God's power and seeming powerlessness in relation to Israel, we need to distinguish between what God is in himself and how God acts relationally. Parents in themselves have authority, wisdom, and power, but in relation to an older wayward child, they may not choose to exercise this power in the way that they would like. Similarly, God is willing to limit the exercise of power, authority, and sovereignty in relation to humanity, which reveals the profoundly relational character of God.[17]

Yahweh's silence in the face of Israel's outward confession and repentance breaks the cycle of sin-oppression-deliverance-rest. This challenges the contemporary community of faith to break perpetual cycles of co-dependence/dysfunction and patterns of abuse/forgiveness or confession/restoration when no real changes take place.

Contemporary forms of Protestantism, evangelicalism, and the charismatic movement in Asia often focus on the "bright" side of God or the more buoyant, triumphalist, and optimistic side of Christianity, with little teaching about God's absence, the dark night of the soul, or our disobedience. Yet the Old Testament is full of the mystery, silence, and apparent absence of God. These themes need to be woven into the teaching and preaching ministry of the church in order to prepare people for times of difficulty and darkness.

Moreover, God's relationship with his people is initiated by God's love and maintained by God's faithfulness, but God also calls his people to respond faithfully. When God's people cease to live faithfully, this passage suggests not only that their relationship with Yahweh suffers, but also that Yahweh suffers and is even diminished. When this happens, God cannot work, which has serious consequences for the quality of life that God's people can enjoy and their ability to impact the world. As the story of Jephthah shows, it can also lead to tragedy.

10:17–11:11 THE RISE OF A SELF-MADE MAN

After revealing God's frustrated inner state, one would expect the next scene to involve God's intervention by raising up a judge or by pronouncing judgement against Israel through an increase in oppression. Yet the narrative falls

---

17. On this, see Fretheim, *The Suffering of God*, 72–78.

silent about what God is going to do and returns to the situation confronting Israel – their military problems. The next scene opens with the two sides – the oppressor and the oppressed – in opposite camps, ready to do battle (10:17). The story is set in the Transjordan regions, in Gilead, opposite the region where most of the Israelite tribes live. As with most judges, Jephthah's leadership is limited to a specific tribe and does not encompass the whole of Israel.

Perhaps Israel's dialogue with Yahweh and their belief that they have done the right thing emboldens them to fight their oppressors, for there is a marked difference between the military circumstances of each side. Webb notes that whereas the Ammonites are summoned, a technical term for being called to arms by the commander of the army, the Israelites assemble, indicating that "Israel is without effective leadership and hence extremely vulnerable in the face of this new threat."[18] Indeed, the next verse (10:18) highlights the acute need for Israel to have someone lead them in battle. Instead of conferring about the best military strategy to fend off the attack of the Ammonites,[19] the people and the captains of Gilead ask each other who among them will lead the fight. Apparently, there are no takers, and as the situation grows desperate, they jack up the reward – whoever leads the fight "will be head over all who live in Gilead" (10:18), the highest tribal office in ancient Israel before the monarchy.[20] This prepares the way to introduce Jephthah.

From the anticipated battle scene, the narrative shifts to Jephthah: "Now Jephthah the Gileadite was a mighty warrior" (11:1a, ESV).[21] This opening statement raises expectations that the search for a military commander is over. The phrase "mighty warrior" was also used to describe Gideon (Judg 6:12a) when he led the fight against the Midianites. Yet the next phrase contrasts Jephthah's military capabilities with his personal history: "but he was the son of a prostitute" (11:1b, ESV). Jephthah is of ambiguous and mixed heritage: "an outsider without inheritance rights and . . . extolled as a hero."[22]

Though illegitimate, Jephthah enjoyed the security of his father, Gilead's, household as a child. However, Gilead's wife also bore sons, and when they grew up, they rejected Jephthah and drove him away, not wanting to divide

---

18. Webb, *Judges: Integrated Reading*, 49.
19. Ibid.
20. Boling, *Judges*, 195.
21. The sentence begins with a disjunctive phrase that breaks the temporal movement of the narrative. This serves to introduce background material regarding Jephthah through a flashback. The temporal movement is resumed again in 11:4, with the elders deciding to bring Jephthah back to be their champion against the Ammonites.
22. Matthews, *Judges & Ruth*, 117.

up their inheritance with another person, especially an illegitimate outsider (11:2). Having been rejected by his brothers, banished from his father's house, and deprived of an inheritance, Jephthah lives in the land of Tob of Syria, gathering around him a group of mercenaries who go out raiding with him (11:3).[23] Capitalizing on his strength as a mighty warrior, Jephthah gains a reputation for leading a bandit group that can be called upon in times of war. So while McCann's depiction of Jephthah as a "guerilla fighter"[24] is contemporary and dramatic, Jephthah is a rogue bandit who lives by plundering others (11:3). Apparently, the elders of Gilead recognize Jephthah's military exploits, for when the Ammonites begin to fight, they send for him. Ironically, they ask Jephthah to stop the plundering of the Ammonites, while he himself makes his living through plunder.

The dialogue between the elders of Gilead and Jephthah form the center of episode two:

> Elders of Gilead: "Come and be our commander and fight against the Ammonites." (6)
>
> Jephthah: "Did you not hate me and drive me away from my father's household? So why do you come to me now? Is it because you are hard pressed?" (7)
>
> Elders of Gilead: "Not so.[25] We have returned to you now so that you can come with us and fight against the Ammonites. Then you shall be our head–over all the inhabitants of Gilead." (8)
>
> Jephthah: "If you take me back to fight against the Ammonites and the Lord gives them over to me, I will surely be your head." (9)
>
> Elders of Gilead: "The Lord be a witness between us if we do not do according to your word." (10)

---

23. The phrase *'anashim reyqim* (11:3; "scoundrels," NIV; "outlaws," NRSV; "worthless fellows," ESV) does not seem to refer to immoral men (Burney, *Judges*, 308; see also Boling, *Judges*, 171; Webb, 223, n. 20), but rather to those who, like Jephthah, have been pushed out or opted out of the mainstream socio-economic and political structures of Israelite society. Thus, they made their living by fighting or killing for a wage or by raiding outlying villages, which would correspond to today's mercenary soldiers. See Judg 9:4; 1 Sam 22:2; 2 Chr 13:7.
24. McCann, *Judges*, 80.
25. Reading with LXX. See Boling, *Judges*, 198.

"So Jephthah went with the elders of Gilead and the people made him head and commander over them. Then Jephthah spoke all his words before the Lord in Mizpah." (11) (trans. mine)

There are several similarities between the dialogue of the elders of Gilead with Jephthah in episode two and Israel's dialogue with Yahweh in episode one.[26] Just as Israel's confession to Yahweh was motivated by the necessity of their situation rather than a genuine desire to serve him, so the Gileadite elders' decision to invite Jephthah back into the fold as their military leader comes out of their need for someone to bail them out of trouble, rather than a renewed fondness for their brother. In this utilitarian move, the elders of Gilead seek to use Jephthah in the same way that Israel tried to use Yahweh for their own selfish purposes.

Some Asian cultures that are driven by economics put a high stock on performance, productivity, profits, and success. These values, though not bad in themselves, can permeate Christian ministry, thereby excluding and devaluing people. Thus holistic and caring values, rather than utilitarian ones, should characterize any Christian community. For example, a seminary might retain a support structure for a professor who is suffering from a debilitating illness and can no longer teach, mentor students, or write. As Christians, we must not reduce our relationship with God and others to a "tit for tat" – I will do this if you will do that.

In Jephthah's narrative, the wording of the Gileadite elders' initial offer reveals their true motives. Rather than asking Jephthah to be "head (*rosh*) of all the inhabitants of Gilead," which was their original promise (10:18), they ask him to be their *qatsin*, their military field commander.

Yet Jephthah is shrewd and knows how to strike a bargain in his favor. Using the psychological advantage that he has been grievously wronged, he makes the elders feel guilty: "Aren't you the ones who hated me and drove me out of my father's house?" he demands.[27] Then he puts them on the defensive: "So why do you come to me now? Is it because you are in trouble?" Jephthah successfully manipulates his advantage, for the elders change their invitation from the temporary and limited role of a military field commander (11:6) to the more permanent role of a political leader (11:8–9). This clever move disconcertingly reveals that Jephthah is not content to help the Gileadites out

---

26. Polzin, *Moses and the Deuteronomist*, 178.
27. The assumption here is that the elders supported the decision of Jephthah's family to disinherit him or they did nothing to prevent his disenfranchisement.

of their difficulty, for he is not satisfied to be a military commander; rather, he wants power – to be the "head," the supreme leader of Gilead. However, he masks his political ambitions with pious language: "If you take me back to fight against the Ammonites and the Lord gives them over to me, I will surely be your head" (11:9, trans. mine). "By invoking Yahweh . . . he elevates victory to the status of divine endorsement of himself and so further enhances his own authority vis-à-vis the elders."[28]

Apparently, Jephthah's calculating strategy works, since the Gileadites install him both as head (*rosh*) and military leader (*qatsin*) (11:11). Nevertheless, the manner in which Jephthah is selected as "deliverer" is disturbing. Instead of turning to Yahweh, the elders find their own leader; instead of Yahweh calling forth and empowering an unlikely candidate, the people choose a likely candidate – a mighty warrior. In Yahweh's absence, the people do their own scheming. Yahweh only comes into the conversation when Jephthah and the elders seal their pact "before the Lord" (11:11), thus legitimizing the self-interests of both Jephthah and the Gileadites. In this act, Yahweh is "relegated to the position of confirming the elders' own selection of the highest leadership."[29]

In the midst of our busy rounds of Christian activity, life work, and business, we often push God to the side. We may identify ourselves as Christians but live as functional agnostics, making our own plans and appointing people to key positions within the church or parachurch organizations without prayer and careful discernment. Or God may be part of our conversations and activities, but rather than looking to the Lord to move things, we drag God into the picture to give our actions credibility and sanctity. In this way, we place ourselves at center stage and push God to the margins. This reveals the great disconnect between human scheming and pious language, for pious language is merely a ploy to cover up our manipulative human schemes.

Jephthah's experience of rejection shapes his life, his relationship to others, and eventually the way he operates as deliverer and leader of Israel. He becomes opportunistic, shrewd, skilled in negotiations, and manipulative – a self-made man! Although these qualities contribute to Jephthah's public successes, the next episode reveals how they also lead him into a heartbreaking personal tragedy.

---

28. Webb, *Judges: Integrated Reading*, 52.
29. Boling, *Judges*, 198. See also Trible, *Texts of Terror* 95.

The Jephthah narrative contains an insightful implicit psychological profile of the outworking of rejection. Jephthah, the rejected, finds a new identity as a mercenary soldier leader on the periphery of society. He is willing to return to the fold, but only on his terms. He takes steps to ensure that he is not rejected again by negotiating to become the ruler of the people of Gilead. Sadly, this is not a move of reconciliation for either party. The rejected weak man now becomes powerful. Because the scenario is cast in power terms, there is no healing for Jephthah or for those who rejected him. This lack of healing plays itself out in the rest of the narrative.

11:12–28 STRONG LEADERSHIP AND PUBLIC SUCCESS

Jephthah's difficult family circumstances and the troubling nature of his rise to leadership do not prevent him from exercising his authority and confidently taking on the mantle of leadership. Shortly after being installed, he sends a message to the king of the Ammonites (11:12): "What do you have against me that you have attacked my country?" Jephthah's language shows authority, assertiveness, and confidence. It also exhibits his leadership ability, executive qualities (taking immediate action about a problematic situation), and skill as an astute negotiator with considerable rhetorical facility. Instead of preparing to do battle as the elders of Gilead expect him to do, he sends envoys to find out the cause of the Ammonites' plan to attack. Even though he is a mighty warrior, his first resort is not the force of arms.

However, Jephthah's language also reveals a troubling sense of entitlement to the status and privileges of kingship. Despite Abimelech's failed attempt at monarchy, Jephthah indirectly raises the matter again by using the phrase, "What do you have against me," which is used by one ruler to another.[30] Furthermore, Jephthah's assertion, "you have come to *me* to fight against *my* land" (11:12, emph. mine), casts the attack of the Ammonites as a personal affront, conveying the belief in the ancient Near East that the king owns the land, and so those who seek to possess it are taking it away from the king rather than the people. The Ammonite king's reply also reflects this view of the king's ownership of the land: "When Israel came up out of Egypt, they

---

30. Literally, the Hebrew expression for "what we have against each other" is a common question used by an aggrieved person who feels that he or she is being treated in an unfair way or being attacked without any reason. See 2 Sam 16:10; 1 Kgs 17:18; 2 Kgs 3:13; 2 Chr 35:21. See Boling, *Judges*, 202. The closest parallel is 2 Chr 35:20–21, in which Pharaoh Necho sent messengers to King Josiah of Judah, who had attacked him without provocation.

took away my land from the Arnon to the Jabbok, all the way to the Jordan. Now give it back peaceably" (11:13).

What is at stake here is the issue of who has the right to live in the land. The Ammonite king argues that Israel grabbed the land previously, and he is just re-claiming it. In response, Jephthah embarks on a long interpretation of Israel's history of conquest. This casts Jephthah – who is already identified as a "mighty warrior," a military commander, and head of Gilead – as a leader with king-like status over all Israel as well as a national historian. The long speech also depicts Jephthah as a master of words, skilled in the art of rhetoric and argumentation.

Block summarizes Jephthah's arguments against the Ammonite king's allegations, noting their impressive breadth, logic, and articulateness. Using historical (vv. 16–22), theological (vv. 23–24), personal (v. 25), and chronological arguments (vv. 26–27), Jephthah seeks to silence all objections to Israel's claim on parts of the Transjordan regions. Jephthah portrays Israel as a tolerant nation that respects territorial integrity, suggesting that Israel is the non-aggressor, whereas the Ammonites violate territorial space through aggression. Yet Jephthah's speech is primarily political,[31] for it is not intended as a dialogue with the Ammonite king in order to reach a compromise about the disputed territories. Rather, Jephthah seeks to establish the "wrongdoing on the part of the Ammonites for their military aggression against Israel,"[32] probably to help galvanize his base and push the Gileadites to fight against the Ammonites.

In this episode, Jephthah's extensive verbosity points to an important theme within the narrative cycle, which is "a concern for words, their power and their importance."[33] Earlier, in episode one, Israel uses the power of confession language to try to get Yahweh to save them from their enemies. In the same way, in episode two, the elders of Gilead use words – the promise of political reward – to get Jephthah to fight their enemy. In this same episode, Jephthah uses the language of guilt to get the political reward he wants – to be head of Gilead – even before he wins the battle. Moreover, both the Gileadites and Jephthah seal their agreement with words before the Lord (11:11),[34] with the Gileadites binding themselves with an oath (11:10) and

---

31. Block, *Judges*, 361–363.
32. Ibid., 363.
33. J. Cheryl Exum, "On Judges 11," *A Feminist Companion to Judges*, ed. Athalya Brenner (Sheffield: Sheffield Academic Press, 1993), 132.
34. Ibid., 133.

calling on Yahweh as witness, even though Yahweh is silent. In episode three, Yahweh is still silent. The spotlight is on Jephthah, who speaks and negotiates with the Ammonite king, utilizing religious language and arguing that he has the approval and support of Yahweh. Predictably, the Ammonite king refuses, which sets the stage for the Gileadites' war against the Ammonites.

In this third episode, Jephthah proves that he is ready for a leadership role in Israel: he acts quickly, radiates confidence and authority, has in-depth knowledge of his nation's history and religious traditions, as well as those of the other nations surrounding Israel, and displays considerable skills in diplomacy and negotiations. However, as with Gideon, there are hints of trouble since Jephthah's language reflects an inflated role for himself: "attacked *my* country" (11:12), "you are doing *me* wrong," "waging war against *me*" (11:27, emph. mine). By identifying himself as the primary actor, Jephthah relegates Yahweh to a secondary role, mentioning God only as it suits his sense of history and interpretation (11:21, 23, 27).

The fact that human action rather than divine action is at the center of this story raises doubts about whether the wounded and rejected Jephthah could ever be a good leader. First, the Gileadites choose Jephthah rather than Yahweh. Second, although it is possible that Yahweh could transform Jephthah, Jephthah is clearly too full of himself and too intent on gaining a victory that will be his passport to the acceptance and respect of his community. As a result, he marginalizes Yahweh.

This episode raises a number of relevant issues for Asian Christians, who live in the midst of great religious and ethnic diversity, fragile political democracies, and often without stable leadership and support for churches and Christian organizations. In this context, there is a tendency to grasp prematurely for leaders who look good, can achieve, and even "save" the church or group. Deeply embedded in the psyche of some Asian cultures is a desire for a tribal leader whose wisdom, skills, and prowess will save the people. This not only makes people look to others instead of looking to God, but it also places such "omni-competent" leaders in unhealthy roles. Moreover, such grasping after one powerful and charismatic leader weakens the movement of the gospel, which encourages maturity and the importance of relying on the gifts of all. Thus churches and Christian organizations need to choose leaders who have shown their skills and commitment over time rather than insisting on short-term "imports" to save the day.

11:29–40 TRAGEDY IN THE MIDST OF VICTORY

The Ammonite king's refusal to withdraw his troops provides the opportunity for Jephthah to prepare for battle. At the same time, it provides an occasion for God's involvement in the Israelite's situation: "Then the spirit of the Lord came upon Jephthah, and he passed through Gilead and Manasseh. He passed on to Mizpah of Gilead, and from Mizpah of Gilead he passed on to the Ammonites" (11:29, NRSV).

Though Yahweh is absent when the Gilead elders choose Jephthah and continues to be absent in the negotiations between Jephthah and the Ammonite king, Yahweh re-enters the story through the spirit of the Lord and plays a prominent role in mustering the troops for battle. As discussed earlier, the spirit of the Lord figures prominently just before a judge's battle with the enemies of Israel, endowing the judge with strength before his encounter with Israel's foreign oppressors. The coming of the spirit signals the granting of victory, without the need for pledges or promises on the part of the judge. After the spirit comes upon Jephthah, "he advanced relentlessly upon the Ammonites,"[35] showing a determination to press and deal a decisive blow against them.

The spirit's presence in empowering Jephthah reveals an ambiguity about God's involvement, which is similar to the ambiguous wording in Judges 10:6b regarding God's feelings of compassion for and impatience with his suffering and stubborn people. On the one hand, God is remote and uninvolved in the selection of Jephthah as the military and political leader of Israel. On the other hand, he makes available the resources of his spirit to ensure that Jephthah is victorious against the oppressors of Israel. This suggests that God wants to alleviate Israel's suffering; yet he does not want to take part in his people's foolish and manipulative schemes. So even though Jephthah and the elders of Israel marginalize Yahweh and only use his name to legitimize their schemes, Yahweh joins his people at the crucial stage, when the defeat of the Ammonites through the spirit-empowered leadership of Jephthah will result in a temporary reprieve of Israel's misery.

Jephthah may be uncertain about God's help in his fight against the Ammonites, since he knows that he is not God's direct choice, but has risen to his leadership position through his own manipulation. Perhaps this awareness causes him to make the vow that has such dire consequences. Moreover,

---

35. Tony Cartledge, *Vows in the Hebrew Bible and the Ancient Near East* (Sheffield: JSOT, 1992), 177.

he is named as both commander and leader before he proves himself, and so he may have a lingering fear that a defeat will relegate him to his previous status of being rejected by the community and stripped of his status and power. Thus he has to achieve victory at all costs.

> And Jephthah made a vow to the LORD, and said, "If you will give the Ammonites into my hand, then whoever comes out of the doors of my house to meet me, when I return victorious from the Ammonites, shall be the LORD's, to be offered up by me as a burnt offering." (11:30–31, NRSV)

Jephthah's vow follows the structure of many vows in the Old Testament. It begins with a condition: "If you . . . ," which is a plea for divine action. This condition is then followed by a promise: "then I will . . . ," which stipulates the worshipper's response when God delivers on the petitioner's plea.[36] Typically, a vow arises from a situation of distress, and what is promised is often a sacrifice, including burnt offerings.[37] Thus in terms of the form – the petition for victory in battle[38] and the promise of a burnt offering – there is nothing unusual about Jephthah's vow.

The timing of the vow, however, is strikingly different. Jephthah makes his vow after the spirit of the Lord comes upon him, so he already has the empowerment he needs for victory. Thus he is not in a situation of dire need, which is typical of petitioners who make vows.[39] In fact, God responds before Jephthah even asks for help. Webb shows that the vow is an intervening episode that interrupts the narrative flow of Jephthah's military campaign against the Ammonites.[40]

"Then the spirit of the LORD came upon Jephthah.

> A and he passed (*'abar*) through Gilead and Manasseh. He passed (*'abar*) on to Mizpah of Gilead, and from Mizpah of Gilead he passed (*'abar*) on to the Ammonites" (v. 29)
>
> B "And Jephthah made a vow to the LORD . . ." (vv. 30–31)

---

36. Cartledge, *Vows in the Hebrew Bible*, 16–17.
37. Ibid., 13, 29.
38. See Num 21:2.
39. See Cartledge, *Vows in the Hebrew Bible*, 178.
40. Based on the structure of Webb, *Judges: Integrated Reading*, 62–63.

A' "So Jephthah crossed over (*'abar*) to the Ammonites to fight against them; and the LORD gave them into his hand" (v. 32). (NRSV)

The fourfold repetition of the word *'abar* ("to cross over" or "pass on") links together the route of Jephthah's inevitable march to victory. In the pattern of the spirit's working in the book of Judges, the coming of the spirit is followed by A and A', so that B is unnecessary. In this structure, the vow is extraneous, since it is not integral to the victory march. Jephthah's endowment with the spirit directly leads to his victory over the Ammonites.[41] Thus the vow does not cause the victory, and the action of the spirit of Yahweh does not cause the vow.

The second difference between Jephthah's vow and other vows in the OT is the content of Jephthah's promise. While animal sacrifices in the form of a burnt offering are common pledges in a vow,[42] Jephthah's ambiguity about his burnt offering – whether a human being or an animal – is unusual. The syntactical structure of the sentence is also unusual, which literally reads "the one that goes forth from the doors of my house to meet me" (11:31, trans. mine). Most English versions have smoothened out the translation, following the Septuagint, which drops the first part, "the one who goes forth,"[43] rendering it as "whatever comes out" (NIV, ESV) or "whoever comes out" (NRSV, NJPS). The rendition of the different translations as either "whatever" or "whoever" raises the question of the identity of the burnt offering, whether Jephthah primarily means an animal or a human being, or whether he has his daughter in mind when he utters the vow. David Marcus argues that Jephthah has in mind a human being rather than an animal, because the phrases he uses in the vow are only applied to human beings and never to animals.[44] On the other hand, Boling thinks that Jephthah has animals in mind, arguing that the structure of Iron Age houses, which integrated livestock pens at the basement,[45] meant that it would be easy to imagine animals wandering out of their pens when people arrive.

Jephthah's language, however, could be deliberately ambiguous. On the one hand, the narrator could be making the reference imprecise (whether

---

41. Webb, *Judges: Integrated Reading*, 63.
42. Cartledge, *Vows in the Hebrew Bible*, 29, n. 1. See also Lev 22:18.
43. It is regarded as a dittography, a doubling of a phrase or word due to scribal error.
44. David Marcus, *Jephthah and his Vow* (Lubbock, TX: Texas Tech Press, 1986), 13–14.
45. Boling, *Judges*, 208.

animal or human being) in order to heighten suspense and maximize the emotional impact when the daughter herself comes out to meet her father, and Jephthah discovers to his consternation that he unwittingly committed to sacrifice his only offspring. On the other hand, Cartledge thinks that Jephthah is deliberately ambiguous as "a cunning attempt to promise one thing while hoping for a lesser outcome."[46]

Numbers 21:2 reflects a close parallel to Jephthah's vow, as it employs almost identical language. Yet Jephthah's pledge differs from the Numbers passage in that his pledge is not related to his request. This stands in stark contrast to all the recorded vows in the OT, where there is a close relationship between the condition and the promise, sometimes even employing identical language.[47] Following this pattern, the most logical promise for Jephthah would be to devote the areas he conquers, but instead he promises a sacrificial burnt offering.[48] Cartledge thinks that Jephthah wants to promise something very precious to match his request and will approximate the value of the spoils of battle – a human sacrifice! Nevertheless, he hopes that the one who meets him will be something or somebody besides his daughter, hence the ambiguity in his statement.[49]

There are several ways to understand the nature of Jephthah's vow and what it means for our time. A naïve reading of the narrative would suggest that it is about keeping one's promises to God, regardless of the cost. Thus if we promise to serve God or the community in a particular way, we must keep our promises, even if circumstances radically change.

Another reading would be to cast the story into the framework of the unfortunate. Jephthah's vow was never meant to have such tragic consequences. He did not intend for his words to lead to such terrible results. This way of reading suggests that life is not in our control. Bad things can happen to people, regardless of their intentions.

A poetic reading would interpret the passage based on the formal structure of Greek tragedy. In this structure, a deity exploits flaws within the human figure through the power of fate, resulting in an unmitigated tragedy.[50]

---

46. Cartledge, *Vows in the Hebrew Bible*, 179.
47. Marcus, *Jephthah and his Vow*, 19. See Gen 28:20–22; 1 Sam 1:11; 2 Sam 15:7–8.
48. Jephthah may have avoided promising this because he needed the spoils of battle for his band of professional raiders (Cartledge, *Vows in the Hebrew Bible*, 179).
49. Cartledge, *Vows in the Hebrew Bible*, 179–180.
50. See J. Cheryl Exum, "The Tragic Vision and Biblical Narrative: The Case of Jephthah," in *Signs and Wonders: Biblical Texts in Literary Focus* (Atlanta, GA: SBL, 1989), 59–83.

A feminist reading would interpret the narrative as a reinforcement of patriarchal values and domination.[51] The clear message in the mouth of the daughter (11:36) is that whatever the father has said (as foolish or tragic as it may be) will determine her fate. In other words, men determine the lives of women. Or, to put it more brutally, the male (in this case the father) is so powerful in a patriarchal society that even his foolish and tragic words determine the life of the female.

A Girardian reading would recognize that a sacrifice has to be offered if there is going to be victory. In a successful event, a scapegoat is necessary. Thus Jephthah's victory over the Ammonites requires a "pure" offering that will justify the killing of many.

While various arguments can be presented for each of these readings, there is another angle for understanding Jephthah's motivations in making this vow, which can be discerned by tracing the tangle of events that led up to this tragedy. Many of our present-day struggles and conflicts can be traced back to earlier factors that have shaped us, our families, and our communities. As shown earlier, Jephthah coped with the experience of marginalization and rejection by becoming opportunistic and utilitarian in his approach to life. In this episode, he brings this attitude into his relationship with God.

With his status, reputation, fortune, and acceptance within the community at stake, Jephthah characteristically tries to bargain with God: "If you will give me victory, I will offer as a burnt offering the very first one who meets me." In some of the nations around Israel, it was thought that a human sacrifice would gain the favor of the gods, thus guaranteeing victory in battle. For this reason, the covenant in Deuteronomy warns Israel against imitating the nations around them by offering their children as sacrifices to their gods (Deut 12:29–31).[52] Even though the reference to a human person is ambiguous, as discussed above, the suggestion remains that Jephthah thinks he can buy Yahweh's favor by approximating the value of a human sacrifice. This reveals how much his thinking mirrors the Canaanite nations around Israel, a theme that resonates with the whole book of Judges.[53]

---

51. For feminist readings of the Jephthah story, see Esther Fuchs, "Marginality, Ambiguity, Silencing: The Story of Jephthah's Daughter," in *A Feminist Companion to Judges*, ed. Athalya Brenner (Sheffield: Sheffield Academic Press, 1993), 116–130 and Exum, "Tragic Vision: The Case of Jephthah" above. See also Mieke Bal, *Death and Dissymmetry*, 41–68.
52. Janzen, "Why the Deuteronomist," 344. This is also one of the practices condemned by the Deuteronomist (2 Kgs 16:3; 17:17; 21:6).
53. Block sees the theme of the whole book as the Canaanization of Israel (*Judges*, 58). See also Janzen, "Why the Deuteronomist", 341.

The action of the spirit of Yahweh is not enough for Jephthah. He feels he has to cover all the bases and ensure victory at all cost, lest he fail. For Jephthah is not fighting the Ammonites because he cares about the oppression of Israel; nor is he fighting to defend the name of Yahweh. He is fighting because there is so much at stake for him personally. He is fighting for his own acceptance, his own security, his own desire for a place in the world.[54] Yet through his desire to save himself, he unwittingly sacrifices his own daughter. He survives life and rejection by mastering the art of diplomacy and manipulation, but in the process he harms the very person he truly cares about.

HARMFUL EFFECTS OF MINISTERING OUT OF REJECTION

When people who exercise Christian leadership are highly insecure, a volatile mix occurs. Christian leaders may use the guise of spirituality to cover their own needs and insecurities. Though Jephthah sounds spiritual when he utters his vow, it is really covering up his desire to manipulate and marginalize God. In the same way, rather than looking to God as our source and inspiration, our piety can get tacked onto our religiosity. This happens when we drag God into our conversation and activities in order to gain credibility – and not because we are depending on God to move.

The story of Jephthah's daughter also reminds us that we can end up sacrificing our families and personal lives at the altar of public success. We may be a successful Christian leader, admired by people, producing desired outcomes, involved in big projects, while our personal life and family life is barren and full of conflicts. In both the secular world and within the Christian community, fathers and mothers often engage in the headlong pursuit of public success at the cost of their children, spouses, and friends.

Moreover, the story emphasizes the importance of coming to terms with painful feelings of rejection, abandonment, and neglect that arise from the way our family or community treated us. If we do not face these feelings, we may end up ministering out of our insecurity instead of putting our security in God. Christian ministry should never become a tool to overcome feelings of rejection. Rather, Christian ministry should be for others and not for our own needs. When utilitarian values and insecurity infect a Christian ministry, they often destroy the life of the leader as well as those who are closely connected with the leader.

---

54. See Trible, *Texts of Terror*, 96.

> Asian Christians who live in formerly colonized countries will also need to be careful that they do not act or react out of an institutionalized sense of inferiority caused by the colonial experience. Churches and organizations in these regions will need to journey through Christian healing processes so that their leadership can emerge from grace and gifting rather than wounding.

After the vow, Jephthah goes on to achieve a great victory: "He devastated twenty towns from Aroer to the vicinity of Minnith, as far as Abel Keramim. Thus Israel subdued Ammon" (11:33). However, Jephthah's great public drama in routing the Ammonites is overshadowed by the personal tragedy that strikes when he returns home.

Having heard of Jephthah's triumph, his daughter – his one and only offspring – rushes out with festive garments, tambourines, and a celebratory dance to welcome her father home, unaware that she has been used as a bargaining chip to gain her father's victory. Jephthah's shock and grief at her appearance is evident when he cries out: "Alas, my daughter! You have brought me very low, and you have become the cause of great trouble to me. For I have opened my mouth to the Lord, and I cannot take back my vow" (11:35, ESV). Jephthah's peculiar speech couches the tragedy as something that his daughter has caused.[55] Instead of taking responsibility for his actions, Jephthah focuses on his own loss rather than his daughter's. Instead of saying, "I caused this," he blames his daughter.

Sadly, when victimization takes place, the victim often gets the blame. You are poor because you do not work hard enough. You are abused because you incited the abuse. Tragically, victims often internalize the blame and believe that they are at fault. Meanwhile, those who are responsible for the pain deflect the blame from their own mistakes.

The daughter does not immediately realize how her father's vow will impact her life. She only thinks about her father's loss. She is his one and only child. Her father has no other son or daughter to carry on his name and

---

55. In Jephthah's speech in 11:35, the first verb used is (*kara'*, "brought very low") is in causative form (*hiphil*) in Hebrew. The next verb (*'akar*), used here as a participle, means "to bring disaster or ruin" (*HALOT* 2, study ed., 824). This is especially significant since the participial form of the verb *'akar* is used in connection with trouble that comes about as the result of committing a transgression (Josh 6:18; 7:25; 1 Kgs 18:18) or that is perceived to come from an action deemed wrong or inappropriate (Gen 34:30; 1 Sam 14:29; 1Kgs 18:17. See also See Trible, *Texts of Terror*, 102).

heritage. With her gone – the joy of his heart – her father will spend the rest of his life in perpetual grief.

In interpreting this passage, one question that often arises is, Did Jephthah really offer his daughter as a burnt offering? In a burnt offering (*'olah*), the sacrifice is wholly burnt up at the altar, symbolizing the offerer's devotion. The smoke is said to go up to gain the deity's favor and assistance.[56] One line of interpretation suggests that the daughter is not literally sacrificed, but becomes a consecrated virgin for the rest of her life, hence the use of the phrases, "lament my virginity" (11:37, 38, trans. mine); "she had never known a man" (11:39, ESV).[57] However, the language of the text seems to be ambiguous: "I will offer him (it)[58] as a burnt offering" (11:31); "he did to her as he had vowed" (11:39). Those who think that Jephthah's daughter is not sacrificed interpret these phrases in a figurative way. However, when used elsewhere in the OT, these phrases always have a literal sense.[59] Some argue that if the daughter is offered as a burnt offering, there would be condemnation from the biblical writer, since human sacrifices are condemned in Scripture;[60] yet such condemnation is notably absent in the story.[61] However, as shown in earlier chapters, the book of Judges uses a highly ironic tone that does not express verbal condemnation, but suggests disapproval of an action by interpreting the narrative in light of the cyclical framework. This framework traces the progressive Canaanization of the Israelites and the progressive deterioration of conditions that results from Israel's continued apostasy against Yahweh.

Those who argue that Jephthah's daughter is not literally offered as a burnt offering point to the repeated use of the phrase, "lament my virginity" (11:37, 38), as an indication that she is committed to perpetual celibacy as a sign of dedication to God (similar to the Nazirites). However, the emphasis of the Hebrew word, *bethulim*, for "virginity" (NRSV, ESV, NASB) does not convey only a lack of sexual relationship, but that the woman has reached puberty and has not yet given birth to a child.[62] Thus the phrase stresses her

---

56. Gary Anderson, "Sacrifice and Sacrificial Offerings," *ABD* 5: 877–878.
57. Marcus, *Jephthah and his Vow*, 50–52, argues for this interpretation.
58. The Hebrew has a masculine singular pronominal suffix, which can refer to a male human being or animal, hence the pronoun can be translated "he" (human being) or "it" (animal; see NIV, ESV). NRSV retains the ambiguity by not translating the pronoun.
59. See the arguments and counter-arguments in Marcus, *Jephthah and his Vow*, 25–26.
60. See Block, *Judges*, 366–367 n. 90, for discussion and references.
61. Marcus, *Jephthah and his Vow*, 47–48.
62. Block, *Judges*, 374 n. 124, citing Peggy Day, *Gender and Difference in Ancient Israel* (Minneapolis, MN: Fortress, 1989), 59.

unfulfilled state in regards to bearing a child. In ancient Israel, offspring are important because they not only carry the family name, but also are tied to the rights of inheritance. For this reason, barrenness is seen as a curse, and so the lamentation of Jephthah's daughter focuses on her not being able to experience the joys of motherhood or produce children who will continue the family line and inheritance.

Despite the pain of her lot, Jephthah's daughter does not blame her father, but accepts that the vow cannot be broken and her death is inevitable. She accepts her limited circumstances within the patriarchal culture, where men decide the fate of women. But even as she accepts the limitations of her culture and the pain of her circumstances, she exercises agency – the power to act.

> She said to her father, "Let this be done for me: let me be for two months, and I will go with my friends and weep upon the hills and there lament my virginity." (11:38, trans. mine)

Even though she cannot control the fate of death, she has the power to decide to spend the rest of her brief life in the manner that she chooses. "Within the limits of the inevitable, she takes charge to bargain for herself."[63]

Many studies have been done to research the structural forces that lead to poverty, marginalization, and abuse. Yet such studies often neglect the individual agent's perceptions, decisions, and transformations in the process. Though we may feel caught in a web of forces beyond our control, and we may feel paralyzed by our family background, limited circumstances, the choices of authority figures, or our own personalities and mistakes, we can still make decisions. Though we may not be able to fight a fatally flawed system and change it, we all have the power to live with integrity and hope. The story of Jephthah's daughter reminds us that we are never completely powerless.

For the last two months of her life, Jephthah's daughter chooses to spend her time with friends rather than with her father, which may imply recognition that her father is responsible for her fate. Her desire is to be with her friends and weep with them about her fate.

In the company of Jephthah and his daughter, we see the negative and positive sides of community. Jephthah, the outcast from an unloving family, builds his own communal alternative, a *barkada,* which is a Filipino term

---

63. Trible, *Texts of Terror*, 103.

for in-group (11:3). In this group of bandits, Jephthah finds a new sense of family and identity. Tragically, this is not a healing community for Jephthah. Yet for Jephthah's daughter, the experience of community is marked by solidarity, vulnerability, and comfort rather than violence (11:37, 38). In this productive and healing community, people do not run away from their hurts and losses, but openly face and grieve them. Such communities need to be formed as small groups within the churches of Asia, where along with prayer and Bible study, life is shared not only in terms of its joys, but also its sorrows.

The response of Jephthah's daughter also points towards the significance of lament. Readers may ask: "Why does God not rescue the daughter from the consequences of the vow made by her father? Why does God allow Jephthath to think that his vow is what ensured his victory?" Questioning God, "why? where? how long?" during situations of deep distress is part of the OT tradition of lament. Asian Christians know something about lament, not only from the masses still living in poverty and those who experience political difficulties, as in Myanmar, but also from those experiencing overcrowding, loss of a good environment, and the damage from ongoing calamities, such as typhoons, volcanic eruptions, and earthquakes. Yet a lament is not just a heart cry, but a cry to God and before God. This cry is not merely angry or disappointed, for it is a cry to Yahweh for hope and comfort in the midst of loss. The cry of lament knows perseverance in the midst of distress and difficulty. Lament is often regarded as a passive response to a situation, but Brueggemann points out that grief and pathos are actually a form of protest, because they refuse to deny the true nature of a situation.[64] Neither Jephthah nor his daughter is delivered. Yet Jephthah's cry expresses despair for himself and blame for others; whereas his daughter's cry expresses both devastating loss and courageous acceptance.

Jephthah's daughter dies a cruel and early death, but her legacy remains. For year after year, the women of Israel remember her: "She became a tradition in Israel; every year, the daughters of Israel would go to commemorate the daughter of Jephthah the Gileadite, four days in the year" (11:39b–40).[65] The verb *tanah* (piel: "to commemorate") means "to recount," but in this

---

64. Walter Brueggemann, *The Prophetic Imagination* (Minneapolis, MN: Fortress, 1978), 51.
65. "She became a tradition in Israel" is from Trible, *Texts of Terror*, 106–107. The verb "became" is in feminine form while *hoq* (translated in most versions as "custom") is in masculine, which is peculiar (Soggin, *Judges*, 214). Most versions (NIV, NRSV, NASB) consider the use of the feminine as impersonal (see GKC § 144b), hence the translation "it became a custom." But "she" instead of "it" is a plausible translation, with *hoq* being translated as "tradition" instead of "custom."

passage it refers to "repetition within an antiphonal performance."⁶⁶ The picture is of women retelling the story of this young daughter's life, possibly through chant, dance, and tears. In contrast to Jephthah, whose mighty deeds will always be overshadowed by his tragic vow, his daughter's courage in the face of her tragic fate will be remembered and lamented by her sisters. Likewise, her fellow sisters in Asia – who suffer under the same patriarchal system, where the male head of a household or clan determines the fate of women and children – can lament along with her for their pain, abuse, rejection, and victimization. In this way, her Asian sisters are walking along the road towards healing and systemic change.

12:1–7 UNRESOLVED ISSUES

Jephthah's tragic flaw resides in his deep insecurities, which lead him to try to manipulate God by uttering a vow that condemns his daughter to an early death and an unfulfilled life while also condemning him to lose his only child and the heir of his line. Even after his daughter's death, Jephthah finds no reconciliation, for the last episode of the story portrays an angry Jephthah and a divided Israel.

After the sacrifice of Jephthah's daughter, the scene shifts abruptly to the Ephraimites as they are called to arms against Jephthah. The narrative does not mention Jephthah's feelings or grieving, nor how the Gileadites and the larger Israelite community regard the tragedy. The text is silent, as if conniving with the characters to deny, ignore, and move away from the pain and loss.

As with Gideon's fight against the Midianites (8:1–3), the Ephraimites confront Jephthah for not including them in the battle for victory against the Ammonites. But rather than merely complaining to Jephthah, they threaten to burn his household (12:1). On the heels of the death of Jephthah's daughter, the threat seems inconsiderate and selfish, since the Ephraimites are thinking only about how they were excluded, instead of recognizing and appreciating what it cost Jephthah to gain the victory.

Filipinos refer to this attitude as crab mentality, which is described as pulling down others who are ahead of you so that everyone is on the same plane. While this may equalize things, it can also kill individual initiative and punish those who do the hard work. Instead of getting credit for the

---

66. *HALOT* 4:1760.

good they have done, they are bashed for their accomplishments. In the long-term, this attitude retards the progress of the whole group, since no one will dare to dream or work harder than others, because they fear being criticized and shunned.

When the Midianites complained to Gideon, his response was conciliatory and self-deprecating, thereby abating their anger. Yet when the Ephraimites confront Jephthah, he meets their anger head-on. Rather than putting salve on their wounded pride, he emphasizes that they were not there when he needed them and boasts that he risked his life and won the battle without them (12:2–3). The phrase, "I took my life in my hands," is also used in 1 Samuel 19:5, 28:21 and Job 13:14, where it means to put one's life in danger. Although the Ephraimites did not share in the sacrifice, Jephthah focuses on his own achievements and emphasizes their failure to contribute, which goads them to greater hostility.

The Ephraimites express their resentment against Jephthah and the Gileadites through a taunt: "you . . . are renegades from Ephraim and Manasseh" (12:4). While the Hebrew term for "renegade," *palit*, generally refers to those who have escaped from being killed in war, in this context it takes on a derogatory sense, as those who deliberately take flight in the heat of battle; hence, it is tantamount to being branded disloyal, a traitor, or a coward. Perhaps they are referring to Jephthah's original raiding band of mercenaries and outlaws, which formed the core of the Gileadite army (11:3). Or perhaps they are looking down on the small Gileadite force as "mere fugitives" (leftovers) in comparison with the combined might of Ephraim and Manasseh – thereby implying that the Gileadites have no reason to exalt themselves for the victory.

Evidently, the slur rankles the Gileadites, for they strike the Ephraimites, killing 42,000 (12:4, 6). Even though the Ephraimites confronted Jephthah with the intention of starting a fight, the war could have been prevented if both sides had been willing to back down. The senselessness of this war is brought to the fore when the Ephraimite war fugitives are identified as they flee back to their home base on the other side of the Jordan. Those who can say, "Shibboleth," are allowed to go on, but those who say, "Sibboleth," are identified as Ephraimites and struck down. If it were not for the sword that struck those whose pronunciation was different, the identification marker might be humorous. But there is no humor in ethnic cleansing.

After leading Israel for six years, Jephthah dies and is buried (12:7). There is no further mention of his daughter. Thus Jephthah–the self-made man, diplomat and negotiator par excellence, who is looked upon to deliver Israel from its oppressors – dies with many unresolved issues.

USING PEOPLE AND USING GOD

This sad saga of a fractured man and self-made hero raises a number of challenging issues. The first part of the narrative depicts the danger of utilitarianism when Jephthah, the devalued Gileadite, becomes the rejected son of the community (11:1–3) and then is reclaimed because of the pragmatic victory he can achieve over the Ammonites (11:6). The elders of Gideon do not care about Jephthah as a person, but only about what he can do for them. Such arrangements always come at a price, and Jephthah's price is to become the ruler and commander (11:8, 10).

Some might try to read the narrative in positive terms: a bad son (11:1), who associates with the wrong group (11:3), can now be used for good purposes in the fight against the Ammonites. But such a convenient reading goes against the text, since Jephthah recognizes that he is being used (11:7), and the elders admit that they only want Jephthah for what he can do (11:8).

At the heart of utilitarianism is a sheer pragmatism that values productivity, achievement, and outcomes without considering the people who produce these outcomes. Such pragmatism has impacted the Christian church in Asia, with Chinese and South Korean churches in particular mixing Western economic and management models with their cultural ideas of power and productivity and then mixing those ideas with a misreading of the biblical text that celebrates work and neglects the Sabbath. Whether practiced in the community or the church, utilitarianism raises three major theological concerns.

First, people matter more than outcomes. The doctrine of the *imago Dei* highlights that people made in God's image should not be used, pushed, or exploited, but should be treated with love because they are loved by God.

Secondly, focusing on the ends without thinking about the means goes against the whole tenor of the biblical story, where only righteous ways produce good outcomes. From this perspective, we cannot use or exploit others in the interests of productivity, efficiency, profit, or success.

Thirdly, the OT themes of shalom and sabbath completely undermine utilitarianism. In utilitarianism, you use people to achieve your outcomes, but in shalom, goodness comes to all – the whole community, all who are blessed. In utilitarianism, people are regarded as achievers, but in the biblical celebration of Sabbath, people are regarded as worshippers.

This has significant implications for the Asian church, where workers are often exploited rather than seen as beloved members of the community. Thus Christian work cannot be informed by capitalism's management models, but must be upheld by values that build the beloved community, bring shalom, empower the least, and honor and bless all.

However, throughout the Jephthah narrative, utilitarianism is not only evident in how people treat one another, but also in how people treat God. Israel, the elders of Gilead, and Jephthah all use God, and this leads to God's marginalization. The marginalization of Yahweh in the book of Judges poses many challenges for us today. Even though the idea that God is central to human affairs may be exhorted as a theological principle and vision, the reality is that God is often marginalized in the world. And even though God may seem to be at the center of a faith community that speaks to and about God, the truth is that God is often marginalized in the church. Thus believers may push God to the periphery of their lives or try to use God to benefit their careers. In the midst of our religious activities and strategies for witness and service, we lose sight of God when we focus on what we are doing instead of what God is doing. Thus we work *for* God but not *with* God.

This highlights the theological and ethical tensions between who God is in terms of power, sovereignty, and lordship and how God is acknowledged in terms of the decisions we make and the way we live. As Christians, we must not use God as a way to fit in with our cultural values, personal dreams, or group agendas. Furthermore, our Christian ministries must not be used for our own purposes. Finally, we must resist every form of bargaining with God. Instead of saying, "I will do this for you, God, if you will do this for me," our response should be, "Lord, help me to do your will and serve your purposes in this world. Amen."[67]

---

67. There are other vows in the OT that are not characterized by bargaining with God, but by a genuine desire to honor and please God. An example is Samson's Nazirite vow, which will be discussed on pp. 174–175.

JUDGES 13:1–16:31

Reversal of Expectations

Whenever a nation is in crisis, people look for a great leader who can turn things around and lead them out of their difficulties. Some may romanticize about the "good old days" when so-and-so provided direction and decisive leadership during times of great distress. Such reminiscing is often accompanied by a wish that another leader will arise with similar qualities.

The birth of a child may also be accompanied by grandiose hopes, particularly if the child comes from a line of rulers – such as the heir to the British throne or the child of a political family or tribal chieftain. Along with the biological family members, the people of the surrounding community or nation rejoice, since the child is often seen as the bearer of good tidings.

When a society approaches an election, similar phenomena can occur – unless the people have become cynical about the political process. For changes in political leadership often revive anticipations that the promises of the past can still be realized. Many politicians exploit this human tendency to hope, making promises that a great future lies ahead or "the best is yet to come."

In Judges 13, such great expectations and hopes accompany the birth of Samson. Certain "signs" at his birth construe hopes that he will become a great leader in the future. Yet his life is a failure and disappointment, even though he unwittingly accomplishes God's purposes. Although the narrative focuses on Samson's life and exploits, it is placed within the broader context of a people who continue "to do evil in the eyes of the Lord." This context provides commentary about the kind of society that produces a leader such as Samson. As such, the Samson narrative leads us to ask, "What kind of people do we need to become in order to produce a certain type of leader?" rather than, "What kind of a leader do we deserve?" For the Samson narrative challenges our normal expectations about what a judge should be and how God should act. Through a series of inversions, the narrative subverts both the characters' expectations as well as the reader's.

JUDGES

OVERALL NARRATIVE STRUCTURE

The Samson narrative cycle can be broadly divided into two parts:

13:1–25	Samson's Birth
14:1–16:31	Samson's Exploits and Death

Structurally, 13:1–25 stands out from the rest of the narratives in the Samson cycle, because it focuses on Samson's parents and their reactions to the announcement of his birth. Chapters 14 through 16 relate the various accounts of Samson's confrontations with the Philistines and the realization of his mission, which was announced before his birth (13:5b). These chapters can be divided into two narrative movements. The first movement (14:1–15:20) deals with Samson's relationship with a Timnite woman and the consequences that result from this relationship, which establishes the tone for the subsequent episodes. The second narrative movement (16:4–31) traces Samson's folly with Delilah, which has nearly fatal consequences. The verses in 16:1–3, where Samson's visits a Gaza prostitute, act as a bridge between the narrative about the Timnite woman and the narrative about Delilah.[1] These three incidents can be structured as follows:

First Narrative Movement (14:1–15:17)	The Timnite
Bridge Narrative (16:1–3)	The Gaza Prostitute
Second Narrative Movement (16:4–30)	Delilah

Chapters 14 through 16 can also be structured according to Samson's encounters with the Philistines:

Episode One (14:11–19)	The Wedding Feast and the Riddle
Episode Two (15:4–17)	Killing with an Ass's Jawbone
Episode Three (16:1–3)	The Prostitute in Gaza
Episode Four (16:4–30)	Samson and Delilah

THE SAMSON NARRATIVE AS DRAMATIC COMEDY: THE TRAGIC HERO WHO OVERCOMES

Many people read Samson as a tragic character since he dies at the end of the narrative and he seems to have lived a failed life. Indeed, certain pathos

---

1. Cheryl Exum, "Aspects of Symmetry and Balance in the Samson Saga," *JSOT* 19 (1981): 3–29, lays out the structure of the narrative based on repetitions and key words.

enters the story when Samson unwittingly breaks his vow and the presence of Yahweh departs from him, leaving him vulnerable to his Philistine captors (16:20–25). Nevertheless, despite these tragic elements, the story ends with the fulfillment of Samson's mission and his incorporation back into his family and community. Narratively, this plot line expresses a "comic vision,"[2] where the hero begins within a harmonious society; that harmony is challenged as the hero becomes alienated from himself and society; then the plot turns upward as the hero reaches a point of self-recognition, overcomes complications, and is reintegrated into society.[3]

Because of the shape of the narrative, some treat the Samson narrative as comedy rather than tragedy and regard Samson as a comic hero rather than a tragic one. The extraordinary circumstances of Samson's birth generate great expectations for his future. But as the narrative develops, Samson gets into one scrape after another because of his weakness for women, becoming alienated from his parents, his Israelite identity, and Yahweh. Before the end of the story, Samson is reconciled to Yahweh and to his roots, since he is buried in Israelite territory with his father.[4] Moreover, his death (16:30b) realizes the promise of his birth: that he would "begin to deliver Israel from the hand of the Philistines" (13:5b, NRSV).

The narrative also employs comic devices, such as incongruity, mockery, and surprise, especially in the incidents between Samson and the Philistines.[5] In addition, the various characters of the story (Manoah, the Philistines, the Timnite woman, and Delilah) reflect comic types, such as tricksters, pedants, fools, and rogues. Even Yahweh takes on the qualities of a trickster. Verbal humor is present in the dialogue within the riddle incident (14:10–19) and

---

2. According to William Whedbee, this comic vision is expressed through a U-shaped plot line, which "leads ultimately to the happiness of the hero and his restoration to a serene and harmonious society" ("The Comedy of Job," *Semeia* 7 [1977]: 4). See also Cheryl Exum and J. William Whedbee, "Isaac, Samson, and Saul: Reflections on the Comic and Tragic Visions," *Semeia* 32 (1984): 5–40.
3. Northrop Frye, *A Natural Perspective: The Development of Shakespearean Comedy and Satire* (New York: Harcourt, Brace, and World, 1965), 76–78; *Anatomy of Criticism: Four Essays* (Princeton, NJ: Princeton University Press, 1957).
4. The comic plot of the Samson story, along with the humorous techniques used in the narrative, is discussed in Athena E. Gorospe, "Comedy and Humor in the Samson Narrative (ThM diss., Asia Graduate School of Theology, 1995).
5. Commentators have noted the humorous quality of Samson's escapades. See Soggin, *Judges*, 249; James Crenshaw, *A Secret Betrayed: A Vow Ignored* (Atlanta, GA: John Know, 1978), 127–129; James Wharton, "The Secret of Yahweh: Story and Affirmation in Judges 13–16," *Int* 27 (1973): 52–54.

between Samson and Delilah (16:4–21a). For all these reasons, it is more appropriate to consider the narrative a comedy rather than a tragedy.

13:1–25 GREAT EXPECTATIONS AND THE REVERSAL OF ROLES

The story is introduced with the usual framework: "The Israelites continually did evil in the sight of the Lord, so the Lord gave them into Philistine control for forty years" (13:1, trans. mine). The framework is even more incomplete than that which is used to introduce the Jephthah cycle, as it does not mention God becoming angry or Israel crying out. As in the Jephthah narrative, the standard elements from earlier accounts – of God raising up or calling a deliverer and the land having rest–are also absent in the Samson narrative. The language is terse, as if the narrator is in a hurry to mention the formula and then move into the heart of the story. With the further deterioration of conditions in Israel, the formula may be outliving its usefulness.

Judges 13 narrates the circumstances surrounding Samson's birth. In the following, I discuss the whole chapter in relation to the characterizations of Samson, Samson's father Manoah, his unnamed mother, and lastly, the divine visitor.

Samson: A Child of Promise

The birth of Samson is accompanied by great expectations, as three of the four characteristics of heroic origins are present: the annunciation scene, the birth narrative, and the call story (he is called to be a Nazirite).[6] These features indicate that Samson is destined for greatness.

The annunciation episode features a "type scene" similar to other birth announcements in the OT. Type scenes, according to Alter, are a literary convention used in narrating the crucial junctures in the lives of heroes, such as their birth, betrothal, and death. These narratives are stylized to follow a set of predetermined motifs.[7] In a type scene, both the narrator and the audience have certain expectations about how the narrative should progress.

---

6. See James Nohrnberg, "Moses," in *Images of Man and God: Old Testament Short Stories in Literary Focus,* ed. Burke O. Long (Sheffield: Almond Press, 1981), 36. Nohrnberg cites four motifs used in literature to mark an individual of heroic origins: the birth story, the annunciation story, the call story, the nobody story (where the individual is obscure or has some oddity or in circumstances that make him an unlikely candidate for a hero). When more of these motifs are present in a story, the individual will become a greater hero.
7. Alter, *Art of Biblical Narrative,* 50–51.

The annunciation of the birth of the hero is one such type scene, which has three major thematic components: a) the initial barrenness of the wife; b) the divine promise of future conception; and c) the birth of a son.[8]

In the OT, the closest parallel to the above structure appears in Genesis 18:1–15, when Yahweh announces to Abraham that his barren wife Sarah will bear a son.[9] In the NT, there is a parallel announcement for the birth of John the Baptist to Zacharias (Luke 1:11–25).[10] The birth of a child to a barren woman is also present in the stories of Rebekah, who bore Jacob and Esau (Gen 25:21–26), and Hannah, who bore Samuel (1 Sam 1:1–20). These children were born at a period of great transition in the life of Israel, and they played a pivotal role in this transition.[11] Thus, there is the expectation that the birth of Samson will usher in a new era in the life of Israel, one that is not marked by the apostasy of the earlier periods.

In each birth narrative, whether Isaac, Samuel, or John the Baptist, the reader bears witness not only to the miracle of conception and birth, but also to the promise of a hoped-for deliverer. Indeed, the birth of Samson is presented as the fulfilment of God's promise to a barren woman: "The angel of the Lord appeared to her and said, 'You are barren and childless, but you are going to become pregnant and give birth to a son'" (13:3).

This verse forms an *inclusio* with 13:24, which records the fulfillment of the promise: "The woman gave birth to a boy and named him Samson."[12] Upon this child of promise, the parents pin their hopes – not only for the joy of having offspring, but also for the visible evidence of the continuity of the family line. Moreover, the disclosure of the emissary of Yahweh regarding the child's mission – "he shall begin to deliver Israel from the hand of the Philistines" (13:5, NRSV) – raises hopes that he will be the instrument of a great deliverance that will loosen the shackles of Philistine control over Israel.

---

8. Ibid., 49.
9. For further discussion, see Gorospe, "Comedy and Humor," 208–212.
10. The birth of Jesus was also preceded by an announcement to the mother; however, Mary was not barren, but rather unmarried and a virgin, a twist in the features of the annunciation type scene that points to the greater significance of Jesus' birth.
11. Jacob and Esau were born in the transition of Israel from a small family to a powerful clan that would be the precursor to the birth of a nation. Samuel was born in the transition of Israel from a tribal confederacy to a monarchy. Isaac marked the beginning of the fulfillment of God's promise of "a great nation" to Abraham. The birth of John the Baptist was the precursor to the coming of the Messiah.
12. The pattern of promise and fulfillment is noted by Cheryl Exum, "Promise and Fulfillment: Narrative Art in Judges 13," *JBL* 99 (1980): 43–59.

Through the mission of this promised son, there is the hope of a brighter future.

> ## CHILDREN OF PROMISE IN ASIAN CULTURE
>
> The God of the Bible is a God of life,[13] families, continuity, and promise. In a birth narrative of promise, there is always the possibility that a child will become a Watchman Nee, a Mother Teresa, a Billy Graham, or a Dietrich Bonhoeffer, and so the birth of any child is a seen as a sign of hope.
>
> Because Asian cultures place a strong value on the importance of the family, the gift of children is important. However, some parents view their son or daughter as a "deliverer." Parents of devout families may dream that their child will become a pastor or a great spiritual leader in the church or the wider community. Such dreams have led to the practice of dedicating the eldest child to the Lord.
>
> Some parents hope that their children will do better educationally, relationally, and economically, thereby bringing great honor and security to the family. For example, a family member who works overseas as an OFW (Overseas Filipino Worker) is seen as an "economic deliverer" because of the regular remittances that are used not only for the family's daily fare, but also for medical needs, shelter and household repairs, debt repayment, or education. Moreover, a son or daughter who earns a degree in higher education, receives or wins a prestigious award, or is promoted to a prominent position brings honor not only to the family, but also to his or her town or ethnic group. Thus when a child fails, there is often grief and shame within the immediate family as well as the kin group or community.

The lofty mission foretold for Samson, the promised son, is matched by stringent requirements regarding his lifestyle. He is to be a Nazirite, even from his mother's womb (13:5b, 7b). In Numbers 6:1–21, a Nazirite is described as someone who makes a special vow of dedication to the Lord. The rules for a Nazirite, according to Numbers 6:1–21, are the following: a) no wine or intoxicating drink or any product of the grapevine; b) no cutting of hair; c) no going near a corpse, which is regarded as polluting. This vow is temporary and voluntary.

Yet Samson's Nazirite status is peculiar for several reasons: a) it is instituted at birth, even while in his mother's womb, and so the regulations of

---

13. On this theme, see Gustavo Gutierrez, *The God of Life* (Maryknoll, NY: Orbis, 1991).

the Nazirite apply to his mother upon pregnancy; b) the Nazirite status is conferred upon Samson for the whole of his life, so it is not temporary, but for his lifetime; and c) God confers the Nazirite status upon Samson; it is not something he enters voluntarily.[14] Samson's status may have depicted an earlier stage in the development of the Nazirite, where an individual was called to a lifelong special relationship with God, as represented by unshorn hair.[15] Later on, the Nazirite became temporary and was marked by a vow.[16]

In the Jephthah narrative, we see an example of a vow made out of a deep sense of insecurity, which should never have been uttered. Yet there are also legitimate ways to make vows. Asian Christians living in cultures with deep religious traditions may explore appropriate ways of making vows and promises to God, such as dedicating their children to God's service, or making promises to God in terms of self-giving, or committing to be generous with their resources. Some may commit to a life of singleness. Others may promise to return to their troubled homeland. Some may commit to downward mobility for the sake of the gospel. As an Asian Christian leader once observed, "I have seen many missionaries and I know many Asian churchgoers, but I have hardly seen any holy men and women." Thus in order to resist the pragmatic Christianity that has been imported from the West, Asian Christians may feel called to take vows that reflect the practices of Christian religious orders. If ordinary Christians commit to a life of prayer in the midst of daily work, for example, we may begin to see holy women and men, along with a Christianity of depth, grace, and missional relevance.

Samson's early years suggest that he is well on his way to fulfilling the great expectations that greeted his birth: "He grew and the LORD blessed him, and the Spirit of the LORD began to stir him while he was in Mahaneh Dan, between Zorah and Eshtaol" (13:24b–25). This verse observes that Samson's childhood is characterized by blessing, and the language echoes the childhoods of Samuel, John the Baptist, and Jesus. This may indicate that the narrator is using formulaic language to emphasize Yahweh's favor and presence during Samson's childhood.[17] In addition, the spirit of the Lord is already

---

14. For further discussion see Block, *Judges*, 403.
15. Tony W. Cartledge, "Were Nazirite Vows Unconditional?" *CBQ* 51 (1989): 411–412. According to him, the text does not show Samson making a vow; in addition, the only prohibition that seems to have applied to him is the uncut hair and not the ban on alcoholic drinks.
16. Cartledge, "Nazirite Vows," 413.
17. Compare the account about Jesus: "And the child grew and became strong; he was filled with wisdom, and the grace of God was on him" (Luke 2:40); "And Jesus grew in wisdom and stature, and in favor with God and man" (Luke 2:52). See also the accounts of John the

evident in Samson's life, even before his first battle against Israel's oppressors. In the accounts of the other judges, the spirit of the Lord figures prominently just before a judge goes into battle (see 3:10; 6:34; 11:29).

Thus Judges 13 is marked by spiritual encounters, words of promise, spiritual entreaty, worship, obedience, and the shaping and formation of Samson's early life. With Yahweh's blessing and spirit on the boy (13:24–25), and with the promise that Samson will begin to deliver the Israelites from the oppression of the Philistines (13:5) after a long period of Philistine domination (13:1), the reader expects purposeful liberating action, particularly since Samson is born for this purpose (13:3) and is being raised within the disciplined lifestyle of the Nazirite vow (13:4–5, 12–14). Out of such promise, preparation, and faithfulness, the reader anticipates a devout and disciplined son, a faithful servant of Yahweh.

But between a promise and its fulfillment, there is the long road of obedience. Samson's anticipated role is clearly circumscribed and limited, since the emissary of Yahweh uses the revealing phrase, "begin to deliver" (13:5), to describe his mission. The remainder of Samson's saga reveals how he partially lives up to this expectation. Yet his partial victory lies in the ruins of his own life, and his death marks this "boy of promise" with sadness and disappointment.

Samson's Father: A Pious Pedant

Yet even before Samson embarks on his career, the reader's expectations are subverted by the depiction of Samson's father, the pious Manoah, who mistakenly assumes that his devoutness entitles him to be the proper recipient of divine revelation instead of his wife.

The opening lines of the narrative immediately put the spotlight on Manoah: "There was a certain man of Zorah, of the tribe of the Danites, whose name was Manoah . . ." (13:2a, ESV). Because he is named, and his lineage is mentioned, he is given clear identity and status.[18] This pattern of naming continues throughout the annunciation episode. Manoah's name is mentioned sixteen times in chapter 13, which is a remarkable reiteration,

---

Baptist: "And the child grew and became strong in spirit and he lived in the wilderness until he appeared publicly to Israel" (Luke 1:80), and Samuel: "And the boy Samuel continued to grow in stature and in favor with the Lord and with people" (1 Sam 2:26); "The LORD was with Samuel as he grew up, and he let none of Samuel's words fall to the ground" (1 Sam 3:19–20).
18. Mark Greene, "Enigma Variations: Aspects of the Samson Story: Judges 13–16," *Vox Evangelica* 21 (1991): 58.

since he is only described as the father of Samson in chapter 14.[19] In contrast, Manoah's wife is unnamed and unidentified:[20] "and his wife was barren and had no children" (13:2b, ESV). The anonymity of Manoah's wife remains throughout the annunciation and the birth accounts, which identify her as "the woman" or "his wife."[21] Hence, the woman has no identity of her own, since she is defined only in relation to her husband.[22] Generally, in biblical narrative, the main protagonists are named while secondary characters are unnamed.[23] The naming of Manoah, along with the anonymity of his wife, creates the expectation that Manoah will be the main character in the story,[24] while his wife will play the part of the agent.[25]

Aside from the pattern of naming, the structure of the story also highlights the figure of Manoah. The central and most extensive portion of the annunciation episode consists of his dialogue with the angel of Yahweh (vv. 11–18), as the following structure shows:

1. Problem: The Woman's Barrenness (2)
    a. The First Appearance (3–8)
        (1) First Appearance to the Woman (3–5)
        (2) The Woman Tells Her Husband (6–7)
        (3) Manoah's Plea for Another Visit (8)
    b. The Second Appearance (9–18)
        (1) Second Appearance to the Woman (9)
        (2) The Woman Tells Her Husband (10)

---

19. Excerpts for the following section are taken from Gorospe, "Comedy and Humor," 182–217. See also Athena Gorospe, "Inversions of Expectations and Roles in Judges 13: A Study in Literary Method," *Phronesis* 2, 2 (1995): 27–42.
20. Scholars point out the peculiarity of the woman being nameless, since she is the main protagonist in the story. See James Crenshaw, "The Samson Saga: Filial Devotion or Erotic Attachment," *ZAW* 86 (1974): 473; Soggin, *Judges*, 233; Exum, "Promise and Fulfillment," 45; Robert Alter, "Samson Without Folklore," in *Text and Tradition: The Hebrew Bible and Folklore*, ed. Susan Niditch (Atlanta, GA: Scholars, 1990), 51. This is exceptional since in biblical stories of barren women who have conceived, the names of the women are always mentioned (Exum, "Promise and Fulfillment," 48).
21. "The woman" is used in vv. 3, 6, 9, 10, 24 (narrator's term), v. 13 (the term of the emissary of Yahweh) and v. 12 (Manoah's term for his wife, which can be translated "this woman"). The husband, too, is also described thrice by the narrator as "her husband" (vv. 6, 9, 10), but in each instance, the narrator merely assumes the perceptual vantage point of the woman.
22. Adele Reinhartz, "Samson's Mother: An Unnamed Protagonist," *JSOT* 55 (1992): 26–27.
23. Reinhartz, "Samson's Mother," 26–27.
24. Greene, "Enigma Variations," 57.
25. Adele Berlin, *Poetics and the Interpretation of Biblical Narrative* (Sheffield: Almond Press, 1983), 32, defines an agent as a character whose importance lies only in his or her function in the plot or as part of the setting.

(3) Manoah's Dialogue with the Messenger (11–18)
    (a) First Interchange (11)
    (b) Second Interchange (12–14)
    (c) Third Interchange (15–16)
    (d) Fourth Interchange (17–18)
2. The Recognition Scene (19–23)
3. Resolution: The Woman Gives Birth to a Son (24b)

At the beginning of the account of the first visit, the narrative hints that things are not what they seem to be: "The emissary of the Lord appeared to *the woman* and said to *her* . . . (v. 3, trans., emph. mine)."[26] The focus on the woman contrasts sharply with the spotlight on Manoah in verse 2. The messenger promises the woman a son, gives her instructions about the regulations she should observe, and foretells the future son's career as a deliverer of Israel (vv. 3–5). The close interdependence between the mother's actions and the future son's life[27] suggests the importance of the woman in Yahweh's plan of deliverance.

Without responding to the visitor, the woman leaves to tell her husband about the encounter (vv. 6–7). Manoah implores God for another visit (v. 8), which can be interpreted as a longing for the prophetic word – a sign of deep piety. Yet the content of Manoah's prayer discloses his misgivings about his wife's testimony: "Please, Lord, let the man of God that you sent come again to us and instruct us what we shall do to the boy who is to be born" (13:8). The emphasis on "us" reveals a desire on Manoah's part for a visitation that will include him. His request for information, which was already given to the woman, suggests skepticism at his wife's report.

Verse 9 renews the reader's expectations about Manoah's importance – "And God listened to Manoah" – but that expectation is immediately shattered by the next phrase: "and the emissary of God came again to the woman while she was sitting in the field." Contrary to Manoah's request to be included in the next visitation, the messenger appears to the woman alone. The narrative specifically emphasizes this: "but Manoah, her husband, was not

---

26. The translations in the rest of this chapter are mine, including emphasis, except when a Bible version is stated.
27. Esther Fuchs, "The Literary Characterization of Mothers and Sexual Politics in the Hebrew Bible," *Semeia* 46 (1989): 156.

with her" (v. 9b). Despite Manoah's desire to be at the center of prophetic revelation, he is deliberately excluded from the scene of the second visit.[28]

Nevertheless, the woman – the ever dutiful wife – runs in haste to her husband before the messenger can utter a word (v. 10a). Her behavior towards her husband remains conscientious and respectful, but her report doubly emphasizes that the appearance is meant for her: "Behold, the man appeared to me, who came that day to me" (v. 10b).[29] Without waiting for a reply, the woman hurries back to the visitor, leaving Manoah to "follow" after her (v. 11). The one who thinks of himself as a more dependable receiver of revelation must now follow after the woman whose credibility he has questioned. Without the initiative of his wife, Manoah would not have had the opportunity to have a personal encounter with the messenger of God. Nevertheless, Manoah dominates the following scene (vv. 11–18), excluding his wife, who quietly listens at the sidelines.

Each of the four exchanges in the series consists of Manoah asking a question, and the messenger responding to his queries. The first question seeks to confirm the veracity of the woman's report, that this is indeed the visitor who spoke to her. The visitor answers without elaboration: "I am" (v. 11). In the second question, Manoah comes to his main agenda, which is to gather more information concerning God's plan for the child: "What shall be the boy's manner of life[30] and what is he to do?" (v. 12). The visitor simply repeats the information that he originally gave to the woman (vv. 13–14).[31] Yet he offers the most complete information to the woman while withholding significant information from Manoah.[32] This upholds the reliability of the woman's report while deflating Manoah's sense of his own credibility and importance. As Polzin comments, "The knowledgeable Manoah remains ignorant" and "his unknowing wife becomes knowledgeable."[33]

As if sensing the messenger's evasive answers, Manoah stops asking questions and invites the visitor for a meal. In the ancient Near East, travelers

---

28. Exum, "Promise and Fulfillment," 53.
29. Ibid., 47.
30. The noun *mishpat* (literally, "judgements" or "regulations"; "rule" in the NIV and the NRSV) means "manner of life" in this verse (Soggin, *Judges*, 234). See Deut 18:3 and 1 Sam 3:11.
31. Twice, the messenger of Yahweh points to the information given to the woman, in v. 13 and v. 14.
32. Exum ("Promise and Fulfillment," 58) and Polzin (*Moses and the Deuteronomist*, 183) note this. In responding to Manoah, the messenger omits the information about the boy's Nazirite status (with the regulation of unshorn hair) and his destiny as a deliverer of Israel.
33. Polzin, *Moses and the Deuteronomist*, 183.

who arrive at a strange town have claims to protection and full sustenance.[34] Manoah's offering is part of his culture's hospitality. Nonetheless, his offer reveals his lack of awareness about what is happening, which is stressed by the narrator: "For Manoah did not know that he was the emissary of the LORD" (v. 16). The offer of food is refused (v. 16a), which hints that the visitor is more than human, since in the ancient Near East the gods do not eat with humans.[35] Moreover, the refusal also provides a further clue to the visitor's divine identity[36] when the messenger bids Manoah to turn the offer of a meal into an offering to Yahweh (v. 16b), implying a connection between the meal offering to the visitor and the grain and burnt offering to Yahweh. In spite of these apparent gestures, Manoah still fails to perceive the visitor's identity.

Manoah's obliviousness in this dialogue achieves its climax with his fourth question: "Who . . . Your name"[37]? (v. 17). The query accentuates the fact that Manoah has failed to pick up the hints given by the messenger, for he still has no clue about the visitor's real identity.[38] As in the other exchanges, the messenger refuses to answer Manoah's question directly, offering a reticent, even mysterious reply: "Why do you ask my name, seeing it is beyond comprehension?" (v. 18).

Throughout these exchanges, Manoah's inquisitiveness and insistence on answers and explanations[39] contrast sharply with the demeanor of his wife, who remains in respectful silence, even though the visitor's message has a direct bearing on her life. Manoah's repeated attempts to get answers are frustrated again and again by the messenger's evasive and restrained responses. The patriarchal head of the household tries different ways to get center stage and take control, but these are not appreciated by the emissary of Yahweh, who says: "listen to your wife" (v. 13); "I can't accept your food" (v. 16); "I won't reveal my name" (v. 18).

After Manoah offers the grain and burnt offering, both he and his wife witness the miraculous ascent of the emissary of Yahweh with the flame of the sacrifice, "and they fell on their faces to the ground" (vv. 19–20). The

---

34. Roland de Vaux, *Ancient Israel: Its Life and Institutions,* Vol. 1 (New York: McGraw Hill, 1965), 10.
35. Sasson, *Judges 1–12,* 334–335.
36. Exum, "Promise and Fulfillment," 51.
37. The Hebrew uses the pronoun for "who," rather than "what." Boling (*Judges,* 222) thinks that the use of the wrong pronoun is deliberate to indicate Manoah's confusion.
38. Exum, "Promise and Fulfillment," 54. Manoah's lack of perception is emphasized in v. 16: "Manoah did not realize that it was the angel of the LORD" (NIV).
39. Webb, *Judges: Integrated Reading,* 174.

individual reactions of the couple to the divine manifestation reveal their interpretation of the divine messenger's appearance. With a consistent and religiously narrow frame of mind, Manoah interprets the manifestation as a form of judgement, and so he expresses a fear of death: "We shall surely die, for we have seen God" (v. 22). According to his stock of religious knowledge, anyone who sees God must die. Yet Manoah's terror is sharply incongruous with the brash attitude he displayed in his dialogue with the divine messenger; his awed response to God's holiness is the diametrical opposite to his earlier inquisitiveness about the visitor's words and identity.

The wife's prosaic and down-to-earth comment (v. 23) provides comic relief to the seriousness of the situation, since it is highly incongruous with the solemnity of the annunciation and the awesomeness of the miraculous ascent. Throughout the account, the narrator omits any reference to the woman's inner thoughts, while her husband's reactions and opinions are explicitly stated. Thus it is quite surprising for the woman to voice her objections to Manoah's conclusions. We will see more of her reaction in the next section.

What makes Manoah's response foolish is not its incorrectness but its inappropriateness. When he should have responded with awe, he reacted with skepticism. But when it was time for him to respond with gratitude and trust, he became apprehensive and terrified. In contrast, Manoah's wife was awed by the first visit because she perceived the visitor's divine identity. However, as she understood more of God's plan, she became more confident and assured, which enabled her to respond in trust at the end of the episode.

Manoah, the head of the household, while a good and pious man, is hardly the true spiritual leader in this story. In spite of his spiritual and pious pretensions, he is clearly not as discerning as he thinks he is, for his humble and unpretentious wife understands the mystery of God's ways. Thus a role reversal takes place, where the slightly comic and bumbling Manoah, despite all his efforts to do the right thing, fails to understand what is going on until much later.

Some men who regard themselves as the head of the household may not consider the counsel or opinion of their wives in making major decisions because they believe that their reasoning is better or their judgement is superior. Indeed, some women may not be able to articulate their intuitions clearly. This can lead to decision-making troubles, especially in relationships where the man is very logical while the woman is more intuitive. The wife may be hesitant without being able to explain fully the reasons for her reservations. Instead of listening to her intuitions and waiting until things become clearer, the husband may go ahead and make a decision because his reasons seem very logical and practical. The result is disaster, for the wife ends up resenting her husband because she feels that she has not been carefully listened to, and the husband often ends up making a deficient decision.

This pattern can also be expressed in relationships between colleagues in an organization or between the leaders of a church. Some are more intuitive and others are more logical. Often, the ones who can set forth their reasons in a logical and clear way win the day. But it is important to listen carefully and to ask questions patiently of those who may not be able to articulate their reservations immediately. Learning to wait until intuition becomes more clear may prove more valuable for the group in the long term.

In the portrayal of Manoah as somewhat pedantic, the narrative also mocks those who take pride in their religious orthodoxy while missing the underlying spirit. The pedant's moralizing tendency, as expressed in general maxims and universal statements, results in a lack of perception about the reality of his own faults and an inability to adapt to circumstances that demand fresh responses. Such inflexibility results in Manoah's failure to respond correctly after the ascent of the emissary of Yahweh, since he cannot apprehend a reality beyond the narrow confines of his knowledge about religious regulations. As David Gunn says, "There is Manoah who must be sure, must map out the future, must fit his experience to the rules of the religious life."[40] In this he is not unlike the friends of Job, who "say the right things about God but who become ridiculous in their approach because of the irrelevance of their counsel."[41]

This also echoes Jesus' rebuke to the Pharisees, who tithed their spices while neglecting the weightier matters of the law in terms of practicing justice and demonstrating the love of God to others (Matt 23:23; Luke 11:42). Our eyes can easily become myopic, focusing on strict adherence to legalistic details while missing the big picture of what is behind those details. Thus there can be outward conformance without heartfelt devotion or self-sacrifice without love (see 1 Cor 13:3). When we no longer discern the presence of God, our lives of faith become joyless and obligatory.

---

40. David Gunn, "Samson," a paper read at a seminar in the biblical studies department at the University of Sheffield, 1982, quoted by Webb, *Judges: Integrated Reading*, 174.
41. Whedbee, "Comedy of Job," 13.

Samson's Mother: A Woman of Discernment

The root word *ra'ah*, whose basic meaning is "to see,"[42] is repeated several times in the annunciation episode as well as in the rest of the Samson narrative. According to Greene, the repetition of this word serves as a thematic device to emphasize the importance of "right seeing."[43]

In 13:3, the emissary of Yahweh "appeared" for the first time to the woman. The underlying root word for "appear" in this verse is *ra'ah*, which is a Hebrew verb form that functions as a technical term for divine manifestation.[44] So even though the characters do not immediately recognize the true nature of the visitor, the narrator clearly indicates the visitor's divine identity to readers.

Even though the woman refers to the visitor as "man of God" (v. 6) to her husband, which is a common designation for a prophet of God, her description of the visitor indicates that she perceives his otherworldly quality, although in a very indistinct way[45]: "A man of God came to me, and his countenance (*ra'ah*) was like the countenance (*ra'ah*) of an angel of God, very awesome" (v. 6a). Her reticence in asking the visitor's name and origin (v. 6b) may come from an intuitive sense about his transcendent nature. Thus, the woman speaks better than she knows.[46] Through this, "the narrator . . . has Manoah's wife come very close to the truth in her groping way."[47]

The woman's report to her husband about the second visit is even more ambiguous. She drops the term "man of God" and simply calls the visitor "the man," possibly indicating that she is unsure whether the man is a prophet or not. Yet she uses the technical term for divine manifestation (*niphal* form of *ra'ah*), which is used by the narrator in verse 3, and which may indicate her growing discernment about the visitor's supernatural identity.

After the visitor's miraculous ascent, his identity as a deity is conclusively established. The narrative emphasizes how the couple witness the divine manifestation, enclosing the miraculous event with this same phrase: "while Manoah and his wife were watching (*ra'ah*)" (vv. 19b, 20b). The repetition of

---

42. It occurs seven times in the annunciation episode and nine times in the rest of the Samson narrative (chs. 14–16).
43. Greene, "Enigma Variations," 48.
44. Soggin, *Judges*, 115. The verb form of *ra'ah* is in the *niphal*. For example, see Gen 12:7; 17:1; 26:2, 4; Exod 3:2; Judg 6:12.
45. Exum, "Promise and Fulfillment," 48.
46. Boling, *Judges*, 220–221.
47. Ibid., 221.

the phrase and the root word *ra'ah* function as a framing device to stress the event which brought about a change in the couple's perception.

After this miraculous event, the angel no longer "appeared" to Manoah and his wife (v. 21a), and then the narrative says: "Then Manoah knew that he was the emissary of Yahweh" (v. 21b). Ironically, Manoah only comes to "see" the divine nature of Yahweh's emissary after he ceases his divine manifestation. The narrator's comment in verse 21b – "then Manoah knew that he was the emissary of Yahweh" – is the antithetical parallel of verse 16b –"for Manoah did not know that he was the emissary of Yahweh." These two phrases enclose the events that led Manoah from a condition of "not knowing" to a condition of "knowing," or from a position of "physically seeing" but "not truly seeing" to a position of "not physically seeing" but "truly seeing." Notably, only Manoah undergoes a change of perception, since his wife has already discerned the real nature of the visitor.[48]

Yet even though Manoah finally "sees" (recognizes) the visitor's deity as a result of "seeing" (physically viewing) his marvelous ascent, he still cannot "see" (discern) the divine plan behind the manifestation. He fears instant death because he and his wife have seen (*ra'ah*) Yahweh (v. 22). However, as Manoah's wife explains, Yahweh himself has shown (*hir'eh*, which is another form of the verb *ra'ah*)[49] them these things (v. 23). If Yahweh has caused them to see his wonders, why should he now kill them for seeing him?

From the woman's point of view, Manoah's fear is absurd for three reasons (v. 23).[50] First, the fact that God has accepted their offerings indicates God's favor, not his judgement. Second, the spectacular display of a miracle is futile if God intends for them to die.[51] Third, the announcement involves the promise of the birth of a son, a prophecy that cannot be fulfilled if the woman dies. The woman's logical and practical approach diverges considerably from her husband's rigid, orthodox understanding. Her commonsensical estimation of the situation is a far more accurate reading of God's intention than her husband's religiously correct perception.[52]

---

48. Crenshaw, *A Secret Betrayed*, 78; Exum, "Promise and Fulfillment," 53, n. 25.
49. The Hebrew verb form is in the *hiphil*, which transforms the root into causative, "he caused to see," or in other words, "to show."
50. Greene, "Enigma Variations," 58.
51. Fuchs, "Literary Characterizations," 156.
52. E. John Hamlin describes Manoah's faith as "traditional and rational, but slow to recognize the presence of God." The woman's faith, on the other hand, is described as "intuitive faith." See *Judges: At Risk in the Promised Land*, International Theological Commentary (Grand Rapids, MI: Eerdmans, 1990), 131–132.

The repeated use of variant forms of the root word *ra'ah* in this chapter illumines the real meaning of discernment. Manoah, though seeing, does not really perceive, while his wife, who is in the background and is largely unseen, has a more perceptive reading of the meaning behind the miraculous events.

In the OT, discernment is connected with wisdom, which is represented by several words. Perhaps the closest root word to discernment is *bin* ("to perceive"), which suggests seeing beyond the external to grasp the deeper meaning of things. Hence, discernment is connected with having insight and right judgement.[53] The woman in Judges 13 is able to perceive the divine character of the visitor and the meaning of his message, and so she is able to make the right judgement regarding the appropriate response to the messenger's disappearance.

Discernment need not be mystical. As in the story, it is very practical, for in order to make the right judgement, one must be able to grasp the contextual features of a particular situation.[54] Asian cultures know full well that book knowledge, theoretical mastery, and strict adherence to rules are not sufficient to make one wise. For this reason, elders, who have long experience, practical know-how and skill, are regarded with respect.

The danger, however, is to equate practicality with discernment. Action people, in their desire for quick solutions and results, may leave no space and time for the attainment of insight. Moreover, the stress on "what works" may supersede "what is right" and "appropriate" for a certain situation. It is therefore important for Christians to draw from the resources of the wisdom tradition, which are ingrained in many Asian cultures. All our actions must spring from true insight.

Divine Messenger: The God Who Hides and Reveals

As in the Gideon narrative, the emissary of Yahweh in this chapter mysteriously appears at a crucial time to bring a message of hope. The mystery of Yahweh's activity is foreshadowed by the secrecy of the messenger's identity in chapter 13. The messenger does not tell his name to the woman (v. 6), and when his name is asked by Manoah (v. 17), the messenger's reply is cryptic. He says that his name is *peli'y*, which means "wonderful, marvelous" (v. 18).[55] *Pele'*, the root word the angel uses to describe his name, is used elsewhere

---

53. See Helmer Ringgren, "*bin, bināh, t^ebhûnāh*," TDOT 2:100–102.
54. On this, see Martha Nussbaum, *Love's Knowledge: Essays on Philosophy and Literature* (New York: Oxford University Press, 1990), 37–38.
55. The adjective is attested only in the feminine (*pil'iyah*; read as *pel'iyah*) in Ps 139:6.

in the OT to express a phenomenon that is unexplainable, incomprehensible, and inaccessible (hence, the NIV's translation "beyond understanding").[56] It also describes a kind of knowledge that is so high that it cannot be attained (Ps 139:6). In the Psalms, it is often used to extol the marvelous works of Yahweh.[57]

In verse 19, the narrator describes Yahweh as "the one who works wonders" (ESV).[58] The wonders may refer to the barren woman conceiving and giving birth, the messenger ascending with the flame of the sacrifice,[59] or to the whole paradox of Yahweh's work in Samson's birth, life, and mission. But the narrative emphasizes the incomprehensibility of God's action, which human beings can never fully grasp.[60]

What is particularly striking in this account is the encounter between the emissary of Yahweh as a transcendent spiritual figure and Manoah and his wife. At the very heart of the OT is the idea that Yahweh, though powerful, majestic and transcendent, is a God who draws near to his people. God drew near to Moses with revelatory clarity, as God drew near to Joshua and Gideon, as God draws near to this insignificant couple of the tribe of Danites (13:2).

Theologically, the presence or dynamism of Yahweh is not only manifested in word and deed, but also through appearance or encounter, which can be revealed in the presence of the spirit, dreams, visions, or through intermediary figures sent by Yahweh. We have seen in the Gideon narrative how Yahweh makes use of intermediary figures, and this occurs throughout the OT story (Gen 18; Exod 3). Since appearance and presence can be ambiguous, both word and spirit are important in the process of discerning the meaning and source of a supernatural encounter. However, as chapter

---

56. The word connotes the meaning of something extraordinary or miraculous (Pss 118:23; 139:14). The participle is often used to refer to Yahweh's wonders and mighty deeds on behalf of his people, especially in connection with the "signs and wonders" which accompanied their deliverance from Egypt (Exod 3:20; 34:10; Judg 6:13; Neh 9:17). The essence of this divine activity is not just in its miraculous nature, but in its "unexplainability," except as being due to God's care or retribution (in *TWOT* 2:723). The root is also used for a situation that is so difficult that it is virtually impossible to find a solution (Gen 18:14; Deut 17:8; Jer 32:17, 27), or for things that are so wonderful that they go beyond one's understanding (Prov 30:18; Job 9:10; 37:5; 37:14).
57. Pss 72:18; 75:1 [Heb. 75:2]; 77:14 [Heb. 77:15]; 86:10; 89:5 [Heb. 89:6].
58. In Hebrew, the phrase, "the one who does wonders" *maphli' la'asot* (Judg 13:19), is peculiar. Gesenius for this).
59. J. Conrad, "*pl'; pele*'," *TDOT* 11: 539.
60. *TDOT* 11: 535.

13 shows, religious experience is not simply intellectual or rational, but also experiential, existential, and revelatory.

> ## SPIRITUALITY OF PRESENCE
>
> Presence or encounter is also at the heart of Christian religious experience. This is particularly relevant for Asian Christians, who live in settings characterized by gurus and holy men and women of other religious traditions, where religious experience is paramount and spiritual encounters are normative. Whereas the reformation tradition elevated the significance of the word, and contemporary evangelical Christianity linked word and deed in acts of healing and service, the third component in this story – the source of word (Judg 13:3–5) and deed (Judg 13:24) – is the power of presence and encounter. The emphasis on presence and encounter is part of the contemplative tradition, which has been part of the long march of the church in history, especially renewal and revival movements within the church, including contemporary charismatic renewal. In the Asian "spiritual" world, the persuasive power of Christianity for personal transformation and mission cannot be merely intellectual, for it must also include the spirituality of presence.

14:1–16:3 COMIC REVERSAL IN THE SAMSON-PHILISTINE EPISODES

Judges 14:1–16:3 is dominated by Samson's encounters with the Philistines, which all follow a predictable pattern. First, each begins with Samson in an advantageous position. Secondly, the Philistines try to bring him down by resorting to trickery, each time using a woman to cover up their schemes. Thirdly, the Philistines' plot seems to succeed and Samson appears to be defeated. Fourthly, Samson escapes from their trap and turns the table against them.[61]

14:1–16:3 The Samson-Philistine Rout: Overture

In the first incident (14:1–19), Samson gains an advantage over the Philistines by giving them a riddle, which is known only to him. The Philistines, who neither want to lose face nor their clothes, embark on a scheme to discover the answer to Samson's riddle by shrewdly playing upon his feelings for his

---

61. Portions of the following material are taken from Gorospe, "Comedy and Humor," 54–96.

wife. The Philistines succeed so that on the seventh day, they triumphantly announce the answer, gleefully anticipating the new changes of clothes and the impoverishment of this cocky, inferior Israelite.[62] However, Samson goes to Ashkelon, slays thirty Philistines, disrobes them, and gives their garments to the ones who have won the bet. Thus the Philistines obtain their wager at a bloody price, while Samson loses nothing.

In the second incident (15:4–17), Samson sets fire to the Philistine grain fields after the Philistines take away his Timnite wife.[63] With their harvest up in smoke, the Philistines counter-retaliate by burning his wife and father-in-law. Samson offers yet another counter-retaliation by slaughtering the Philistines,[64] but the Philistines strike back by employing a clever ruse. They threaten Samson's countrymen and pressure them into delivering Samson securely bound with ropes. The Judahites deliver Samson, with his hands fettered, to the Philistines. When the Philistines see Samson coming to Lehi, bound and helpless, they shout in triumph (15:14). The picture, in Boling's words, is that of "Samson with his hands tied walking straight into a pack of Philistines clamoring for revenge."[65] But at the Philistines' approach, Samson breaks his bonds, picks up an ass's jawbone, and slays one thousand of his arch-enemies. Thus the Philistines, instead of capturing Samson, are reduced to a bloody mass. After his mass slaughter, Samson raises his voice for a victory song (15:16):

> "With the jawbone of an ass, heap upon heaps;
> With the jawbone of an ass, I have killed a thousand men."

---

62. The clothing involved in the bet consisted of a light undergarment, which was very highly valued, as can be gleaned from 2 Kgs 5:5, where it is one of the gifts offered by Naaman to Elisha, along with silver and gold (Gray, *Judges*, 330). Cundall and Morris (*Judges*, 166) think that the average person at that time would possess only one such garment. Thus, the Philistines equate their losing in the bet to becoming impoverished (14:15).

63. Although the burning of the fields is used elsewhere in biblical literature to attract someone's attention (2 Sam 14:28–31), the mode which Samson uses is a novel one. He catches three hundred foxes (or jackals, according to Soggin [*Judges*, 246] and Boling [*Judges*, 235]), tied each pair tail to tail, put a torch in between each pair of tails, and sent the foxes off into the Philistine fields. The ease with which Samson accomplishes the complicated feat of catching three hundred foxes and tying their tails in pairs highlights the magnitude of his prowess (Exum, *Symmetry and Balance*, 17).

64. The meaning of "hip and thigh" or "leg on thigh" (15:8) is unknown. Possibly, it is a technical military expression (Soggin, *Judges*, 246) or a term referring to some sort of wrestling match (Cundall and Morris, *Judges*, 170), but Gray thinks that these meanings are not at all clear (*Judges*, 332). Based on the phrase that follows it, "with great slaughter," the term may likely be an idiom for total defeat or total routing of the enemy.

65. Boling, *Judges*, 238. Just as a lion roars when it is about to attack and kill its prey (14:5), the Philistines "roar" in voracious anticipation of tearing Samson to pieces.

Ironically, in spite of the Philistines' triumphant shouts, Samson utters the victory song in the end.

In the third episode (16:1–3), Samson goes to spend the night with a prostitute in Gaza. Upon hearing this, the Philistines plot together about how best to seize him. They decide to wait by the city gates, so that when Samson comes out, tired and depleted from a night of spent passion, they can easily lay hold of him. They wait eagerly, certain that the dawn will bring their mortal enemy into their hands. As they crouch by the gates, along comes Samson, uprooting the very doors of the gates which are hiding them. He takes hold of everything – the doors, the posts, the bar, and all – and carries them on his shoulders. Samson goes on to Hebron, while the men who have conspired against him are left stunned and exposed by the sudden removal of their hiding place. Once again, victory has eluded the Philistines. Once again, Samson slips away from their grasp.

14:1–16:3 Retaliations and Counter-Retaliations: A Closer Look at Violence and Comedy

The use of scenic repetition – where the same characters are placed in different settings, encounter the same series of incidents, with more or less the same reactions and consequences – makes Samson's encounters with the Philistines comic.[66] Such scenic repetition is reminiscent of the slapstick head hitting that occurs in *Charlie Chaplin* movies, where Chaplin hits someone in the head; that person hits him back; Chaplin strikes a stronger blow; then his opponent give a counter-blow. On and on, they hit each other, using different implements until the violence escalates and the scene degenerates into a farce, with everyone striking everyone else, except the one who committed the original action. Or, in the case of the *Three Stooges*, the characters repeatedly slap each other in the face with a pie or cake until the episode ends with everyone covered in pastry. In the Samson story, the actions of retaliation and counter-retaliation intensify until the whole incident culminates in a bloodbath (15:8, 15).

Aside from the almost mechanical repetition of events, the comedy is heightened by the skillful use of comic reversal. This common device is in used in many comic plays, where there is an inversion of roles, such as "the robber robbed," "the cheat cheated," or "the villain who is the victim of his

---

66. Henri Bergson, "Laughter," in George Meredith, *Comedy* (Doubleday AB; Garden City, NY: Doubleday, 1956), 119.

own villainy."⁶⁷ In the three episodes outlined above, the Philistines are presented as cunning conspirators who delight in their own abilities to maneuver events. However, by trying to make a fool out of Samson, they become greater fools themselves. Notwithstanding their meticulously planned schemes, Samson manages to escape right under their very noses.

The violence of these episodes can be problematic for readers, especially since Samson's bouts against the Philistines seem to be linked with the spirit "rushing upon him" (Judg 14:19; 15:14, ESV). Three of the four episodes in Samson's encounters with the Philistines end in violence.⁶⁸ At the conclusion of each confrontation, we get a vision of spilled blood, mangled limbs, and piles of corpses.

One way to interpret this violence is to consider the comic genre, since violence is by no means alien to comedy. According to Edwin Good, comedy is full of violence because it proposes a new order of society or the renewal of the old one.⁶⁹ The violence is used as a means of removing or renewing the characters that block the movement towards a new society. This pattern expresses the "comic vision" noted above.

Strangely, however, the violence in comedy is not meant to evoke sympathy or outrage in the readers. In the Samson story, for instance, we feel no pity for the Philistines, and we remain unmoved even though they are flattened to death. As Exum and Whedbee observe, "The narrative allows no place for remorse over the Philistine casualties of Samson's pranks and angry outbursts."⁷⁰

The reason for this lack of feeling for the Philistines' plight is the narrator's use of comic distance. In order to make his readers laugh at the objects of his ridicule (in this case, the Philistines), the narrator must relate their experiences from the standpoint of emotional detachment. If too much sympathetic feeling comes in, arousing the readers' pity for the Philistines, then the violence that befalls them will no longer be laughable. As Bergson puts it, "the comic demands something like a momentary anaesthesia of the

---

67. Bergson, "Laughter," 122.
68. This is true of the first and second episodes, as noted above, as well as the final episode with Delilah, which will be discussed in the next section. Although the third episode with the Gaza prostitute does not end in slaughter, it has the potential to explode into a very violent situation.
69. Edwin Good, "Apocalyptic as Comedy: The Book of Daniel," *Semeia* 32 (1984): 45.
70. Exum and Whedbee, "Reflections on the Comic and Tragic Visions," 33.

heart."⁷¹ Indifference and absence of charitable feelings are laughter's natural environment.

14:1–16:3 Mocking the Enemy: A Closer Look at Satire as a Tool

The skirmishes between Samson and the Philistines contain two elements that characterize satirical works. First, these episodes use wit and humor that borders on the fantastic, grotesque, and absurd. Secondly, an object of attack is present within each of the episodes.⁷² Even as the narrator describes the Philistines' astuteness in conjuring up stratagems, he also jeers at their cowardice and shortsightedness. He portrays them as being too petrified to confront Samson directly, and so they resort to burning Samson's wife and father-in-law to get back at him (15:6). The Philistines' cowardice is also evident in the way they recruit assistance from women (14:15; 16:5) and even their own enemies, the Israelites (15:9–10), to ensure that Samson will be out of action before they confront him.⁷³ When the Philistines finally summon enough courage to capture him, they do it with a whole battalion of men during the secrecy of night (16:2).⁷⁴ Thus the Philistines' overweening pride is brought down, and they are exposed as being dimwitted and weak rather than clever and strong.

The Samson-Philistine episodes bear a remarkable similarity to other comic narratives in the OT. Earlier in the book of Judges, the Moabites were the objects of amusing ridicule in the Ehud story (3:15–30), and Shamgar killed six hundred Philistines with an oxgoad, a humble farming implement (3:31).⁷⁵ The ark narratives (1 Sam 4–7) are also replete with comic moments, such as the repetitious falling down of the image of Dagon on the threshold of its own temple, with its head or one of its limbs cut off (1 Sam 5:3–5). Moreover, the scene of Dagon lying before the ark of Yahweh with only the

---

71. Bergson, "Laughter," 63–64.
72. Northrop Frye, *Anatomy of Criticism: Four Essays* (Toronto, ON: University of Toronto Press, 2006), 224.
73. Exum notes how the Philistines use intimidation to secure the aid of a third party to gain an advantage over Samson ("Symmetry and Balance," 17).
74. One ludicrous scene is Samson's battle with the Philistines using a donkey's jawbone. Samson's twofold repetition of the term for the weapon, which he uses in his triumphant shout ("with a jawbone of an ass"), emphasizes the ineptitude of the Philistines, who can be knocked to the ground with just a swing of a donkey's bone.
75. Webb takes note of Shamgar's makeshift weapon, thus marking him as a "non-professional, makeshift warrior" (*Judges: Integrated Reading*, 132). This gives the story a grotesque, satirical quality.

trunk of its body remaining conveys the absolute futility of the Philistine god before Yahweh, the God of Israel. Finally, of all the diseases that could have plagued the inhabitants of Ashdod, who took the ark, Yahweh sends the undignified disease of tumors, which may be hemorrhoids[76] (1 Sam 5:6–12). After noting the similarities of the ark narratives with the Samson narrative, H. W. Hertzberg observes:

> The audience would have been overcome with laughter on hearing how the God of Ashdod fell down on his nose before the ark of Yahweh or on listening to the consummate way in which the God of the stolen ark dealt with those who had taken it.[77]

One possible way to look at these satirical accounts is to see them as resistance stories. James Wharton suggests that these stories, in their earliest stages of composition, were actually indirect expressions of Israelite aggression against the Philistines when the Philistines were still rulers over Israel.[78]

14:1–16:3 Resisting the Powers: A Closer Look at Humor as a Weapon

Studies have shown that humor often serves as an outlet for tension and frustration.[79] Moreover, it has been used as a form of non-violent resistance against oppression and domination. For example, M. J. Sorenson shows how humor played a part in the Serbian Otpor movement, which challenged Milosevic in the 1990s, by building solidarity among the oppressed and strengthening

---

76. The word for "tumors" (1 Sam 5:6, 9, 12; 6:4, 5 in the NIV) is written in the Hebrew text (*kethib*) as *'opalim*, usually meaning "hills" or "mounds," but it can also mean "swelling," according to P. Kyle McCarter, Jr., *1 Samuel*, AB (Garden City, NY: Doubleday, 1980), 123; "a thickening of tissue" in *HALOT*, study ed., 1: 861. In public reading (*qere*), however, the word is read as *tekhorim* (1 Sam 5:6, 9, 12; 6:4, 5, 11, 17), which means "hemorrhoids" (*HALOT*, study ed., 1:374).

77. Hans Wilhelm Hertzberg, *I & II Samuel: A Commentary*, OTL (London: SCM, 1964), 63. Another tale which provides a parallel to the satirical humor in the Samson narrative is the story of David and Goliath. Here the description of Goliath's military accessories is exaggerated to provide a striking contrast to the weakness and vulnerability of David. The narrator's mockery of Philistine strength can be detected in the way he relates the account of David's slaying of Goliath: "So David prevailed over the Philistine with a sling and with a stone, and struck the Philistine and killed him; there was no sword in the hand of David" (1 Sam 17:50, ESV). It is interesting to note that, in the same way that Samson is able to defeat a whole mob of attacking Philistines with an inconsequential weapon (Judg 15:15–16), David also vanquishes a heavily armed Philistine giant with a sling (1 Sam 17:40).

78. This is presupposed in the text in Judg 14:4b: "for at that time they [the Philistines] were ruling over Israel."

79. Jacob Levine summarizes the results of these studies in *Motivation in Humor* (New York: Atherton, 1969), 10–20.

their capacity for resistance. Humor helps the oppressed overcome apathy and reduces their fear by casting the oppressor in a less than dignified light.[80] In light of the Philistine oppression of Israel during Samson's time, the mockery of the Philistines within these episodes may have originated as protests against Philistine domination and superiority.

In biblical history, the skirmishes between the Philistines and the Israelites (particularly the tribes of Judah and Dan) arose because of the proximity of their territories. The Philistines occupied the coastal plain, while the Danites and the Judahites dwelt in the Shephelah, the fertile hilly region overlooking the southern coast of Palestine. Not content to stay in that narrow strip of land near the seashore, the Philistines began to move inland, pressuring and displacing the Israelite inhabitants of the lowlands next to the coast, perhaps with the desire to control not only the sea routes, but also the overland routes.[81] Hence, they sought to subdue the Israelites, who were living near the trade routes on the central ridges of Palestine. The Samson narratives show that the Philistines were successful in their bid to control the southern and central tribes of Israel (Judg 14:4; 15:20; 15:11). In the opening chapters of the book of Samuel, we see Philistine supremacy over Israel reaching its height with the capture of the ark of Yahweh (1 Sam 4:10–11).

The success of Philistine expansionism was largely due to their superior military technology, especially in the production of military armaments.[82] Because of the advanced state of their metal craft, they were able to control the trade of metallurgy. This was a great disadvantage to the Israelites, who had to go down to the Philistine coast and pay a fee before they could have their farming and domestic implements sharpened (see 1 Sam 13:19–22). According to the biblical account, part of the Philistine strategy for the continual subjugation of Israel was to outlaw blacksmiths (1 Sam 13:19). Thus, during Saul's reign as king, "there was neither sword nor spear found in the hand of any of the people" (1 Sam 13:22). In addition to this, the Philistines had excellent military organization and strategy. They established military posts and garrisons at strategic points in their conquered territories

---

80. M. J. Sorensen, "Humor as a Serious Strategy of Nonviolent Resistance to Oppression," *Peace & Change* 33 (2008): 160–190. Online: http://onlinelibrary.wiley.com/enhanced/doi/10.1111/j.1468-0130.2008.00488.x/.
81. Benjamin Mazar, ed., *The World History of the Jewish People*, Vol. 3: *Judges* (Tel Aviv: Rutgers University, 1971), 172.
82. The description of Goliath's military armor and weapons (1 Sam 17:5–7) provides a glimpse of the state of Philistine technology.

so that they could immediately dispatch professional, mobile military units to squelch any attempts at rebellion.[83]

Philistine rule was greatly resented by the Israelites. The books of Samuel show that Israel's aversion to Philistine oppression indirectly led to the formation of the monarchy.[84] Before the monarchy, there was no centralized administrative system that could develop a disciplined and organized military force to check Philistine advances,[85] and so the Israelites remained the "underdogs" in the Philistine-Israelite conflict. Since Israel was incapable of launching a successful military offensive, they had no choice but to allow the Philistines to encroach upon their territories and to exact tribute from the people. This position of helplessness produced feelings of suppressed hatred and contempt among the Israelites. Because the Israelites could not fight back through military strength, they may have resisted their enemies by poking fun at them. Wharton suggests that these stories act as "a low-risk outlet for anger, fear, and hope among people who had little means to press their cause against the Philistines."[86]

In the three Samson episodes noted above, there is a clear note of aggression against Philistine supremacy and a ridicule of the Philistines' overweening pride in their own political and military power. Samson accomplishes some of his greatest feats in Ashkelon and Gaza, centers of Philistine political power. Moreover, he is depicted as carrying away the very gates of Gaza–the concrete symbols of the city's strength – to Israelite territory. These episodes display how the Philistines, in spite of their avowed strength and cleverness, can be defeated by an oversized, oversexed, overindulgent buffoon.

It is probably not a coincidence that Samson, Shamgar, and David all use inferior weapons in their battles against the Philistines. Since the Philistines had control of the metal trade, the only weapons that the Israelites could use were farming implements, animal bones, and slingshots. Ironically, the Israelites still win their battles in spite of substandard weapons. This unexpected reversal communicates both to the Philistines and the Israelites that superior military technology is no guarantee of military victory. In this way, the stories may have functioned as a morale boost for the Israelites, who felt their military inferiority keenly.

---

83. Mazar, *World History*, 175.
84. C. H. Gordon, "Cultural and Religious Life," in *The World History of the Jewish People*, Vol. 3: *Judges*, ed. Benjamin Mazar (Tel Aviv: Rutgers University, 1971), 59.
85. John Bright, *A History of Israel*, 3d ed. (Philadelphia, PA: Fortress, 1981), 162–182.
86. Wharton, "The Secret of Yahweh," 54.

"Laughter," according to Bergson, "appears to stand in need of an echo."[87] Thus laughter needs to be shared with a group, where it can become a social force for molding human relationships. For the Israelites, the very act of laughing at the Philistines helps build up solidarity, "defining a certain 'us' over against a certain 'them.'"[88] Such group solidarity helps fire their imaginations about the possibilities for the future, when Israel will no longer be the "underdog," but will wield power over her oppressors. As Wharton observes:

> A community inclined to tell such stories and cherish them in tradition cannot be counted on, indefinitely, to put up with Philistine tyranny. "Some day," the stories say, "Samson's jokes on the Philistines will all come true in a new way."[89]

These stories also act as a polemic against the god of the Philistines, for the object of satirical attack was not just the Philistines, but, more importantly, their god Dagon.[90] The ancient Near East had the common belief that a god was ultimately behind every victory or defeat in battle.[91] The final act (16:23–30) in the contest between Samson and the Philistines opens with the Philistines offering a sacrifice to Dagon for the capture of Samson (16:23). The Philistines think that the capture of Samson is due to their god's power:

> "Our god has given into our hands our enemy,
> the ravager of our lands, who multiplies our dead." (Judg 16:24)[92]

The narrator, however, has already made it clear to the readers that Yahweh's departure is the reason behind Samson's capture (16:20). Thus the Philistines' praise to Dagon is ironic, since the Philistine god and their own cleverness have nothing to do with the capture at all. Unwittingly, the

---

87. Bergson, "Laughter," 64.
88. Wharton, "The Secret of Yahweh," 53.
89. Ibid.
90. Dagon was a well-known Semitic corn god who was adopted by the Philistines as they settled in the corn-growing coastal plain (Gray, *Judges*, 337). He was the chief deity of Ashdod (1 Sam 5:1–7) and was worshipped in Ugarit and Gaza (Myers, "Judges," 796–797). He was once known as the father of Baal. In contrast to Baal, however, who was known as the storm god, Dagon was regarded as the god of the harvest (Soggin, *Judges*, 255).
91. William Hamblin, *Warfare in the Ancient Near East to 1600 B.C.: Holy Warriors at the Dawn of History* (London/New York: Routledge, 2006), 186.
92. Since Samson destroyed the Philistine harvest in one of his pranks, it is appropriate for Dagon to be the focus of praise in this episode (Stanislav Segart, "Paranomasia in the Samson Narrative in Judges XII-XVI," *VT* 34 (1984): 459. The song resounds with the first-person plural suffix, *-enu*: "our god" (*'eloheynu*), "into our hands" (*beyadenu*), "our enemy" (*oyebenu*), showing how the Philistines attribute their victory over Samson to the power of their god Dagon and to their own cleverness as well.

Philistines are praising the God of Israel.[93] The end of the episode clearly identifies Yahweh as the most powerful God of all, for he strengthens Samson to deal one final blow against the Philistines (16:28–30).

> ## HUMOR IN FILIPINO CULTURE AND THE CHRISTIAN LIFE
>
> In the Philippines, humor functions culturally to diffuse tension, especially in awkward or hostile social and political situations. Thus during the 1986 Philippine People Power Revolution, during a face-off between the people and the army, humor served to ease the tension, which helped keep the critical situation from erupting into violence.[94] Moreover, even before the peaceful revolution on the streets, resistance against the dictatorship solidified through jokes, parodies, and satirical songs and plays. According to one survey, Filipinos value humor more than good looks.[95]
>
> Just as humor has a place in the Bible, humor also has a place in the Christian life. Laughter and tears form the fabric of human existence and express what it means to be made in the image of God. God has a sense of humor, too, and this theme will be explored further within the "The Divine Trickster" section below.[96] Moreover, humor keeps us humble, as we learn not to take ourselves seriously and to laugh at our own mistakes and foibles. In addition, humor has a social and political function by helping us to challenge oppression and injustice without resorting to physical violence.

14:1–16:3 Samson as a Comic Hero

Preachers who give a sermon on the story of Samson are confronted with the difficulty of interpreting Samson's character. The interpretation goes along two lines. On one hand, Samson is regarded as a tragic hero–someone whose positive qualities have destined him for great things, but whose story ends in tragedy because of his own faults. The account of his birth shows the promise of Samson. However, because of a fatal flaw – his passion for women

---

93. Boling, *Judges*, 251.
94. Known also as EDSA Revolution, this event put an end to fourteen years of martial law and dictatorship under the Marcos regime.
95. "Nine in 10 Filipinos value humor over good looks, says survey," *Manila Bulletin* (February 13, 2014). Online: http://www.mb.com.ph/nine-in-10-filipinos-value-humor-over-good-looks-says-survey/ (accessed: August 31, 2015).
96. See also Cheryl Taylor, "A Theology of Humor," in the Network for Women in Ministry. Online: http://ag.org/wim/0805/0805_Theology_Humor.cfm (accessed: August 31, 2015).

— Samson violates his vows and as a consequence, he fails in his mission to deliver Israel from the Philistines. His disappointing life finally ends in a tragic death.[97] Thus, the story of Samson depicts "the failure of a charismatic leader, and divine powers wasted."[98] The lesson that is often drawn from this is that those who begin well may not end well, and therefore we should be vigilant up to the end.

Technically, however, a figure can only be properly called a tragic hero if he or she is a victim of both a fatal flaw and of circumstances beyond his or her control, as in Greek tragedies.[99] One example of a tragic hero from the biblical story is King Saul, who had a moral fault, but was also caught in the complexities and ambiguities of Israel's transition to a monarchy. Although there are tragic elements in the Samson story, as mentioned earlier, Samson's life is not characterized by the inevitability of doom, which marks the destiny of tragic heroes. Instead, we encounter a character who has great freedom, succeeds repeatedly in getting out of the Philistine traps, and exhibits independence from physical, cultural, and social bonds.

Moreover, unlike tragic heroes, Samson's defects are earthier, done out of spite rather than from a deliberate moral choice. Thus in Humphrey's analysis, the story has "seeds for the tragic vision . . . but they fail to take root and blossom when mixed with the figure of Samson" because "Samson's failings are all too human and narrow," arising "more from a deep-seated passion than from conscious choice."[100]

On the other hand, some think that Samson is portrayed as an antihero, whose characteristics are totally opposite to those of a true hero, and whose example should not be followed.[101] A tragic hero is presented initially in a positive light, whereas an antihero is portrayed negatively from the beginning.[102] Thus events that seems to show the hero in a positive light only act as foils to heighten the antihero's negative qualities. Moreover, the tragic hero is shown

---

97. See John McKenzie, *The World of the Judges* (London: Chapman, 1967), 159 and Leland Ryken, *Words of Delight: A Literary Introduction to the Bible* (Grand Rapids, MI: Baker, 1987), 149, who both regard Samson's relationship with women as his fatal flaw because it leads to the breaking of his Nazirite vows.
98. Gerhard von Rad, *Old Testament Theology*, Vol. 1 (Edinburgh: Oliver and Boyd, 1962), 334.
99. This is the definition given by W. Lee Humphreys, "From Tragic Hero to Villain: A Study of the Figure of Saul and the Development of 1 Samuel," *JSOT* 22 (1982): 100.
100. W. Lee Humphreys, *The Tragic Vision and the Hebrew Tradition*, Overtures to Biblical Theology (Philadelphia, PA: Fortress, 1985), 70.
101. Soggin, *Judges*, 258. See also Klein, *Triumph of Irony*, 109–139.
102. C. F. Kraft, "Samson," *IDB* 4: 200.

to be the victim of his own internal weakness as well as inevitable external circumstances, whereas the antihero's failure is entirely his own fault.[103]

What makes the Samson narrative even more difficult as moral story is that the text does not explicitly condemn Samson's actions. Although the lack of explicit ethical evaluation is common in biblical narratives, this is more marked in Samson's story. There is no recurring refrain, as in the last part of the book of Judges, which brings the different episodes under the rubric of a religious, moral, or political evaluation. Moreover, the text makes no connection between Samson's questionable behavior and the work of the spirit of Yahweh who comes upon him (14:19; 15:14). In addition, despite Samson's violent and immoral acts, Yahweh affirms him by answering his prayer (15:18–19), and the prayer itself shows Samson's dependence on Yahweh for his needs.[104] Thus positive elements are present within the story, which do not fit with conventional antiheroic attributes.

Without dismissing the tragic elements of the story or the negative depiction of Samson, the most helpful way to resolve the ambivalence and ambiguity in the characterization of Samson is to see him primarily as a comic hero. As with other comic heroes, Samson is resilient and extricates himself from what appear to be deadlock situations,[105] such as when he escapes from the Philistines' grasp again and again. He also exhibits great freedom and is not tied down by the rules that govern ordinary men, especially the trappings of culture and civilization. Furthermore, Samson's characterization displays an absence of development, which is a typical feature of comic heroes,[106] who are portrayed as static characters rather than dynamic personalities. Moreover, the same comic devices employed in the depiction of the

---

103. The difference between the two can be better understood if one analyzes the function in the Samson narrative of the annunciation scene (chapter 13), the notes on the spirit's endowing Samson with extraordinary strength (14:6, 19; 15:14), and the divine responses to prayer (15:18–19; 16:28–30). In the tragic hero paradigm, these episodes would express Samson's positive traits and manifestations of his inherent greatness, which is then marred by outward circumstances and his own disastrous choices. In the antihero model, these positive events are seen to have an ironic function as the narrator's means of bringing into clearer focus Samson's negative qualities.
104. While acknowledging the self-centeredness of Samson's prayers, Exum nevertheless maintains that these prayers serve to demonstrate his dependence upon Yahweh, who responds to human need ("Theological Dimension," 4–45).
105. This is in contrast to the characterization of the tragic hero who, when faced with the inevitable, has no recourse but to suffer the consequences of unjust fate or his own moral failure. See Wylie Sypher, "The Meanings of Comedy," in *Comedy*, ed. George Meredith (Garden City, NY: Doubleday, 1956), 48–49.
106. Exum and Whedbee, "Isaac, Samson, and Saul," 33.

Philistines, such as comic repetition and reversal, are also used to characterize Samson. Like Ehud, he is rendered as a trickster figure, able to break the rules and overstep boundaries.

By reading Samson as a comic hero, the reader cannot simply condone or condemn him. Samson breaks the conventional biblical rules that connect ethical behavior with spiritual fruitfulness, virtue with ministry, and character with effectiveness. Because one cannot regard him as a virtuous or ethical model, the reader must suspend judgement as Samson gets into one comic scrape after another, waiting to see how the narrative will play out. In the final scene (16:4–30), the narrative does not let Samson get away with his rash behavior, since he becomes a victim of his own tricks, which is also a characteristic of comic heroes. Though this fourth episode begins in the same way as the three episodes discussed above, a surprising twist sets this final incident apart from the rest.

16:4–31 COMEDY TURNS TO TRAGEDY AND THEN COMES FULL CIRCLE

16:4–19 Love Play in the Samson-Delilah Interchange

The Delilah episode is the climax of the threefold structure outlined above, which traces Samson's involvement with three women. The first and last episodes correspond closely to each other. Both episodes record the Philistines' attempts to discover Samson's secrets by inducing a woman to entice him (14:15b; 16:5b) him. Both Samson's Timnite wife and Delilah try to exploit Samson's emotional and sexual vulnerability by reproaching him for falling short of love as evinced by his lack of openness (14:16; 16:15).[107] In both incidents, Samson finally yields to the women's pressure and reveals his secrets–not because he wants to prove his love, but because he simply gets tired of all the crying and nagging (14:17; 16:16–17).

Yet Samson's capitulation in the Delilah episode is preceded by a long verbal interchange, where each tries to conquer the other through the power of words. This interchange is divided into four enticement scenes (16:6–9, 10–12, 13–14, 15–20), which follow a highly symmetrical four-part structure, as outlined below:

---

107. The word for entice (*patah* in the piel, which NIV translates as "coax" in 14:15 and "lure" in 16:5) usually means "to deceive" or "to fool a person." This may include a sexual element, since it is used to refer to the seduction of a virgin in Exod 22:15 and to the seduction of a youth in Prov 16:29.

1) Delilah's Entreaties
   "Please tell me where your strength is found . . ." (vv. 6, 15)
   and "how you may be bound" (vv. 6, 10, 13a).
2) Samson's Responses
   If he is bound in a certain way, he will "become weak like any other man" (vv. 7, 11, 13b, 17).
3) The Enactment
   Delilah follows Samson's instructions (vv. 8–9, 12, 14, 18–19).
4) The Escapes
   Samson escapes from his bonds (vv. 9b, 12b, 14b), except in the final episode, where his strength leaves him (vv. 19–20).

This repetitive structure only changes in the fourth scene, where Delilah's entreaty begins with a reproach: "How can you say you love me when your heart is not with me?" (v. 15). This shift indicates the climax of the whole interchange and prepares readers for the change that comes in part four of the above outline: Samson's failure to escape.

A major motif in the Samson-Delilah dialogues is that of binding. Both the Philistines and Delilah believe that the source of Samson's strength lies in magic, and they will only be able to extend their authority over the magical power if they discover the proper binding ritual.[108] Thus the Philistines adjure Delilah to: "See where his great strength lies and by what means . . . we may bind him" (16:5). And Delilah pleads: "Please tell me wherein your great strength lies, and how you might be bound" (16:6).

Samson's responses to Delilah exploit this erroneous magical notion: "If anyone ties me with seven fresh bowstrings that have not been dried, I'll become as weak as any other man" (16:7); "If anyone ties me securely with new ropes that have never been used, I'll become as weak as any other man" (16:11); "If you weave the seven braids of my head into the fabric on the loom and tighten it with the pin, I'll become as weak as any other man"

---

108. The motif of binding (and loosing) is widespread in many religions, where it is believed to be connected with mythical events (Grolia Piccaluga, "Binding," in the *Encyclopaedia of Religion*, Vol. 2, ed. Mircea Eliade [New York: Macmillan, 1987], 217). The tying of knots, especially, is seen as having the power to hinder or impede the actions of persons or things (Walter Dilling, "Knots," in the *Encyclopaedia of Religion and Ethics*, Vol. 7, ed. James Hastings [Edinburgh: T & T Clark, 1918], 747). Mircea Eliade discusses the role of magical bonds in Semitic religions, where its connection with divine or demonic power is almost universal (*Images and Symbols: Studies in Religious Symbolism* [New York: Sheed and Ward, 1969], 92–124). Semitic parallels are given in 108–110.

(16:13b). The magical undertones of Samson's replies are evident in his use of the number seven (fresh bowstrings and new ropes),[109] along with the action of weaving, which is regarded as a more powerful way of binding.[110]

By couching his responses in the form of a magic ritual, Samson intends to mislead Delilah about the true nature of his strength.[111] The repeated phrase, "I'll become weak like any other man," implies that because Samson's strength is not like any other man, it must be supernatural and therefore magical, as the Philistines and Delilah believe.[112] Through the proper binding act, this supernatural power can be broken, and Samson will be like any other man, susceptible to natural attacks. Thus Samson plays a joke on Delilah and the Philistines, since the actual secret of his strength is unrelated to any instruments of binding.[113]

One wonders why Samson agrees to be bound when Delilah clearly states that her objective is to subdue Samson. Moreover, Delilah repeatedly tests Samson by declaring, "Samson, the Philistines are upon you!" (16:9, 12, 14, 20). Is Samson too gullible to walk into the Philistine trap with open eyes?

Aside from the fact that Samson may have become too confident of his abilities to get out of traps, the dynamics of their conversation can only be understood in light of the different levels operating in their communication. On the obvious level (one evident to the reader), the interchange is a contest of wits, where Delilah's goal is to learn the secret of Samson's strength in order to bind him, while Samson's goal is to keep Delilah from learning his secret in order not to be bound. A subtext of the conversation, however, is a love play between two lovers who desire to gain each other's unreserved surrender. While Delilah's persistent attempts arise from mercenary objectives – to get the promised reward from the Philistines (16:5) – she communicates to Samson that she wants his total sexual vulnerability, expressed by her use of the word "subdue" (16:6).

---

109. In antiquity, seven is a number used frequently in religious rituals and magical incantations. See R. Campbell Thompson, *Semitic Magic* (London: 1908), 166, for an example. The insistence on the use of new objects that are not marred by common use also gives a suggestion of magic (Gray, *Judges*, 335; see also Piccaluga, "Binding," 218).
110. According to Piccaluga, the reason for this is that weaving, as well as spinning, are activities that involve countless loops, ties, and knots and are therefore much more difficult to unravel ("Binding," 219).
111. John Vickery, "In Strange Ways: The Story of Samson," in *Images of Man and God: Old Testament Stories in Literary Focus*, ed. B. O. Long (Sheffield: Almond Press), 70.
112. Othniel Margalith, "Samson's Riddle and Samson's Magic Locks," *VT* 36 (1986): 229.
113. Robert Alter, "Samson Without Folklore," in Niditch, *Text and Tradition*, 53.

The word "subdue" (*'anah*) can mean "to overpower" or "to humiliate, afflict or oppress."[114] These seem to be the senses in which the Philistines use the word in their instructions to Delilah (16:5) as well as Delilah's real intent in using the word in her entreaty to Samson (16:6). However, "subdue" can be understood as "to cause one to feel dependent,"[115] and it also has sexual overtones.[116] Thus Delilah's use of the word may carry a deliberate misdirection, referring to sexual subjugation.

On the other hand, Samson's continuance in the love play comes from his intense passion, as expressed by the narrator at the beginning of the episode: "After this he loved a woman in the valley of Sorek, whose name was Delilah" (14:4). As a lover, Samson sees their dialogue as a form of coquetry, which is expected to culminate in the total conquest by the man and the complete surrender of the woman. Read on the level of a love play, the phrase, "I shall become weak and be like any other man" (16:7, 11, 13, 17), can be understood as a lover's declaration of his willingness to become completely vulnerable to his beloved, if she can only discover the right way to subdue him.

So Samson plays the game of love, becoming bolder each time around, until during the third scene, he mentions his hair and flirts dangerously close to the truth. As Samson's estimation of his own cleverness grows, he ironically becomes more oblivious to Delilah's hidden intentions.

The interplay between Samson and Delilah in this story highlights the seductive power of playing games. In contemporary terms, one can see Samson playing games all night in a Macau casino. He is just that kind of guy. At the heart of any game is the intoxicating elixir of power. While games can be fun, they are also about winning, which is about having power over others. So the games we play can become dangerous and backfire. Games of power are always dangerous since they are open to manipulation. Sadly, we all play games of power – in the bedroom, in church, at work, in the public sphere. The challenge for Christians is to refuse to be drawn into games of power.

In Delilah's fourth attempt to discover the secret of Samson's great strength, her entreaty gives way to reproach: "How can you say, 'I love you,' when your heart is not with me?" (ESV). She continues with a litany of Samson's offenses (16:15), nagging him day after day "until he was sick (*qatsar nefesh*) to death of it" (16:16). We encountered the phrase *qatsar nefesh* (literally,

---

114. *DCH* 6: 497–498.
115. *HALOT* 2: 853.
116. *'anah* is used when a woman is humiliated through rape (Gen 34:2; 2 Sam 13:12, 14, 22, 32; Judg 19:24) or by forcible marriage or sex (Deut 21:14).

nefesh (literally, "life is shortened") in the Jephthah narrative in reference to Yahweh's growing impatience with the Israelites. In the Samson narrative, the phrase clearly indicates that Samson has reached the limit of patience or endurance. However, as discussed on p. 146, the phrase can also mean "to be diminished" or "to be weakened."[117] Thus the author may be playing on both meanings. Samson is growing extremely impatient because of Delilah's constant barrage of words, but Samson may also be weakening. In fact, he is "rendered so powerless that in the next verse he finally does reveal the secret of his strength which leads directly to his own death."[118]

The secret is that Samson's strength cannot be diminished by any form of binding, because he is already bound. He declares, "I have been a Nazirite dedicated to God from my mother's womb" (16:17). As explained earlier, a Nazirite is a person bound to Yahweh by virtue of a special vow or, in the case of Samson, by a special calling before he was born. Thus the key to unmanning Samson is not to bind him, but rather to unbind him from being a Nazirite, which Delilah does by shaving his hair, the symbol of his "bound" life.[119] Yet on another level, even though Samson cannot be bound by concrete materials, such as ropes, bowstrings, and the twines and twists of weave, or by any form of magical ritual, he can be bound by a woman's words and the power of his own passion. So even as the repetitive dialogue and actions within each enticement scene demonstrate that Samson is physically able to get out of Delilah's trap again and again, they also reveal how he is progressively "weakening" until he becomes "bound" at the end.

The account in the final enticement scene stresses the importance of Samson telling Delilah "all his heart." The reference to the heart, in relation to the disclosure of Samson's secret, is repeated four times from different vantage points.[120] First, Delilah tells Samson, "your heart is not with me" (16:15), and so from her viewpoint, his lack of disclosure indicates a lack of love. Next, the narrator relates how Samson succumbs to the pressure to prove his love and so "told her all his heart" (16:17). When Delilah realizes

---

117. See Robert Haak, "A Study and New Interpretation of *qsr nps*," *JBL* 101 (1982): 161-167, based on a study of Ugaritic texts.
118. Haak, "*qsr nps*," 166.
119. Hair is also often associated with sexuality and virility, so that some scholars see the shaving of Samson as a symbol of "sexual stripping and subjugation." See Susan Niditch, "Samson as Culture Hero, Trickster, and Bandit: The Empowerment of the Weak," *CBQ* 52 (1990): 616.
120. When the same information is redundant, it may mean that a different point of view is entering the narrative. See Adele Berlin, *Poetics and the Interpretation of Biblical Narrative* (Sheffield: Almond Press, 1983), 73.

that Samson has told her "all his heart," she shares this knowledge with the Philistines (16:18, 2x).

At this point, the comic tone shifts to a somber mood. The game between the two lovers is now seen for what it really is – a story of betrayal and humiliation. In this game, Delilah emerges as the victor, having gained not only Samson's sexual surrender, but also the secret of his strength. After putting Samson to sleep "on her knees" (ESV) – a phrase that has sexual connotations–and then shaving him, "she began to subdue him and his strength left him" (16:19). The consummation of the strongman's sexual subjugation also marks his descent into the lowest point of the story.

16:20–22 Samson's Lowest Point

With the shaving of Samson's hair and the subsequent breaking of the vow that binds him to Yahweh, Samson's journey reaches its lowest depths. The narrator summarizes the pathos of Samson's predicament: "He awoke from his sleep and thought, 'I'll go out as before and shake myself free.' But he did not know that the LORD had left him" (16:20b).

All along, Samson has presumed that any attempt to capture him can be thwarted by his incredible strength, as proved by his previous encounters with the Philistines. Flushed with self-confidence, he regards his strength as his own possession.[121] This confidence disappears when Samson finds himself at the mercy of his Philistine captors. Too late, he realizes that Yahweh – not himself – is the real source of his strength. This is expressed in the parallel construction: "his strength left him" (16:19b) and "the Lord had left him" (16:20b). The last phrase begins emphatically with a disjunctive phrase, which emphasizes the contrast between Samson's presumption of freedom and security and the reality of his peril and vulnerability to being captured.

Thus Samson is bound and brought to Gaza, the place of his previous victory, which becomes the place of his degradation,[122] for his hands are fettered, his eyes are gouged out (an action done to one's enemy because it puts him in disgrace),[123] and he is made to work in a mill doing manual labor that is typically done only by women, asses, and slaves.[124] His extreme humiliation is completed when he is made to play the fool in front of the Philistines. The

---

121. Wharton, "The Secret of Yahweh," 61.
122. Wharton thinks that the different stories in chapter 16 are tied together by their setting, which is the locality of Gaza ("The Secret of Yahweh," 62). Gaza is the place of Samson's initial victory (16:1–3), his deepest humiliation (16:21–27), and his final victory (16:28–30).
123. Myers, "Judges," 795. See 1 Sam 11:2; 2 Kgs 25:7.
124. Cundall and Morris, *Judges*, 179.

strong and invulnerable Samson, whom everyone feared, is reduced to an object for other people's amusement.

However, as Vickery notes, amidst "the stark horror of Samson's blinding and imprisonment," we find "a laconic observation" in verse 22: "But the hair of his head began to grow again after it had been shaved."[125] Unknown to the Philistines and even to Samson, Yahweh is at work behind the scenes, working to accomplish the mission entrusted to Samson, which is to deliver Israel from Philistine domination (13:5). The growth of Samson's hair signals the return of his strength.

16:23–30 The Upward Turn

Samson's upward ascent begins during a Philistine assembly to honor Dagon for their triumph over Samson. The scene is one of merriment, contentment, and satisfaction, with the Philistines congratulating themselves for having caught "the big fish." The phrase "to be merry" ("in high spirits," NIV) describes physical satisfaction, contentment, and confidence.[126] The reference to the "three thousand men and women"[127] and the "lords of the Philistines" in the five principal Philistine cities (16:27) shows that this gathering has considerable social and political importance.

To cap their celebration, the Philistines decide to bring out Samson for public display, so that they can make him the object of their jokes and laughter (16:25, 27). They watch with amusement as this clumsy giant, once so strong and fearsome, fumbles his way around, providing the evening entertainment for the Philistines. But while Samson's enemies are having fun at his expense, the narrator foreshadows the coming reversal by focusing on the pillars: "they stood him among the pillars" (v. 25); "put me where I can feel the pillars that support the temple" (v. 26). Samson's prayer to Yahweh reveals his growing self-realization:[128]

---

125. Vickery, "In Strange Ways," 72.
126. The literal rendering is, "When their hearts were good." This phrase is often used to describe exhilaration from the effects of wine. See Gray, *Judges*, 337; see 1 Sam 25:36; Esth 1:10; Eccl 2:3.
127. A flat roof cannot possibly support three thousand people (Gray, *Judges*, 337–338). McKenzie comments: "The presence of three thousand people on the roof of such a building would have brought it down without any push from Samson" (*World of the Judges*, 157). The impossibility of this situation may have been the reason that the LXX reads "seven hundred." Boling suggests that the roof does not refer to the roof of the temple but to a nearby structure from which the crowd watched (*Judges*, 251).
128. Exum, "Theological Dimensions," 42.

Sovereign LORD, remember me. Please, God, strengthen me just once more, and let me with one blow get revenge on the Philistines for my two eyes[129] (16:28).

Even though the prayer is somewhat self-centered, since it contains only a petition for personal vindication, Samson acknowledges that strength and victory over the Philistines can come only from Yahweh. This prayer parallels Samson's first prayer (15:18), which he utters before Yahweh's departure from him.

As Samson calls on Yahweh, he grasps the central pillars of the house and pushes them with all his might, so that the building tumbles down "on the rulers and all the people in it" (16:30). The catastrophic consequences of Samson's last feat lie not only in the drastic diminution of the Philistine ranks (three thousand die at one blow!), but also in the severe crippling of the Philistine political power base (all the rulers of the Philistines were there). Thus, the Philistines' greatest triumph turns into an ignominious defeat. But since Samson dies with the Philistines, there cannot be any counter-retaliation.

The episode ends with an ironic observation from the narrator (16:30b): "So the dead whom he killed in his death were more than those whom he killed in his life" (trans. mine). With the restoration of his relationship with Yahweh, Samson finally pulls his last and greatest feat. His death, together with three thousand Philistines, is the ultimate trickery on the Philistines.

13:1–16:31 DENOUEMENT: THE DIVINE TRICKSTER

Throughout the Samson narrative, Yahweh is portrayed as the unseen hand who works out an inexorable plan behind human events, often without the knowledge of the human characters, and frequently at their expense. In this way, Yahweh resembles a trickster figure, who converts to his advantage the ignorance and foibles of the people around him.

Moreover, Yahweh acts in ways that are contrary to what is expected. Manoah expects the messenger to give him a prominent role in the revelation of his son's birth, but the most important role is given to the woman instead. Samson's parents object to his desire to marry a Philistine woman, since this is against Israel's cultural norms. However, contrary to their objections and expectations, Yahweh uses this very desire as an opportunity to accomplish

---

129. The natural reading of the MT is: "let me be avenged for one of my two eyes." Gray and others, however, takes the reading of the LXX: "let me avenge myself of a single vengeance for my two eyes" (*Judges*, 338).

Yahweh's plans against the Philistines. Samson presumes that the strength that comes from Yahweh will always be there to rescue him from the traps of his opponents, so he is surprised by the weakness that comes upon him after he reveals the secret of his strength to Delilah. The Philistines expect Yahweh's power to be cut off after they capture Samson, so they are caught unprepared by Samson's renewed strength, which eventually leads to the Philistines' demise.

As the characters' expectations are undermined, the readers' expectations are frustrated by Yahweh's unexpected and often puzzling actions. Yahweh affirms the woman instead of the man, playfully twitting Manoah for his obtuse piety. Yahweh's intentions run contrary to Hebrew culture and laws in terms of intermarriage with non-Israelites, who may influence Israel to worship other gods. Yahweh does not immediately punish Samson for his violent and erotic actions, but rather seems to be affirming him by endowing him with the spirit's supernatural strength at critical points in his career. Unknown to Samson and the Philistines, Yahweh secretly uses their trickery to accomplish God's own purposes. The raising up of an amoral character such as Samson to deliver Israel has the character of a divine joke against the Philistines and the Israelites.

The freedom to act in ways that are contrary to conventional experiences and standard norms is a characteristic of the trickster. Yahweh refuses to conform to the ideas that others – including the readers – have about God. Just when people think they have captured the divine essence, Yahweh eludes their grasp. As Webb points out, "God acts in this story with a freedom which sets very definite limits to the kind of knowledge which mortals can have of him."[130]

To speak of Yahweh as a divine trickster[131] may be considered irreverent by some, since it seems to connote the image of a God who loves to deceive people for the sake of enjoyment and avaricious appetites. Certainly, Yahweh does not share the trickster's profane and amoral nature, lust and self-interest, and fondness for deceit. Nevertheless, in this narrative, events are divinely orchestrated so that those who think they have the upper hand because of their trickery become the objects of the divine trick. This surprising inversion of roles bespeaks of a deity who has a comic sense.

---

130. Webb, *An Integrated Reading*, 173–174.
131. The term "divine trickster" is from Exum, "Thematic Instabilities," 424.

The divine trick is directed towards a certain end: to unmask the pretensions of those who put too much confidence in their own knowledge and strength. Yahweh undermines the confidence of those who believe they can predict God's ways and manipulate the divine being into doing what they want. Though Yahweh responds, it is according to Yahweh's own terms, for Yahweh will not be manipulated.[132] In this freedom lies Yahweh's power, for it enables Yahweh to turn defeat into victory, weakness into strength, and the tricks of human beings into something that will accomplish God's ultimate purpose.

GOD'S UNEXPECTED WAYS

The Samson narrative is full of inversions:

> The woman is affirmed more than the man;
> The Nazirite is the profligate;
> The sensuous man is the mighty fighter;
> The man full of puns is the man who prays;
> The man who tricks others is the man betrayed;
> The man who takes women is the man who loses them;
> The man who is bound is the man who is freed;
> The man who is deformed is the man of power.

In light of the earlier Judges stories, one would expect Samson to mobilize others, form an army or guerilla force, and lead them into battle against the Philistine oppressors. But none of this organizing and mobilizing takes place. Samson appears in this saga as a solo hero, with his own countrymen against him. While Samson does cause mayhem among the Philistines, he is no Gandhi mobilizing large groups of people in peaceful resistance, nor a Che Guevarra using violent opposition. He is impetuous, foolish, vindictive, and passionate, but he is used by Yahweh to do God's strange work. Yahweh, the sovereign God, is willing to link his power and action to human agency. In so doing, God works in and through the weaknesses and limitations of such human agency.

This narrative can teach us that as Christians – even though we are committed to virtue and values – should not prescribe how God should work, what God should do, and who God should use. For God has free sovereignty and power, and God's ways are not our ways. Therefore, we must be careful that we do not limit the working of God to those who are socially acceptable

---

132. Greene, "Enigma Variations: Aspects of the Samson Story Judges 13–16," *Vox Evangelica* 21 (1991): 58.

and powerful, particularly if we live in hierarchical and highly stratified societies. God can work even through an unnamed woman and through a marginal and weak figure such as Samson.

JUDGES 17–18

The Domestication of God: Gods, Gold, and Goons

One of the great tragedies in the history of the Christian church is that religion is often combined with physical force to serve the interests of wealth and power. When this happens on a personal basis, the results are tragic. But when nations purport to spread the Christian religion and civilization by occupying another country in the name of God while glorying in their superior military strength and strategies, the consequences are catastrophic. Occupation or colonization may be rationalized in terms of spreading the fruits of democracy, bringing economic and cultural benefits to another country, or sharing the gospel, but lurking underneath these rationales is often a desire for another country's natural and people resources to help in the growth of the colonizing country's economy.

Although God's name may be used frequently to justify our conquests, we must ask, where is God in the midst of colonization, occupation, or violent aggression? While religious language may be on people's tongues, God may be marginalized in the decision-making process. Political and religious leaders may claim to know God's mind about certain matters without devoting time, prayer, and discernment to the process.

In the Gideon story, God is marginalized by the way Gideon highlights his own part in the deliverance while minimizing God's role. In response, God withdraws his presence and support for Gideon's vindictive actions and memorial projects. Jephthah marginalizes God by manipulating God's favor and power to meet his needs for acceptance and status. As a result, Yahweh's power is diminished.[1] The pattern of marginalization in the Samson narrative revolves around the obsessive desire of Samson and the Philistines to possess knowledge that will enable them to gain power over the other without acknowledging God as the true source of knowledge and power.

In Judges 17–18, God is not only marginalized, but domesticated when God is used to serve the characters' personal, familial, and tribal interests.

---

1. See the section "The Diminishment of Yahweh" on pp. 140–147.

JUDGES 17–21 OVERVIEW OF CONCLUDING CHAPTERS

Judges 17–18 is a part of the broader unit of chapters 17–21. These last five chapters break the pattern of the deteriorating cyclical framework that structures the lengthy account of individual deliverers from Ehud to Samson (3:16–16:31). Moreover, many scholars see Judges 17–21 as a double conclusion corresponding to the double introduction in Judges 1:1–3:6.[2] Whereas chapters 17–18 talk about the deterioration of religious life (which corresponds to the religious problem set forth in 2:1–3:6), chapters 19–21 show the social depravity and political instability pervading Israel (which corresponds to the military problem of 1:1–31). This correspondence, however, may be artificial, since the introductory passage in 1:1–3:6 can also be divided into five sections, detailing the account of Israel's failure to conquer the land with multifaceted explanations for those failures.[3] Although the introductory passage in 1:1–31 and the concluding passage in 20:1–48 correspond, in that both show the tribes of Israel engaged in a divine war (chapter 1) and its perversion (chapter 20), there is no corresponding parallel in the first chapters with the events of chapters 19 and 21. Thus, it is best to see chapters 17–21 as a conclusion that does not necessarily correspond to the introduction.

Rather than featuring stories of deliverance or battles against Israel's oppressors, we find in these last chapters stories of individuals and their families, whose actions are connected with affairs that impact a whole tribe or several tribes of Israel.[4] Satterthwaite believes that this "alternation between the individual and the tribal levels is meant to suggest a sickness in Israel which permeates all levels of society, personal, familial, and national."[5] In the following, I explore the common features of chapters 17–21 so as to provide a framework for understanding Judges 17–18.

17–21 Anonymity

One distinguishing feature of these concluding chapters is that most of the characters are anonymous.[6] In Judges 17–18, Micah is the only one named repeatedly, and only a passing reference is given to the name of the Levite priest as Jonathan, the son of Gershom, the son of Moses (18:30). In Judges

---

2. Cheryl Exum, "The Centre Cannot Hold," 413, 425; Cundall and Morris, *Judges*, 18–25; Younger, *Judges/Ruth*, 30–33; McCann, *Judges*, 27; D. W. Gooding, "Composition," 75–77.
3. These introductory passages are discussed in the opening sections on pp. 12–35.
4. McCann, *Judges*, 119.
5. Philip Satterthwaite, "'No King in Israel': Narrative Criticism and Judges 17–21," *TynBul* 44 (1993): 77.
6. Klein, *Triumph of Irony*, 142–143.

19–21, only the tribes are named, while the names of significant characters – whose actions set the stage for the intertribal wars – are withheld (the Levite, the concubine, the father of the concubine, the host). This anonymity focuses the narrative on social roles and social relationships rather than on the individuality of the characters. Thus the individual characters are presented as archetypes, and their actions represent the degeneration happening within the society as a whole.[7] By being cast as archetypes, their particular ways of living and acting provide a window into what ails the Israel nation as a whole: "everyone did as they saw fit" (17:6; 21:25).

17–21 Use of Irony

The seemingly matter-of-fact storytelling of these chapters paints a frightening picture of Israel. Despite the trappings of religiosity, there is an underlying chaos and dysfunction in the characters' dealings with each other. Both family life and institutional life appear to be okay on the surface, but inside there is inner corrosion – just as termites attack an inner wall that may look sound, but then it suddenly collapses. Thus there is a lack of cohesion, integrity, and authentic spirituality.

Although there are few explicit markers about how the events in these chapters should be interpreted, there are implicit signs that the characters' actions are not ideal, but are being criticized and mocked. The key to interpreting this section is to recognize the extensive use of irony.[8]

Irony, according to E. M. Good, is "a conflict marked by the perception of the distance between pretense and reality."[9] There are different types of irony, but comic works tend to rely on rhetorical irony, where the author makes readers understand that they should not take seriously what is said explicitly, but should follow the opposite implicit meaning.[10] Rhetorical irony is common in everyday conversation. For example, when we say that a person is "nice," we may actually mean the opposite. This creates incongruence or lack of correspondence between what is said and what is actually true. In this way, irony is used as a form of critique or protest, since it shows the distance

---

7. Marais, *Representation in the Old Testament,* 133. See also E. J. Revell, *The Designation of the Individual: Expressive Usage in Biblical Narrative,* Contributions to Biblical Exegesis and Theology 14 (Kampen: Kok Pharos, 1996), 190–94; J. M. Hudson, "Living in a Land of Epithets: Anonymity in Judges 19–21," *JSOT* 62 (1994): 49–66.
8. See Dale Ralph Davis, "Comic Literature – Tragic Theology," *WTJ* 46 (1984): 159–161.
9. Edwin M. Good, *Irony in the Old Testament,* 14.
10. See Klein's discussion of irony in *Triumph of Irony,* 195–199.

between what is and what ought to be,[11] "testifying in favor of one thing as over against another."[12]

The problem with the use of irony is that it relies on the audience's recognition that the speeches of the characters and the narration itself have a double-edged meaning, so that they say one thing, but the "audience with a wider context of knowledge, understands another."[13] There is a danger that the message may be completely lost if the audience misses out on the irony. On the other hand, because the audience may be resistant to direct indictments, they may not see that a direct rebuke applies to them. Thus an ironic tale may lead audiences to better self-recognition as they see their inconsistencies in the light of the characters' inconsistencies.

Within the book of Judges, the use of irony in the stories enables the narrator to convey an indirect message to his implied Israelite hearers about what kind of society they have become. As they laugh, feel scandalized, or lament about the follies and fates of the characters, they may well be laughing and lamenting about themselves.

17–21 "There Was No King in Israel": Concluding Refrain

Similar to the middle part of the book of Judges (3:7–16:31), a clear refrain, although deteriorating, ties the concluding chapters (17–21) together, so that Judges may be called a book of pitiful refrains. Earlier, the narrator uses the phrase, "again the Israelites did evil in the eyes of the LORD." The additional word "again," which may also be translated "continually," points to the breathless repetition in evildoing that marks the life of Israel with God, so that a sense of fatalism and resignation permeates the later parts of the book.

In chapters 17–21, the new refrain is the phrase, "in those days there was no king in Israel; everyone did what was right in his own eyes."[14] This refrain is placed at the end of the first episode (17:6) and also at the end of the whole section (21:25), acting as an *inclusio* that frames the stories of these last chapters. The totality of the word "everyone" (which can also be translated as "all people" in the NRSV) suggests a grey landscape of unrelenting despondency. Instead of the earlier signs of hope in raising up deliverers, there is now only a dull uniformity of hopelessness.

---

11. Edwin Good, *Irony in the Old Testament*, 30.
12. Ibid., 32. See also Carolyn Sharp, *Irony and Meaning*, for a theoretical discussion of irony.
13. Good, *Irony in the Old Testament*, 31.
14. Modified from the ESV. The NIV translation, "everyone did what he saw fit," is more idiomatic. I have chosen a more literal translation in order to parallel "Israel did evil in the eyes of the Lord" and "everyone did what was right in his own eyes."

JUDGES 17–18

A shortened form of the refrain, "in those days there was no king in Israel," is used as a transition device between episodes (18:1; 19:1). As a transition device, the phrase seems to act as a conclusion to the previous episode and an introduction to the next one.[15] This phrase serves as a guide for evaluating the events in the last chapters of Judges, because the narrator does not make any other explicit evaluation of the characters' actions. The narrator seems to narrate the story from a neutral viewpoint, although the use of ironic descriptions reveals the narrator's true sympathies. But is this refrain a lament for a king who will make all things well, or does it imply support for a future Davidic kingship? This question is difficult to answer, for it depends on how we view the composition of the book of Judges as a whole and, in particular, these last chapters. Were these chapters written or redacted during the time of the united monarchy or the divided monarchy? During what period? Were they produced during or after the exile?

One interpretation is that the phrase, "in those days there was no king in Israel; everyone did what was right in his own eyes," indicates that the only solution to the anarchy existing in Israel during that time (as shown by the stories in chapters 17–21) is for Israel to have a king. This king is understood to be a Judean king,[16] which is seen to be the legitimate king, unlike the line of Saul (who was from the tribe of Benjamin), or the kings of the northern kingdom of Israel. This reading would set this material during the time of the early monarchy, when there was a power struggle between the house of Saul and the house of David as to which king was legitimate. Yet there are some objections to this view. First of all, there is a very strong criticism of the monarchy in other parts of Judges, as seen in the Gideon and Abimelech narratives.[17] Secondly, even though the different tribes are shown in a negative light, Judah itself is not exempt from criticism.[18] Judah's victories in chapter 1 are countered by its failure to drive out the inhabitants of the plain (Judg 1:19). The men of Judah hand Samson over to the Philistines (Judg 15:9–13).[19]

---

15. Yairah Amit, "Hidden Polemic in the Conquest of Dan: Judges xvii–xviii," *VT* 40 (1990): 5–6; W. J. Dumbrell, "'In Those Days There Was No King in Israel; Every Man Did What Was Right in His Own Eyes,' The Purpose of the Book of Judges Reconsidered," *JSOT* 25 (1983): 24.
16. See O'Connell, *Rhetoric of the Book of Judges*, 268–270; Marc Brettler, "The Book of Judges: Literature as Politics," *JBL* 108 (1989): 395–418, and *The Book of Judges*, 111–116; Arthur Cundall, "Judges – An Apology for the Monarchy," *ExpTim* 81 (1969–1971): 178–181.
17. Dumbrell, "In Those Days," 25–26. Marais, *Representation in the Old Testament*, 133. See also Revell, *Designation of the Individual*, 134–135.
18. McCann, *Judges*, 117.
19. See Block, *Judges*, 57, n. 156.

Micah's household priest, a Levite, comes from Bethlehem in Judah. So if the intention of the book is to idealize the Judean monarchy, there are counter-voices that seem to question this proposition.[20]

On the other hand, Gale Yee offers an alternative dating, setting this material during King Josiah's reforms in the seventh century BCE. Yee contends that the portrayal of the chaotic conditions in these chapters is intended to emphasize the urgency of Josiah's religious reforms, which centralized worship in Jerusalem.[21] This centralization of worship was driven by the need to enlarge Josiah's tax fund, since the coffers of the state were depleted when it had to pay tribute to Assyria. Emerging from Assyrian vassalage, Josiah wanted to ensure that the local tax paid to local sanctuaries and religious leaders, such as the Levites – especially in the northern kingdom – would all flow to Jerusalem. To achieve this, Josiah had to destroy all the local sanctuaries and discredit the country Levites who ministered at these sanctuaries.[22] In this context, the refrain, "Israel had no king," along with the other stories in Judges 17–21, were intended to highlight the chaos of a decentralized government and of competing local alliances, thus affirming and consolidating the powers of King Josiah in Jerusalem and also ensuring that the city would have a continuous supply of funds.[23]

Yet W. Dumbrell sets the material at the time of the exile, contending that the phrase is not an apology for the monarchy, but rather points towards what Israel could be after the exile. During the exile, the writers and editors would have already witnessed the utter failure of the monarchy to maintain the nation's socio-political and religious institutions. With no king and no sacral-political institutions, Israel is called to recognize that what has preserved the nation has been Yahweh's commitment and constant interventions.[24] Thus, "despite the disordered political condition of the period and the blatant individualism which characterized it," the ideal of a united Israel is still there, so long as Israel realizes that God alone has made it and can make it possible.[25]

---

20. Moreover, there are positive portrayals of non-Judahite tribes, such as Ehud, a Benjamite, and Deborah, who is from one of the northern tribes.
21. See 2 Kgs 23:1–25 for an account of Josiah's reforms.
22. Gale Yee, "Ideological Criticism: Judges 17–21 and the Dismembered Body," in *Judges & Method: New Approaches in Biblical Studies* (Minneapolis, MN: Fortress, 1995), 154–156.
23. Yee, "Ideological Criticism," 158.
24. Dumbrell, "In Those Days," 29–32.
25. Ibid., 31–32.

JUDGES 17–18

Some commentators believe that this refrain refers to the failure to acknowledge Yahweh as king.[26] As Block puts it, "With this fourfold repeated formula the author of Judges declares that . . . the nation recognized no one, not even God, as king. Thus the episodes that follow are presented as evidence of Israel's complete repudiation of Yahweh's claims on their lives."[27] As noted above, the key to understanding this phrase is to recognize the extensive use of irony in these five concluding chapters. Scholars have commented on the ironic tone behind the phrase, "everyone did what was right in their own eyes," but they have not included, "there was no king in Israel," as part of that ironic treatment. Whether the section was written during the time of the monarchy or the exile, it is safe to say that Israel had already experienced both the glories and failures of the kingship.[28] They would have known that the king could be a positive force for good, but could also lead people to a path that was contrary to the ways of Yahweh. It could be that the phrase was a commentary on the fact that even though there was or had been a king in Israel, this king did not or had not functioned in the way he was supposed to under Israel's covenant with Yahweh – which was to be a covenant administrator and ensure that the covenant was observed in Israel.[29] Despite the presence of a king, it was as if "there was no king in Israel," for "everyone [including the king] did what was right in his own eyes."[30]

JUDGES 17–18 STRUCTURE AND OVERVIEW

Using the refrain above as a framing device, chapters 17–18 can be structured into three episodes as follows:[31]

---

26. Boling, *Judges*, 258, 277, 293–94; Block, *Judges*, 476. Gregory Wong discusses this extensively in *Compositional Strategy of the Book of Judges* (Leiden: Brill, 2006), 212–223. He also discusses other views on 191–212.
27. Block, *Judges*, 476.
28. The phrase "In those days . . ." shows that the material was written much later than the period being described and presumes that Israel already had a king.
29. See Gerbrandt, *Kingship: Deuteronomistic History*, 98–99. What is needed, according to Davis ("Comic Literature," 158), is a particular type of king. The Torah puts clear limitations on kingly authority and rule (Deut 17:14–20; see 1 Samuel 8). The kind of king allowed for by Samuel (1 Sam 8:22) and highly qualified in Deuteronomy (17:16–20) is a king who has Yahweh at the center of his rule–a king who fears Yahweh and does Yahweh's will (Deut 17:19).
30. See E. Aydeet Mueller, *The Micah Story: A Morality Tale in the Book of Judges* (New York: Peter Lang, 2001), 103–123; Satterthwaite, "No King in Israel," 87–88.
31. Amit, "Hidden Polemic," 4–20. This outline is modified from the work of one of my former students, Edwin Tugano, in a class in Old Testament Studies 2, 1994, at Asian Theological Seminary.

Episode One (17:1–6)
- 17:1 — Introduction: "There was a man (*wayhi 'ish*) from the hill county of Ephraim, whose name was Micah"
- 17:2–5 — Plot: Micah-Mother encounter
- 17:6 — Comment: "In those days, there was no king in Israel; everyone did what was right in his own eyes."

Episode Two (17:7–18:1a)
- 17:7 — Introduction: "There was a young man (*wayhi na'ar*) from Bethlehem of Judah, from the tribe of Judah. Now he was Levite and was sojourning there."
- 17:8–13 — Plot: Micah-Levite encounter
- 18:1a — Comment: "In those days, there was no king in Israel."

Episode Three (18:1b–19:1a)
- 18:1b — Introduction: "In those days (*wayyamim hahem*), the tribe of Danites was seeking for themselves a territory to live in."
- 18:2–31 — Plot: Micah-Danites-Levite encounter
- 19:1a — Comment: "In those days, there was no king in Israel."

Aside from the refrain and the parallel introduction of each episode, other elements tie chapters 17 and 18 together. The figure of Micah, the only consistently named character, is prominent in all the episodes, as well as the Levite, thus showing the overlapping interests that impact the family, religious figures, and tribal concerns. References to the "carved image and cast idol" (NIV; 17:3, 4; 18:14, 17, 18, 20, 30, 31), ephod (17:5; 18:14, 17, 20), and teraphim (17:5; 18:14, 17, 18, 20) are repeated[32] in the familial, the cultic, and the tribal spheres, highlighting their role in the plot of the narrative as well as their pervasiveness in the life of Israel during this period.

---

32. John Hamlin, *Judges: At Risk in the Promised Land*, ITC (Grand Rapids, MI: Eerdmans, 1990), 146.

The Hebrew *pesel umassekah* can be two objects (NIV: "a carved image and a cast idol"; NASB: "graven image and a molten image"; ESV: "carved image and a metal image"). Some, however, see it as a hendiadys, meaning that it is a word pair that refers only to one object (see NRSV: "an idol of cast metal").[33] Although the word pair appears together in Judges 17:3–4 (with a singular verb in v. 4) and 18:14, they are separated in 18:17–18 and in other OT texts.[34] Thus it seems likely that the two terms originally referred to two objects, but they were brought together in this story because of a polemical thrust. Since the cast idol (Heb. *massekah*) is identified with the golden calf made by Aaron (Exod 32:4. 8)[35] and the two calves of Jeroboam (1 Kgs 14:9; 2 Kgs 17:16), it is probable that the word was added later to *pesel* as an implicit attack on Jeroboam's actions in setting up an alternate shrine in Dan and Bethel (1 Kgs 12:28–29).[36]

We encountered the ephod earlier in the Gideon narrative. The teraphim could have been statuettes representing dead ancestors, which were used for consulting the dead regarding certain future events.[37] These objects seem to have been used for divination, a "mechanical form of obtaining an oracle" from God.[38] In divination, objects (e.g. lots, animal entrails, dice, etc.) are used to get a word from God, while no such objects are used in prophetic oracles.[39]

Unlike previous stories, the name of God is only mentioned in the speech of the characters (17:2–3, 13; 18:5–6, 10) and never by the narrator himself.[40] Yahweh appears almost absent in this sorry saga, having been replaced by a religiosity and religious structures of the characters' own making. In the following incidents, God is domesticated to assuage a guilty conscience, meet a family's desire for prosperity, and establish a tribal need for settlement. What

---

33. Thus Boling (*Judges*, 256) translates it as one word, "molten figure." Block (*Judges*, 480, n. 19) also sees it as referring to one object and translates it as "a carved image overlaid with molten metal."
34. See Nah 1:14; Deut 27:15. In Isa 30:22; 42:17, they are seen as parallel to each other.
35. See Deut 9:12, 16; Neh 9:18; Ps 106:19.
36. See Jason Bray, *Sacred Dan: Ritual Tradition and Cultic Practice in Judges 17–18* (New York: T & T Clark, 2006), 64–65.
37. For a discussion about the nature of the teraphim, see Karel van der Toorn, *Family Religion in Babylonia, Syria, and Israel: Continuity and Change in the Forms of Religious Life* (Leiden/New York: Brill, 1996), 219–225.
38. Bray, *Sacred Dan*, 111.
39. Ibid., 111.
40. Davis, "Comic Literature," 159.

is remarkable about these episodes is how religious language is used to further the characters' interest and benefits.

17:1–6 GOD'S DOMESTICATION IN FAMILY LIFE

The first episode begins, "There was a certain man . . . ," which is a typical beginning for a narrative in Judges and Samuel, where the character sets in motion or becomes a part of a significant series of events (Judg 13:1; 19:1; 1 Sam 1:1; 19:1, trans. mine). The character's place of origin and name are identified. This man is *Mikayehu* (Micah in English versions), and he comes from the hill country of Ephraim.

On first reading, one may get the impression of a family that puts religion and piety at the center of family life. Micah readily confesses his sin to his mother and returns what he has stolen (17:2a, 3a, 4a); the mother accepts his son's confession and blesses her son by the Lord (17:2b); the mother dedicates the silver that her son returned to the Lord (17:3); Micah has a shrine (*beyth 'elohim* or "house of God") and a priest. The name of the son himself (*Mikayehu* in Hebrew) means, "Who is like Yahweh?," a testimony to Yahweh's incomparability. Thus, religious language and actions converge to show a mother and a son who profess religious devotion and who are involved in overt religious acts.

A closer reading of the story, however, shows a discrepancy between the religious language and apparent piety expressed by the characters and the true interests and devotion demonstrated by their actions. For instance, one would expect that the return of the silver to Micah's mother would bring a change for the better. After all, this act of restitution opens up possibilities for change and transformation. But the hope for change does not occur. In fact, the story spirals downwards, and restitution ends in idolatry.

The motivation for Micah's confession becomes clear in the first part of his confession to his mother: "The eleven hundred pieces of silver which were taken from you, about which you uttered a curse and of which you spoke about in my hearing . . ." (17:2, trans. mine).[41] The confession is triggered by his fear of the curse which his mother has imputed on the thief, rather than

---

41. The sentence is awkward and unfinished so that BHS suggests that one or a few words have dropped out, presumably the content of the curse itself, although no other versions attest to this. Boling thinks that the awkwardness is deliberate on the part of the narrator to show Micah's embarrassment in having to admit his wrongdoing (Boling, *Judges*, 255).

by genuine remorse and recognition of wrongdoing.[42] The amount that he stole – eleven hundred shekels of silver – is staggering, if one considers that the total amount of earrings that the Israelites took from the Midianites as spoil was seventeen hundred shekels.[43] It also reveals the wealth of the mother as well as Micah's insensitive conscience, which should have been troubled by stealing even a small amount.

Without expressing indignation or regret for her son's actions, the mother blesses the son (17:2b) as if what he said is the most wonderful or normal thing in the world. The blessing may have been given in order to counteract the curse.[44] Nevertheless, her blessing serves only to condone her son's behavior. Moreover, the mention of Yahweh's name draws Yahweh into seeming complicity with the actions of both son and mother.

The mother adds insult to injury by dedicating (causative form of *qadash*, "to set apart for holy purposes") the tainted silver to Yahweh in order to make a carved image and cast metal, thinking perhaps that consecrating it will remove its dubious past. Ironically, although the silver is dedicated to Yahweh, it is actually for the use of her son ("for my son"; "I will give it back to you," 17:3). Ostensibly, the mother thinks that Yahweh will be pleased to have a carved image, but in doing so, she is also thinking about how this can benefit her son. Perhaps this is the meaning behind her statement, "Blessed is my son by the Lord" (17:2b, trans. mine).

Behind the thinking of mother and son is the belief that the concrete physical image represents the presence of the deity and therefore can mediate blessings to those who have it, along with curses against the possessor's enemies. The mother, however, does not realize the incongruity of dedicating to Yahweh what is actually abhorrent to God. A comparison with Deuteronomy 12 highlights this incongruity.[45] Deuteronomy 12:3 says that when the Israelites enter the land, they are to cut down the images (*pesilim*, the same root word used in 17:3) of the Canaanite gods. Many other verses warn Israel against making an image,[46] even if that image is that of Yahweh.

---

42. Block, *Judges*, 479.
43. Boling, *Judges*, 249. Boling mentions other examples as comparisons: four hundred shekels for Abraham's burial site (Gen 24:15, 19), fifty shekels that David paid for the threshing floor of Araunah and the oxen (2 Sam 24:24). The Levite in the next episode was only paid ten shekels per year (17:10), aside from his board and lodging and a set of clothes.
44. Matthews, *Judges & Ruth*, 171; Block, *Judges*, 479; Van der Toorn, *Family Religion*, 250.
45. See Matthews, *Judges & Ruth*, 172.
46. See Exod 20:4; Deut 4:16, 23, 25; 5:8; 27:15; Ps 97:7. On the prohibition of a cast image, see Exod 34:17; Lev 19:4; Deut 27:15. The Israelites are also to destroy cast images when they enter the land (Num 33:52).

And yet Micah's mother seems to think sincerely that her act of giving the silver to make an image is a sacrifice that can only lead to prosperity for her son, thus canceling the curse and compensating for the silver that she personally will lose.

The narrative emphasizes that the silver belongs to Micah's mother. Twice, it is reported that the silver was returned to her (17:3, 4). Since the silver is hers, it lies in her power to give it to a silversmith and to hand it back to her son in the form of a cast image. The impression made is that this image, being made of her silver, is also the possession of Micah's mother, to be disposed of in any way she chooses. This is completely opposite to her action of "setting apart" the silver solely for the Lord's use.

The thinking that the silver and the image are really hers and not God's can be seen in the way the mother is free to use only two hundred pieces of silver out of the eleven hundred she dedicated to the Lord (17:4). Thus, as the son steals from his mother, the mother also steals from God, to whom she has verbally committed to give what her son has returned. However, since the silver is hers to begin with and is utilized according to her wishes, she may not have regarded this as stealing, but rather a generous offer that grants favor both to God and to her son.

WHAT IS OFFERED TO GOD BELONGS TO GOD

This narrative helps us to reflect on our attitude towards the things we have handed over to God as an offering for the church and for God's mission. Although ensuring proper stewardship and accountability of God's resources is important, we need to keep in mind that what we hand over as an offering is no longer our possession. In the first place, all that we have belongs to God; we are only stewards. In the second place, to offer something means to relinquish control over it – it is no longer "our right" to dictate the terms of its use.

This echoes Paul's injunction in 1 Corinthians 11:17–34 about the divisions in the Corinthian church regarding the conduct of the Lord's Supper.[47] It seems that the wealthy, who hosted and donated the provisions for the Lord's Supper, also insisted that they, along with their favorites, eat the Lord's

---

47. Anthony Thiselton, *1 Corinthians: A Shorter Exegetical and Pastoral Commentary* (Grand Rapids, MI: Eerdmans, 2006), 180–181.

> Supper in a separate room ahead of the others,[48] with better food and wine.[49] This goes against body life, according to Paul (vv. 24, 29). In 1 Corinthians 11:20-21, a contrast is made between one's own meal and the Lord's meal. Even though the meal for the Lord's Table was provided by the wealthy, once it was given over for the Lord's use, it was no longer private property, but community property.[50] In the same way, what we offer to God is no longer at our disposal, and we hand our "right" of decision over to God.

The carved image and cast idol are kept in the "house of Micah" (17:4), but within Micah's house is also a shrine (literally, "house of god"; 17:5). One would expect that Micah, having made the right move by returning the stolen silver, would make another positive step by giving up the shrine in his house. But he does not. Rather, he intensifies his own homemade religiosity. To the carved image and cast idol, he adds a teraphim and an ephod. With a complete cast of cultic objects, Micah, as the patriarch, now heads over "the house of God" inside his own household.

However, something is lacking, since someone is needed to do the cultic activities appropriate for the teraphim, the ephod, the carved image, and cast idol in the "house of God," as well as to be guardian of the shrine. So Micah installs[51] one of his sons as priest. This is another aberration[52] in that he completely bypasses God's provision that the administrators of the religious ritual activities in relation to the worship of Yahweh should be Aaron and his sons, as well as the Levites, because they have been placed in a special state of holiness (Lev 8-9; 21-22; Num 3, 18).

Lest these actions be seen as positive models advocating normative behavior in Israel, the narrator inserts: "There was no king in Israel, everyone did what was right in his eyes." What the mother and Micah are all about is

---

48. Gerd Theissen, *The Social Setting of Pauline Christianity: Essays on Corinth* (Philadelphia, PA: Fortress, 1982), 161.
49. Jerome Murphy-O'Connor, *St. Paul's Corinth: Texts and Archaeology* (Wilmington, DE: Michael Glazier, 1983), 159–161; Theissen, *Social Setting*, 155–156. The rich patrons brought more than what they needed, but they were eating the extra and better food themselves. See C. K. Barrett, *The First Epistle to the Corinthians*, Harper's New Testament Commentaries (New York: Harper and Row, 1968), 263.
50. Theissen, *Social Setting*, 148–149.
51. Literally, the Hebrew phrase is, "fills the hands of," a standard expression used for installing a priest (Cundall and Morris, *Judges*, 185).
52. Ibid.

something that is right in their own eyes and, implicitly, not right in the eyes of Yahweh.

Ironically, *Mikayehu* means, "Who is like Yahweh?" In many instances where the theme of God's incomparability is taken up in the OT, the focus is on God's uniqueness and superiority over and against idols. Whereas idols are made of fallible materials and by human hands, Yahweh made heaven and earth (Isa 40:18–20; 44:6–18). Whereas idols cannot save, Yahweh both saves and declares his plan of redemption from the beginning (Isa 45:18–46:13). Whereas idols are powerless to do anything and to believe in them is foolish, Yahweh shows his power and wisdom in the way he has established the world (Jer 10:1–16). Whereas Idols "cannot speak; they must be carried because they cannot walk" (Jer 10:5), Yahweh says, "I have made you and I will carry you; I will sustain you and I will rescue you" (Isa 46:4).

But instead of demonstrating the incomparability of Yahweh (as reflected in the name, *Mikayehu*) Micah reduces God to images that can be owned, housed inside the house of another master, tended by a family member who serves as an illegitimate priest, and handled like a domestic servant in a patriarch's household, whose function is subservient to the family interests. In short, Yahweh is treated like an idol, an object that can be owned and possessed. Thus it is no surprise that *Mikayehu*, the name used in verses 1 and 4, is shortened to *Mikah* in verse 5, a diminutive of the longer name. However, the omission of the name of Yahweh in the shortened form may indicate that Micah's behavior no longer reflects the meaning of his longer name, which points to the incomparability of Yahweh.[53] It may also be an attempt to diminish "the status of the character to an unruly child."[54]

In many Filipino homes there is a wall hanging that says:

> Christ is the head of this House,
> the unseen guest at every meal,
> the silent listener to every conversation.

The saying demonstrates a desire for God to be part of the family's life – someone so familiar and intimate that he is invited to sit with the family at the dinner table. But God can be treated so much like a family member that he is expected to further the family's interest and be subservient to the family's needs and agenda. In Filipino society, the security of the family is given primary importance, even if it means compromising other roles and

---

53. Aydeet, *The Micah Story*, 53.
54. Matthews, *Judges & Ruth*, 169.

responsibilities.⁵⁵ This expectation may be projected onto God so that God exists only to advance the family interests. Thus being involved in religious activities can be seen as a means to ensure the well-being of the family rather than as a way of honoring God.

In the West, religion is seen as a very private matter – something between the believer and God. The "I" becomes the center of the gospel: "What's in it for me?" Even though such individualistic thinking may not orient Asian cultures, the family can be substituted for the individual. So, instead, the question becomes: "What's in it for my family?" In this thinking, God is regarded not as someone who calls us into account, but as someone whose main function is to serve human needs. As in the Jephthah story, this challenges the utilitarian thinking that orients some of our Christian activities.

17:7–13 GOD'S DOMESTICATION IN RELIGIOUS LIFE

If Micah is described as a man from the hill country of Ephraim, the opening character in the next episode is a young lad (perhaps to indicate that he is much younger than Micah) from Bethlehem of Judah. Moreover, this young man is a religious leader – a Levite – yet his name is withheld (17:7). Lest one gets confused about how a Levite can come from the tribe of Judah, he is also described as sojourning in Bethlehem, which means that he is not a Judahite but only lives in Judah.⁵⁶ Apparently this Levite was not satisfied with his own land portion in Judah, so he set out looking for greener pastures. And this is how he comes to Micah's house.

Micah, upon learning that the young man is a Levite, immediately offers, "Live with me and be my father and priest" (17:10). The term "father" does not mean to be in authority over or responsible for someone. In relation to the prophets, the term "father" is used to acknowledge their role in discerning God's intentions for specific situations, and so people ask them for guidance about their future actions and present difficulties.⁵⁷ On the other hand, priests act as intermediaries between God and people in terms of their worship life. Micah needs someone to consult about his activities, and he thinks

---

55. Mina Ramirez, *Understanding Philippine Social Realities through the Filipino Family: A Phenomenological Approach* (Manila: Asian Social Institute, 1993), 43–45.
56. The Levites did not have their own tribal territory but were allotted cities and pasture lands in the other land allocations of the other eleven tribes (Num 35:1–5; Josh 21:1–41), so they were in some sense always resident aliens (Boling, *Judges*, 257).
57. The prophet Elisha is called "father" by the king in 2 Kgs 6:21; 8:9; 13:14, particularly in relation to inquiries about present and future situations. See Boling, *Judges*, 257.

a "diviner" will ensure that his endeavors will become successful. Moreover, he needs to legitimize his "house of God" with a "genuine" priest from the chosen Levitical line. Thus, in exchange for the Levite's services, Micah offers him food, clothing, shelter, and a yearly allowance (17:10).

At first glance, there seems to be nothing wrong with the quid pro quo between Micah and the Levite. Micah needs someone to give him religious services while the Levite needs someone to provide for him. Is not the laborer worthy of his wages? Moreover, the Levite is not coerced into this arrangement: "The Levite was willing to live with the man" (17:11, trans. mine). Here, the Hebrew verb "to be willing" (trans., "he agreed," in the NIV, NRSV, NASB) can have the sense of "to be pleased."[58] So he becomes part of the family and is treated like one of Micah's sons. Both Micah and the Levite find the arrangement mutually agreeable – especially Micah, who believes the Lord will be good to him because he has secured the services of a legitimate priest (17:13). So "the scene ends with Micah confident that his future is now well secured."[59]

There are several incongruities, however. First, Micah asks the Levite to be a father to him (17:10), yet he treats the Levite as one of his own sons (17:11).[60] So who is a father to whom? Far from receiving guidance and instruction from the Levite, Micah seems to be the one in control, creating his own web of religious security in order to satisfy his own needs. Moreover, even though Micah does not have qualms in appointing his own son as priest, he is quick to depose his son as soon as he finds a better substitute. Thus, to Micah's eyes, it is better to have a priest than to have no priest, but better still is to have a priest from the line sanctioned by God. In this thinking, Micah reveals how he looks at God. To him, God is a benefactor who can be manipulated to grant certain favors by complying with certain religious formulas. The problem is that Micah is regarding Yahweh as someone whom he can carry around in his back pocket.

This view of God is rooted in the thinking that Yahweh is just the same as the Canaanite idols. Since the idols were thought to represent the gods, what they could do was feared (Jer 10:5; Isa 41:23). But even so, they were made and decorated by human hands (Jer 10:3–4, 9), from the same material that

---

58. *BDB*, 384. Note parallel in Exod 2:21. For the sense of "to be willing, to be pleased, to be keen," see Judg 19:6; 1 Sam 12:22; 2 Sam 7:29; 2 Kgs 5:23; 6:3; Job 6:9, 28. The stronger sense of "being resolved, determined" is found in Deut 1:5; Hos 5:11.
59. Webb, *Integrated Reading*, 184.
60. Block, *Judges*, 489.

people used to warm, feed, and otherwise sustain themselves (Isa 44:12–17), and they had to be carried (Isa 45:20; 46:1, 7; Jer 10:5) or put in place since they could not move on their own (Isa 41:7; 46:7). This meant that they were objects that could be controlled and manipulated. The very nature of the idols themselves engendered the worldview that gods could be influenced to bring blessing to their bearers or owners and woe to their owner's enemies. This thinking was imported into the Israelite religion, so that even Yahweh himself was regarded as someone who could be induced to act in a certain way, just like the images that were used to represent him.

As in the first episode, Micah is seeking to use Yahweh for his own personal purposes, although he thinks he is doing so in a more religiously acceptable way. By employing a religious leader designated in the covenant, he thinks he will also be able to get the blessings of the covenant. He fails to understand that the heart of the covenant is the exclusive worship of Yahweh, with a specific prohibition against images, regardless of whether the image is of Yahweh or another deity.[61]

Asia is home to some of the world's major religions, which have been rooted in the life and mentality of the people for many centuries. Thus when people convert to Christianity, they may bring their previous conceptions about their previous deities and project them onto the God of the Bible. But not only traditional religions shape our view of God. Secular philosophies, a market-driven economy, our personal and national history, and our cultural worldview all play a part in how we view God. In fact, in a world where economic productivity receives the greatest value and people are evaluated for their market value, a mentality that puts an economic tab on religion can easily take root and flourish, masquerading itself as genuine piety.

We have already encountered this utilitarian mindset in the Jephthah narrative, where Jephthah marginalizes Yahweh because of Jephthah's desire to overcome his earlier rejection. In the Micah narrative, Micah both marginalizes and domesticates Yahweh, regarding him as someone whose primary function is to benefit and bless Micah and his household. In this way, worshipping God is seen as religious capital – a good investment – because it will redound to the blessing of the believer. The folly in such thinking is that it reduces God to someone whom we can control and manipulate to serve our own needs and preferences.

---

61. A unique characteristic of the religion of ancient Israel is the absence of images of the deity and its strong prohibition against representing God in any form of image. See Patrick Miller, *The Religion of Ancient Israel* (Louisville, KY: John Knox, 2000), 15–23.

Perhaps one should not expect too much from Micah, the lay person as self-styled religious leader, but certainly we should expect more from the Levite. This "proper" religious leader could be a sign of hope, coming as he does from Bethlehem in Judah (17:9).[62]

Levites were tasked to assist the priests in doing the work of the sanctuary (Num 3:5–38; 4:1–33; 8:23–26; 18:1–7; Deut 10:8). They read the law and, in the post-exilic period, were involved in teaching the law (Neh 8:1–18). In some cases, they functioned as priests themselves.[63] But these roles and tasks, which were related to the maintenance and administration of the sanctuary and the performance of the sacrifices, were rooted in a more fundamental calling and vocation: the Levites were chosen to minister before the Lord (Deut 10:8–9; 18:5–7) in place of the firstborn of Israel (Num 3:11–13, 41–44). Being set apart for the Lord's work, they were expected to put God's interests and service above all.

However, the Levite in this story shows a lack of genuineness in spiritual vocation. While he appears to be strong in his Bethlehemite identity (17:9), he is also purposeless (17:9) – leaving Bethlehem for no apparent reason, without a clear destination (17:8), going forth "to sojourn wherever he might find" (17:8, 9). He is also easily co-opted (17:10) and young (17:11–12), a point made several times in the text. Willful and wandering, he appears to be concerned only about himself (17:9). His youthfulness may suggest that he lacks spiritual formation and maturity. He is easily bought by Micah, and he quickly forgets his vocation of ministering to God in order to offer his religious services to the highest bidder. God's purposes seem to be completely lacking in the motivation and commitments of this Levite.

Perhaps the financial vulnerability of the Levite causes him to seek security by finding a patron, who will provide him with clothing, shelter, and a wage that will sustain him (17:10). Because the Levites did not have land allocation, as did the other tribes of Israel,[64] the Israelite tribes were com-

---

62. The narrative indicates three times that the Levite was from Bethlehem of Judah (17:7, 8, 9).
63. Some see a distinction between the Aaronic priesthood and the Levites. Even though not all Levites might have been priests, there were some who were, as seen in the following verses. In Deut 31:9, the sons of Levi are called "priests." The term "levitical priests" are found in the following verses: Josh 3:3; 8:33; Deut 18:4. Josh 13:14 says that "the offerings by fire to the Lord" is the inheritance of the sons of Levi, while Deut 18:1–5 assumes that the Levites, as all priests, can eat the sacrifices given as the Lord's portion.
64. Deut 10:9; 12:12; 14:27, 29; 18:1, 2; Josh 13:14, 33; 14:3–4; 18:7. The explanation given is that God is their inheritance.

manded to set aside towns and pasture lands, where the Levites could live and tend their flocks and herds (Num 35:1–8; Josh 21:1–41).

Nevertheless, the Levites' provisions might have been inadequate because they were considered a marginalized group that needed the support of the community, along with aliens, widows, and orphans.[65] The cause of the Levites' poverty might have been varied: perhaps the allocated land did not yield enough produce; perhaps the other tribes did not fulfill their responsibility in giving lands, towns, and a portion of their provision, in accordance with what was stipulated in the covenant;[66] or, with the growth of local sanctuaries, there might not have been enough people bringing their tithes, sacrifices, and offerings to the central sanctuary in Jerusalem, causing a drop in the support of the priests and the Levites.

If this is the case, it is not surprising that the Levite of Judges 17 is seeking better pastures and is eager to take advantage of the opportunity to attach himself to a rich patron such as Micah. The offer of free board and lodging, with the chance to practice his religious profession, is just too good to miss. The downside, however, is that he has to compromise his calling in order to serve the interests of his patron. Moreover, the story shows that the problem goes beyond his need for sustenance, since the Levite quickly drops his patron, Micah, when a better opportunity arises, as Judges 18 shows. This reveals the mercenary and opportunistic nature behind the Levite's religious façade.

> **PATRONAGE SYSTEM IN ASIAN CULTURE**
>
> The patronage system[67] is deeply embedded in Asian life and culture. J. K. Chow describes the system as a patron-client relationship, which is characterized by an exchange relation, where "a patron gives the client what he needs, and in turn, gets from the client what he wants."[68] Filipinos, in particular, are drawn towards father figures – *padrinos* – who are perceived as those

---

65. W. O. McCready, "Priests and Levites," *ISBE* 3:966–967. See Deut 14:29; 16:11, 14; 26:11–13.
66. Aydeet, *The Micah Story*, 62.
67. The most extensive study of the patronage system in Corinth is John K. Chow, *Patronage and Power: A Study of Social Networks in Corinth* (Sheffield: JSOT, 1992). Other works that discuss it are: Peter Marshall, *Enmity in Corinth: Social Relationship in Paul's Relations with the Corinthians* (Tübingen: J. C. B. Mohr, 1987), 143–147.
68. Chow, *Patronage and Power*, 31.

> who can provide for their needs, because they have access to resources and are generous to share this with whomever they favor. In return, patrons expect the loyalty of their recipients, which is expressed by undertaking efforts that promote the patrons' interests.
>
> The patronage system is also apparent when wealthy and influential families or church members act as patrons to pastors or church workers. Because of church workers' financial vulnerability, many accept support and favors from patrons who have access to privileges and resources. These patrons often expect a pastor-beneficiary to meet their demands and support their interests, even if these are contrary to the pastor's role as a spiritual leader of the whole congregation. Thus instead of shepherding the whole flock and ministering to God as the primary vocation, the pastor serves the vested interests of just a few families or the richer, more influential members of the church.
>
> The fault in this system does not lie with the religious leaders alone, although a fuller understanding of their vocation is needed. First, we should not perceive religious leaders primarily in terms of how they can serve us and the needs of our families, for religious leaders are accountable to God, and they serve God's interests. Second, the main function of religion is not to bless us. If we hold to this mistaken understanding, then our worship of God will be centered on our personal needs rather than what will glorify God.

18:1–31 GOD'S DOMESTICATION IN ECONOMIC-POLITICAL LIFE

In Judges 18, the focus shifts from individuals and households in Israel to the entire tribe of Dan. In chapter 17, we see the domestication of God within families and among the religious sector in Israel. In chapter 18, the narrator broadens the scope of his observations about what is happening to society by relating the story of the tribe of Dan's search for a settlement.

One wonders why a whole tribe is still looking for land (Judg 18:1). Did not Joshua allocate the land to the different tribes? The original territory allocated to Dan was near the Philistine coast (Josh 19:40–46), from Zorah and Eshtaol (the birthplace of Samson), extending up to Joppa (modern-day Tel-Aviv). It also bordered Judah[69] and Ephraim (hence the mention of the sons of Joseph in Judg 1). The Danites, however, lost this territory, according to

---

69. Cundall and Morris, *Judges*, 187.

Joshua 19:47. Judges 1:34–35 reports how the Amorites pressed the Danites into the hill country and occupied Aijalon and Shaalbim, which were originally part of the Danites' tribal territory. The pressure of living in such limited space while encroaching into the land of other tribes might have forced the Danites to look for another place to live. The other lands nearby had already been allotted to and were already occupied by the other tribes. Moreover, the non-Israelites occupying the land that had been allocated to the Danites were too strong for the Danites to drive out. The only solution was to look for a place unoccupied by the other tribes, which was easier to conquer.

As a first step, the Danites send five men to spy out the land. One gets a feeling of *déjà vu* as one reads the story. Did not Moses send out twelve spies prior to the conquest of Israel (Num 13:1–16)? Did not Joshua do the same (Josh 2:1)? Judges 1:23–24 relates another incident of spying on land immediately prior to making war its inhabitants. Such spying was intended to assess the strength or weakness of the potential foe while also discerning whether the land was economically viable in order to sustain its new inhabitants (Num 13:17–20). In each case, spying was done prior to a military attack in order to conquer the land. Thus when the Danites send men to spy out Laish, it indicates that an attack is about to follow.

Before the spies reach Laish, however, they pass by the house of Micah and spend the night there (18:2), possibly because the house was near a land bridge that led to the northern part of the country.[70] In Micah's house, the spies "recognized" (18:3; NRSV; NJPS; NIV) the voice of the young Levite. This may indicate that they had previous personal acquaintance with the Levite. Most likely, they simply recognize his accent as coming from the south rather than the north,[71] which indicates that he is not from that region, thereby arousing their curiosity.

The young Levite's response to the spies' questions seems to reveal that he is grateful to have found sustenance in the household of Micah (18:4). The spies are not shocked by the information that the Levite was hired to be a personal priest, but seem to take it for granted and expect the Levite to give them guidance (18:5). The Levite does not hesitate to proclaim divine blessing: "Go in peace. Your journey has the LORD's approval" (18:6), implying that it will be successful.

---

70. From their allocated territory near the Philistine plains, the Danites had to pass through the hill country of Ephraim to go north.
71. Boling, *Judges*, 263. Note the translation of the NJPS: "they recognized the speech of the young Levite."

Even though this spy episode follows the general lines of the spy stories in the OT, there are some indications that the elements of the spy story motif are being parodied and inverted to present an anti-conquest theme.[72] Bauer, with modifications by Matthews, presents the typical elements of the spy story: first, spies are chosen or appointed; secondly, the spies' mission is described; thirdly, the execution of the mission is reported; fourthly, the spies return and give their report; fifthly, Yahweh declares the gift of land; sixthly, conquest commences. In Numbers 13–14, however, a move to conquer and possess the land did not happen immediately, because the people were afraid to fight against the well-armed and stronger inhabitants of the land (14:4).

A comparison between Numbers 13 and Judges 18 shows an inversion of the elements of spy stories that are present within each narrative, with an added element showing God's response.

Numbers 13 and 14	Judges 18
1 & 2. God gives a command to spy out the land (13:1–2) and Moses obeys (13:3). Prior to this, God declares that this land has been given to the Israelites (Deut 1:20–21; Josh 1:2–3, 6, 11, 13, 15).	1 & 2. No corresponding command and obedience is recorded. Instead, the spies consult Micah's personal priest to see if they have God's approval for their journey (18:5–6). The Levite, acting as priest, assures them of God's approval.
3. The spies, in their reconnaissance, see a very fertile land, but they also see the sons of Anak, whose great height has sown fear among the inhabitants of the surrounding areas (13:21–22).	3. The spies see a peaceful people rather than a strong, mighty people that they would have difficulty conquering (18:7).

---

72. See Uwe F. W. Bauer, "Judges 18 as an Anti-Spy Story in the Context of an Anti-Conquest Story: The Creative Usage of Literary Genres," *JSOT* 88 (2000): 37–47. See also Matthews, *Judges & Ruth*, 174–175; Webb, *Judges: Integrated Reading*, 185–186.

4. They report the abundance of the land – it is flowing with milk and honey. According to the spies, the inhabitants are "strong, and the cities are fortified and very large." Also they report the presence of the descendants of Anak. They also talk about the other inhabitants – Amalekites, Hittites, Amorites, Canaanites (13:27–29; cf. 32–33).	4. They report that the land is good (although not abundant) and spacious, and they would not lack anything if they live in the land (18:10). They describe the people as unsuspecting, but omit the other description of the narrator, which is that the people of Laish are peaceful. The spies emphasize the weakness of the people (18:10).
5. Caleb encourages the people to "go up and possess the land," for they will "surely be able to do so" (13:30), based on Yahweh's previous promise.	5. The spies encourage their fellow Danites "to go up against the inhabitants of the land." They utter the victory formula: "Do not be slow to go, to enter in and possess the land . . . for God has given it into your hands" (18:9–10), even though there was no prior promise from God.
6. The rest of the spies discourage the people from going, emphasizing the strength of the people (13:31–33). Even when the people grumble, Caleb and Joshua continue to exhort the people not to fear the people of the land. They say: "If the Lord is pleased with us, he will bring us into this land and give it to us" (14:6–9). The people cry and grumble and are unwilling to enter the land. Moreover, they want to go back to Egypt (14:1–4).	6. Six hundred men set out, armed with weapons of war (18:11). But they want tokens of God's presence, so they take Micah's priest and the household gods (18:17–20). They attack Laish, kill the people and burn the city with fire (18:27).
7. God becomes angry with the people (14:11–12).	7. God is silent. There is no word of approval or disapproval.

Interestingly, this comparison highlights the Danites' ready willingness to conquer the land, which should have been Israel's response in Numbers 13–14. On the other hand, there is no indication that God is giving the land to the Danites, and there is no clear command to possess it,[73] and so the Danites should have been more cautious in planning a military attack based solely on favorable circumstances.

Even though the Danites plan to conquer the land without God's initiative, they still seem conscious of the need for divine approval, wanting God's stamp on what they have decided to do without God. So they solicit the go-signal of a bogus priest. The Danite spies no longer seem able to distinguish between a true word from God and what is false. Or they may no longer care if the message really comes from God, so long as they follow the outwardly religious ritual, which they think will ensure a successful plot. In this, they are not unlike Micah, who thinks that employing a false priest to perform religious acts will guarantee his prosperity. In this narrative, we see how Yahweh has become the automated benefactor of Israel, for there is no evidence in the rest of the story that the Danites pray to Yahweh, obey Yahweh's voice, or look to Yahweh to give the victory.

In the Judges and Numbers narratives, both the Danite spies and the twelve spies report that the land they have surveyed is good. The report of the twelve spies in Numbers emphasizes its fruitfulness, confirming God's earlier description of the land as flowing with milk and honey (Num 13:27; see also Exod 3:8, 17; 33:3; Lev 20:24). The report of the Danite spies emphasizes the land's spaciousness, presumably because they have been constricted in a very narrow space as result of pressure from the Canaanites (Judg 1:34), but it also includes a description of the land's material sustenance: "a place where there is no lack of anything in the earth" (Judg 18:10). Having marginalized and domesticated Yahweh, the Danites become blind to who Yahweh really is and are drawn by the hope of material prosperity (18:7, 10).

The above comparison also highlights a contrast between the descriptions of the inhabitants. In Numbers, the Israelites are at a disadvantage because the Canaanite inhabitants are strong and big, and their cities are fortified (Num 13:28–29). Moreover, the narrative mentions the descendants of Anak – the Nephilims – who were semi-divine mythical figures that represented lawlessness.[74] In Judges, the inhabitants of Laish are described by the spies

---

73. This is in contrast to the Numbers story, where such promise is clearly given (Num 13:1; Deut 1:20–21; Josh 1:2–3. See Bauer, "Judges 18: Anti-Spy Story," 38.
74. Bauer, "Judges 18," 39; see also n. 11.

as *boteakh*, which literally means "trusting" or "secure" (Judg 18:10). The NIV, NRSV, and ESV translate the word as "unsuspecting," implying that these people are vulnerable and easy to overcome since they are not prepared for an attack. Interestingly, the spies omit the narrator's other descriptions of the people, who are like the Sidonians – quiet, trusting, lacking nothing, possessing wealth (18:7).[75] This description gives the impression that the people of Laish are living quietly on their own, disturbing no one, with no need to occupy other lands since they are self-sufficient. Moreover, since they are far from their natural allies and have no dealings with others, they do not pose a threat to anybody. By this description, the narrator evokes the sympathies of the reader for these people, who are vulnerable and whose manner of life does not invite attack.

Both the Numbers and Judges episodes contain an encouragement to go up and take the land. Ironically, those who do not have a direct command from God seem to be more confident of God's backing, even to the point of presumptuously uttering the victory formula: "God has put (the land) into your hands" (18:10). In this, they echo the tone of Micah, who self-assuredly says that God will prosper him because he has the Levite for his priest (17:13). And like master, like servant, the Levite places Yahweh at the behest of the Danites, assuring them that the mission is "under the eye of the Lord" (18:6, NRSV, ESV). In contrast, Joshua and Caleb, although confident that they would possess the land despite the superior strength of its inhabitants, nevertheless gave room for God to move: "If God is pleased with us, he will bring us into this land" (Num 14:8). The Levite, however, has no qualms about speaking on God's behalf.

Religious leaders can fall into the trap of claiming that what they say comes directly from God because they have a desire to be credible or authoritative or because they want to say something that will meet people's demand for a direct word from God. One must be careful when one says, "Thus says the Lord," thereby claiming the mantle of prophetic authority. First, such language can easily be abused and become a vehicle for manipulating people. Secondly, instead of patiently discerning God's will through the guidance of the Holy Spirit, people can become dependent on religious figures who give them instant and specific messages from God about what they are supposed

---

75. The Hebrew for the phrases "lacked nothing" and "prosperous" are cryptic, and so English versions and commentators have translated them differently. NASB has "there was no ruler humiliating them for anything in the land," while the NJPS has "with no one in the land to molest them and with no hereditary ruler."

to do. Thirdly, such messages can actually mislead people into paths that are not sanctioned by God, or make people think that God will prosper them because a religious authority says so, even when their lives are not consistent with God's will.

Notably, in verse 10, the Danite spies use the formula that was used earlier in the book of Judges to signal God's granting of victory to the Israelites tribes: "The Lord has given . . . into your/their hand" (Judg 1:2; 3:10; 4:7; 7:9). This suggests that the Danites regard their conquest of Laish as part of God's program for the conquest of Canaan. Yet this is clearly not the case, since: a) there is no instruction from God; b) the inhabitants do not belong to the Canaanites; c) this is not within the tribal territory allocated to the Danites; and d) they are not oppressed by the inhabitants of Laish, who only want to live in peace.[76]

Nevertheless, six hundred Danite men set out, girded with weapons of war, to conquer Laish, whereas the Israelite community in Numbers wanted to retreat and go back to Egypt. Yet the narrator is not simply describing an unholy war by an Israelite tribe, since he makes clear connections with the Micah story and devotes significant narrative space to the Danites' side trip to Micah's house before embarking on their war project (18:2–6; 14–25).

Interestingly, the five Danite spies seem to know how their brothers will react when they inform them about Micah's cultic objects – an ephod, a teraphim, and a cast image (18:14). These are the objects that Micah's mother made, for which Micah built a shrine in his house, which have been used for divination by the Levite priest whom Micah installed.

This long episode reveals that the idols Micah thought would protect him, along with the Levite whom he hired to make him prosperous, do nothing for him in the end. His idols are stolen (18:17–18), his personal priest leaves him for greener pastures (18:19–20), and superior strength prevails (18:26). In the end, Micah looks pathetic as he runs after those who have stolen his gods and his priest and confronts them: "You took the gods I made, and my priest, and went away. What else do I have? How can you ask, 'What's the matter with you?'" (18:24). Ironically, Micah's language reveals that the gods were "made" by him and the priest belongs to him (see 18:27). In this case, they are obviously not powerful enough to do him any good. Moreover, even though Micah claims proprietorship over the gods and the Levite, they

---

76. See Bauer, "Judges 18," 41.

can be stolen or bought with a more attractive offer, highlighting the fact that they can be controlled easily and therefore cannot provide any real benefits.

As for the Levite, he is consistent in his opportunistic and utilitarian nature. Realizing that he has no chance against the Danites' superior strength (18:17–19) and receiving a "better" offer to be father and priest not just to one man, but to a whole tribe, he quickly jumps at the chance and is glad to come along. He does not exhibit even a tinge of conscience at taking Micah's idols, which were only entrusted to him (18:20).

This easily bought, purposeless, and immature Levite is co-opted by the Danites and elevated to become their spiritual leader (18:19), which reflects their low spiritual status. Clearly, they are not interested in having the Levite lead them into greater reverence, devotion, and obedience to Yahweh; rather, they want to facilitate a form of religion that will reinforce their expectations and needs.

Confident of their strength and religious backing, the Danites embark on their planned conquest. In contrast to the earlier part of the book of Judges, when the tribal groups faced strong enemies that sometimes routed the Israelites, this act of territorial expansion is effortless. Unlike the earlier enemies of Israel, the inhabitants of the land are not oppressors. The "enemy" offer no resistance (18:7, 27), and thus they are easily conquered: the Danite soldiers "came to Laish, to a people quiet and unsuspecting, and struck them with the edge of the sword and burned the city with fire" (18:27, ESV). The repetition of the description of the people of Laish as "quiet and unsuspecting" throughout the narrative (18:7, 10, 27) highlights the Danites' wanton brutality. They take whatever they can get, plundering the house of Micah (18:14–26) and then an unsuspecting people.[77] The narrator further emphasizes the helplessness of the people with the description: "there was no one to rescue them because they lived a long way from Sidon and had no relationship with anyone else" (18:28). Clearly, this is not a war for Yahweh and by Yahweh, but a massacre of a defenseless people (18:7, 10, 27).

What makes this incident even more grievous is that the Danites view the massacre as a divine war, with divine sanctions, and they use religious language and symbols to justify their conquest. However, the Danites' land-grabbing is wrapped in superficial piety, for as they fall on the unsuspecting inhabitants

---

77. Linking this to the Joshua account–where the Danites were allotted territory (Josh 19:40–46), which they subsequently lost (19:47) – this account either contradicts the Joshua story or the Danites were on a second excursion in finding a place, but this time on the basis of mercenary brutality.

of the new territory, they never mention Yahweh fighting for them or with them (18:27–31). The entire war venture does not seem to have anything to do with Yahweh, but proceeds on the basis of a co-opted and compromised priest and his religious paraphernalia of ephod, teraphim, and idol (18:20). The Danites are quite happy to steal a priest and idols from Micah, who himself is a thief (18:22–26), and then proceed to steal the land of a people who do not present a threat to them. Hence, in this war project, the Danites are doing their own thing, with superficial nod towards Yahweh. Ironically, the name Dan has its roots in the concept of justice, but the tribe is doing injustice.[78] This leads us to wonder how can there be such a Yahweh "victory" when Israel is doing whatever they see as right (17:6), and the Danites are flaunting their idolatry (18:30). Ironically, the Danites – who should have lost – easily win, but they exclude Yahweh and massacre an innocent people. Hence, as Bauer says, "the legitimacy of the conquest becomes questionable because the ideological grounds for this action are hereby revoked."[79]

Organizational development, whether religious or secular, emphasizes the need for a clear vision and mission. The vision and mission help to define what the organization is all about and distinguish it from other groups, while also laying the basis for the organization's goals and strategies. Yet any human achievement that is not birthed in faith and prayer or any mission or vision that sidelines Yahweh is hollow and will eventually collapse in on itself. Thus our first consideration should be whether the vision and mission of a church or Christian organization is in line with God's purposes for the world. Hence it is not just a matter of "branding" or good marketing strategies or achieving successful outcomes, but about fulfilling the will of God, working out the values of God's kingdom, and participating in God's work in the world.

The last part of this story echoes Gideon's earlier action (8:24–27) of making an ephod that becomes a snare to Israel: "the Danites installed the carved image for themselves" (18:30, trans. mine). The narrator explicitly identifies this carved image, which the Danites kept and used until the captivity, as the one that Micah had made (18:31). Thus the idol made from stolen silver, dedicated under false piety, treated as a precious household lucky charm, administered by a bogus priest in a privately owned "house of god," seized by thieves from another thief, and carried away like stolen property by armed goons, now becomes the religious symbol of a whole tribe.

---

78. Dan is a derivative of the root *dyn*, which means "to plead the cause of someone" in a legal sense so that they receive the right judgement (*HALOT*, study ed. 1:220).
79. Bauer, "Judges 18," 39.

Even though the narrative does not explicitly condemn the installation of the carved image, in contrast to the criticism of Gideon's ephod as a "snare" (8:27), there is a hidden polemic in the last phrase of verse 31,[80] which says that the Danites established their sanctuary "all the time the house of God was in Shiloh" (18:31b). This contrasts the God-designated worship site of Shiloh, which is free from images, with the Danite religious center, which keeps forbidden images. Moreover, even though the purported function of the carved image is for the worship of Yahweh, the narrator mentions twice that the carved image is "for themselves" (18:30, 31). Along with Micah, the Danites are motivated by the impulse to seize religious implements as a *talisman* that will guarantee future prosperity and success.

The last verses of this chapter provide a surprise revelation by identifying the previously unnamed opportunistic Levite priest as Jonathan, who is the son of Gershom, Moses' son. The mention of his lineage underscores the tragic irony that only two generations away from the mediator of the Sinai covenant, which prohibits the making of images,[81] the Israelites are already drifting away from the pure worship of Yahweh into idolatry and syncretistic religion. This should make us aware of how easily we can drift away from a spirituality centered on the biblical God to something that may look like the real deal when it is actually just a farce.

THE DOMESTICATION OF YAHWEH

Towards the end of the book of Judges, the theme of Yahweh's marginalization is re-cast as the domestication of Yahweh. Hence by Judges 17–18, God is treated like a domestic – someone whose primary function is to serve personal, familial, and tribal needs. This domestication is a natural outcome of the marginalization that begins in the middle of the book and becomes increasingly evident in the later narratives for Gideon, Jephthah, and Samson.

While marginalization is about being pushed to the peripheries, domestication suggests taming something for human use and control. Thus we domesticate wild animals by training them to adapt to serve human needs. A domesticated person, on the other hand, is someone whose sphere of interests or preoccupation revolves around the affairs of the home and the family. A domestic refers to a household servant, someone who is hired to do menial

---

80. For the characteristics of hidden polemic in the Hebrew Scriptures, see Yairah Amit, "Hidden Polemic in the Conquest of Dan: Judges XV11–XV111," *VT* 60 (1990): 10–12.
81. Bauer, "Judges 18," 43.

tasks around the house.[82] Domestics do not have any say in household affairs, even though their main occupation has to do with these affairs. The task of domestics is to serve unobtrusively while the main occupants of the house take the limelight.

In this we see that even though marginalization is not the same as domestication, "domestics" often play a marginal role in terms of decision-making. Similarly, when we have a utilitarian mindset in relation to God, we place God in the service of human interests rather humbling ourselves to God's purposes. Jephthah, through his vow, tries to manipulate God into giving him the victory, thereby highlighting Jephthah's skill as negotiator and marginalizing God's power. On the other hand, Micah attempts to domesticate God's power through religious paraphernalia, personnel, and institutions in order to protect his own interests.

At the center of the themes of marginalization and domestication is the issue of power. A marginalized person is powerless, one whose "capacity to do" has been cut off. On the other hand, a domesticated person's power has been harnessed in the service of another. In the book of Judges, as the human characters act on their desire for more power, or to possess the secret of God's power, or to use God's power for their own ends, they marginalize and domesticate God.

---

82. Filipinos are familiar with the phenomenon of domestic servants who migrate and are hired as contract workers overseas. In a foreign environment and with low status positions, they often experience marginalization and become "invisible."

JUDGES 19:1–20:7

When Home Becomes Unsafe

In 1967, Filipinos were shocked by the gruesome story of a woman being hacked to death, with different pieces of her body scattered throughout Metro Manila. Although her murder was never fully resolved, it was suspected that she was a victim of domestic violence.

All around the world, women suffer sexual, physical, and emotional abuse from those who are supposed to look after their welfare. A survey conducted by the Philippines National Statistics Office in 2008 revealed that "one in five women aged 15–49 has experienced physical violence since age 15," while "14.4 percent of married women have experienced physical abuse from their husbands."[1] This does not include statistics of rape and sexual abuse, which are often unreported. Ironically, the home is supposed to be a place of refuge and safety, but the unequal power relations between men and women, which are caused by cultural values and systematic structures, often leave women vulnerable even in their own homes.

Judges 19 plays on the theme of home as a place of welcome, hospitality, and safety, but it shows how the perversion of values in Israelite society as a result of their apostasy has deteriorated these ideals. Whether the home is a domestic dwelling or being with one's people, this narrative reveals how it can become a place of danger, hostility, and violence, especially for vulnerable women and migrants.

19–21 STRUCTURE AND LINKS IN JUDGES

Judges 19 is the inciting story for the broader narrative of Judges 19–21, which, as shown earlier, has links with Judges 17–18. Both Judges 17–18 and 19–21 start with a seemingly simple domestic problem, which becomes more serious and eventually broadens into a tribal crisis involving violence and civil war. Chapters 17–18 begin with a son stealing from his mother, an act that provides the occasion for the practice of idolatry in the home, which

---

1. Philippine Commission on Women, "Statistics on Violence against Filipino Women." Online: http://www.pcw.gov.ph/statistics/201405/statistics-violence-against-filipino-women (accessed September 23, 2015).

then broadens to the idolatry of a whole tribe. Chapters 19–21 also begin with a fractured relationship between a man and a woman, which leads to the woman's brutal murder, which then broadens to inter-tribal conflict and the near extermination of an entire Israelite tribe.

In both stories, a Levite figures prominently and is pivotal in the movement of the plot. In Judges 17 the Levite travels to the north (from Bethlehem to Ephraim), whereas in Judges 19 the Levite travels to the south (from Ephraim to Bethlehem). The Levite, although not directly responsible for the turn of events, is nevertheless complicit in the way the tribes of Israel become involved in violence and then a war that is inconsistent with Yahweh's good purposes.

Indeed, both stories present a parody of divine war. In chapters 17–18 this war is directed against outsiders, but in chapters 19–21 it is directed against an Israelite tribe. In both sections, actions are attributed to Yahweh and are purportedly made for Yahweh, but Yahweh remains detached, never initiates action, and responds when called upon in a distant and uninvolved way.

O'Connell identifies three plot levels in chapters 19–21: a) the recovery of the Levite's concubine (19:1b–9, 10–28); b) the judgement against Gibeah and the Benjaminites (19:10–18; 19:29–20:48); and c) the attempt to restore the remnant of Benjamin (21:1–3, 4–14, 15–23).[2]

These different plot levels overlap with each other so that the resolution of the first becomes the inciting incident for the second, and the second for the third. The first and third incidents correspond in that the ravishment of the concubine in chapter 19 mirrors the handing over of the women of Jabesh-Gilead and the abduction of the women of Shiloh to provide wives for the Benjaminites in chapter 21. Women in these incidents become pawns – ironically serving both as a rallying point to destroy an Israelite tribe, as well as breeding cattle to rebuild the same tribe. As Biddle says, "episodes in this comedy of horrors unfold in a grotesque downward arc that begins with marital strife and ends with captive brides, including along the way betrayal, rape, murder, and the near-eradication of an Israelite tribe."[3]

Because of the length of Judges 19–21, I will focus on Judges 19 first and then turn to Judges 20–21 in the next chapter.

---

2. O'Connell, *Rhetoric of Judges*, 244.
3. Mark E. Biddle, *Reading Judges: A Literary and Theological Commentary* (Macon, Georgia: Smyths & Helwys, 2012), 181.

Plot Structure of Judges 19

The plot of Judges 19, if taken without chapters 20–21, revolves around a woman who leaves her husband's home to return to the home of her father. The movement of the story traces how she comes back to the home of her husband. Utilizing Ska's different moments of the plot,[4] I have structured the narrative in the following way:

1) Exposition (19:1)

    The characters and setting are introduced.

2) Inciting Moment (19:2a)

    The problem is introduced: the concubine leaves her husband.

3) Complications

    a. Complication 1 (19:2b–3)

    The Levite delays in getting back his concubine.

    b. Complication 2 (19:4–10)

    The father-in-law delays the departure of the couple.

    c. Complication 3 (19:11–14)

    The delayed departure means they may have to spend the night in a non-Israelite place, which could be dangerous.

    d. Complication 4 (19:15–21)

    Even though they reach an Israelite city, nobody offers them hospitality, and they are in danger of being attacked in a public place.

4) Climax (19:22–26)

    Even though somebody takes them in for the night, their lives are still endangered. The concubine is raped until near death.

5) Resolution (19:27–29)

    At last the couple reaches home – but the concubine is dead, mangled, and cut into pieces!

---

4. Jean Louis Ska, "*Our Fathers Have Told Us*": *Introduction to the Analysis of Hebrew Narratives*, Subsidia Biblica 13 (Rome: Editrice Pontificio Istituto Biblico, 1990), 21–29. His different moments of the plot are: a) exposition – presentation of information which is necessary to set the stage for the action: setting, main characters and their relationships; b) inciting moment – when the conflict or the problem appears for the first time; c) complication – the different attempts to solve the problem or conflict; d) climax, or turning point; and e) resolution, or denouement.

6) Conclusion/Sequel (19:30–20:7)
   The tribes gather together hear to the Levite's report, which becomes the basis of their war against the tribe of Benjamin.

The above plot shows a movement from "leaving home" to "going home."

19:1 EXPOSITION: THE CHARACTERS

After the evaluative comment that establishes the framework by which the story is to be interpreted ("Israel had no king" [19:1a]), the main character of the story is introduced – a Levite. Like the Levite of chapter 17, he is also described as "sojourning" (ESV),[5] which means that he was a migrant residing more or less permanently in the hill country of Ephraim. This Levite took a concubine from another place – Bethlehem of Judah.

In ancient Israel, a concubine was a secondary wife, not a mistress. She had legal status in the community, but her position was lower than a wife (e.g. Leah and Rachel were wives to Jacob, but their maidservants were concubines). The primary wife made the decisions, and the concubine deferred to her.[6] Often concubines were taken in order to bear children, especially if the primary wife was unable to do so.[7]

However, there is no mention of another wife or children in this story. The concubine may have been a former slave because of family debts, who has been elevated to the status of a concubine because she is the sexual partner of the Levite.[8] The fact that the woman remains a concubine instead of being given the legal status of primary wife, with its greater status, role, and privileges, may indicate the Levite's low regard for her, perhaps because she is unable to bear him children or remains a debt-slave in his eyes. The designation "concubine" may also suggest that the Levite regards her as a mere sexual partner.

Like the wife of Manoah (mother of Samson) and the daughter of Jephthah, the concubine remains nameless throughout the narrative. This anonymity creates distance for the reader, detaching them from the horrendous events that follow.

---

5. NIV translates the Hebrew verb *gur* as "who lived" and RSV as "residing."
6. For example, Hagar, as a concubine, is expected to defer to her mistress, Sarah (Gen 16:6, 9).
7. Gen 16:1–2; 30:1–13.
8. Carolyn Pressler, "Wives and Daughters, Bond and Free: Views of Women in the Slave Laws of Exodus 21:2–11," in *Gender and Law in the Hebrew Bible and the Ancient Near East*, ed. Victor H. Matthews, et al. (Sheffield: Sheffield Academic Press, 1998), 150–154.

> ## OBJECTIFYING GOD AND ONE ANOTHER
>
> Perhaps when God is treated like an object – not only marginalized, but domesticated and used–people begin to treat others as objects as well. When our vision of Yahweh becomes blurred, it impacts our vision of each other. If we can no longer clearly see Yahweh, then we can no longer clearly see our fellow human beings, who are made in God's image and likeness. Since Israel's life was meant to be rooted in Yahweh, the narrative suggests that the dethroning or de-centering of Yahweh throws all of life into chaos. Thus when Yahweh is no longer center stage, it affects both our personal piety as well as our social life as a whole.
>
> We see this clearly in how people treat each other in this story – with inhospitable callousness, brutal violence, and deceit. Vertical distortion leads to horizontal distortion. Therefore the vision of God and the love of God are not simply themes that impact our inner life, but are the glue for social cohesion and human flourishing.

19:2A INCITING MOMENT: LEAVING HOME

The domestic problem is precipitated by the concubine leaving her husband and returning to her father's house. The reason for the spat between the Levite and his concubine is unclear. Many English versions translate 19:2 as she "was unfaithful to him" (NIV; ESV) or "played the harlot against him" (NASB), but others have she "became angry with him" (NRSV; see also NJB) or she "deserted him" (NJPS).[9]

The crux of interpretation lies in the meaning of the verb *zanah*. Its usual meaning in other parts of the OT and in the book of Judges is "to prostitute oneself" (see Judg 2:17; 8:27, 33), where it is used figuratively to describe the way Israel prostitutes itself in worshipping other gods.[10] The noun form of the verb can refer to a literal prostitute (Gen 38:15, 24; Lev 19:29; 21:7; Josh 2:1) or to someone who has become adulterous or unfaithful. It can also be applied to Israel when it adopts other gods aside from Yahweh (Exod 34:15–16: Lev 20:5), turns to wizards and mediums (Lev 20:6), or puts its trust in foreign alliances (Hos 9:1, see also 8:8–10).

---

9. The ESV has a marginal note "to become angry."
10. The more literal meaning of *zanah* as "to prostitute oneself" or "to play the whore" is found in Gen 38:15; Num 25:1; Deut 22:21.

However, in this passage, the verb form of *zanah* seems to be used in a different way. First, if the woman committed a grave sin against her husband, why does the Levite want to bring her back instead of initiating criminal proceedings against her, which might result in her being stoned to death? Why does he think that reconciliation is still possible? Moreover, if she prostituted herself, it would bring shame to her family. Yet rather than joining her supposed lover, she returns to her father's house, and her father welcomes her back into the family fold.[11] This suggests that the offended party may be the concubine rather than the Levite.

One indication of a different meaning can be gleaned from a version of the Septuagint, which translates the Hebrew into Greek with the verb *orgizo*, which means "to become angry." This corresponds with another meaning for *zanah* provided by a more recent Hebrew Lexicon, based on Akkadian (a language related to Hebrew), which is "to be angry, to be offended."[12]

Some scholars think that the concubine's unfaithfulness is the fact that she left her husband.[13] The NJP's translation – "she deserted him" – suggests that she did not have to commit adultery in order to be considered unfaithful. By leaving her husband without permission, she metaphorically commits an act of fornication.[14]

Olson tries to reconcile the two positions: "Since a woman could not initiate divorce in ancient Israel, the very act of a woman's leaving her husband would be construed as committing adultery."[15] Nevertheless, the fact that she leaves her husband suggests that he did something to offend her. Perhaps she wanted the status of a full wife, which the Levite was unwilling to give, or maybe the Levite did not treat her well because of her low status.

Whatever the reason, the text emphasizes that the woman was not driven away, but took the initiative to leave.[16] In contrast to the rest of the narrative,

---

11. Ken Stone, "Gender and Homosexuality in Judges 19: Subject-Honor, Object-Shame?," *JSOT* 67 (1995): 90; Karla Bohmbach, "Conventions/Contraventions: The Meanings of Public and Private for the Judges 19 Concubine," *JSOT* 83 (1999): 90.
12. *HALOT* Akkadian *zenu*, "to be angry, to hate." BHS gives another solution – to read *zanah* as *zanakh*, which means "to reject" or "to spurn." In addition, the construction of *zanah* with the preposition *'al* is peculiar since the usual phrase used is *zanah akharey* ("prostitute after") or *zanah min* ("prostitute from") instead of *zanah 'al*. In Hebrew, the use of a different preposition may signal a change in meaning.
13. Boling, *Judges*, 274. See Ps 73:27.
14. Jacqueline Lapsley, *Whispering the Word: Hearing Women's Stories in the Old Testament* (Louisville, KY: Westminster/John Knox, 2005), 38.
15. Olson, "Judges," 876; see also Soggin, *Judges*, 284.
16. Trible, *Texts of Terror*, 66–67.

the woman acts independently and with self-reliance, which is clearly exhibited when she travels by herself back to her father's house through dangerous territory, without men to protect her.[17] Nevertheless, the woman's departure causes a rift in the domestic relationship and precipitates a crisis that only reconciliation can resolve.

The action of a woman returning to her parents' home when she is having problems with her husband is familiar among Asian audiences. In such situations, the crisis is resolved when the husband fetches the woman from her parents' house and pleads with her to return home with him. If the woman agrees and her parents allow her to leave, then all is well and reconciliation takes place.

19:2B–21 COMPLICATIONS: GOING HOME

19:2b–3 The Levite Delays Reconciliation

Yet four months pass before the Levite takes the initiative to get his concubine back, thus delaying the anticipated reconciliation.[18] In Philippine culture, two to three days would be too long. The long delay probably indicates that the Levite has some qualms about getting his concubine back. His delay in seeking reconciliation may center on how he can uphold his honor.[19] Perhaps he is offended by her leaving, or pridefully thinks that she should be the one to apologize and come back, or is unsure if he wants her back. Or perhaps he feels shamed by her walking out on him, since many – particularly his fellow males – may think he is unable to keep "his woman."[20] If he sees her primarily as a sexual partner, his own need may be driving him to seek her out.

Nevertheless, after four months, he decides to go "after her," "to speak upon her heart" (NIV: "to persuade") about coming back. The idiom "speak upon her heart" (19:3a) seems to denote an assuring tone by someone who is either the offended party,[21] or the one who has offended,[22] or it can simply be a general encouragement from someone in a higher social position (Ruth

---

17. Karla G. Bomhbach, "Conventions/Contraventions: The Meaning of Public and Private for the Judges 19 Concubine," *JSOT* 83 (1999): 89–90.
18. See Lapsley, *Whispering the Word*, 38.
19. The fact that his concubine left him was a blow to his honor, but her failure to return might be seen as a greater dishonor.
20. Stone, "Gender and Homosexuality," 96.
21. In this way Joseph spoke to his brothers who betrayed him and sold him into slavery (Gen 50:21). The phrase is also used to describe how God comforted Israel after a period of discipline for their sins (Isa 40:2) and also how God wooed Israel to himself (Hos 2:16).
22. In Gen 34:3, Shechem spoke in this way to Dinah after sexually violating her.

2:13; 2 Sam 19:7; 2 Chr 30:22; 32:6). In some instances, it can indicate a wooing tone (Hos 2:16; see also NJPS "to woo her and win her back") or affectionate speech (NRSV, NASB "to speak tenderly to her"). But since the "heart" is regarded in the OT as the seat of the will rather than the emotions, some see the idiom as an appeal to the will,[23] which is reflected in the NIV's "to persuade."

In any case, the use of the idiom can support the reading that either the woman or the man is the offended party. Thus either the man comes to assure the woman that it is okay for her to return home, or the man comes to plead with the woman to return. But the intention of the action is clear – "to bring her back" (19:3). The fact that he brings along a servant and a couple of donkeys demonstrates his determination to return with his concubine.

All seems well since the woman (presumably having met her husband outside) takes him into her father's house,[24] indicating that she is ready for reconciliation. Her father ("the father of the girl") is glad to meet his daughter's husband (19:3). Perhaps the father-in-law is happy that there is going to be reconciliation at last, and so he welcomes his son-in-law with open arms. On the other hand, if the daughter has been sold as a slave to pay for the family's debts, then the father's welcome can be interpreted as a form of servility.

19:4–10 The Father-in-Law Delays Departure

The function of this section in relation to the whole plot is not easy to understand. First of all, if the father is eager for the reconciliation of his daughter and son-in-law, why does he keep delaying their departure? Secondly, why is there such a drawn out narration of this episode? The inciting moment when the woman leaves her husband takes up only half a verse, while the climax itself – the events leading to the rape and the report of the rape – takes only five verses, but this episode covers seven verses, which is about twenty percent of the whole story.

---

23. Jean-Marc Babut, *Idiomatic Expressions of the Hebrew Bible: Their Meaning and Translation through Componential Analysis*, BIBAL Dissertation Series 5 (North Richland Hills, TX: Bibal Press, 1999), 76–77.
24. The LXX, however, has a different reading: "and he came to the house of her father" instead of the MT's "she brought him to the house of her father." The LXX's reading does not record the woman's reaction to her husband's arrival. This is more consistent with the Septuagint's translation that "she became angry with him" (19:2), indicating that perhaps she is not yet ready for a reconciliation.

Various views on the function of this episode have been suggested.[25] It can be considered as a simple literary device to delay the climax and lure the readers into a sense of security so that the ending becomes more shocking. On the other hand, some regard the hospitality and generosity of the father-in-law as a foil to the lack of hospitality shown by the people of Gibeah.[26] The Levite's refusal to extend his stay and "spend the night" in the house of his father-in-law for the third time leads to devastating consequences.

Not all see the father-in-law's hospitality in a positive way, however. In terms of the overall plot, the father-in-law's repeated attempts to keep the couple from leaving only serve to delay the return of the woman to her own home. The hospitality seems excessive and coercive, and it eventually leads to the couple's harm. Three days would have been a respectable amount of time for a visit, especially since the purpose is to bring the woman home. But "by enjoying the lavish hospitality," the company is "left stranded in an inhospitable world."[27]

Moreover, the verbs used for the father-in-law's actions to detain the Levite indicate some pressure. The verb for "prevailed upon" in the NIV (*khazaq* in Hebrew) means "to hold fast or firmly" (19:4); in 19:7, the father-in-law explicitly "presses" him to stay.

Such pressure is familiar in some parts of Asia, where hosts may feel that they have not extended the appropriate hospitality if they do not insist that the visitor extend his or her stay. (In the Philippines, one offers food to the visitor several times before accepting the refusal as final.) The assumption here is that guests are far too embarrassed to express a desire to stay because they do not want to impose on the host. Nevertheless, there are cases when the pressure for people to accept welcome may prove harmful rather than helpful. It can even make them feel uncomfortable, since they may feel forced to accept in case their refusal is misconstrued as ungratefulness. True hospitality involves giving space to the other, which includes giving them the freedom to accept or decline our hospitality.

One issue in the Judges episode is whether it shows solidarity between the father and the daughter to the exclusion of the Levite, or if it highlights

---

25. Lapsley, *Whispering the Word*, 39–41, sees the father-in-law's efforts as a way of ensuring that the Levite reconciles with his concubine before leaving. However, the fact that the concubine meets him and brings him inside the house already signals the reconciliation, even without the verbal exchange.
26. Susan Niditch, "The 'Sodomite' Theme in Judges 19–20: Family, Community, and Social Disintegration," *CBQ* 44 (1982): 366–367
27. Marais, *Representation*, 139.

the camaraderie between the Levite and the father-in-law to the exclusion of the woman. The former is supported by the repeated use of "the father of the young woman" (19:3, 4, 5, 6, 8, 9; trans. mine) in this section, which stresses the woman's relationship with the father, rather than the term "concubine," which highlights her connection with the Levite.[28] If the daughter's connection with the father is at the forefront, then the father's action in detaining the Levite can be interpreted as a hesitancy to let his daughter leave, out of concern for her safety in the Levite's house.[29]

On the other hand, the camaraderie between the Levite and the father-in-law, aside from the repeated use of "father-in-law" and "son-in-law," is indicated by the references to the two of them eating and drinking together (19:6, 8). As the two are involved in a subtle power game to decide when "the young woman" (19:3–5, 8–9) is going home, the subject of their conversation – who demonstrated independence and self-reliance before – fades into the background and once again becomes "the concubine" (19:9).[30]

The second interpretation seems more plausible since the woman is never referred to as "daughter" or "young woman" only, but is always named in relation to her father. The repeated use of father-in-law and son-in-law is a reminder that the woman is the link between the two men, but her wishes are completely sidelined.

19:11–14 Threats in the Midst of Strangers

Before this incident, the verb "spend the night" (*lyn*) is repeated several times, with the Levite "spending the night" in the house of his father-in-law (19:4), and the father-in-law insisting that he spend the night and enjoy himself (19:6, 7, 9).[31] But the Levite can no longer be prevailed upon to spend one more night and finally goes on his way, traveling as far as Jebus, which is later called Jerusalem (see 19:10).

At this point in the narrative, the verb "spend the night" begins to take on ominous tones. The delay in travel means that they will have to spend the

---

28. Yani Yoo. "Han-Laden Women: Korean 'Comfort Women' and Women in Judges 19–21," *Semeia* 78 (1997): 39–40.
29. Koala Jones-Warsaw, "Toward a Womanist Hermeneutic: A Reading of Judges 19–21," in *A Feminist Companion to Judges,* ed. Athalya Brenner (Sheffield: Sheffield Academic Press, 1993), 22.
30. See Bomhbach, "Conventions/Contraventions," 93–94; see also Lapsley, *Whispering the Word,* 40–42.
31. David Penchansky, "Staying the Night: Intertextuality in Genesis and Judges," in *Reading Between Texts: Intertextuality and the Hebrew Bible,* ed. Danna Nolan Fewell (Louisville, KY: Westminster/John Knox, 1992), 78, 86 n. 6.

night midway, since daylight is almost gone and the nearest place is Jebus, a non-Israelite town (19:11). Even with the servant urging the Levite to spend the night in Jebus (19:11), the Levite insists on traveling further – "we will not turn aside into a city of foreigners, who do not belong to the people of Israel" (19:12, NRSV), but will "spend the night at Gibeah or at Ramah" (19:13, NRSV). The Levite's use of *nokri* (foreigner) to refer to the people of Jebus emphasizes their otherness and indicates that, in his thinking, they will not be sympathetic to his need.[32] So even though it is late, and travel is dangerous, they go on until sundown, when they reach Gibeah, an Israelite territory belonging to the tribe of Benjamin (19:15).

19:15–21 Threats in "Home"

There has always been a strong ethnic and tribal identity among Asians, and so we prefer to be with our own people, especially when traveling and living outside the country. This not only reflects our preference for people who share our own cultural customs and traditions, but also our feeling that it is safer to be with those whom we consider as our own family. We see this among Filipinos who meet each other for the first time overseas. Even though they may not know each other, there is a desire to help and look out for each other in practical ways, as if with their own family.

So the Levite's desire to spend the night in Israelite territory is understandable. Travel in the ancient Near East was fraught with the risks of robbery, rape, and even death,[33] particularly in the evening when travelers were more vulnerable to attacks, so the question of where to spend the night was crucial. For this reason, hospitality was particularly valued.[34] Among one's people, one could expect not only welcome, but also practical provisions such as food, shelter, and the pleasure of company.

So it is with some shock that the Levite and his party find themselves in Gibeah – in home territory, so to speak – but with nobody to welcome them. Whereas they fully intend to "spend the night in Gibeah" in order to avoid the risks of being in a non-Israelite city, they just sit in the town plaza, and no one offers to take them in for the night (19:15). What a forlorn feeling to expect welcome from one's own people and to be met with indifference and

---

32. Ilse Müllner, "Lethal Differences: Sexual Politics as Violence Against Others in Judges 19," in *Judges, A Feminist Companion to the Bible (Second Series)*, ed. Athalya Brenner (Sheffield: Sheffield Academic Press, 1999), 136.
33. Travelers are aware that harm might befall them on the journey (Gen 28:20–21; 42:38) and so God's protection, guidance, and help are gratefully received (Ps 107:4–9; Gen 35:2–3).
34. See Gen 18:1–6; 19:1–9; 24:15–33; Exod 2:15–22; 1 Kgs 17:8–16.

neglect, perhaps even suspicion and fear. This is even more appalling since God's covenant people are enjoined to be generous and kind to strangers as well as to Levites residing within their midst.[35] Moreover, a deserted town plaza – a place of interaction after the day's work is over – indicates that all is not right in this city, foreshadowing the horrifying events to come.

In this dejected and forlorn state, the Levite and his company are approached by the comforting presence of an old man coming in from his evening work in the field. The narrator informs us that this old man is not originally from Gibeah, but is a sojourner – a resident alien like the Levite – who is originally from the hill country of Ephraim, whereas the people of Gibeah are from the tribe of Benjamin (19:16). The visual perspective now shifts to the old man, who sees the travelers in the middle of the town and inquires about their identity (19:17).

The Levite stresses that they are fellow Hebrews traveling from Bethlehem of Judah to the hill country of Ephraim. The mention of "the house of the Lord" (19:18) the tabenacle in Shiloh is odd since it is not mentioned elsewhere in the story. This may have been a scribal error or a deliberate ploy by the Levite to gain sympathy from the old man, since it clearly does not fit the narrative movement of the story.[36]

The Levite's speech emphasizes that "no one has taken me in for the night" (19:18), but he adds that he has ample provisions for himself and for those with him, including his animals, implying that he will not be a burden to his host (19:19). The old man, perhaps feeling the plight of a fellow sojourner, assures the Levite of safety and provisions (the mention of shalom – "all is well" – indicates his positive response to the Levite's request).[37] But he begs him not to spend the night in the plaza (19: 20–21), which again hints of the danger ahead. In retrospect, one realizes that perhaps nobody takes them in because they do not want to invite trouble into their own homes.

In this episode, a dichotomy is presented between Jebus/Gibeah, foreigner/own people, sojourner/local resident, and outsider/insider. One would expect safety, security, and welcome to be found in an Israelite city such as

---

35. Exod 22:21; 23:9; Lev 19:33–34; Deut 10:18–19; Deut 26:12–13.
36. The reference may have been a scribal error, in which the personal suffix "my" in Hebrew is taken for the abbreviation of the name Yahweh. If not taken as an abbreviation, the phrase could also be translated "my house," referring to the Levite's house, instead of "the house of the Lord" (see NRSV; NJB).
37. I disagree with Matthews, who thinks that the old man, as a sojourner, inappropriately asks questions of the guest (*Judges*, 184, 186). This may be seen as invasion of privacy in Western societies, but in Asian societies would be regarded as an attempt to establish a connection.

Gibeah, among one's own people, and from local residents rather than outsiders. Ironically, Gibeah proves to be inhospitable, the Israelites unwelcoming, and the local residents insensitive to the vulnerable plight of travelers who need a place to stay for the night. One wonders if the Levite and his small entourage might have been safer in the foreign city of Jebus rather than the Israelite city of Gibeah.

One of the most frequently asked questions in theological discourse and in the history of the church is: what does Jerusalem have in common with Athens? Or, said differently, what do Christians have to do with the world? Or, what does prayer have to do with politics? In some circles the answer is straightforward: nothing. Such Christians have a world-denying form of Christianity. Others believe that prayer does have something to do with politics, which reflects a world-formative Christianity.

Judges 19 indirectly throws up this question, since the Levite and his small band would most likely have been safer in Jebus than in Gibeah. This suggests that we cannot conclude that Gibeah – our religious community – is safe and that Jebus – the worldly community–is unsafe. This brings us back to the theological question, what does Jerusalem have to do with Athens, or what does Jebus have to do with Gibeah? The answer is: everything.

This has important implications for Asian Christianity, which cannot afford to be esoteric and isolationist. It also cannot afford to have an ecclesio-centric view of the purposes of God in the world, meaning that God is only concerned about the church. God is the God of the heavens and the earth. God has all humanity in view. God is at work in our world. There are times when the church may need to learn from the world about how to be good citizens and neighbors or exemplary employees and community workers.

One also wonders why a sojourner in Gibeah readily extends hospitality, while the local residents do not.[38] Even today, migrants and other internationals often welcome and extend help to other migrants, because they can identify with the feelings of being a stranger, while the local inhabitants – who have the resources, connections, and knowledge of the local culture – can be the most unwelcoming. This points to our need to be sensitive to those who belong to other cultures and to extend hospitality rather than favoring those who belong to our own ethnic group or geographical region.

---

38. Matthews thinks that the old man's offer of hospitality is inappropriate, since as a sojourner he does not have legal basis to do so (*Judges*, 185–186). The tone of the narrative, however, seems more sympathetic to the old man.

Notably, fellow Israelites, such as the Levite and the old man from Ephraim, are seen as outsiders by their own countrymen in this episode. This highlights the tribal fragmentation within Israel at that time, which is portrayed in different forms earlier in the book of Judges. While disunity is expressed in terms of the lack of intertribal cooperation in the Deborah story, it is expressed through tribal infighting in the Gideon narrative, manipulation in the Jephthah story, and betrayal in the Samson story. In this narrative, the lack of cohesion and solidarity is expressed in the failure to exercise hospitality.

19:22–26 CLIMAX: OUTCAST AND DISGRACE OUTSIDE THE HOME

19:22–23 A Vile and Disgraceful Thing

The peaceful picture of comfort, eating together, and merriment (19:21–22a), which is reminiscent of the young woman's house in Bethlehem,[39] is shattered by violent pounding at the door. The narrator's previously neutral stance after the implicit evaluation in the ironic introduction becomes explicitly evaluative, for "wicked men" (literally, "men of belial") surround the house and demand that the host hand over his male guest, so that they can have sex with him (19:22b). The narrator's description of these men as "men of belial" is used in other parts of the OT to refer to those who lead people astray to worship other gods (Deut 13:15), are disrespectful of God's holy sacrifices (1 Sam 2:12), make false accusations (1 Kgs 21:10, 13), or plot evil and spew out evil speech (Prov 16:27). In other words, they represent a perverse lot. The narrator's forceful language – "surrounded the house," "pounding at the door" (19:22) – emphasizes that these men pose a very dangerous threat to the people inside the house.

The old man – referred to as the "owner of the house," perhaps to emphasize his jurisdiction over what happens there – describes their act as "vile" and "outrageous" (19:23). But from the old man's point of view, what exactly is this "vile" and "outrageous" thing?

Excursus: parallels to Genesis 19

Perhaps the parallel story of Lot and the two angels in Sodom (Gen 19:1–29) can shed light on these questions. The similarities between these two passages

---

39. Niditch, "Sodomite Theme," 367.

are numerous.⁴⁰ In Genesis, the two visitors are also going to spend the night in the town plaza when Lot urges them to spend the night in his house (Gen 19:2–3; see also Judg 19:17–20). They are also in the midst of feasting and eating when the men of the city (Sodom) surround the house and demand that Lot bring out his guests so the men of the city can have sex with them (Gen 19:4–5; see also Judg 19:22).

Lot admonishes the men to refrain from carrying out their intensions, stating, "they have come under the shelter of my roof" (Gen 19:8, trans. mine), which is parallel to the language of the old man in Judges: "inasmuch as this man has come into my house" (Judg 19:23, trans. mine). Both passages share this emphasis on the protection due to a guest. As mentioned earlier, hospitality was a high moral value in the ancient Near East,⁴¹ and so attacking a vulnerable traveler was seen as particularly reprehensible.⁴² Perhaps the "outrageous" thing in the Judges narrative is that the men of Gibeah are violating the code of hospitality by attempting to molest a visitor. In the norms of hospitality, the host was duty-bound to protect and give security to the people he had welcomed into his house.

19:24 An Outrageous Action

The most shocking thing in both episodes is that the host offers the women in the household as a substitute to dissuade the men from sexually assaulting the male guest. Lot volunteers his two virgin daughters – "let me bring them out" and "do what you like with them" (Gen 19:8) – which is almost a word-for-word repetition of what the old man says to the wicked men of Gibeah when he offers them his virgin daughter and the concubine of his guest (see Judg 19:24).

---

40. See Stuart Lasine, "Guest and Host in Judges 19: Lot's Hospitality in an Inverted World," *JSOT* 29 (1984): 37–59; Daniel Block, "Echo Narrative Technique in Hebrew Literature: A Study in Judges 19," *WTJ* 52 (1990): 325–341; see also Block, *Judges*, 532–534; Trible, *Texts of Terror*, 75–76. Scholars have postulated a literary dependence of one on the other, but some think that the two stories are just drawing from a shared language of hospitality and travel (Niditch, "Sodomite Theme," 375). The similarities, however, invite an intertextual reading. See Penchansky, "Staying the Night," 77–78.
41. See p. 251. For example, the Moabites and the Amalekites are to be barred from joining the assembly of the Lord because they did not offer hospitality to the Israelites (Deut 23:3–6),
42. Although there is no specific law that deals with a prohibition to attack a traveler, there are laws that prohibit killing by treachery (Exod 21:14) or deliberately lying in wait to ambush an unsuspecting victim (Num 35:20–21; Deut 19:11–12). Part of the general breakdown of society, as the prophets see it, is the existence of marauding bands who rob travelers (Hos 6:9) or people who plot an ambush with deceit and violence (Jer 9:8 [7]; Mic 7:2; Hos 7:6). The Amalekites are to be blotted out from remembrance because they attacked the Israelites on their journey while the Israelites were faint and weary (Deut 25:17–19).

The language of Judges 19, however, is even more shocking – "Debase them . . . only do not do this disgraceful thing to this man" (19:24, trans. mine). In other parts of the OT, *'anah* ("to debase") is used in the general sense of "to oppress," as in a master-slave relationship,[43] "to afflict,"[44] "to humble,"[45] or "to humiliate."[46] In sexual situations, *'anah* is used in the sense of being humiliated,[47] where it means "to become socially debased."[48] As a result of sexual relations that do not go through acceptable and proper societal processes, the woman suffers dishonor and is demeaned. The old man's use of *'anah* in imperative form explicitly gives permission for the men to sexually humiliate the women as long as they spare his male guest from the same humiliation.

This has led some to conclude that the code of hospitality at that time was applied only to male guests.[49] Others have argued that this does not reflect the culture of ancient Israel, since women were a legal extension of their husbands and therefore accorded the same protection.[50] The old man's strange action suggests that something more is happening than a violation of the hospitality code.

Elsewhere in the OT, the term for "outrageous" (NIV: "disgraceful"; ESV: "vile") – *nebalah* – is used to describe deplorable sexual behavior, such as Shechem's rape of Dinah (Gen 34:7), Amnon's rape of his half-sister Tamar (2 Sam 13:12, 13), sexual promiscuity (Deut 22:21), and adultery (Jer 29:23).[51] In fact, the rape of the concubine is described by the Levite himself and the rest of the Israelite community as *nebalah* (20:6, 10). Ironically, from the old man's perspective, this is not the case, and so he pleads with the men not to pursue their "outrageous" plan, but permits them – even begs them

---

43. Gen 15:13; 16:6; Exod 1:11, 12; Deut 21:14; 26:6; Isa 60:14.
44. Gen 31:50; Exod 22:21, 22; Num 24:24; Ruth 1:21; 2 Sam 7:10; 1 Kgs 11:39; 2 Kgs 17:20; Isa 53:4; 58:10; 64:11; Lam 3:33; Nah 1:12; Zeph 3:19.
45. Deut 8:2, 16; Isa 58:3.
46. Judg 16:5, 6, 19.
47. Aside from the key texts above, see also Lam 5:11; Ezek 22:10, 11.
48. Ellen van Wolde, "Does *'Innâ* Denote Rape? A Semantic Analysis of a Controversial Word," *VT* 52 (2002): 540–544.
49. Trible, *Texts of Terror*, 75.
50. Jan Fokkelman, "Structural Remarks on Judges 9 and 19," in *'Sha'rei Talmon': Studies in the Bible, Qumran, and the Ancient Near East Presented to Shemaharyu Talmon*, eds. Michael Fishbane, Emmanuel Tov and Weston W. Fields (Winona Lake, IN: Eisenbrauns, 1992), 44 n. 20; Matthews, *Judges & Ruth*, 187.
51. The word *nebalah* is also used to describe Achan's sin in taking the devoted things (Josh 7:15), despicable, lying, or disgraceful speech (Isa 9:17; 32:6; Jer 29:23; Job 42:8), and idolatry (Jer 16:18).

– to do another "outrageous" act in its stead. The nice, hospitable, and generous old man turns out to be not so nice after all.

Some have zeroed in on homosexuality as the old man's particular objection, so that he willingly offers the women in order to prevent this from happening.[52] Based on this perspective, heterosexual sex – no matter how violent – is considered less offensive than homosexual sex.[53]

Yet the prospect that raised the old man's horror is not homosexuality, per se, but the act of homosexual rape. In an anthropological analysis, Ken Stone shows the interplay of shame and honor in this text as it relates to issues of sex, power, and hospitality. In a society of strict role differentiation and hierarchical relationships between male and female, the sexual subjugation of a man by another man is considered more shameful because it is seen as the "feminization" of the male, forcing the male to take on the position of a female, which is "associated with lower status and power."[54] This results in humiliation and loss of honor for the man, who now becomes a sexual object rather than the sexual subject, which is perceived as his proper role in this society.[55]

Read from this angle, the intent of the mob is not just to have sex with another man, but to assert their power over two weak outsiders – the old man and the Levite – who do not have the means to defend themselves. In the same way, the old man's horrendous offer of the women in exchange for the protection of the man is meant to spare his male guest the disgrace of being "feminized" and humiliated. Obviously, the old man has more sympathies for his fellow male and shows no concern at all for the plight of the women. For him, the rape of the women is less abominable than the rape of men.

Thus as Niditch comments, "this passage is perhaps less about views of homosexuality, which priestly writers do condemn (Lev 18:22), than about a larger theme in sexual ethics in which one partner subdues, owns, and holds unequal power over the other."[56] Yet in this case, the power of subjugation is wholly given to the men. While it is considered reprehensible for men to be sexually subjugated by other men, the unequal exercise of sexual power is regarded by the male characters in the narrative as more acceptable if it is in relation to men over women.

---

52. Niditch, "Sodomite Theme," 368–369.
53. Jones-Warsaw, "Womanist Hermeneutics," 23–24.
54. Stone, "Gender and Homosexuality," 97.
55. Ibid., 100.
56. Niditch, *Judges*, 193.

The shame attached to male rape is highlighted in a recent report of the American Psychological Association regarding its occurrence in the US military. Even though fifty percent of the survivors of sexual assaults are men, very few report the incident and seek treatment because of the belief that "real men/strong men don't get raped." The fear of being "feminized" and stigmatized as weak and unable to defend themselves against assault leads not only to the underreporting of such incidents, but also to severe sexual trauma.[57] The act of trying to cover up and cope with sexual humiliation sheds light on the Levite's drastic action and coldhearted disregard towards his concubine in the next scene.

19:25–26 The Levite's Callous Defense of His Honor

With wicked men outside, refusing the offer of the host, the Levite – now simply referred to as "the man," perhaps to emphasize his maleness – takes matters into his own hands, possibly in appreciation for the host's desire to protect him and also to prevent the men from making him a sexual object. He thrusts his concubine outside into the hands of the waiting mob, and there follows the most sickening and heartbreaking part of the story: "and they raped her and abused her throughout the night" (19:25).

The coming of dawn often symbolizes new hope, but for this woman, the dawn only reveals the horrors of the night. The woman walks slowly towards the house where her master is staying (19:26). One can imagine her appearance after being gang-raped again and again throughout the night–bruised, battered, stunned, barely breathing, stumbling, as she painfully drags herself towards the only familiar place, where she hopes she can still find succor. Before she can enter, however, she collapses at the entrance of the house (19:26). There she lies, and nobody opens the door for her. Nobody is on the lookout or even cares to see how she has fared after being sacrificed to prevent her master's disgrace. She comes home, crying out for help, but the door is shut.

In the same way, many Asian women and children cry out for help after being sexually abused and exploited. There are the "comfort women" who were forced to give sexual services to soldiers during the war.[58] There are the children who have been bought (sometimes from willing parents), recruited,

---

57. Carol O'Brien, Jessica Keith and Lisa Shoemaker, "Don't Tell: Military Culture and Male Rape," *Psychological Services* 12/4 (2015): 357–65. Online: http://www.apa.org/pubs/journals/releases/ser-ser0000049.pdf.
58. On this and its interface with Judges 19, see Yoo, "*Han*-Laden Women," 37–46.

and transported in order to supply the burgeoning sex trade.[59] And there are the victims of sexual violence in the home, who have not been able to speak out because of shame, fear of repercussion, guilt of betraying a relative or a member of the family, thinking that it is their fault, or feeling that nobody will believe them anyway. They all cry out for help, but the church often shuts its door.

19:27–29 RESOLUTION: GOING HOME

The narrative continues: "her master got up in the morning and opened the door of the house and stepped out to continue on his way" (19:27a), ready to resume his journey as if the horrors of the night before did not happen, indifferent to the woman he had come so far to bring home, who depended on him for safety and security, and whom he cruelly handed over to the mob in order to spare his dignity. But his preparations for the journey are interrupted because the woman described by the narrative as "his concubine" – as if stressing his obligations towards her – is lying at the entrance, "her hands on the threshold" (19:27b), blocking his way.

The man's impatient reaction to the body of his concubine crumpled at the door is more appropriate for a child having a tantrum than someone who has suffered violence the whole night: "Get up; let's go" (19:28a), as if he expects her to take hold of herself and follow him. When she does not respond, he picks her up like a piece of unwanted baggage, dumps her on the donkey, and leaves for home (19:28b). Unlike the scene at the father-in-law's house, there are no extended goodbyes or offers of hospitality. The man is obviously in a hurry to depart; the unexpected appearance of his concubine at the entrance causes a delay in his departure and seems to have annoyed him.

The arc of this narrative, from leaving home to going home, does not have a happy or even a bittersweet ending. Rather, the story of reconciliation ends in a violent and deeply disturbing note. For upon reaching home, the Levite "took a knife and cut up his concubine, limb by limb, into twelve parts and sent them into all the areas of Israel" (19:29). This horrific conclusion raises several questions. Was the concubine dead when the Levite saw her in the morning? Or did she die on the way home? Or was she still breathing when the Levite hacked her into pieces? The fact that she did not respond

---

59. On the use of biblical texts, including Judges 19, to address issues of sex trafficking, see David G. Garber, "Awakening Desire Before It Is Season: Reading Biblical Texts in Response to the Sexual Exploitation of Children," *RevExp* 105 (Summer 2008): 453–469.

when the man called her (19:28) may mean that she was already dead, but the narrator leaves this ambiguous.[60] Whether she was dead or alive, she was not treated with the care and respect that she deserved. In ancient Israel, the body of the dead was treated with respect and honor,[61] but the Levites' treatment of his concubine's battered body shows a complete disregard of her relationship to him.

In ancient Israel, the action of hacking an animal into pieces and then distributing the pieces to various territories was generally recognized as a call to arms.[62] Saul cut up a team of oxen and sent them throughout the territory of Israel as a way of calling the Israelites to unite in fighting against the Ammonites (1 Sam 11:7). The kind of knife (*ma'akeleth*) mentioned here is a butcher's knife that was used for slaughtering animals for the sacrifices (see Gen 22:6, 10). The word for "cut" (*natah*) is the same word used when Saul cut up the oxen for the military muster and is also used in various contexts to refer to the cutting up of animals for various offerings and sacrifices.[63]

Thus the woman, after acting independently and leaving her husband, entrusted herself to the same man, but was treated like sacrificial cattle upon reaching home, and her body was used as a means to vindicate the Levite's lost honor by raising the indignation of the rest of the Israelite tribes. For even though the men of Gibeah did not humiliate the Levite directly, they did so indirectly by sexually assaulting his concubine.[64] As a concubine, the woman was regarded as an extension and possession of her husband so that her sexual humiliation became the means by which the men of Gibeah, after an unsuccessful first attempt, were able to shame her husband and assert their power over him.[65]

If one views the rape of the concubine as a deliberate affront to the Levite's honor, this makes his actions more comprehensible, although no less reprehensible. Yet his anger is directed towards the wrong person – his concubine – as seen in his harsh and indifferent attitude towards her. Without

---

60. The LXX resolves the ambiguity by adding, "and she did not answer for she was dead" at the end of 19:28.
61. Roland de Vaux, *Ancient Israel: Its Life and Institutions* (London: Darton, Longman & Todd, 1961), 56.
62. Block, *Judges*, 548.
63. See Exod 29:17; Lev 1:6, 12; 8:20; 1 Kgs 18:23, 33.
64. Stone, "Gender and Homosexuality," 100–101.
65. For example, Reuben brought shame to Jacob by sleeping with his father's concubine (Gen 49:3–4; see also 35:22). Absalom also dishonored David when he had sex with his father's concubines in the sight of all Israel (2 Sam 16:20–22), which was also his way of asserting supremacy over his father's right to the throne.

acknowledging his responsibility for what happened, his anger towards those who sought to humiliate him spills over to the person who has nothing to do with those who disgraced him. In fact, the Levite's desire to defend his honor causes him to be selfishly indifferent and cruel towards the woman who is wholly dependent on him and whose honor and welfare he is responsible to protect.

According to a study made by the Center for Disease Control and Prevention in Atlanta, men who feel stressed because others see them as less masculine may try to compensate by engaging in violent behavior.[66] In Filipino culture, the pressure for men to preserve a macho image may lead to domestic violence, since men who feel insecure may vent their anger about themselves onto their wives and children.

When the Levite and his entourage are standing in the middle of Gibeah, forlorn and unwelcome, the reader's sympathies align with the Levite, which makes his harsh and cruel action at the end of the story even more shocking and confusing. Similarly, the excessive hospitality of the woman's father is puzzling, since his insistent generosity ends up endangering his guest. Likewise, the old man – a migrant himself – appears to be a positive and appealing figure when he welcomes the strangers who are shut out by the local inhabitants.[67] But where the woman's father offers excessive hospitality, the old man exercises selective hospitality, valuing only the honor of the man and disregarding the welfare of the women.

The bottom line, as Müllner puts it, is that "all the characters are given positive and negative attributes, and all are both victims and offenders."[68] Even the woman's action in leaving her husband and then taking him to her father can be seen both in a positive and negative light. "Thus in this narrative, the usual assumption that victims are not guilty does not apply."[69] "The characters are . . . complex, capable of demonstrating the best in human behavior and the worst."[70]

Consistent with the ironic tone of the epilogue, which will be discussed in the next section, the narrative seems to represent the perversion of good values. Hospitality and honor are good values in Asian society. However, the

---

66. Reuters, "Pressure to be 'Manly' May Lead to Violence," Sept. 25, 2015. Online: http://www.reuters.com/article/us-health-genderroles-men-violence-idUSKCN0RP27P20150925.
67. Webb, *Book of Judges*, 467.
68. Müllner, "Lethal Differences," 137.
69. Ibid.
70. Butler, *Judges*, 425.

practice of hospitality can be manipulative – to gain something in return – or extended towards certain people while excluding the rest. On the other hand, the desire to preserve and fight for one's honor and dignity may indicate a healthy respect for oneself and commendable loyalty to one's family, but it can also degenerate into an insensitive disregard of loved ones in order to protect the family's name.

19:30–20:7 EPILOGUE: THE LEVITE TELLS THE STORY

Most commentators include this section (except for 19:30) in the next story, since it sets the stage for the war of the Israelite tribes against Benjamin. However, the story of the Levite and his concubine actually ends in 20:7, since the Levite still plays a key role in the assembly that leads to the war. After the assembly, he is no longer part of the war scenes. Thus it is best to see an overlapping of plot levels, as mentioned at the beginning of this chapter, so that the conclusion of one story actually acts as the introduction to the next. In this case, the Levite's story acts as the impetus and rationale for the war against Benjamin. Therefore, I will use 19:30–20:7 to reflect on the ending of the Levite story, but I will use the same section to discuss the introduction to the story of the war against the Benjaminites in the next chapter.

As expected, the tribes of Israel are shocked at the mangled body parts scattered before them: "Everyone who saw it was saying to one another, 'Such a thing has never been seen or done, not since the day the Israelites came up out of Egypt'" (19:30a). The Exodus was the most significant event in the life of Israel, since it was the founding event that led to the formation of the nation. Thus to mention this incident in connection with the Exodus shows the extent of its impact in the life of the community. In fact, its effect is so great that it galvanizes the fragmented tribes into unified action in order to respond to the situation.

It is not clear who is giving the imperatives in the second half of 19:30 – "We must do something! So speak up!" The arrangement of the text in the MT seems to suggest that the Israelites themselves are speaking. However, the community assembly has not yet convened at this point, and they have not heard firsthand the Levite's testimony, so the exhortation to act seems premature.[71]

---

71. On the other hand, Block (*Judges*, 548) observes that the exhortation sounds as if it is coming from the narrator himself. He translates, "Apply yourselves to it," as, "Think about her," with the feminine direct object pronoun referring to the concubine instead of the situation

The LXX attributes the imperatives to the Levite himself. After "until today," it adds: "and he [the Levite] commanded the men he sent, 'Say this to all the men of Israel, "Has anything like this happened from the day the Israelites came up out of Egypt until today? Consider it, take counsel, and speak out."'" Aside from the fact that the omission in the MT can be explained by scribal error,[72] the Levite himself uses similar language in 20:7: "Put together a plan and get counsel here." Yet the addition seems repetitive,[73] so that the NRSV, following the LXX, attributes the whole verse to the Levite and omits the reaction of the Israelites.

The MT's version can be explained by what often happens in oral cultures. Whenever something scandalous and particularly horrifying takes place, people in a community engage in a lot of village chitchat to dissect the event and forcefully express their sentiments about what should be done, and soon a public opinion is formed about the matter. Presumably, the Israelite village chitchat took place before the public assembly in 20:1–7,[74] or else it would not have been possible to mount such a big and unified gathering. Thus, with the tide of public opinion on his side, it is quite easy for the Levite to convince the assembly to punish Gibeah, since he is merely echoing what they were already thinking beforehand.

The Levite is introduced by the narrator to the public assembly as "the Levite, the husband of the murdered woman" (20:4). Here the narrator takes on the point of view of the assembly, which sees the Levite as the aggrieved party – the victim – because his "wife" has been murdered. Note that the word used to refer to the concubine is not *pilegesh* (concubine) but *'isshah* (woman/wife), emphasizing the solidarity between the man and his wife, which has been sundered by the brutal murder. The word "murder" (*ratsa*) is not used in the narrator's account in chapter 19, but is used here to express the strong feelings of the community about the incident – the woman was murdered, leaving her husband tormented and devastated. Although *ratsa* can be used to refer both to premeditated and accidental killing,[75] there is an

---

(both are grammatically possible). The appeal may be the narrator's own call to his immediate readers to ponder the concubine's fate, although Block himself acknowledges that this kind of call is rare in Hebrew narrative.

72. See Webb, *Book of Judges*, 471 n. 50. It is possible that the LXX is the more original text and that a section has been inadvertently omitted by a scribe due to the repetition of the word "today."
73. Ibid.
74. Ibid., 473.
75. Block, *Judges*, 553.

active sense to the term so that it is understood that the woman did not just die consequently, but was killed through an overt act. The use of the term *ratsa*, however, raises a question for the reader about who actually killed her (an ambivalence noted earlier).[76]

Many commentators point out how the Levite's version in his testimony to the assembly differs from the narrator's account in chapter 19.[77] He begins consistently enough – he and his concubine came to Gibeah, which belongs to Benjamin, to spend the night (20:4). However, whereas the narration in chapter 19 emphasizes the company of the Levite and his servant – to the exclusion of the concubine, who does not speak nor is she consulted about where to spend the night (19:11–13) – the Levite's report puts the concubine at the forefront. This is understandable, since the horrible fate of the concubine provides the reason for the gathering. But as the Levite continues to testify, his account diverges significantly from the narrator's.

First, instead of attributing the attack to a few goons in the city, the Levite states that the citizens or leading men[78] of the city threatened him. Second, he says that they were intending to kill him, whereas the narrator's account says that the men wanted to have sex with him (20:5; see also 19:22).

Even more telling, the Levite does not mention the lack of hospitality shown to him by the people of Gibeah. With the high value given by the community to hospitality, this is striking, since this fact would have bolstered his case that the citizens of Gibeah were wicked and heartless. Moreover, the Levite omits all references to the old man and everything that transpired before the rape and death of his concubine.

Twice the Levite uses the word "against me," emphasizing that the men rose up "against me" and at night surrounded the house "against me" (20:5, ESV), revealing that he was really the target of the attack. He continues: "They were intending to kill me, but they raped my concubine instead, and she died" (trans. mine). Both phrases begin with a disjunctive clause, putting "me" and "my concubine" in parallel. The Levite may have wanted to convey to the assembly that the men's object was his concubine, and in order to get what they wanted, they had to kill him first. But a close reading of his speech reveals that he was the real target. The Levite never explains why the men

---

76. Ibid., Schneider, *Judges*, 267; Webb, *Book of Judges*, 475–476.
77. Block, 553–555; Schneider, *Judges*, 267–268; Butler, *Judges*, 442–443; Lasine, "Guest and Host," 48–49; Younger, *Judges, Ruth*, 370–371; Olson, "Judges," 884–885; Niditch, *Judges*, 202; Klein, *Triumph of Irony*, 177.
78. Baalim can be translated as "lords, masters," or "citizens."

would go after his concubine if he was the real object – a marked inconsistency in his story – but the Israelite assembly never asks.

The most blatant omission, however, is the lack of detail about the circumstances of her death: "They raped my concubine and, she died." Between the first and second clauses is a time gap of several events: the concubine reached the house where her master was towards dawn; the Levite saw her at the threshold in the morning; he told her to get up, implying that she was still alive; then he slung her body onto the donkey and traveled home. Somewhere in this continuum of events, she died, but the Levite makes it appear that she died immediately after being raped, implying that the men of Gibeah killed her.

The last part of the Levite's story reflects the subsequent events: he cut his concubine's body up and sent her throughout the territory of Israel, omitting any reference to the butcher's knife, which the narrator mentioned in chapter 19 to show how her body was treated like cattle. In addition, the Levite expands the description of Israelite territory to include a reference to the "inheritance of Israel," suggesting that God's gift of the land is being threatened by what has happened.[79] He closes his testimony with a call to action, the urgency of which is shown in the NJPS translation: "Now you are all Israelites; produce a plan of action here and now!" (20:7). The Levite makes it appear that the identity of being an Israelite itself is under threat, hence the need for the tribes' immediate, concerted action.

Obviously, the Levite has his own agenda. He clearly wants revenge on the people of Gibeah. But why does he involve the whole town and not just the culprits? And is his grievance solely related to what the men of Gibeah did to his concubine? His explanation to the assembly seems to suggest that this is the case: "for they have done what was shameful and outrageous in Israel." The word "outrageous," *nebalah*, is used again, but from the lips of the Levite. In addition, he uses the word *zimma*, translated by Block as "lewd," a technical expression for shameful behavior.[80] Clearly, he is referring to the sexual violation of his concubine.

Commentators see the Levite as an indifferent, selfish individual whose only concern is his own welfare and who never wants to face up to his own responsibility about what happened.[81] Webb describes him as a truth-manip-

---

79. Webb, *Book of Judges*, 476; Block, *Judges*, 554.
80. Block, *Judges*, 553.
81. Younger, *Judges, Ruth*, 371; Block, *Judges*, 554; Olson, "Judges," 885.

ulator, manipulating not only the facts, but Israel itself, for his own ends.[82] Indeed, there is some support for this reading in the Levite's behavior and speech. But something more seems to be going on, aside from his desire to save his own skin while seeking revenge on the people of Gibeah.

As noted above, an underlying dynamic in this story is the interplay of shame/honor and powerlessness/power over, especially as it relates to sexual violence and being treated as an outsider/insider.[83] The attempted sexual violence of the men of Gibeah on the Levite has completely humiliated him and made him feel weak and powerless – just like a woman – but he cannot admit this to an assembly of men, since that would result in greater shame and dishonor. Thus he omits the incident that would expose him to the ridicule of his fellow males.[84] Moreover, since the old man protected him from dishonor, he may have felt bound to shield the old man from criticism or possible sanctions by the community.

Moreover, the lack of hospitality shown by the people of Gibeah – and not just by a few "worthless men" – placed him in an outsider status, thus making him an easy target for those "worthless men." Thus he may have blamed the whole city for putting him in a vulnerable situation. By being able to marshal the full military force of the tribes of Israel through the symbol of his concubine's desecrated body and his own misleading story, the Levite gains back his honor and assert power over those who have dishonored and disempowered him.

---

82. Webb, *Book of Judges*, 476.
83. On this, Stone comments: "It is not her welfare that motivates his call for retaliation, but rather the damage that he believes has been done to his own honor" ("Gender and Homosexuality," 101).
84. See Müllner, "Lethal Differences," 137–138.

JUSTICE: RESTORING AGENCY AND EMPOWERING THE VULNERABLE

Who is to blame for the concubine's sexual assault and death? Is it the mob of worthless fellows who wanted to humiliate the outsiders by asserting sexual control? Is it the Levite who pushed his concubine into the mob and treated her callously afterwards? Is it the old man who was only willing to protect his male guest? Is it the citizens of Gibeah for failing to provide the hospitality that would have kept the Levite's party safe? Often a situation of injustice is not the fault of one person alone; rather, the whole system is responsible for protecting the vulnerable. In the work of justice, isolated intervention may do some good, but it will never be enough since systematic factors need to be identified and addressed. This story brings up the concubine's lack of voice and powerlessness. Throughout the story, the men make the decisions for the woman, a situation that lends itself to abuse. Women must be empowered to take initiative and helped to make decisions for their own lives and their families. Doing justice involves restoring agency to those whose capacity to act has been removed or stunted.

For this reason, the story of Jephthah's daughter is more hopeful than the concubine's story. For Jephthah's daughter, when faced with her tragic fate, is able to exercise agency. "Let this be done for me," she says. Even though she cannot control the fate of her death, she can still decide to spend the rest of her brief life in the manner that she chooses.

The Levite's concubine was treated like an object: she was silenced and cut off from her agency. In order to help oppressed women, we must affirm their voices and empower their ability to exercise agency for the betterment of their lives. For all our desire to be generous and offer concrete help, we cannot be too interventionist in our approach. For when we decide what is good for others, we take away their capacity to act, and this makes them more vulnerable to abuse.

JUDGES 20:1–21:25

A Society That Has Gone Awry

Unity – whether it involves a family, community, a church, or a nation – is something for which we all aspire. Because of the positive emotional response generated by the word "united" or the phrase, "we are all in this together," such rhetoric is used by anyone who wants to galvanize people into action, whether for the good of all or in support of one's personal or institutional agenda. Tragically, not all united efforts automatically lead to the good of a community. We see this clearly in the last chapters of the book of Judges.

Chapter 20 opens with an event that has never happened before in the book of Judges: Israel is galvanized into action, united against a perceived threat. The narrative emphasizes phrases such as, "all Israel," "as one man," and "united."

Previously, the judges had repeatedly tried to get Israel to act as one against the threat of the Canaanites, but they were not successful. Deborah reproached the tribes who did not join their brothers in fighting against those who were oppressing them and occupying their land inheritance (5:16–17, 23). In the Samson narrative, there was not only lack of cooperation, but also outright betrayal as the tribe of Judah handed Samson, their fellow Israelite, over to the Philistines (15:9–13). In the Gideon narrative, the Ephraimites censured Gideon for not letting them share in the glory of victory, but then were somewhat pacified by Gideon's words. Yet with Jephthah, the conflict between the Gileadites and the Ephraimites foreshadowed the civil war in chapter 20 (12:1–6). The narrator does not elaborate on this foreshadowing. Despite the great numbers of Ephraimites that were killed during that time (12:6), the theme of fragmentation is not fully explored until the last part of the book in order to showcase the disintegration of the spiritual and social fabric of Israel's national life.

Nevertheless, the opening of chapter 20 creates expectations that, at last, the long-awaited unity is going to take place. The fact that the community is shocked by what happened to the Levite's concubine (19:30) seems to show a moral sensitivity that is not present in the earlier stories, particularly since it involves giving voice to the suffering of the nameless woman and protesting against the injustice done to her. In the face of a morally reprehensible act (*nebalah*), the community comes together, ready to go to war if necessary, to root out the evil from their midst (see 20:13).

20:1–17 A WAR BETWEEN BROTHERS

20:1–7 Convening the Religious Assembly

The turnout to the great assembly is massive and impressive, gathering together "all the Israelites . . . from Dan to Beersheba and the land of Gilead" (20:1).[1] This comprised the geographical scope of ancient Israel, from its northernmost to its southernmost cities, along with the land across the Jordan River given to the tribes of Reuben, Gad, and the half-tribe of Manasseh.[2] Such an assembly has not gathered since the time before Joshua's death, when he convened all the tribes at Shechem for a covenant renewal ceremony (Josh 24).[3] After this covenant ceremony, the tribes scattered to claim their own land inheritances.

For the assembly at Mizpah in Judges, the narrative does not mention a convener – so it seems to have come from a snowballing of emotions as a result of the Levite's call to arms, which ultimately culminates in a community meeting that maps out the community's response. The expression "as one" (20:1) or "in one body" (NRSV) shows the remarkable solidarity and unity among the different tribes, whose narrow-mindedness and self-interest were evident earlier in their lack of involvement in the oppressive situations of other tribes as well as their lack of support for the victories those other tribes achieved.

The narrator is careful to point out that the community is rallying for religious reasons. First, there is the use of the word *'edah* (20:1; translated "congregation" in the NRSV and ESV). Although *'edah* can have the general meaning of a "company," it is used to refer to Israel as a legal and cultic community under Yahweh.[4] Specifically, it can refer to "all free adult men" in Israel "empowered with making decisions for the entire nation" and organized according to the tribes and/or their representatives.[5] The setting for the assembly is religiously significant, since Mizpah was one of ancient Israel's religious sites, being a part of Samuel's annual circuit, along with Bethel and Gilgal (1 Sam

---

1. Younger, *Judges, Ruth*, 370.
2. Num 32:1–5, 28–33; see also Josh 1:12–14.
3. Boling, *Judges*, 283.
4. Block, *Judges*, 551.
5. H.-J. Fabry, "*ēdâ*," *TDOT* 10: 470, 474–475.

7:16). Samuel summoned Israel to Mizpah (1 Sam 7:5–7; 10:17), and Israel also went forth to battle against the Philistines from Mizpah.[6]

More importantly, the narrative mentions that the congregation is gathering "to the Lord" (20:1, ESV, NASB; "before the Lord" in the NIV).[7] The phrase *el-Yahweh* ("to the Lord"), however, is peculiar, since the phrase, *lipne-Yahweh*, is typically used whenever Israel as a community gathers "before the Lord."[8] To do things "before the Lord" (*lipne-Yahweh*) is to conduct oneself "in the presence of" Yahweh.[9] This shift in terminology may signal that the gathering does not have a clear divine stamp. Nevertheless, from the people's perspective, they are present for the Lord, and so a better translation may be, "All the Israelites assembled . . . for the Lord at Mizpah" (20:1, trans. mine).

One might have expected such a terrible crime to lead to self-searching among the Israelites so that the religious gathering would be for fasting, prayer, and repentance, as in Judges 2:4, when the angel of the Lord rebuked "all the Israelites" so that the people wept. The only other time the phrase "all the Israelites" (literally, *kol beney-yisrael*, "all the sons of Israel") is used in the book of Judges (aside from 20:1 and 2:4 mentioned above) is in 8:27.[10] In Judges 2:4 and 8:27, the context is the breaking of God's covenant, which may suggest a similar context for 20:1. Contrary to the expectations of a religious gathering for worship and soul-searching, however, 20:2 opens with the chieftains and foot soldiers in the forefront. This is indeed a religious gathering, but it is a gathering for war. Even before ascertaining the facts, people have come fully prepared to fight.

The narrative again emphasizes the totality of the turnout in verse 2: "the chiefs of all the people, of all the tribes of Israel" (ESV, emph. mine). In addition, the huge number of military men – four hundred thousand – plus their skill – they are all swordsmen – indicates that this is not going to be a mere

---

6. In this verse, Mizpah is a hilltop location in the territory of Benjamin, 7.5 miles north of Jerusalem, and should not be confused with Jephthah's house in Gilead. See Niditch, *Judges*, 202, see 1 Sam 7:11; Josh 18:26.
7. Most translate this as "before the Lord" (NRSV, NIV, NJPS), although ESV and NASB have "to the Lord."
8. In all occurrences of the community assembling "before the Lord," whether for worship, repentance and fasting, or going out to battle, the phrase is always *lipne-yhwh*, except in 1 Sam 10:17, where the subject is Samuel, who calls Israel "to the Lord" at Mizpah, where the usage of the preposition "to" is directional.
9. H. Simian Yofre, "*pānîm*," *TDOT* 11:608. The phrase can "express the viewpoint of Yahweh and his assessment of persons and situations" (*TDOT* 11:611, citing Gen 6:11; 7:1; 10:9; Lev 16:30; Deut 24:4; Eccles 2:26).
10. Boling, *Judges*, 283.

skirmish, but an all-out war. The narrative accentuates the religious nature of the gathering with the phrase, "the assembly of God's people." Here the word for assembly is not *'edah,* but the synonymous term *qahal,* which can likewise have a technical theological meaning as "the cultic community," although it can also be used in a more general sense.[11] But the phrase "God's people" clearly qualifies the purpose of this assembly as religious. Interestingly, both *'edah* and *qahal* are used only in chapters 20–21 in the book of Judges, implying that no such assembly was summoned beforehand, despite all the external threats that Israel experienced.

The narrative implies that the people believe that they are gathering for God by using the verb *yatsab* ("presented themselves," ESV; "took their places," NIV). Elsewhere, the verb is used in the context of Israel's tribes presenting themselves before the Lord in relation to momentous transitional events: a) for the covenant renewal in Joshua 24:1 and b) after the division of the land and the selection of the first king at the establishment of the monarchy in 1 Samuel 10:19.[12] The tribes in this incident also seem to regard their assembly as critical for Israel. Nevertheless, the narrator downplays the event by using the phrase, "present themselves in the assembly of the people of God," rather than the more direct, "present themselves before God/the Lord," which is used in the other two incidents. Ironically, even though the people believe that they are gathering for the sake of God, the narrative does not mention them seeking God's guidance or help, nor does it record any prayers.

Verse 3 shatters the idea of unity among all the Israelite tribes, for even though "all" Israel assembled, the tribe of Benjamin is missing: "The Benjaminites heard that the Israelites had gone up to Mizpah" (20:3a). But why isn't Benjamin included among "all the Israelites"? Are they no longer members of the *'edah* and the *qahal,* the cultic and legal community? It seems that Benjamin is treated like an outsider, hearing only about the assembly secondhand.[13] Why were they not told about the assembly? If the evildoers were only a few worthless men of Gibeah, why was the whole tribe excluded? Did the rest of the Israelite tribes feel that the whole tribe of Benjamin was to blame for what happened? Or were they convinced that the Benjaminites would be recalcitrant and refuse to punish the perpetrators?

---

11. H.-P. Müller, "*qāhāl,* assembly," *TLOT* 3:1119.
12. The meaning of *yatsab* [hitpael] as "present oneself" is also found in Exod 8:20; 9:13 (Moses before Pharaoh); Deut 31:14 (Joshua and Moses before the Lord); 2 Chr 11:13 (priests and Levites); and Job 1:6; 2:1 (heavenly beings).
13. Block, *Judges,* 552; Webb, *Book of Judges,* 475.

Ironically, the gathering is supposed to include "all Israel," "from Dan to Beersheba," "all the people," "all the tribes," but these phrases seem to be the narrator's tongue-in-cheek way of showing that the perception of unity is a farce. Moreover, since the affected party is excluded from the decision-making on what is supposed to be done, there is no opportunity for a dialogue about how best to settle the matter. Thus a truly concerted, united effort does not take place.

Nevertheless, the rest of the eleven tribes are careful to lay the legal basis for their show of force. The Levite is asked to speak in the assembly as the aggrieved party and the primary witness to the crime (20:3b). As discussed earlier, the Levite omits some incidents, particularly his part in the whole affair, and there are inconsistencies in his statements. Yet the tribes never fully clarify what happened. They never interrogate the Levite, and they do not test his statements for inconsistency,[14] which probably would have taken place if representatives of Benjamin had been present in the assembly. There is no calling of other witnesses (such as the servant), which is stipulated in the law: "On the testimony of two or three witnesses a person is to be put to death, but no one is to be put to death on the testimony of only one witness" (Deut 17:6; see also Deut 19:15). And yet, the Israelite tribes are ready to exterminate one of their tribes on the basis of one witness. More importantly, there is no attempt to seek God's mind about the matter.[15] The tribes are all set for armed action, and the Levites' testimony demonstrates publicly that what the tribes have already decided is justifiable and legitimate.

20:8–11 Finalizing the Plan

As stated earlier, the plan for armed action is already in place before the Levite gives his testimony. Nevertheless, the testimony serves to strengthen the resolve of the tribes to punish Gibeah: "None of us will go home. No, not one of us will return to his house" (20:8b). The intention to start a war is left out, because it is already clear to everybody what is going to be done. The only thing left is to finalize the details.

The plan involves all the tribes, and it is structured in such a way that the contribution of each tribe is central to the arrangement. First, they are to draw up lots to determine which tribe will be in the frontlines and which will form the rear (20:9). Secondly, they make plans for the supplies – each tribe will contribute people to bring provisions for the troops, going into detail

---

14. Klein, *Triumph of Irony*, 177–178.
15. Matthews, *Judges & Ruth*, 94; Klein, *Triumph of Irony*, 175.

about how many people will be needed (20:10). It is a pretty good plan – detailed, clear assignment of responsibility, involving everybody – "from all the tribes of Israel" (20:10).

The intention is "to do[16] to Gibeah of Benjamin according to all the disgrace (*nebalah*) that they did in Israel." Here the word *nebalah* ("outrage," "disgrace," "sacrilege") appears again. In 19:23–24, it is used by the old man, who refers to the plan of the wicked men of Gibeah to sexually violate the Levite – a fellow male – as *nebalah* without seeing that his own action – offering his own virgin daughter and the Levite's concubine to the men to be raped – as equally disgraceful. The word is uttered again by the Levite in 20:6, whose use of the word contains a double-meaning. On one hand, he is clearly communicating to the Israelite assembly that the gang-rape of his concubine is an outrage; on the other hand, he hides from the assembly what he really considers an outrage – being sexually molested and shamed by fellow males, a perspective he shares with the old man. Like the old man, he never sees his own actions – deliberately thrusting his concubine out to be raped, emotionally withdrawing from her because of the shame, and treating her body in a dehumanizing way – as equally reprehensible.

In 20:10, the Israelites use *nebalah* to describe the brutal gang-rape of the concubine. But like the old man and the Levite, they cannot see their own actions – in excluding and warring against one of their own tribes and in turning away from Yahweh to other gods – as a greater sacrilege than the men of Gibeah's actions. Here the narrator again exploits the use of irony, since Israel is never outraged by its own sin of idolatry.

Nebalah comes from the root word *nbl* – of which the noun form is often translated as "fool" and the adjective as "foolish."[17] These translations, however, do not fully express the force of the meaning of *nbl*, which has a religio-ethical and wisdom component.[18] The connection of *nbl* with the wisdom tradition shows that the fool is not so much lacking in mental

---

16. The Hebrew text has three infinitives one after the other, which makes for awkward translations, literally, "to do in their coming to Gibeah." The LXX reads, "to the ones going [referring to the troops] to do . . ." See also Soggin, *Judges*, 291; see also Block, *Judges*, 556 n. 314.
17. See Prov 17:7, 21; 30:22, 32.
18. J. Marböck, "*nāḇāl*," *TDOT* 9:163; *TLOT* 2:713. A *nabal* (fool) is a "person who brings disaster, a 'carrier of ruin' for both self and others" (*TLOT* 2:714). Hence a foolish act involves a breach of relationships – whether with Yahweh or other human beings – and destroys the bonds of human society (*TDOT* 9:166–169). The abstract noun *nebalah* is an act which "was understood to impugn the community of Israel as a religious and ethical entity" so that "the person who commits the *nebalah* callously disregards not only the norms of the community but also human warnings and pleas" (*TDOT* 9:168).

cognition, but rather lacking in moral discernment, showing a "breach of insight and integration into the good order guaranteed by God."[19] The old man, the Levite, and the eleven tribes of Israel are morally scandalized by the actions of the men of Gibeah, but in reality, they are as morally compromised as these men. Tragically, they are blind to their own actions, and this is disgraceful and outrageous (*nebalah*).

This is reminiscent of Jesus' words in the Sermon on the Mount:

> "Why do you look at the speck of sawdust in your brother's eye and pay no attention to the plank in your own eye? How can you say to your brother, 'Let me take the speck out of your eye,' when all the time there is a plank in your own eye? You hypocrite, first take the plank out of your own eye, and then you will see clearly to remove the speck from your brother's eye. (Matt 7:3–5)

Church people can so easily express outrage over the low standards of morality in society, especially regarding others' sexual purity. However, they may be blind to their own failures in other areas, such as a lack of integrity in financial matters, gossiping and backbiting, judgemental attitudes, using power for their own interests, domestic abuse. As Christians, we may be steeped in orthodox teachings, yet lack wisdom and discernment about how our knowledge should be applied.

In response to what the Israelites consider *nebalah*, "all the men rose up together as one" (20:8a); "all the Israelites got together and united as one against the city" (20:11). These verses reiterate the unity and solidarity of 20:1. The addition of the word "united" (*khaver*) emphasizes the sense of companionship and partnership among the different tribes as they plan and implement the assault on Gibeah. The word *khaver* itself, however, does not necessarily have a positive meaning, since people can be "companions" in doing evil.[20] As Matthews comments, "it is a true irony that the one occasion in the Book of Judges when 'all the men of Israel gathered . . . united as one' (v. 11) is in a war against their own kin."[21]

---

19. *TLOT* 2:713.
20. Elsewhere the nominative *khaver* is translated as "companion" (Pss 45:8; 119:63; Song of Songs 1:7; Isa 1:23). *Khaver* is used in both negative and positive contexts (*NIDOTTE* 2:17). The verb form, *khbr*, is often used to indicate political and military alliances (George J. Brooke, "hbr," *NIDOTTE* 2:16; see Gen 14:3).
21. Matthews, *Judges & Ruth*, 195.

Moreover, the narrative highlights the exclusion of Benjamin from "all" the people of Israel. In ancient Israel, to be cursed is to be expelled from the community, the tribe, or the people who live under blessing.[22] Thus in a society where exclusion is a form of community censure, the Israelites communicate to Benjamin that they have been punished before they have been given a chance to be heard. As Soggin observes, "the absence of Benjamin form the debate presages no good."[23]

20:12–17 Challenge and Refusal

Hence it is no surprise that the tribe of Benjamin does not respond positively to the challenge of the assembly to hand over the perpetrators of the crime. First, rather than addressing the leaders of Gibeah, the assembly sends the message "throughout the tribe of Benjamin" (20:12) after the Israelite army is already gathered in front of Gibeah, ready to begin the assault. Even though the message gives Benjamin the chance to be involved in the concerted action (perhaps by joining the assault and pressuring the leaders of Gibeah to turn over the culprits), it does so without giving Benjamin the opportunity to be part of the decision-making.

Secondly, the message sent to the Benjaminites is in the form of an accusation, immediately assigning guilt: "What about this awful crime that was committed among you?" (20:12b). Such a confrontational message would put anybody on the defensive. God, in confronting the first man and woman about disobeying God's command, first gives them the opportunity to own up to what they did (Gen 3:9–13). The same is true when God confronted Cain regarding the murder of Abel, his brother (Gen 4:9–10). But here, the assumption of guilt – which was implied in the exclusion of Benjamin from the assembly – becomes more explicit.

Thirdly, the accusation is followed immediately by a demand: "Now then, give up the men, the worthless men who are in Gibeah, in order that we may execute them . . ." (20:13a, trans. mine). The use of "worthless men" (literally, "men of belial") – the same description used by the narrator in 19:22[24] – is surprising, since the Levite referred to the men as "citizens/lords of Gibeah" in his testimony (20:5). This makes one wonder whether the Israelites are as ignorant about what really happened as the Levites' suppression of certain incidents might lead one to think.

---

22. Josef Scharbert, "'rr," *TDOT* 1:409.
23. Soggin, *Judges*, 290.
24. Webb, *Book of Judges*, 480.

The Hebrew word for "execute" (*mut*) in this verse is not the general word used for killing as a violent, bloody act (*harag*; see 20:5),[25] nor does it express the moral and religious assessment of *ratsa* ("to murder"; see 20:4).[26] Rather, the word *mut* is used in relation to capital crimes and includes the idea of God's judgement.[27] Clearly, the rest of the tribes see themselves as a legal body authorized to mete out the death penalty to the criminals in Gibeah.

The reason for the death penalty is that "we may purge the evil from Israel" (20:13b). Here the idea of corporate guilt comes into play. In ancient Israel, the sin of an individual or a few was seen to affect the whole community. Therefore, the whole community, along with the ones who directly committed the crime, was subject to God's judgement. Hence the whole community needed to root out the sin in its midst by executing the death penalty on the originators of evil so that God's wrath could be averted and blessing and shalom could flow back to the whole nation.

This is exemplified in the treatment of Achan and his family in Joshua 7.[28] In this passage, Achan took for himself the goods which God previously commanded the people to destroy. Achan's action is described as *nebalah* (Josh 7:15), affecting the whole community, so that Israel was defeated in the battle against Ai. To prevent further defeat, the whole community executed the death penalty on Achan and his whole household (Josh 7:24–26) so that the nation of Israel would not be given over to destruction (Josh 7:11–12).[29]

The same reasoning applies to the Israelite assembly's desire to execute the criminals of Gibeah. Hence at first glance, the intention of the Israelite tribes against Gibeah seems honorable – they want to ensure that the sin of a few will not spread and contaminate the rest. They are trying to preempt what could possibly take place in the future that could lead to the destruction of the whole community.

Nevertheless, they pronounce the death penalty without clear instructions from God; they do not follow due process; and they do not attempt to dialogue with Benjamin before making judgements and demands. All this suggests that something is gravely remiss in the community's discernment about the situation. Rather than seeing what happened to the concubine

---

25. *TLOT* 2:662.
26. Ibid., 663.
27. W. R. Domeris, "*rṣḥ*," *NIDOTTE* 3:1189.
28. Matthews, *Judges & Ruth*, 194, draws out a parallel between Judg 20 and Josh 7. See also Niditch, *Judges*, 203.
29. For a discussion of the concept of corporate punishment in Josh 7, see Joel Kaminsky, *Corporate Responsibility in the Hebrew Bible* (Sheffield: Sheffield Academic Press, 1995), 67–95.

as a mirror to recognize what has happened to Israelite society as a whole, they use the incident to assign guilt and make war on one of their tribes. Moreover, they want to "purge evil (*ra'ah*) from their midst," yet they ignore the fact that they have continually done evil (*ra'ah*) in the sight of the Lord by worshipping other gods and goddesses (3:7, 12; 4:1; 6:1; 10:6; 13:1).

The intertribal war could have been averted if the tribe of Benjamin had responded in a positive way, "but the Benjaminites were not willing to listen to the voice of their brothers, the Israelites" (20:13, trans. mine). "Judged without a hearing, the Benjaminites turn a deaf ear to 'their brothers.'"[30] "The failure of negotiation has been made all but inevitable by developments that have occurred in the previous episodes."[31]

The emphasis on the word "brothers" (20:13, 23, 28; 21:6; "fellow Israelites" in the NIV) highlights the conflict of relational interests at play in this story. As in the story of Abimelech, the Benjaminites show a preference for their immediate kin,[32] even though the rest of the Israelite tribes can be considered as their "brothers." Hence loyalty to the immediate kin trumps issues of justice and national interest. At the same time, the emphasis on "brothers" also puts into relief the breakdown of relations within the community. Ideally, fellow Israelites would be able to give and receive admonitions that could result in each other's greater good. But with the Israelites' unilateral demand and the Benjaminites' refusal, the stage is set for an all-out war among "brothers."

Without waiting for the rest of the Israelite tribes to go on the offensive, the tribe of Benjamin immediately musters an army from all its towns. The fighting force involves large numbers – twenty-six thousand swordsmen, excluding Gibeah. On the other hand, the Israelite tribes have four hundred thousand swordsmen – all warriors. The disjunctive clause in verse 17 serves to contrast the respective military forces of Benjamin with the rest of the Israelite tribes.[33] While the Israelite tribe is larger, the account carefully points out the special skill of the seven hundred chosen men from Benjamin; like Ehud, their left hand is strong, which can be very advantageous in battle, since the direction of the sword's blow cannot be anticipated. Aside from this skill, these men are also described as not missing a target (20:16).

---

30. Klein, *Triumph of Irony*, 180.
31. Webb, *Book of Judges*, 479.
32. Niditch, *Judges*, 203.
33. In Hebrew narrative, a disjunctive clause begins with a non-verb and has several functions, one of which is to provide contrast.

Nonetheless, the contrast in the description between the "sons of Israel" and "sons of Benjamin" emphasizes how Benjamin is no longer regarded as belonging to "the sons of Israel."

While conflicts cannot be prevented, there are some things that can be done to prevent them from escalating into violence and bloodshed, such as giving people the opportunity to explain their side, listening genuinely without jumping to conclusions, adequately investigating the cause of the conflict, trying not to favor family and friends, addressing issues of justice, using inclusive processes that give paramount importance to those who will be affected, and the discipline to avoid using military or institutional force. These elements of conflict resolution are all lacking in this Judges narrative.

The vision of shalom is an overarching theme in the biblical narrative. Shalom not only describes peace with God through Christ and inner peace through relationships of goodness with others, but also praying and working for peace in our world. In our present-day world of conflict and strife, Christians ought to be engaged in just peacemaking and conflict resolution as a way of outworking God's mission in the world. While peacemaking begins in our homes and personal relationships and within the life of the church, it must also spill out into the wider society. In various periods of the history of the church, and also in our present time, Christians have too readily supported the way of force and war without fully exploring the ways of peace.

Yet peacemaking is a long process that requires patience, repentance, and justice – often without immediate fruit. The process can be very risky and dangerous, but it is an expression of the way Christ lived his life on earth. Hence we must encourage and come along side those who work for peace.

20:18–48 PARODY OF A DIVINE WAR

The account of the battle between the Israelite tribes and Benjamin is remarkable because of its length and attention to detail.[34] Moreover, certain portions – particularly the last part – are repeated with some expansions, omissions, or nuanced differences in detail. The repetitions and omissions showcase a classic example of the existence of several sources that have been joined together.[35]

---

34. Block, *Judges*, 557.
35. See Simon De Vries, "Temporal Terms as Structural Elements in the Holy-War Tradition," *VT* 25 (1975): 89–92; Boling, *Judges*, 288; Soggin, *Judges*, 294; Gray, *Judges*, 280–282; Burney, *Judges*, 447–458.

Whether composite or not, the account can be read as a narrative whole,[36] with the repetitions presenting different viewpoints about the battle.[37]

Several commentators have drawn parallels between Judges 20 and Judges 1, along with other narratives featuring Yahweh involved in fighting a war.[38] The parallels suggest that the writer is using earlier war motifs to present a view of Israel that is opposite to the depiction in Judges 1 or any war fought with divine involvement. As Marais puts it, the similarity "evokes the frame of reference of the conquest of the land, but, in contrast, focuses on the fact that the conquest was unsuccessful and that the tribes spent their time conquering each other."[39]

The section can be divided into three parts, based on the account of the three battles waged between the eleven tribes and Benjamin. Younger notes that they follow the same pattern: a) pre-inquiry actions; b) inquiry; c) Yahweh's response; and d) result.[40] Thus, according to Younger, the battle narrative can be structured as follows:

Battle 1 (20:18–21)	Israel Fails
Battle 2 (20:22–25)	Israel Fails
Battle 3 (20:26–48)	Israel Succeeds[41]

This structure could be further modified by a more detailed structure of 20:26–48, detailing the battle from the perspective of the majority of the Israelite tribes and then from the viewpoint of Benjamin. Thus the third battle can be structured accordingly:

---

36. See Satterthwaite, Philip E., "'No king in Israel': Narrative Criticism and Judges 17–21," *TynBul* 44 (1993): 75–88; E. J, Revell, "The Battle with Benjamin (Judg 20:29–48) and Hebrew Narrative Techniques," *VT* 35 (1985): 417–433.
37. Webb, *Book of Judges*, 491; Matthews, *Judges & Ruth*, 197; Klein, *Triumph of Irony*, 183. On the other hand, some see the repetitions as reflecting the general messiness and complications of war (Webb, *Book of Judges*, 489). According to Niditch, the repetitions point "to the very nature of war as an often pointless round of battles; power rises and falls, and justice is difficult to determine." It is not clear, however, in what way the repetitions achieve this.
38. Olson, "Judges," 885; Marais, *Representation*, 140; Niditch, *Judges*, 204; Webb, *Book of Judges*, 482–483; Hudson, "Anonymity in Judges 19–21," 49; Wong, *Compositional Strategy*, 32–35; Younger, *Judges*, 374–375.
39. Marais, *Representation*, 140; see also Hudson, "Anonymity," 53.
40. Younger, *Judges/Ruth*, 372. Niditch, *Judges*, 203, sees a similar pattern: muster (vv. 14, 15, 17, 19, 22, 29, 32); request for an oracle by the Israelites (vv. 18, 23, 26–28); response of the deity (vv. 18, 23, 28); going forth to battle (vv. 20, 21, 24, 25, 30, 31); the battle (vv. 25, 31, 33, 34, 35, 36–37, 39); and the outcome (vv. 39–48), although she does not use the pattern to produce a structure.
41. Younger, *Judges*, 373.

Battle 1 (20:18–21)   First Loss of Majority Israel[42]
Battle 2 (20:22–25)   Second Loss of Majority Israel
Battle 3 (20:26–48)   Benjamin's Defeat
    From the Perspective of Majority Israel (20:26–36)
    From the Perspective of Benjamin (20:37–46)
    The Outcome of the Civil War (20:47–48)

20:18–21 The First Encounter: Israel Loses

As in Judges 1, the Israelites consult the Lord about who should be the first to start the attack against the Benjaminites (see 20:18). The response is the same as in Judges 1: Judah is to lead the attack (20:18; see also 1:2). In Judges 20, however, the place of consultation is Bethel, presumably because, at that time, the ark of the covenant resided there, along with the high priest (see 20:27–28); whereas in Judges 1, Bethel was not yet in Israelite hands (see 1:22).

A glaring gap in chapter 20 is the lack of a divine command to fight the Benjaminites. In Judges 1, this command is given beforehand (see Josh 1:1–5; 3:9–10), so that the tribes are just carrying out God's previous instruction. Thus in Judges 20, the Israelites show a great deal of presumption by taking God's approval for their plans for granted, since they only ask God to help them with a minor detail – who should lead the attack – rather than asking God if the whole plan is a good idea. As Boling says, they have neglected "to ask the prior question: 'Shall we go or not?'"[43]

Perhaps it is going too far to say with Klein that the Israelites' question is an empty formality since their plan is already set.[44] Although there seems to be a genuine desire to solicit God's involvement in what they are doing, they only want God's participation in the details, but not in the conception of the project itself.[45]

Thus it is not surprising that the formula for victory is lacking,[46] in contrast with other narratives in Judges where God is shown to be fighting on

---

42. I am using the term "majority Israel" rather than "Israel" to highlight the fact that Benjamin was still part of Israel, even though the majority of the tribes banded against Benjamin.
43. Boling, *Judges*, 286.
44. Klein, *Triumph of Irony*, 178–179.
45. Wong (*Compositional Strategy*, 34. n. 17) observes that in similar situations, when there is no clear directive to go to war, the prior question in oracular inquiries is to ask whether to go to war or not.
46. Webb, *Book of Judges*, 482–483.

behalf of Israel (see 1:2; 3:28; 4:7; 7:9). But even without God's assurance of presence and victory, the Israelites push through with their plan since they get an answer from God about the only the detail with which they feel God can help them. They encamp against Gibeah in the morning and go on the offensive, fully confident that God is on their side, and that victory is assured. After all, they are on the side of what is right, and they are to be God's judicial instrument to punish wrongdoing.

Hence it is an unexpected blow when Israel is defeated by the smaller Benjaminite force. The losses are heavy as the Benjaminites march out of Gibeah to fight the united force of the eleven tribes – twenty-two thousand Israelites that day. One cannot help asking, Is Yahweh fighting for Benjamin? If so, why did God answer the Israelite tribes by telling them to have Judah lead the battle, as if to say, "Go ahead with your plan." Is God just leading them on? But did God really say "yes"?

The stories of the seer Balaam (Num 22–24) and the war alliance between Ahab and Jehoshaphat (1 Kgs 22) present similar situations. In Numbers 22:12, God told Balaam not to comply with the request of the dignitaries of Moab to go with them and curse Israel. But when the men appeared a second time to offer a greater reward, and Balaam asked them to stay to seek God's mind on the matter again, God told Balaam to go ahead (Num 22:15–20). Yet subsequent events show that this was not what God wanted (Num 22:22–35). But due to Balaam's insistence, God allowed him to have his way, which led to his being dishonored and humiliated before the king of Moab (24:10–11).

In 1 Kings 22, Ahab asked Jehoshaphat to enter into an alliance with him to fight Syria, but before the planned attack, Jehoshaphat wanted to inquire first from the Lord whether to push through with it, or not (vv. 3–5). When they consulted Micaiah the prophet, he said, "Attack and be victorious, for the LORD will give it into the king's hand" (v. 15), yet he only said this because this was what the king wanted to hear (see v. 13). Even though Micaiah eventually prophesied disaster (vv. 17–23), the two kings went ahead, with disastrous consequences for Ahab, who died in the battle (vv. 29–39).

What these two stories show is that there are some cases when God seems to give a positive signal to a certain undertaking, but only because those concerned have already made up their minds before consulting God. In such cases, divine consultation functions to provide religious legitimacy to what people have already decided to do. In other words, it is a token way of soliciting God's help in some small detail so that they can secure God's cooperation for the whole venture. It is a bit like trying to make people feel good by seeking their advice, so that they will not derail the plan that has already been set in motion. In such cases, solicitation for help and advice becomes largely manipulative and political.

It is interesting that the eleven tribes relate with Benjamin the same way that they relate with God. While completely marginalizing God in the process of making the decision to fight against Benjamin, they bring God in at the end to help make their project successful, yet without giving God any power to challenge their plans. God responds to the small part they ask him to play, but God withholds his presence and blessing on the whole enterprise.

Even in the sphere of Christian ministry, we often treat God as a stamping pad to bless plans and projects that we have devised without God's guidance and approval. This reveals that we do not genuinely want to obey God, but only to ensure that God cooperates with our own ventures. The problem with this is that we treat God like a political tool to advance our own interests rather than the God who is to be worshipped and obeyed.

20:22–25 The Second Encounter: Israel Loses Again

Even as the huge losses of the first day jolt majority Israel out of their self-confidence and self-righteousness, they line up for battle again on the second day. However, the fact that they do not change their strategy, but go into battle formation at the same place where they fought on the first day, reveals that they have no doubts about the rightness of their cause and that they will prevail in the end. So they "strengthened themselves" (NRSV: "took courage"; NIV – "encouraged one another") to fight on resolutely (20:22).

Nevertheless, there is weeping before the Lord and a twinge of doubt about whether they are on the right course, for they ask: "Shall I again do battle with Benjamin my brother?" (20:23a, trans. mine). As some have noted, there is now a reference to "Benjamin my brother."[47] For the first time, majority Israel acknowledges the huge strain on the bonds of kinship that their decision to war against Benjamin has caused.

But the fact that they go into battle formation before inquiring from God whether they should continue the war against Benjamin shows that they have already made up their minds before they ask. Not surprisingly, God's answer is the same as before: "Go up against them" (20:23c). As in the first

---

47. Klein, *Triumph of Irony*, 181.

day, majority Israel experiences huge losses, although fewer than the first day – eighteen thousand experienced swordsmen (20:25).

20:26–46 The Third Encounter: Benjamin Is Defeated

This third day of battle opens differently from the first two days. First of all, there is the sudden entry of a named character: Phinehas, son of Eleazar, from the priestly line of Aaron (20:28), presumably the high priest during that time. This is a surprise, since all of the characters have remained unnamed up to this point, but it provides a foil to the other named priest in a sea of anonymous characters in chapters 17–21: Jonathan – son of Gershom, son of Moses – who is the illegitimate priest of the Danite shrine (Judg 18:30). These two priests are contrasted with the two unnamed Levites – also of the priestly line – who are central to the action of Judges 19–21. As mentioned on p. 239, the naming of Jonathan shocks the reader into realizing that idolatry and syncretism were already prevalent in Israelite society a mere two generations away from Moses, the Exodus, and the giving of the law at Sinai. In the same way, the naming of Phinehas shows that the disintegration of Israel's communal life is already apparent one or two generations away from Joshua, the conquest, and the division of the land.[48]

In the third divine inquiry, majority Israel is no longer certain if they should go ahead with their plan – "they had lost confidence in their own capabilities."[49] Instead of asking God to help them with a bit of war strategy, as in the first battle, or lining up in war formation before consulting God, as in the second battle, the Israelites army[50] troops to Bethel to inquire of the Lord. But the manner of inquiry has changed, for the weeping is now accompanied by fasting and the offering of burnt and peace offerings (20:26). The additional note that "they stayed before the Lord" (*lipne-Yahweh*) and "they offered . . . offerings before the Lord" (*lipne-Yahweh*) seems to indicate that they intend to stay and delay the war until they are sure of God's "go" signal – something they should have done in the first place.

Moreover, the question is framed differently: "Shall I march out in battle again against the Benjaminites my brother or shall I give up?" Again there is an intensification of the relational aspect, which is emphasized with the use

---

48. Hudson, "Anonymity," 64–65.
49. Marais, *Representation*, 141.
50. In a military context, "all the people" in this verse refers to members of the army and not to all the people of Israel (Webb, *Book of Judges*, 485).

of the first person pronoun – "my brother."[51] More significantly, the addition of the phrase, "shall I give up," indicates that majority Israel is now open to the possibility that the war is a mistake, and they are willing to quit if God should say so.[52] The attitude of arrogance implied by their asking God for help with only minor details is gone. They realize their utter dependence on God for the outcome of the battle.

With the Israelites' new humility, God's response changes from a terse reply to a speech that includes the promise of victory: "Tomorrow, I will give him [Benjamin] into your hand" (20:28).

20:29–36a The third battle from Israel's perspective

The change in majority Israel's attitude is accompanied by a corresponding change in strategy. Instead of lining up in the same battle formation as in the previous two encounters, the plan now includes an ambush. While the main force is drawing the Benjaminites away from the city, the men in ambush place themselves in position.

With two successful military encounters behind them, now the Benjaminites become overconfident. They pursue the fleeing Israelites, breaking ranks as they reach the main roads to Bethel and Gibeah. Because they strike down thirty men, they think that they are winning again. Even though the Benjaminites are trapped between two forces – the fleeing Israelites, who now suddenly turn to face them, and the ten thousand men in ambush, who now march out in front of the city–they still do not realize that they are close to ruin.

God's involvement in the battle now becomes clear as the Lord fights for majority Israel against Benjamin: "The LORD defeated Benjamin before Israel . . ." (20:35). As a result, the army of Benjamin is soundly defeated – 25,100 swordsmen – and then the Benjaminites realize that they are beaten (20:36a).

God's involvement connects this war with the other wars fought in Judges (see 4:15; 7:22). In these wars, God is portrayed as an active participant, fighting on behalf of his people. However, in this narrative, the opponent is one of the tribes of Israel, and God is fighting with the rest of the tribes against their brothers. If war is an instrument of divine judgement,[53] does the fact that God fights for majority Israel mean that God shares their moral outrage against the tribe of Benjamin for refusing to hand over the culprits of

---

51. Webb, *Book of Judges*, 486.
52. Klein, *Triumph of Irony*, 182.
53. Robert Good, "The Just War in Ancient Israel," *JBL* 104 (1985): 385–400.

Gibeah? If so, then why did God allow Israel to be defeated twice, with such grave losses – forty thousand experienced swordsmen, who can no longer fight in Israel's war? In fact, despite the confidence shown by the eleven tribes on their moral rightness at the beginning, the losses caused them to doubt if God was really fighting on their side, leading them to wonder if God was fighting for Benjamin instead.

The rape of the concubine was, indeed, a *nebalah*, and Benjamin's indifference in dealing with the offenders, along with their readiness to fight for those who did wrong, is morally indefensible. Nevertheless, the process majority Israel used to reach the decision to war against Benjamin, along with their self-righteous arrogance in marginalizing God in the decision-making process, is also unjustifiable. Thus, as Webb observes, Yahweh was on no one's side.[54] God chastised both parties.[55] Although one side gained the victory in the end, there were great consequences for the whole Israelite society.

20:36b–46 The third battle from Benjamin's perspective

To show what it is like to be on the other side – the one considered to be in the wrong – the narrative repeats the events leading to the defeat of Benjamin, but from their own psychological viewpoint. While verses 29–36a emphasize the victory for majority Israel, verses 36b–46 highlight the losses for Benjamin. Even though God fights against Benjamin in the third battle, the narrative does not minimize or gloss over Benjamin's loss.

> We are taken inside the heads of the defeated Benjaminites to see what they now see and see it through their eyes . . . By lingering for a while on what has just happened; the narrator underlines the magnitude and significance of it. And by showing it through the eyes of the defeated Benjaminites, he enables us to feel it as they do and produces a degree of empathy with them.[56]

The second account (v. 36b) begins by giving more details about the strategy that leads to the Benjaminites' defeat. This explains how the Benjaminites – though strong and skilled warriors–get into a position that they did not anticipate, and therefore are unable to fight back. The explanation helps to mitigate the pain of loss by showing that the Benjaminites are not slack in battle, but are outmaneuvered. Because the Israelites allow the Benjaminites

---

54. Webb, *Judges: Integrated Reading*, 194.
55. Marais, *Representation*, 141.
56. Webb, *Book of Judges*, 491.

to advance,[57] the ambush force is able to rush towards the city and strike it while the army pursues the retreating Israelites (v. 37).

The next verses graphically recount how the turn in the battle is viewed from both sides, but the focus is on the changing emotions of the Benjaminites, which shift from confidence (v. 39b) to confusion (v. 40) to terror (v. 41) as they realize the disaster overtaking them. This turn is signaled by the rising smoke from the city. To the majority Israelites, the smoke is a positive sign, since it signals when they are to turn from being pursued and engage the Benjaminites directly (vv. 38–39a). However, the smoke confuses the Benjaminites, who only later realize that their city is burning (v. 40). At this point of confusion and uncertainty, the full force of the Israelites bears upon them. Realizing the futility of struggle, they turn around and flee towards the wilderness, but the battle catches up with them (v. 42).

The verbs used to describe the routing of the Benjaminites underscore the totality and brutality of their defeat: *hishkhit* (*shakhat*) ("to exterminate, slaughter," v. 42), *hidrik* (*darak*) ("to crush, trample", v. 43), *'alal* ("to glean," that is, to eliminate whatever remains," v. 45), and *hikka* ("to strike down," v. 45). The narrative becomes repetitive, adding to the atmosphere of turmoil and unrest as simultaneous actions happen at once, and the Benjaminites are pursued relentlessly by the majority Israelite army until they are struck down. In addition, the constant repetition of the numbers of Benjaminites killed is like a somber refrain bearing witness to their devastating losses: eighteen thousand, five thousand, one thousand, twenty-five thousand. Though the numbers do not add up, they show clearly that nearly all the fighting men of Benjamin are decimated. The twice-repeated reference to the Benjaminites as "valiant fighters" (vv. 44, 46) accentuates the wasteful nature of this war and the worthiness of the men who are being sacrificed for unclear causes and ends.

This reveals that waging wars, even those for so-called righteous causes, is fraught with ambiguities. Who is right? Who is wrong? Who is the winner? Who is the loser? Since all sides suffer the loss of lives and property, as well as the rending of the social fabric, no one ever really "wins" in war. It is even more tragic if the ones who are involved are near kin, such as the people of North and South Korea, or those who have lived alongside each other in peace previously, such as the Muslims and Christians in the southern

---

57. The text reads, "the Israelites gave ground to the Benjaminites."

Philippines, who now inflict violence against each other because of territorial disputes and ideological, religious, and ethnic differences.

20:47–48 Epilogue: The Aftermath of the Intertribal War

The last part of chapter 20 records two events, which foreshadow and set the stage for the attempt to restore the remnant of Benjamin.[58] First, the narrative repeats the information that some of the Benjaminites fled to the Rock of Rimmon (v. 47),[59] adding here the detail that six hundred Benjaminites lived there for four months. The significance of this information will become clear in chapter 21.

The second event depicts majority Israel doing a complete sweep of the Benjaminites. Although this tribal destruction is never commanded by God, the men of Israel set fire to cities and put to sword all that remains, whether people or animals (20:48). The practice of totally destroying cities, along with all the inhabitants and property, for religious reasons is commonly known as *kherem*,[60] but the narrator never uses that word here – although it is used by the Israelites later in 21:11. Nevertheless, the narrative uses other terminologies associated with *kherem*: "put to the sword" (vv. 37, 48), "set on fire" (v. 48), "cut down" (*hishkhit*, vv. 35, 42), "strike down" (*hikkah*, vv. 45, 48). Although these phrases are common in war accounts, *kherem* terminology implies the destruction of everything until no survivors are left .[61]

The idea behind *kherem*, in the context of war, is to destroy totally all inhabitants and goods (whether animals or property) of a city or populace because of a) their moral depravity and b) because their corrupt practices in close proximity to Israel pose a threat to Israel's faithfulness to their covenant and consequently their continuance in the land. The emphasis of *kherem* is the dismantling of structures that are opposed to Israel's covenant with Yahweh rather than on the capricious killing of people.[62] *Kherem* was primarily directed against the seven Canaanite nations (Deut 7:1–2; 20:16–18) who were occupying the land that God had promised to Israel. However, in some

---

58. This is the third plot level identified by O'Connell in *Rhetoric of Judges* (244). These three plot levels were identified on p. 242.
59. This detail is mentioned previously in v. 45.
60. See comment on Judg 1:17.
61. *TDOT* 5:183.
62. Paul Copan, *Is God a Moral Monster? Making Sense of the Old Testament God* (Grand Rapids, MI: Baker, 2011), 170–173. On God and violence in *kherem* texts, see Elmer A. Martens, "Toward Shalom: Absorbing the Violence," in *War in the Bible and Terrorism in the Twenty-First Century*, eds. Richard S. Hess and Elmer A. Martens, Bulletin for Biblical Research Supp. 2 (Winona Lake, IN: Eisenbrauns, 2008), 45–50.

cases, it was applied to Israelite cities who had been led astray to worship other gods (Deut 13:12–18).

Apparently, the Israelites think that they are carrying out God's intention for *kherem* when they apply it to their kin, the Benjaminites. However, although Yahweh promises them victory, they are never commanded to subject the whole tribe to *kherem*. Yet the eleven tribes interpret this destruction as a natural follow-up to their victory, following the pattern of their wars against the Canaanites. Ironically, they failed to enact *kherem* in their wars with the Canaanite nations, but they effectively carry it out on their brother tribe.

The case of an Israelite city being led astray to idolatry as a reason for subjecting it to *kherem* (see Deut 13:12–18) cannot be applied to Benjamin in this case, since the reason for the war is not idolatry.[63] Nevertheless, the Israelites think that the Benjaminites are committing religious apostasy. There is another irony here, since the book of Judges repeatedly shows that all Israel followed after other gods; hence all Israel should be subjected to *kherem* and not just Benjamin. In fact, the reason God handed them over to the Canaanite nations was because of their idolatry.

Nevertheless, even if the Benjaminites were suspected of committing religious apostasy, the requirements of Deuteronomy 13:12–17 state that a thorough investigation must be done before the judgement of *kherem* can be applied (Deut 13:14). However, as noted above, this is not followed in this case. Again, in their overzealousness, Israel misreads the situation and overstretches a principle, misapplying an instrument for justice to the wrong people – with disastrous consequences.

Social and religious institutions are established to support the values of justice and goodness within a community. Yet sometimes, the power of institutions can be administered without wisdom, discernment, or proper due process. Some examples include: declaring war in the name of peace and justice without considering the long-term and widespread consequences, harshly applying the law for first-time offenders with minor offenses, indiscriminately using police force to arrest and pursue suspected criminals without regard for human rights, or punishing prisoners without providing a way for their restoration into normal society.

It is naïve to think that religious institutions are exempt from the misuse of power or that they are never abusive in their policies and strategies. The

---

63. The case of Achan (Josh 7) was not a case of idolatry, but it was still related to the seven Canaanite nations.

religious leaders during Jesus' time, for all their piety, condemned Jesus – an innocent man – to death. In some periods of the Christian church, the powers of the state were co-opted by the church and brought to bear upon those who were perceived to be religious heretics. Many a saint was burned at the stake in the name of God based on the authority of the church. Today, leaders of religious organizations may subtly use their positions and authority to marginalize those who disagree with them or who threaten their power base.

This highlights the need for those who hold the power of institutions to facilitate the common good rather than personal self-interests and to be discerning about how they carry out their responsibilities. Hence it is not enough for leaders to be competent and strong; they must also be people of discernment and foresight. A servant leadership is called for within the faith community and in Christian organizations.

21:1–23 REPARATIONS FOR A LOST TRIBE

21:1–4 Skewed Judgement

In chapter 21, the lack of judgement exhibited by majority Israel's leaders continues, degenerating into a farce as they face the long-term consequences of their hasty decisions. Yet rather than recognizing their folly, they stand by their poor judgement and compound the situation by making one imprudent decision after another. If not for the grave consequences, the mental calisthenics of the Israelite tribes can be considered laughable – a "comedy of correctness."[64] In chapter 20, there is "show of legality first (vv. 12–13), followed by full scale military action," whereas the sequence in chapter 21 is "fight first and think later (vv. 16–22)."[65]

As chapter 21 opens, the Israelites begin to see the impact of subjecting Benjamin to *kherem*.[66] Earlier in the narrative, while the tribes were assembled at Mizpah and emotions against the Benjaminites were running high, the Israelites made a joint pledge not to return to their own houses until they had carried out their plan against Gibeah. Moreover, they swore an oath that they would never give any of their daughters as wives to Benjamin (21:1).

In Deuteronomy 7:1–2, the command for *kherem* against the seven nations occupying Canaan is followed by the instruction, "you shall not intermarry with them, giving your daughters to their sons or taking their

---

64. Boling, *Judges*, 294.
65. Ibid.
66. Webb, *Book of Judges*, 496.

daughters for their sons" (Deut 7:3). Thus the oath that the eleven tribes entered into was a by-product of their notion that the tribe of Benjamin, their brother, was to be treated like one of the Canaanite nations surrounding them. Ironically, they seemed to have no scruples when it came to intermarrying with the Canaanites themselves.[67]

Yet when they made these oaths at Mizpah, they did not think through the consequences for them as a nation.[68] As soon as they realize that the tribe of Benjamin will be cut off so that there will no longer be the twelve tribes of Israel, the Israelites all troop to Bethel and stay there until evening, as they did before going out to battle against Benjamin (21:2; see also 20:26). They must be thinking that since they were able to get an answer from God before the battle, repeating the assembly will guarantee the same results. Here, the narrator creates distance between their actions and God's personal involvement by stating that they wept "before Elohim" instead of "before Yahweh" (21:2).[69]

The eleven tribes begin to lament loudly before God: "LORD, God of Israel . . . why has this happened to Israel? – Why should one tribe be missing from Israel today?" (21:2–3). The question is a theological one[70] – one that is often asked when calamity strikes a community. But here, the catastrophe does not have to do with natural disasters, but with the fragmentation of national community life and the possible extinction of one tribe.[71] In a culture where the vision of shalom and well-being includes all the members of the family together (Ps 128), to have one tribe missing is felt keenly as a grievous loss.

The irony is that even as the tribes weep about the situation before God and question why this huge loss has happened in the great tradition of the lament, they never reflect on their role in bringing it about, nor on the limitations they imposed on themselves to restore Benjamin by virtue of their own thoughtless oaths. In the structure of the psalms of lament, the questioning is either followed by a confession of sin, an assertion of innocence, or imprecation on those who caused the calamity. Then the lament moves to an expression of confidence in God.[72] In Israel's lament, however, there is

---

67. See Block, *Judges*, 569.
68. Schneider, *Judges*, 278–279.
69. Block, *Judges*, 570, thinks that the narrator's preference for Elohim instead of Yahweh when describing Israel's actions reveals "that he recognizes their insincerity."
70. Lapsley, *Whispering the Word*, 38.
71. Cundall and Morris, *Judges*, 208.
72. See the structure of the psalms of lament in Federico G. Villanueva, *The Uncertainty of a Hearing: A Study of the Sudden Change of Mood in the Psalms of Lament* (Leiden: Brill,

no confession, no protestation of innocence, and no imprecation. Moreover, there is no answer from God – not even a terse reply. God is totally silent.[73] Hence there is no expression of confidence, which assumes God's response to the lament.

"Early the next day the people built an altar and presented burnt offerings and fellowship offerings" (21:4). With no word from God, the people resort back to the old formulas and practices, thinking that these will be enough to discern God's will about the matter.[74] Having done that, they are now ready to propose a solution.

The response of the people is similar to the scene in 2:1–5, when the people also wept and offered sacrifices after being rebuked by the emissary of Yahweh for entering into covenants with the people of the land, the consequence of which was that they would become so entangled with the Canaanites that the latter would not be driven out. Yet in chapter 21, the weeping does not arise because of Canaanite encroachment, but because Israel's strength as a nation is being decimated by the loss of one whole tribe, where strength is defined in terms of military force. As Block points out, the term for "missing" (*paqad*) in 21:3 is used for the mustering or roll call of troops.[75] Except for the six hundred men who fled into the wilderness of Rimon (20:47), all the valiant fighters are gone (20:44, 46); all the towns, with their inhabitants, including animals, have been struck down and set on fire (20:48). Not only is the present military force diminished, there is no hope of building it up again, since there are no wives and no offspring. With the present and future diminishment of the military force, Israel's tenuous hold on their tribal territories will soon give way to the relentless Canaanite advance.

21:5–14 Making Amends: Part One

This section reveals another detail that has been left out regarding the events that transpired in Mizpah, which is that the tribes also made an oath among those who assembled that anyone who did not join the assembly "was to be put to death" (21:5). The oath is described as a great or solemn (*gedullah*) oath (21:5), underscoring the seriousness of the participants who uttered it. In ancient Israel, to violate an oath involved grave consequences, incurring

---

2008), 43–44.
73. Klein, *Triumph of Irony*, 187; Younger, *Judges*, 380.
74. See Boling, *Judges*, 291.
75. Block, *Judges*, 570 n. 369.

human or divine sanctions.[76] Ironically, however, the Israelites only remember the oath because of the expediency of the moment–their need to provide wives for the tribe of Benjamin.

The phrase, "he shall surely be put to death" (*mut yumat*), is a familiar one from the law materials of the OT. It is used for what the community considers as capital crimes.[77] The formula is used to refer to execution by human hands, whether by the community or the avenger of blood, in contrast to the penalty, "he shall be cut off."[78] Similar to the scenario in 20:13, the Israelite assembly sees itself as the legal body that can mete out judgements to the rest of the community. The fact that the Israelites continue to refer to the gathering at Mizpah as the assembly "to the LORD" (*leYhwh*) reveals that they believe their actions not only have God's approval, but also will redound to God's benefit.

The next phrase, "the Israelites had a change of heart regarding Benjamin their brother" (21:6, trans. mine), forms an ironic contrast to the harshness of the preceding and following verses, as well as to the drastic measures that Israel employed to punish Benjamin in chapter 20. The tribes did not feel any compunction in decimating the whole tribe of Benjamin or in putting to death anybody who did not participate in their plan. They did not show any remorse about excluding one of their tribes from the gathering in Mizpah. But here, they finally relent and show some concern for their brother's plight. The Hebrew form of the verb for "change of heart" (*nikham*) is variously translated as "grieved for" (NIV), "had compassion" (ESV; NRSV), "felt/were sorry" (NJB; NASB), and "relented" (NJPS). In this context, however, the word does not seem to indicate emotional pain because of what Benjamin has gone through. Rather, the use of *nikham* shows that the attitude of the tribes towards Benjamin has changed – they no longer want to obliterate the tribe, but rather to build it up.[79]

Aside from the military reason, the change of attitude of the rest of the tribes towards Benjamin may also have to do with the loss of inheritance rights and land in situations where there are no living descendants. The image evoked by the phrase "cut off" (21:6) is that of a tree that has been hacked

---

76. Yael Ziegler, *Promises to Keep: The Oath in Biblical Narrative* (Leiden: Brill, 2008), 3.
77. Karl-Johann Illman, *Old Testament Formulas about Death* (Meddelanden Fran Stiftelsens för Akademi Forskningsinstitut 48; Finland: Abo Akademi, 1979), 122–126.
78. Block, *Judges*, 573 n. 376. The formula, "he shall be cut off," may, in some instances, mean execution by or exclusion from the human community, but at other times the offender's punishment is left in God's hands. See G. F. Hasel, "*kārat*," *TDOT* 7: 348.
79. See H. Simian-Yofre, "*nhm*," *TDOT* 9:350.

down, its strength and capacity to produce life diminished. In a culture where children are seen as a blessing and childlessness as a curse, the lack of offspring to continue the line and the tribe's name is seen as a very grave tragedy.

So Israel is in a quandary: how can they be consistent with their pledge not to give their daughters as wives to Benjamin, and yet at the same time act like a dutiful brother in ensuring that the line of Benjamin will continue? Although not the same practice, this duty springs from the same motivation as that of a levirate marriage, where a family member (a brother or a relative) sees it as his responsibility to marry his brother's widow in order to raise up offspring for his dead brother and ensure that his name and line will continue.[80] However, the reason for majority Israel's change of heart is not because of what the tribe of Benjamin suffered in terms of the death of their kin and the destruction of their towns, but rather is oriented by their own territorial interests.

Israel embarks on a creative solution to this dilemma – they are to exterminate the inhabitants of Jabesh-Gilead for not joining the war against Gibeah, something they discover after the roll is called (21:9). Thus, just as the Israelite assembly subjected the whole Benjamin tribe to *kherem* for protecting the men of Gibeah, now they plan to subject all the inhabitants of Jabesh-Gilead to *kherem* for not cooperating in the war (21:10–11).[81] In chapter 20, the guilt is extended to those who are harboring the evildoers, while in chapter 21 it is extended to those who did not take part in punishing the evildoers.

Here, once again, the concept of corporate guilt underlies the Israelites' actions. However, as in chapter 20, the wisdom of their actions is questionable. First, there is no directive from God, for God is totally silent throughout the episode even though the Israelites plea for God to respond. Moving forward with such a drastic action without divine confirmation is rash and totally imprudent, especially since it is carried out against their fellow Israelites. Even though God allowed them to be defeated twice before in their battle against the Benjaminites, they never reflect critically on their previous actions. If they had acknowledged the flaws in their previous treatment of Benjamin, they would have seen that the inhabitants of Jabesh-Gilead, rather

---

80. Aside from the protection and provision of the widow, the levirate system ensures that the dead brother retains his "name" or title to his landed inheritance because the offspring of the levirate marriage would receive his name and inheritance. See Westbrook, *Property and the Family*, 77.
81. Block, *Judges*, 574.

than being defiant, were the only ones level-headed enough not to be "guilty of overreacting."[82]

Secondly, the situation does not call for such drastic measures. There is no threat of idolatry or turning away to other gods, as in Deuteronomy 13:12–18. The city's lack of cooperation does not warrant such actions either. Even in the war against the Canaanites, who were oppressing the Israelites, Deborah only reproved the non-cooperative tribes, but they were never placed under *kherem* (4:16).[83] Moreover, although Jabesh-Gilead did not participate in the foolish war, they were never belligerent; hence it was another case of "overkill" to send "12,000 of their bravest men" on an unprepared city. This harks back to the attack of the Danites on Laish, a people "quiet and unsuspecting" (18:7).[84]

Another signal that this is a misapplication of *kherem*, as in chapter 20, is that the Israelites carry it out selectively. The idea behind *kherem* is that something is no longer available for common use, since it has been devoted to God. This is one of the main reasons for the command of complete destruction so that whatever is devoted God becomes permanently inaccessible to human use.[85] The first instruction to the men who attacked Jabesh-Gilead seems total – "Go, strike the inhabitants of Jabesh-Gilead with the edge of the sword; also the women and the little ones" (21:10; ESV). However, the *kherem* is later limited to all the men, as well as all the women who "have known a man," that is, those who have had sexual relations with a man (21:12). By implication, this means sparing the virgins who, as part of the spoils of battle, can then be given as wives for the remaining Benjaminites.

In this way, the Israelites plan to circumvent the commitments they made at Mizpah not to give their daughters as wives to the Benjaminites, while also fulfilling their brotherly duty (21:7) towards them. Moreover, they will be able to carry out their oath to execute those who did not participate in the war. It is like hitting three birds with one stone. Thus the Israelite tribes try to make amends with one tribe by enacting more violence on another tribe. Because intertribal violence is what caused the rupture in the fabric of community life to begin with, it is a matter of making up for a failing by

---

82. Boling, *Judges*, 292.
83. The actions of the Israelites are more comparable to that of Gideon, who harshly treated the men of Succoth and Peniel because they did not support him in his war against the Midianites (8:13–17), an action that springs more from vindictiveness rather than a concern to preserve the community's purity.
84. Younger, *Judges*, 381.
85. *TDOT* 5:184. J. P. U. Lilley, "Understanding the *Herem*," *TynBul* 44/1 (1993): 176–177.

doing another one. As Lapsley comments: "In an absurdly ironic effort to mend the tear, they further rip the fabric of Israel by destroying more of their own people."[86]

The Israelites might have been following the precedence of Numbers 31:1–18 in the war against the Midianites. The laws in Deuteronomy distinguish between nearby nations and distant nations. Nearby nations consist of the six or seven nations inhabiting Israel's territories. These are to be completely exterminated because their structures and lifestyle are inimical to God and present a religious threat to Israel (Deut 20:16–18). In such cases, Israel is not allowed to take the spoils of battle. However, in the case of distant nations, who war against Israel after being offered peace, only the grown men are to be killed, while women and children are to be spared and spoil can be taken (Deut 20:18–14). Captive women may even become wives and be set free if the husband gives notice of divorce (Deut 21:10–14). Nevertheless, since Midianite women led Israel astray to worshipping Baal-Peor through sexual seduction (Num 25:1–9), *kherem* was also applied to them. Thus in Numbers 31:1–18, only the virgins, who could be easily assimilated into Israelite society, were spared.[87]

In Judges, the virgins are also spared as spoils of battle for the purpose of providing wives to the Israelites. But the larger purpose of *kherem*, to prevent religious apostasy, is forgotten. Moreover, fellow Israelites are treated like other nations simply because they do not side with the majority – Benjamin like the nearby nations and Jabesh-Gilead like the distant nations. Here again, we see a utilitarian approach to sacred institutions, for the Israelites use institutional mechanisms to justify their actions, but they only choose those parts that suit their purposes. This is a bit similar to 1 Samuel 15:9, when "Saul and the army spared Agag and the best of the sheep and cattle, the fat calves and lambs – everything that was good," while Saul believed (or perhaps tried to convince himself) that he had carried out the Lord's command (1 Sam 15:13–15, 20).

Sometimes, what seems to be zealousness for God may actually reflect a moral rigidness that comes out of our need to control and impose on others our view of the world. This is the case with religious fundamentalism. Fundamentalism originally had a more positive sense, meaning adherence to a core set of beliefs, but in some quarters it now has a negative connotation

---

86. Lapsley, *Whispering the Word*, 59.
87. For more discussion, see Baruch Levine, *Numbers 21–36*, AB (Garden City, NY: Doubleday, 2000), 464–470.

because this adherence is associated with intolerance of other views to the point of persecution, anti-intellectualism, separatism, unloving acts, and the use of political power to exclude those who deviate from these beliefs. While moral convictions are important, and we should not be wishy-washy about what we believe, our religious beliefs should never support acts of violence, persecution, or exclusion against others who hold different views.

The virgins are spared so that they can become a reconciliatory peace offering to the alienated Benjaminites.[88] Presumably, since the Israelites are responsible for the near extinction of the tribe of Benjamin, their way of making amends is to provide a way by which the line of Benjamin can continue. Again, there is an attempt at reparation, but there is no admission of guilt or expression of remorse. The vindictive attitude of the Israelite tribes towards Benjamin has changed – they are now sorry *for* Benjamin; however, they never said they were sorry *to* Benjamin.

In response to Israel's conciliatory gestures and offer of peace, Benjamin returns to the fold, and the virgins of Jabesh-Gilead are given to them as wives (20:13–14). In this, the Benjaminites have no choice. The proffered peace is wholly on the Israelites' terms. Benjamin is in a weak and humiliated position, and so they are in no position to demand anything. They can only accept what is offered in bitter gratitude, which is made even more humiliating since they are forced to accept the favor of their conquerors.

As in Judges 19, women in this chapter are treated as mere property to serve the interests of men: "they gave them [the Benjaminites] *the women* whom they had saved alive of *the women* of Jabesh-gilead" (21:14, ESV, itals. mine). Whereas the concubine in chapter 19 was sacrificed to save the men's life and preserve their honor, women in this story are saved to ensure the survival of one tribe and to serve as pawns to be bartered in exchange for peace.

JUST REPARATIONS

One of the issues in reconciliation is the need for just reparation. In situations where one's actions have caused much damage, simply saying, "I am sorry," or "forgive me," may not be enough. Genuine remorse for the harm that one has caused others needs to be accompanied by deeds that seek to repair the damage. This is demonstrated in the way the Philippine government has

---

88. See Webb, *Book of Judges*, 501.

> attempted to recognize, support, and provide financial reparation to the victims (and/or their families) of summary execution, torture, enforced or involuntary disappearance, and illegal detention during the Marcos dictatorship.[89]
>
> But how does one make reparation for mass killing or genocide? The Israelite tribes obviously thought that providing wives who could bear children for the remaining Benjaminites would compensate for the mass destruction of families and the loss of lives, livelihood, and property. Yet they never admitted wrong, and they never allowed the ones who had lost their families to tell their stories and share their pain. Moreover, they never accepted responsibility for their violent actions and never expressed a willingness to shoulder the corresponding consequences themselves. Instead, they compensated for the damage they did by doing more damage to other people. This narrative highlights that making amends is not a straightforward task, but needs much thought and prayer as well as an in-depth understanding of the real offense so that just reparation can be made.

21:15–23 Making Amends: Part Two

Yet the efforts of majority Israel to make amends fall short, since the four hundred virgins from Jabesh-Gilead are not enough for the six hundred remaining Benjaminites (21:14). At this point in the narrative, the narrator takes on the point of view of the Israelites by expressing that it was the Lord who "had made a gap in the tribes of Israel" (21:15). The Israelites expressed this sentiment indirectly in their prior prayer of lament (21:3).[90] The word for gap, *peretz*, is used to refer to a break in a city wall, rendering a city defenseless against attack,[91] which again supports the view that the Israelites see the problem in terms of a reduction of military resources. Yet the Israelites blame the diminished state of the Israelite army on God. Furthermore, according to them, God is responsible for the breach, and the people are the ones who relent (*nikham*, v. 15) concerning Benjamin (thereby implying that God has not relented). God is silent and withdrawn, whereas the rest of the

---

89. Republic Act 10368, "Human Rights Victims Reparation and Recognition Act of 2013," February 25, 2013.
90. The point of view of the people is signaled by the disjunctive clause, "As for the people, they felt had a change of heart towards Benjamin" (21:15a). See also Lapsley, *Whispering the Word*, 60.
91. J. Conrad, "*pāraṣ, pereṣ, pārîṣ*," *TDOT* 12:106.

tribes proactively provide a solution. God is the culprit, whereas the Israelites heroically and generously extend help to their fellow Israelite tribe.[92]

This narrative challenges us not to devise our own foolish attempts at restoration when pride and folly propel us towards wrong decisions. While restoration is a great theme in the biblical narrative, and God's desire is to repair, rebuild, heal, and make new, our life in the presence of God, guided by the wisdom of God, moves us to do good. Our greatest sin is to usurp God by seeking to be our own gods and to make our own way in the world. Thus when the folly of our ways bears its unwelcome fruit, our instinct is to patch things up without proper and careful processing. Most often what is needed is a deeper repentance, where we place Yahweh at the center – rather than at the periphery – of our existence and action in the world.

It is not entirely clear why the Israelite religious assembly decides to engage in another unorthodox and extreme act of violence to secure wives for the two hundred remaining Benjaminites. If their concern is only for the preservation of the Benjaminite line, the four hundred pairs would have been sufficient to produce children to ensure the perpetuation of descendants. But clearly, the Israelites do not think that the first attempt to make amends is adequate. Perhaps they feel that full reparation can only happen if they exhaust all the possibilities. Or perhaps they figure that it is a waste of two hundred able-bodied men if they cannot produce offspring to repopulate Benjamin and increase the military force along with their hold on Israelite territory.

During this assembly, the elders offer a plan. In ancient Israel, the clan elders (*zeqanim*) decided on disputes and gave counsel. Because of their age, experience, and stature, they were expected to be invested with wisdom in decision-making. The elders in the book of Judges, however, seem to be as undiscerning and utilitarian as the rest of Israelite society.

The elders agonize about Benjamin's situation as they deliberate about how to make things right. First, they take note of the facts – all the women have been destroyed out of Benjamin (21:16), and there are not enough virgins from Jabesh-Gilead to go around. Secondly, they identify the need – the tribe of Benjamin must produce descendants to be able to continue their hold on their territory or else a whole tribe will be "wiped out" (21:17). Thirdly, they look at the blockages – they cannot give their daughters as wives to the Benjamin survivors, since they have taken an oath not to, and breaking that oath would put a curse upon themselves. Fourthly, they come

---

92. See Block, *Judges*, 580.

up with an innovative solution to obtain wives for Benjamin without technically violating their oath. Lastly, they anticipate the problems that may arise once they implement the solution. Their deliberation exemplifies systematic, innovative, objective-based problem-solving, with foresight about possible consequences.

Remembering the yearly feast in Shiloh, when young women go out dancing, the elders instruct the remaining unattached Benjaminites to: "Go and hide in the vineyards and watch. When the young women of Shiloh come out to join in the dancing, rush from the vineyards and each of you seize one of them to be your wife. Then return to the land of Benjamin" (21:20–21).

At certain periods of Israel's history, Shiloh functioned as one of the central sanctuaries.[93] The nature of this yearly festival in Shiloh is not entirely clear. 1 Samuel (1:3, 29) speaks about Elkanah and his household traveling to Shiloh every year for a sacrifice. Thus this may be one of Israel's annual feasts, such as the feast of tabernacles, which is celebrated at the end of the harvest, and this may be implied by the reference to a vineyard. On the other hand, this could be a local feast. Regardless, the feast highlights how easily Israel "moves on" from the major conflict that tore the nation apart by celebrating a "feast to the Lord" with dancing and music, without grieving for the thousands who died or the massive destruction. Moreover, there is no self-reflection about their complicity.

This highlights the fact that decision-making should never be evaluated in terms of effectiveness or outcomes alone. Rather, we need to consider the ethics and morals of any decision in terms of our life and relationship with God. Furthermore, we need to be sensitive to the circumstances of any mediation or reparation in situations of conflict, particularly when death and destruction have been involved.

The elders' motive for providing wives for the rest of the Benjaminite tribe may not be as disinterested as they seem to suggest. At first glance, they seem to be concerned for Benjamin, but, as discussed above, they are most

---

93. In Joshua, Shiloh is the site of the tent of meeting and of the Israel camp as they are dividing the land still needing to be possessed by the various tribes (Josh 18:1–10; 19:51). Judges 18:31 provides the detail that the house of God was in Shiloh. Indeed, the book of Samuel further corroborates that the house of God (tabernacle) was in Shiloh (1 Sam 1:24; see also Ps 78:60), where also resided the ark of God (1 Sam 4:3–4) and the priests who offered sacrifice there (1 Sam 1:3, 9; 2:14; 14:3). In Jeremiah, however, Shiloh is said to have come under God's judgement and has been destroyed (Jer 7:12, 14; Jer 26:6, 9). So perhaps the reason for the detailed description of the location of "Shiloh" (21:19) and the further qualifier that it is "in Canaan" (21:14) is that at the time of the writing of this story, Shiloh had ceased to exist.

concerned about the diminishment of the military force. At the same time, they are worried about the consequences for the territorial borders of Israel if Benjamin lacks descendants. This is revealed in 21:17, where the elders vehemently insist: "A possession for the survivors of Benjamin so that a tribe may not be blotted out from Israel!" (trans. mine).

The Hebrew word for possession, *yerushah* (translated in the NIV as "heirs"), refers to one's legal property,[94] which in this case is the land allocated to Benjamin. On the other hand, the verb for "blotted out," *makhah*, is connected not only with the extinction of life,[95] but also with lack of remembrance, especially of the name.[96] In ancient Israel, the "name" is bound up with establishing ownership of property so that if there are no descendants to take on the father's name, it means the loss of the family's property as well.[97] Thus the concern of the elders is not so much that the remaining Benjaminite survivors will have offspring for the sake of the well-being of Benjamin; rather, they do not want Israel as a nation to lose more land to the surrounding nations.[98] Thus the change of majority Israel's attitude towards Benjamin does not spring from compassion towards their brother, but rather the need to preserve their own interests.

Moreover, the means by which they choose to solve the problem is bizarre. While the young women are going off innocently to dance and celebrate in the feast of the Lord, there are sinister plans to abduct them and take them away from their fathers' houses without any negotiations with the families or input on the women's part. This is especially significant since they will be spirited away far from their homes[99] without the dowry that will provide

---

94. *HALOT* 2:442. See Deut 2:5, 9, 12, 19; Josh 1:15; 12:6; Jer 32:8. See N. Lohfink, "*yāraš, y^erēšâ, yeruššâ*," *TDOT* 6:371, 376. Some LXX manuscripts read, "how will there be survivors in Benjamin," which some commentators adopt (Burney, *Judges*, 491; Soggin, *Judges*, 299; Moore, *Judges*, 450; Boling, *Judges*, 292) because the context of a tribe being blotted out seems to demand it. However, if the survivors die without a son, their tribal possession "would be deemed never to have accrued" to them (Westbrook, *Property and Family*, 141). Since tribal identity is bound up with their land, the name of the tribe would also be obliterated in Israel.
95. See Gen 6:7; 7:4, 23; 2 Kgs 21:13.
96. Deut 9:14; 25:6; 2 Kgs 14:7; Pss 9:5; 109:13.
97. S. Bendor, *The Social Structure of Ancient Israel* (Jerusalem: Simor Ltd., 1996), 125. See Num 27:4.
98. Technically, the rest of the tribes could divide up Benjamin's allotted territory if the tribe dies out, or they could claim it by right of conquest, but they may not be able to defend this territory because of the diminished military force.
99. Even though the father or the eldest brother has the final say on whom the young women in their household are going to marry, sometimes the women's opinions are solicited, as in the case of Rebekah in relation to becoming Isaac's wife (Gen 24:50–58).

a means of sustenance if their husband dies or a bride price to compensate their families for their loss.[100]

The Benjaminites are instructed to "hide in the vineyard" (21:20). The word for hide (*'arab*) is used in contexts where someone or a group waits in concealment in order to attack, kill, or victimize someone, whether in military ambush, assassination, or seduction.[101] Although there is no killing or seduction in this story, there is clearly victimization. The verb used for taking the woman is *khatap*, which involves forcible seizing (21:21). In the only other instance in which this verb is used in the OT, where it is also used with the verb *'arab*, the victims are the poor and innocent (Ps 10:8–9).[102]

Matthews draws parallels to Deut 22:28–29 and Exod 22:16–17, in which a man who has seduced or sexually forced an unengaged woman needs to pay the bride price to the father and make her his wife. In the case of a forceful sexual encounter, the man is not allowed to divorce her,[103] since a woman who is no longer a virgin can no longer be married off. Hence the woman loses out in the long term since, not having a husband or legitimate children, she has no economic security. On the other hand, the father loses out as well since he never receives the bride price, which compensates for the loss of his child in marriage.[104] As in earlier instances, the tribes are using existing mechanisms allowed by the law, but twisting them to suit their purposes. As Webb notes, the cases in Deuteronomy and Exodus regulate "isolated

---

100. The bride price is different from the dowry. The dowry comes from the bride's family, and the bride brings this to her husband's house upon marriage. The bride price comes from the groom and is given to the bride's family to compensate for her loss as an economic contributor to her family of origin. See Richard Nelson, "What is Achsah Doing in Judges?" in *The Impartial God*, ed. Calvin J. Roetzel and Robert L. Foster (Sheffield: Sheffield Phoenix Press, 2007), 16 n.10.
101. Deut 19:11; Ps 59:4; Prov 1:11; Mic 7:2 (assassination); Josh 8:2–21; Judg 9:25–43; 16:2 (military ambush); Job 31:9; Prov 7:12 (seduction); Ps 10:9; Jer 9:7 (general victimization). When directed at individuals, it is often used in connection with lying in wait for someone in order to kill him.
102. See Alice Bach, "Reading the Body Politic: Women and Violence in Judges 21," in *Judges: A Feminist Companion to the Bible, Second Series*, ed. Athalya Brenner (Sheffield: Sheffield Academic Press, 1999), 152; Block, *Judges*, 581.
103. Matthews, *Judges & Ruth*, 200.
104. Carolyn Pressler, *The View of Women Found in the Deuteronomic Family Laws* (Berlin/New York: De Gruyter, 1993), 41; Christopher Wright, *Deuteronomy*, NIBC (Peabody, MA: Hendrickson, 1996), 244–245. Wright, however, does not consider the payment as bride price, which tends to reduce the practice to economic terms. Rather, the "custom of exchanges of money and other gifts between families . . . is usually a part of the cementing of relationships and investing in the stability and permanence of a new union" (246).

acts of passion"; they are not the "planned act of large-scale abduction" found in Judges 21.[105]

Nevertheless, the elders anticipate the objections that will be made by the fathers and brothers, whose consent will not be asked and to whom a bride price will not be paid. They cast their appeal in terms of a favor to them for the sake of the Benjaminites (21:22).[106] Again, they identify themselves as the heroes, since their intervention makes it possible for the remaining Benjaminites to have wives. Moreover, some quick thinking enables them to reason out a way for the men of Shiloh to avoid breaking their oath at Mizpah, for they never give their consent voluntarily. Thus the incident ends with good closure on all sides:

> So that is what the Benjaminites did. While the young women were dancing, each man caught one and carried her off to be his wife. Then they returned to their inheritance and rebuilt the towns and settled in them. (21:23)

Each of the Benjaminites now has a wife, and the survival of the tribe is guaranteed with the descendants that are sure to follow. The reference to returning, rebuilding, and resettling shows a return to normalcy after the ravages of war. The broken relationship between the Israelite tribes and Benjamin has been settled. The problem has been solved, and everyone can now move on. But is everything really back to normal?

The whole of chapter 21 is narrated in a matter-of-fact, nonchalant tone, as if the killing of the men and women of Jabesh-Gilead, the saving up of the virgins for the Benjaminite escapees, and the abduction of the women of Shiloh are the most natural things in the world. This narration contrasts with that of Judges 19. While the narrator in both chapters withholds explicit and extensive moral evaluation, the narrator in chapter 19 employs a scenic style that gives us a blow-by-blow account of the events leading and following the gang-rape of the concubine. Thus even though the narration is not emotive, we enter into the concubine's plight and imagine her suffering as well as the abuse and callousness of the perpetrators.

In contrast, chapter 21 employs a summary report of the violence and abuse from the point of view of the Israelite assembly and the elders. The perspectives of the inhabitants of Jabesh-Gilead, the Benjaminites, and the

---

105. Webb, *Book of Judges*, 507.
106. The MT reads with a double accusative, "Grant us/them a favor," which can be read, "Grant us a favor for their sakes."

victimized women are completely inaccessible, and so we cannot sympathize with their plight. Even though the actions in chapter 21 are equally horrendous, the incidents are reported with detachment. Instead, the narrator provides us with a generous glimpse of the mental calisthenics of the Israelite assembly and the elders, as revealed in their speeches and plans of action.

The difference in narration techniques contrasts the reactions of the Israelite assembly to the "outrageous" (*nebalah*) crime against the concubine in chapter 20 with their indifferent dealings with the inhabitants and virgins of Jabesh-Gilead and the young women of Shiloh in chapter 21. Their skewed attitudes also mirror the callous treatment of the Levite towards his concubine – perspectives which reveal that a whole society has gone awry.

RECOVERING GRACE AND LOVE IN THE CHURCH

One of the challenges facing the contemporary church is that the pragmatism and utilitarianism that so characterize the modus operandi of the modern world have also infected the ways we do ministry. We feel the need to step up and make things happen, emphasizing outcomes and productivity, to the point that we sacrifice prayer, character, beauty, and being. We no longer focus on what will advance God's mission or express the values of God's kingdom – by caring for the vulnerable and doing justice or by loving people and doing good to them – but on what will be marketable and attract money, people, and influence. While we have a responsibility to assess the effectiveness of our efforts and to find solutions that are acceptable to the majority and demonstrate a responsible expenditure of resources, we must never sacrifice the soul of our institutions and the mission to which God has called us. For "What does it profit [us] if [we] gain the whole world, but lose or forfeit [ourselves]?" (Luke 9:25, NRSV). While there will always be pressure to follow the quick, easy, or most practical route, what is most important is to assess whether that route will be good for the institution in the long-run by asking if it expresses the ethos of our Christianity community and if it affirms the value of people and the gifts they bring to our community.

For God does not work pragmatically, but redemptively. God seeks out the broken in order to bring restoration and the wounded in order to bring healing. This is not a functional way of operating, but the way of grace and love. This way needs to be recovered in our churches and institutions, which have become captive to the utilitarian and the pragmatic.

21:24–25 EPILOGUE: THE IRONIC AND INCOMPLETE ENDING

The ending of Judges echoes the ending of the Joshua era, with the Israelites leaving the place of assembly and returning to their own inheritance (Judg 21:24; see also Judg 2:6; Josh 24:28). The crisis is over, and now they can go back to tending their own land and their own household affairs. All's well that ends well, and life can go on as usual.

The last verse of Judges, however, shatters this perception. The conclusion of the book echoes the formula: "In those days Israel had no king; everyone did as they saw fit" (21:25). As shown earlier, this refrain offers a sad commentary about the devolution of the spiritual and social life of Israelite society as a result of not acknowledging the kingship of Yahweh. As Younger comments:

> Thus, the reader will find no "Hollywood" ending in the final chapter. Instead, one is left with an overburdening sense of discomfort. Israelite degeneracy has reached its nadir. When the book finally ends, the reader can breathe a sigh, but more because the discomforting story is finished than because he or she experiences a final, positive feeling.[107]

The story of Judges, however, continues in the books of Samuel. Thus, to properly appreciate this period in the life of Israel, one must connect it to the stories in Samuel, which recount the establishment of the Israelite monarchy and the story of the last judge, the prophet Samuel.

---

107. Younger, *Judges*, 383.

BIBLIOGRAPHY

Ackroyd, Peter R. "Composition of the Song of Deborah." *VT* 2 (April 1952): 160–162.

Albertz, Rainer. *A History of Israelite Religion in the Old Testament Period. Vol. 1. From the Beginnings to the End of the Monarchy.* Louisville, KY: Westminster/John Knox, 1994.

Alter, Robert. *The Art of Biblical Narrative*. New York: Basic, 1981.

———. "Samson without Folklore." In *Text and Tradition: The Hebrew Bible and Folklore*. Edited by Susan Niditch. Atlanta, GA: Scholars, 1990.

Amit, Yairah. *The Book of Judges: The Art of Editing*. Leiden: Brill, 1999.

———. "Hidden Polemic in the Conquest of Dan: Judges xvii-xviii." *VT* 40 (1990): 4–20.

Assis, Ellie. *Self-Interest or Communal Interest: An Ideology of Leadership in Gideon, Abimelech, and Jephthah Narratives (Judg 6–12)*. Leiden: Brill, 2005.

Babut, Jean-Marc. *Idiomatic Expressions of the Hebrew Bible: Their Meaning and Translation through Componential Analysis*. BIBAL Dissertation Series 5. North Richland Hills, TX: Bibal Press, 1999.

Bach, Alice. "Reading the Body Politic: Women and Violence in Judges 21." In *Judges: A Feminist Companion to the Bible, Second Series*. Edited by Athalya Brenner. Sheffield: Sheffield Academic Press, 1999.

Bal, Mieke. *Death and Dissymmetry: The Politics of Coherence in the Book of Judges*. Chicago, IL: University of Chicago Press, 1988.

———. *Murder and Difference: Gender, Genre, and Scholarship on Sisera's Death*. Translated by Matthew Gumpert. Bloomington, IN: Indiana University Press, 1988.

Barr, James. *Old and New in Interpretation*. New York: Harper & Row, 1966.

———. *The Scope and Authority of the Bible*. London: SCM Press, 1980.

Bendor, S. *The Social Structure of Ancient Israel: The Institution of the Family (Beit'ab) from the Settlement to the End of the Monarchy*. Jerusalem: Simor Ltd., 1996.

Bergson, Henri. "Laughter." In *Comedy*. Edited by George Meredith. AB. Garden City, NY: Doubleday, 1956.

Berlin, Adele. *Poetics and the Interpretation of Biblical Narrative*. Sheffield: Almond Press, 1983.

Biddle, Mark E. *Reading Judges: A Literary and Theological Commentary*. Macon, GA: Smyths & Helwys, 2012.

Bledstein, Adrien Janis. "Is Judges a Woman's Satire of Men Who Play God?" In *A Feminist Companion to Judges*. Edited by Athalya Brenner. Sheffield: Sheffield Academic Press, 1993.

JUDGES

Block, Daniel. "Echo Narrative Technique in Hebrew Literature: A Study in Judges 19." *WTJ* 52 (1990): 325–341.

———. *Judges, Ruth.* NAC. Nashville, TN: Broadman & Holman, 1999.

Bluedorn, Wolfgang. *Yahweh versus Baalism: A Theological Reading of the Gideon-Abimelech Narrative.* Sheffield: Sheffield Academic Press, 2001.

Bohmbach, Karla. "Conventions/Contraventions: The Meanings of Public and Private for the Judges 19 Concubine." *JSOT* 83 (1999): 83–98.

Boling, Robert G. *Judges.* AB, Vol. 6. Garden City, NY: Doubleday, 1977.

Boogart, T. A. "Stone for Stone: Retribution in the Story of Abimelech and Shechem." *JSOT* 32 (1985): 45–56.

Bowman, Richard G. "Narrative Criticism: Human Purpose in Conflict with Divine Presence." In *Judges & Method: New Approaches in Biblical Studies.* Edited by Gail A. Yee. Minneapolis, MN: Fortress, 1995.

Bray, Jason. *Sacred Dan: Ritual Tradition and Cultic Practice in Judges 17–18.* New York: T & T Clark, 2006.

Brenner, Athalya, ed. *A Feminist Companion to Judges.* Sheffield: Sheffield Academic Press, 1993.

———. *Judges: A Feminist Companion to the Bible*, Second Series. Sheffield: Sheffield Academic Press, 1999.

Brettler, Marc Zvi. "The Book of Judges: Literature as Politics." *JBL* 108 (1989): 395–418.

———. *The Book of Judges.* London and New York: Routledge, 2002.

———. *The Creation of History in Ancient Israel.* London and New York: Routledge, 1995.

Bright, John. *A History of Israel.* 3rd ed. Philadelphia, PA: Fortress, 1981.

Brown, F., S. R. Driver, and C. A. Briggs. *The Brown-Driver-Briggs Hebrew and English Lexicon.* Peabody, MA: Hendrickson, 2001.

Brueggemann, Walter. *The Prophetic Imagination.* Minneapolis, MN: Fortress, 1978.

Burney, C. F. *The Book of Judges with Introduction and Notes, and Notes on the Hebrew Text of the Books of Kings with an Introduction and Appendix.* New York: KTAV Publishing House, 1970.

Buttrick, George. *Interpreter's Dictionary of the Bible.* 4 vols. New York: Abingdon, 1962.

Camp, Claudia V. "Wise and Strange: An Interpretation of the Female Imagery in Proverbs in Light of Trickster Mythology." *Semeia* 42 (1988): 14–36.

Cartledge, Tony. *Vows in the Hebrew Bible and the Ancient Near East.* Sheffield: JSOT Press, 1992.

———. "Were Nazirite Vows Unconditional?" *CBQ* 51 (1989): 409–422.

Childs, Brevards. *Biblical Theology of the Old and New Testaments.* Minneapolis, MN: Fortress, 1992.

Bibliography

Claassens, L. Juliana. "The Character of God in Judges 6–8: The Gideon Narrative as Theological and Moral Resource." *HBT* 23 (June 2001): 51–71.

Clines, D. J. A., ed. *Dictionary of Classical Hebrew.* Sheffield: Sheffield Academic Press, 1994.

Coats, George W. *Moses: Heroic Man of God.* Sheffield: JSOT Press, 1988.

Coogan, Michael. "A Structural and Literary Analysis of the Song of Deborah." *CBQ* 40 (April 1978): 143–166.

Copan, Paul. *Is God a Moral Monster? Making Sense of the Old Testament God.* Grand Rapids, MI: Baker Academic, 2011.

Craigie, Peter C. "A Note on Judges 5:2." *VT* 18 (July 1968): 397–399.

———. "Some Further Notes on the Song of Deborah." *VT* 22 (July 1972): 349–353.

Crenshaw, James. "The Samson Saga: Filial Devotion or Erotic Attachment." *ZAW* 86 (1974): 420–504.

———. *A Secret Betrayed: A Vow Ignored.* Atlanta, GA: John Knox, 1978.

Cross, Frank Moore and David Noel Freedman. *Studies in Ancient Yahwistic Poetry.* Grand Rapids, MI: Eerdmans, 1997.

Crüsemann, F. *Der Widerstand gegen das Königtum.* Wissenchaftliche Monographien zum Alten und Neuen Testament 49. Neukirchen: Neukirchener Verlag, 1978.

Cundall, Arthur E. and Leon Morris. *Judges and Ruth: An Introduction and Commentary.* TOTC. Leicester: IVP, 1968.

Cundall, Arthur. "Judges – An Apology for the Monarchy." *ExpTim* 81 (1969–1971): 178–181.

Day, Peggy, ed. *Gender and Difference in Ancient Israel.* Minneapolis, MN: Fortress, 1989.

Davis, Dale Ralph. "Comic Literature – Tragic Theology." *WTJ* 46 (1984): 156–163.

De Vaux, Roland. *Ancient Israel: Its Life and Institutions,* Vol. 1. New York: McGraw Hill, 1965.

De Vries, Simon. "Temporal Terms as Structural Elements in the Holy-War Tradition." *VT* 25 (1975): 89–92.

Dilling, Walter. "Knots." In *Encyclopaedia of Religion and Ethics*, Vol. 7. Edited by James Hastings. Edinburgh: T & T Clark, 1918.

Dorsey, David. "Judges." In *The Literary Structure of the Old Testament: A Commentary on Genesis to Malachi.* Grand Rapids, MI: Baker Academic, 1999.

Dumbrell, W. J. "'In Those Days There Was No King in Israel; Every Man Did What Was Right in His Own Eyes,' The Purpose of the Book of Judges Reconsidered." *JSOT* 25 (1983): 23–33.

Eliade, Mircea. *Images and Symbols: Studies in Religious Symbolism.* New York: Sheed and Ward, 1969.

Emerton, John A. "The Second Bull in Judges 6:25–28." *Eretz Israel* 14 (1978): 52–55.

Enriquez, Virgilio. *From Colonial to Liberation Psychology: The Philippine Experience*. Manila: De La Salle University Press, 1994.

Eslinger, Lyle. *Into the Hands of the Living God*. LHB. Sheffield: Almond Press, 1989.

Exum, J. Cheryl. "Aspects of Symmetry and Balance in the Samson Saga." *JSOT* 19 (1981): 3–29.

———. "The Centre Cannot Hold: Thematic and Textual Instabilities in Judges." *CBQ* 52 (July 1990): 410–429.

———. "Feminist Criticism: Whose Interests Are Being Served?" In *Judges and Method: New Approaches in Biblical Studies*. 2nd. ed. Edited by Gale Yee. Minneapolis, MN: Fortress, 2007.

———. "On Judges 11." In *A Feminist Companion to Judges*. Edited by Athalya Brenner. Sheffield: Sheffield Academic Press, 1993.

———. "Promise and Fulfillment: Narrative Art in Judges 13." *JBL* 99 (1980): 43–59.

———. "Samson's Women." In *Fragmented Women: Feminist (Sub)Versions of Biblical Narratives*. Valley Forge, PA: Trinity Press International, 1993.

———. "The Tragic Vision and Biblical Narrative: The Case of Jephthah." In *Signs and Wonders: Biblical Texts in Literary Focus*. Atlanta, GA: SBL Press, 1989.

Exum, J. Cheryl and William Whedbee. "Isaac, Samson, and Saul: Reflections on the Comic and Tragic Visions." *Semeia* 32 (1984): 5–40.

Fewell, Danna Nolan. "Deconstructive Criticism: Achsah and the (E)razed City of Writing." In *Judges & Method: New Approaches in Biblical Studies*. Edited by Gail A. Yee. Minneapolis, MN: Fortress, 1995.

Fewell, Danna Nolan and David M. Gunn. "Controlling Perspectives: Women, Men, and the Authority of Violence in Judges 4 and 5." *JAAR* 58 (September 1990): 389–411.

Fokkelman, Jan. "Structural Remarks on Judges 9 and 19." In *'Shaʾrei Talmon': Studies in the Bible, Qumran, and the Ancient Near East Presented to Shemaharyu Talmon*. Edited by Michael Fishbane, Emmanuel Tov, and Weston W. Fields. Winona Lake, IN: Eisenbrauns, 1992.

Fretheim, Terence. *The Suffering of God: An Old Testament Perspective*. Philadelphia, PA: Fortress, 1984.

Frye, Northrop. *Anatomy of Criticism: Four Essays*. Toronto, ON: University of Toronto Press, 2006.

———. *A Natural Perspective: The Development of Shakespearean Comedy and Satire*. New York: Harcourt, Brace, and World, 1965.

Fuchs, Esther. "The Literary Characterization of Mothers and Sexual Politics in the Hebrew Bible." *Semeia* 46 (1989): 151–166.

Bibliography

———. "Marginality, Ambiguity, Silencing: The Story of Jephthah's Daughter." In *A Feminist Companion to Judges*. Edited by Athalya Brenner. Sheffield: Sheffield Academic Press, 1993.

Garber, David G. "Awakening Desire Before It Is Season: Reading Biblical Texts in Response to the Sexual Exploitation of Children." *RevExp* 105 (Summer 2008): 453–469.

Gerbrandt, Gerald Edie. *Kingship According to the Deuteronomistic History*. Atlanta, GA: Scholars Press, 1986.

Goldingay, John. *Old Testament Theology, Vol. 1: Israel's Gospel*. Downers Grove, IL: IVP, 2003.

Goldstein, Jeffrey H. and Paul E. McGhee. *The Psychology of Humor: Theoretical Perspectives and Empirical Issues*. New York/London: Academic Press, 1972.

Gordon, C. H. "Cultural and Religious Life." In *The World History of the Jewish People, Vol. 3: Judges*. Edited by Benjamin Mazar. Tel Aviv: Rutgers University, 1971.

Good, Edwin. "Apocalyptic as Comedy: The Book of Daniel." *Semeia* 32 (1984): 41–70.

———. *Irony in the Old Testament*. Philadelphia, PA: Westminster Press, 1965.

Good, Robert. "The Just War in Ancient Israel." *JBL* 104 (1985): 385–400.

Gooding, D. W. "The Composition of the Book of Judges." *Eretz Israel* 16 (1982): 70–79.

Gordon, Wenham J. *Genesis 1–15*. WBC. Waco, TX: Thomas Nelson, 1987.

Gorospe, Athena E. "A Biblical Model of Empowerment: The Story of Gideon." In *Church and Poverty in Asia*. Edited by Lee Wanak. Mandaluyong City: OMF Lit, 2008.

———. "Comedy and Humor in the Samson Narrative." ThM diss., Asia Graduate School of Theology, 1995.

———. "Inversions of Expectations and Roles in Judges 13: A Study in Literary Method." *Phronesis* 2/2 (1995): 27–42.

———. "Old Testament Narratives in Context: Moses' Reverse Migration and the Hermeneutics of Possibility." In *The Gospel in Culture: Contextualization Issues through Asian Eyes*. Edited by Melba Maggay. Mandaluyong City: OMF Lit, 2013.

Gottwald, Norman K. *The Tribes of Yahweh*. Sheffield: Sheffield Academic Press, 1999.

Gray, John. *Joshua, Judges, and Ruth*. NCB. Grand Rapids, MI: Eerdmans, 1986.

Greene, Mark. "Enigma Variations: Aspects of the Samson Story: Judges 13–16." *VE* 21 (1991): 53–79.

Gunn, David. "Samson." A paper read at a seminar in the biblical studies department at the University of Sheffield, 1982.

Gutierrez, Gustavo. *The God of Life*. Maryknoll, NY: Orbis, 1991.

Haak, Robert. "A Study and New Interpretation of *qsr nps*." *JBL* 101 (1982): 161–167.

Habel, Norman C. "The Form and Significance of the Call Narratives." *ZAW* 77 (1965): 297–323.

Hackett, Jo Ann. "In the Days of Jael: Reclaiming the History of Women in Ancient Israel." In *Immaculate and Powerful: The Female in Sacred Image and Social Reality*. Edited by Clarissa W. Atkinson, Constance H. Buchanan, and Margaret R. Miles. Boston, MA: Beacon Press, 1985.

Hamlin, E. John. *Judges: At Risk in the Promised Land*. International Theological Commentary. Grand Rapids, MI: Eerdmans, 1990.

Hamblin, William. *Warfare in the Ancient Near East to 1600 B.C.: Holy Warriors at the Dawn of History*. London/New York: Routledge, 2006.

Handy, Lowell K. "Uneasy Laughter: Ehud and Eglon as Ethnic Humor." *SJOT* 6/2 (1992): 233–246.

Hauser, Alan J. "Judges 5: Parataxis in Hebrew Poetry." *JBL* 99/1 (March 1980): 23–41.

———. "Two Songs of Victory: A Comparison of Exodus 15 and Judges 5." In *Directions in Biblical Poetry*. Edited by Elaine R. Follis. Sheffield: JSOT Press, 1987.

Hertzberg, Hans Wilhelm. *I & II Samuel: A Commentary*. OTL. London: SCM, 1964.

Hudson, J. M. "Living in a Land of Epithets: Anonymity in Judges 19–21." *JSOT* 62 (1994): 49–66.

Humphreys, W. Lee. "From Tragic Hero to Villain: A Study of the Figure of Saul and the Development of 1 Samuel." *JSOT* 22 (1982): 95–117.

———. *The Tragic Vision and the Hebrew Tradition*. Overtures to Biblical Theology. Philadelphia, PA: Fortress, 1985.

Hyatt, J. P. *Exodus*. NCB. London: Oliphants, 1971.

Illman, Karl-Johann. *Old Testament Formulas about Death*. Meddelanden Fran Stiftelsens för Akademi Forskningsinstitut 48. Finland: Abo Akademi, 1979.

Janzen, David. "Why the Deuteronomist Told About the Sacrifice of Jephthah's Daughter." *JSOT* 29 (2005): 339–357.

Jenni, Ernst and Claus Westermann. *Theological Lexicon of the Old Testament, Vol. 3*. Translated by Mark E. Biddle. Peabody, MA: Hendrickson, 2004.

Jones, Gwilym H. "'Holy War' or 'Yahweh War.'" *VT* 25 (July 1975): 642–658.

Jones-Warsaw, Koala. "Toward a Womanist Hermeneutic: A Reading of Judges 19–21." In *A Feminist Companion to Judges*. Edited by Athalya Brenner. Sheffield: Sheffield Academic Press, 1993.

Kaminsky, Joel. *Corporate Responsibility in the Hebrew Bible*. Sheffield: Sheffield Academic Press, 1995.

Bibliography

Klein, Lilian R. "A Spectrum of Female Characters." In *A Feminist Companion to Judges*. Edited by Athalya Brenner. Sheffield: Sheffield Academic Press, 1993.

———. *The Triumph of Irony in the Book of Judges*. Sheffield: Almond Press, 1988.

Koehler, L., W. Baumgartner, and J. J. Stamm. *The Hebrew and Aramaic Lexicon of the Old Testament*. Translated and edited under the supervision of M. E. J. Richardson. 5 vols. Leiden: Brill, 1993–2000.

Koehler, Ludwig and Walter Baumgartner. *The Hebrew and Aramaic Lexicon of the Old Testament*. Study edition. 2 vols. Leiden: Brill, 2002.

Lapsley, Jacqueline. *Whispering the Word: Hearing Women's Stories in the Old Testament*. Louisville, KY: Westminster/John Knox, 2005.

Lasine, Stuart. "Guest and Host in Judges 19: Lot's Hospitality in an Inverted World." *JSOT* 29 (1984): 37–59.

Leach, Maria and Jerome Fried, eds. "Trickster." In *Funk and Wagnalls Standard Dictionary of Folklore, Mythology, and Legend*. 2 vols. New York: Funk and Wagnalls, 1950.

Levine, Jacob. *Motivation in Humor*. New York: Atherton, 1969.

Levine, Baruch. *Numbers 21–36*. AB. Garden City, NY: Doubleday, 2000.

Lilley, J. P. U. "A Literary Appreciation of the Book of Judges." *TynBul* 18 (1996): 101–102.

———. "Understanding the *Herem*." *TynBul* 44/1 (1993): 176–177.

Linao, Rex T. *Community Immersion: Toward Becoming Agents of Community Empowerment*. Quezon City: Great Books Trading, 2004.

Lindars, Barnabas. *Judges 1–5: A New Translation and Commentary*. Edited by A. D. H. Mayes. Edinburgh: T & T Clark, 1995.

Marais, Jacobus. *Representation in Old Testament Narrative Texts*. Leiden: Brill, 1998.

Marcus, David. *Jephthah and his Vow*. Lubbock, TX: Texas Tech Press, 1986.

Maribao, Joel. *Strategies for Empowerment: A Filipino-Christian Perspective*. Manila: Logos Publications of the Divine Word, 1996.

Margalith, Othniel. "Samson's Riddle and Samson's Magic Locks." *VT* 36 (1986): 225–234.

Martens, Elmer A. "Toward Shalom: Absorbing the Violence." In *War in the Bible and Terrorism in the Twenty-First Century*. Edited by Richard S. Hess and Elmer A. Martens. Bulletin for Biblical Research Supp. 2. Winona Lake, IN: Eisenbrauns, 2008.

Martin, Lee Roy. "Power to Save!?: The Role of the Spirit of the Lord in the Book of Judges." *JPT* 16 (April 2008): 21–50.

Matthews, Victor H. *Judges & Ruth*. NCBC. Cambridge: Cambridge University Press, 2004.

Mazar, Benjamin, ed. *The World History of the Jewish People, Vol. 3: Judges*. Tel Aviv: Rutgers University, 1971.

McCann, J. Clinton. *Judges*. IBC. Louisville, KY: Westminster/John Knox, 2002.
McCarter, P. Kyle Jr. *1 Samuel*. AB. Garden City, NY: Doubleday, 1980.
McKenzie, John. *The World of the Judges*. London: Chapman, 1967.
Miller, Patrick. *The Religion of Ancient Israel*. Louisville, KY: John Knox, 2000.
Mitchell, Christopher Wright. *The Meaning of Brk 'to bless' in the Old Testament*. SBL Dissertation Series 95. Atlanta, GA: Scholars, 1987.
Moore, George F. *A Critical and Exegetical Commentary on Judges*. Edinburgh: T & T Clark, 1895.
Mosca, Paul G. "Who Seduced Whom? A Note on Joshua 15:18/ Judges 1:14." *CBQ* 46 (January 1984): 18–22.
Mueller, Aydeet. *The Micah Story: A Morality Tale in the Book of Judges*. New York: Peter Lang, 2001.
Müllner, Ilse. "Lethal Differences: Sexual Politics as Violence Against Others in Judges 19." In *Judges, A Feminist Companion to the Bible (Second Series)*. Edited by Athalya Brenner. Sheffield: Sheffield Academic Press, 1999.
Muraoka, Takamitsu. *Emphatic Words and Structures in Biblical Hebrew*. Leiden: Brill, 1985.
Myers, Jacob. "The Book of Judges." In *The Interpreter's Bible*. Vol 2. New York: Abingdon, 1953.
Nelson, Richard D. "What is Achsah Doing in Judges?" In *The Impartial God*. Edited by Calvin J. Roetzel and Robert L. Foster. Sheffield: Sheffield Phoenix Press, 2007.
Niditch, Susan. "Eroticism and Death in the Tale of Jael." In *Gender and Difference in Ancient Israel*. Edited by Peggy Day. Minneapolis, MN: Fortress, 1989.
———. "Samson as Culture Hero, Trickster, and Bandit: The Empowerment of the Weak." *CBQ* 52 (1990): 608–624.
———. "The 'Sodomite' Theme in Judges 19–20: Family, Community, and Social Disintegration." *CBQ* 44 (1982): 365–378.
———. *War in the Hebrew Bible*. Oxford: Oxford University Press. 1993.
Nohrnberg, James. "Moses." In *Images of Man and God: Old Testament Short Stories in Literary Focus*. Edited by Burke O. Long. Sheffield: Almond Press, 1981.
Noth, Martin. *The Deuteronomistic History*. Sheffield: Almond Press, 1981.
Nussbaum, Martha. *Love's Knowledge: Essays on Philosophy and Literature*. New York: Oxford University Press, 1990.
O'Brien, Carol, Jessica Keith, and Lisa Shoemaker. "Don't Tell: Military Culture and Male Rape." *Psychological Services* 12/4 (2015): 357–365. Online: http://apa.org/pubs/journals/releases/ser-ser0000049.pdf
O'Connell, R. H. *The Rhetoric of the Book of Judges*. Leiden: Brill, 1996.
Ogden, Graham S. "Jotham's Fable: Its Structure and Function in Judges 9." *The Bible Translator* 46/3 (1995): 301–308.

Bibliography

Olson, Dennis. *Introduction, Commentary, and Reflections on the Book of Judges.* NIB, Vol. 2. Edited by Leander Keck and David Peterson. Nashville, TN: Abingdon, 1994.

Ortigas, Camela D. *Training for Empowerment.* Quezon City: Office of Research and Publications, Ateneo de Manila University, 1992.

Pardes, Ilana. "Zipporah and the Struggle for Deliverance." In *Countertraditions in the Bible: A Feminist Approach.* Cambridge, MA: Harvard University Press, 1992.

Penchansky, David. "Staying the Night: Intertextuality in Genesis and Judges." In *Reading Between Texts: Intertextuality and the Hebrew Bible.* Edited by Danna Nolan Fewell. Louisville, KY: Westminster/John Knox, 1992.

Piccaluga, Grolia. "Binding." In the *Encyclopaedia of Religion.* Vol. 2. Edited by Mircea Eliade. New York: Macmillan, 1987.

Polzin, Robert. *Moses and the Deuteronomist: A Literary Study of the Deuteronomic History.* New York: Seabury Press, 1980.

Pressler, Carolyn. *The View of Women Found in the Deuteronomic Family Laws.* Berlin, New York: De Gruyter, 1993.

———. "Wives and Daughters, Bond and Free: Views of Women in the Slave Laws of Exodus 21:2–11." In *Gender and Law in the Hebrew Bible and the Ancient Near East.* Edited by Victor H. Matthews, Bernard M. Levinson, and Tikva Frymer-Kensky. Sheffield: Sheffield Academic Press, 1998.

Radin, Paul. *The Trickster: A Study in American Indian Mythology.* New York: Schocken Books, 1956.

Republic Act 10368. "Human Rights Victims Reparation and Recognition Act of 2013." February 25, 2013.

Reinhartz, Adele. "Samson's Mother: An Unnamed Protagonist." *JSOT* 55 (1992): 25–37.

Revell, E. J. "The Battle with Benjamin (Judg 20:29–48) and Hebrew Narrative Techniques." *VT* 35 (1985): 417–433.

———. *The Designation of the Individual: Expressive Usage in Biblical Narrative.* Contributions to Biblical Exegesis and Theology 14. Kampen: Kok Pharos, 1996.

Ricouer, Paul. "Imagination in Discourse and Action." In *From Text to Action: Essays in Hermeneutics, II.* Translated by Kathleen Blamey. Evanston, IL: Northwestern University Press, 1991.

———. *Time and Narrative.* Vol. 3. Translated by Kathleen Mclaughlin and David Pellauer. Chicago, IL: University of Chicago Press, 1988.

Routledge, Robin. "*Hesed* as Obligation: A Re-examination." *TynBul* 46/1 (1995): 179–196.

Ryken, Leland. *Words of Delight: A Literary Introduction to the Bible.* Grand Rapids, MI: Baker, 1987.

Sasson, Jack M. *Judges*. AYBC. New Haven, CT: Yale University Press, 2004.
Satterthwaite, Philip. "'No King in Israel': Narrative Criticism and Judges 17–21." *TynBul* 44 (1993): 75–88.
Schneider, Tammi J. *Judges*. BerOl. Collegeville, MN: Liturgical Press, 2000.
Sharp, Carolyn. *Irony and Meaning in the Hebrew Bible*. Bloomington, IN: Indiana University Press, 2009.
Sills, David L., ed. *The International Encyclopedia of the Social Sciences*. New York: Macmillan & The Free Press, 1968.
Ska, Jean Louis. *"Our Fathers Have Told Us": Introduction to the Analysis of Hebrew Narratives*. Subsidia Biblica 13. Rome: Editrice Pontificio Istituto Biblico, 1990.
Soggin, J. Alberto. *Judges: A Commentary*. OTL. Philadelphia, PA: Westminster, 1981.
Sorensen, M. J. "Humor as a Serious Strategy of Nonviolent Resistance to Oppression." *Peace & Change* 33 (2008): 160–190. Online: http://onlinelibrary.wiley.com/enhanced/doi/10.1111/j.1468-0130.2008.00488.x/.
Steinberg, Naomi. "Israelite Tricksters, Their Analogues and Cross-Cultural Study." *Semeia* 42 (1988): 1–13.
Sternberg, Meir. *The Poetics of Biblical Narrative: Ideological Literature and the Drama of Reading*. Bloomington, IN: Indiana University Press, 1987.
Stone, Ken. "Gender and Homosexuality in Judges 19: Subject-Honor, Object-Shame?" *JSOT* 67 (1995): 87–107.
Sugirtharajah, R. S. *Asian Biblical Hermeneutics and Postcolonialism*. Maryknoll, NY: Orbis, 1998.
Sypher, Wylie. "The Meanings of Comedy." In *Comedy*. Edited by George Meredith. Garden City, NY: Doubleday, 1956.
Taylor, Cheryl. "A Theology of Humor." In *The Network for Women in Ministry*. Online: http://ag.org/wim/0805/0805_Theology_Humor.cfm.
Theissen, Gerd. *The Social Setting of Pauline Christianity: Essays on Corinth*. Philadelphia, PA: Fortress, 1982.
Thiselton, Anthony. *1 Corinthians: A Shorter Exegetical and Pastoral Commentary*. Grand Rapids, MI: Eerdmans, 2006.
Thompson, R. Campbell. *Semitic Magic*. London: 1908.
Tigay, Jeffrey. *Deuteronomy*. JPSTC. Philadelphia, PA: The Jewish Publication Society, 1966.
Trible, Phyllis. *Texts of Terror: Literary Feminist Readings of Biblical Narratives*. Philadelphia, PA: Fortress, 1984.
Van der Merwe, Christo H. J., Jackie A. Naudé, and Jan H. Kroeze. *A Biblical Hebrew Reference Grammar*. Sheffield: Sheffield Academic Press, 1999.
Van der Toorn, Karel. *Dictionary of Deities and Demons in the Bible*. Leiden: Brill, 1995.

Bibliography

———. *Religious Life*. Leiden/New York: Brill, 1996.

Van Wolde, Ellen. "Does *'Innâ* Denote Rape? A Semantic Analysis of a Controversial Word." *VT* 52 (2002): 528–544.

Villanueva, Federico G. *The Uncertainty of a Hearing: A Study of the Sudden Change of Mood in the Psalms of Lament*. Leiden: Brill, 2008.

Vincent, Mark A. "The Song of Deborah: A Structural and Literary Consideration." *JSOT* 91: (December 2000): 61–82.

von Rad, Gerhard. *Old Testament Theology*. Vol. 1. Edinburgh: Oliver and Boyd, 1962.

Waldman, Nahum M. "The Imagery of Clothing, Covering, and Overpowering." *JANES* 19 (1989): 161–170.

Webb, Barry G. *The Book of Judges: An Integrated Reading*. Sheffield: JSOT Press, 1987.

Webber, R. E. *The Church and the World*. Grand Rapids, MI: Academie Books.

Wenham, Gordon J. *Genesis 1–15*. WBC. Waco, TX: Word Books, 1987.

Wessels, J. P. H. "'Postmodern' Rhetoric and the Former Prophetic Literature." In *Rhetoric, Scripture, and Theology: Essays from the 1994 Pretoria Conference*. Edited by Stanley E. Porter and Thomas H. Olbricht. Sheffield: Sheffield Academic Press, 1996.

Wharton, James. "The Secret of Yahweh: Story and Affirmation in Judges 13–16." *Int* 27 (1973): 48–66.

Wong, Gregory. *Compositional Strategy of the Book of Judges*. Leiden: Brill, 2006.

Wright, Christopher. *Deuteronomy*. NIBC. Peabody, MA: Hendrickson, 1996.

Yee, Gale A. "By the Hand of a Woman: The Metaphor of the Woman Warrior in Judges 4." *Semeia* 61 (1993): 99–132.

Yoder, J. H. *For the Nations: Essays Evangelical and Public*. Eugene, OR: Wipf and Stock, 2002.

Yoo, Yani. "Han-Laden Women: Korean 'Comfort Women' and Women in Judges 19–21." *Semeia* 78 (1997): 37–46.

Younger, K. Lawson, Jr., William W. Hallo, and Bernard Frank Batto, eds. *The Biblical Canon Comparative Perspective: Scripture in Context IV*. Lewiston, NY: The Edwin Mellen Press, 1991.

Younger, K. Lawson, Jr. *Judges/Ruth*. NIVAC. Grand Rapids, MI: Zondervan, 2002.

Zakovitch, Yair. "Sisseras Tod." *ZAW* 93 (1981): 364–374.

Ziegler, Yael. *Promises to Keep: The Oath in Biblical Narrative*. Leiden: Brill, 2008.

Asia Theological Association
54 Scout Madriñan St. Quezon City 1103, Philippines
Email: ataasia@gmail.com Telefax: (632) 410 0312

OUR MISSION

The Asia Theological Association (ATA) is a body of theological institutions, committed to evangelical faith and scholarship, networking together to serve the Church in equipping the people of God for the mission of the Lord Jesus Christ.

OUR COMMITMENT

The ATA is committed to serving its members in the development of evangelical, biblical theology by strengthening interaction, enhancing scholarship, promoting academic excellence, fostering spiritual and ministerial formation and mobilizing resources to fulfill God's global mission within diverse Asian cultures.

OUR TASK

Affirming our mission and commitment, ATA seeks to:

- **Strengthen** interaction through inter-institutional fellowship and programs, regional and continental activities, faculty and student exchange programs.
- **Enhance** scholarship through consultations, workshops, seminars, publications, and research fellowships.
- **Promote** academic excellence through accreditation standards, faculty and curriculum development.
- **Foster** spiritual and ministerial formation by providing mentor models, encouraging the development of ministerial skills and a Christian ethos.
- **Mobilize** resources through library development, information technology and infra-structural development.

To learn more about ATA, visit www.ataasia.com   or   Facebook /AsiaTheologicalAssociation

Langham Literature and its imprints are a ministry of Langham Partnership.

Langham Partnership is a global fellowship working in pursuit of the vision God entrusted to its founder John Stott –

to facilitate the growth of the church in maturity and Christ-likeness through raising the standards of biblical preaching and teaching.

Our vision is to see churches in the majority world equipped for mission and growing to maturity in Christ through the ministry of pastors and leaders who believe, teach and live by the Word of God.

Our mission is to strengthen the ministry of the Word of God through:
- nurturing national movements for biblical preaching
- fostering the creation and distribution of evangelical literature
- enhancing evangelical theological education

especially in countries where churches are under-resourced.

Our ministry

Langham Preaching partners with national leaders to nurture indigenous biblical preaching movements for pastors and lay preachers all around the world. With the support of a team of trainers from many countries, a multi-level programme of seminars provides practical training, and is followed by a programme for training local facilitators. Local preachers' groups and national and regional networks ensure continuity and ongoing development, seeking to build vigorous movements committed to Bible exposition.

Langham Literature provides majority world preachers, scholars and seminary libraries with evangelical books and electronic resources through publishing and distribution, grants and discounts. The programme also fosters the creation of indigenous evangelical books in many languages, through writer's grants, strengthening local evangelical publishing houses, and investment in major regional literature projects, such as one volume Bible commentaries like *The Africa Bible Commentary* and *The South Asia Bible Commentary*.

Langham Scholars provides financial support for evangelical doctoral students from the majority world so that, when they return home, they may train pastors and other Christian leaders with sound, biblical and theological teaching. This programme equips those who equip others. Langham Scholars also works in partnership with majority world seminaries in strengthening evangelical theological education. A growing number of Langham Scholars study in high quality doctoral programmes in the majority world itself. As well as teaching the next generation of pastors, graduated Langham Scholars exercise significant influence through their writing and leadership.

To learn more about Langham Partnership and the work we do visit **langham.org**

www.ingramcontent.com/pod-product-compliance
Lightning Source LLC
Chambersburg PA
CBHW060942230426
43665CB00015B/2033